INTERACTIVE TEAMING

Consultation and Collaboration in Special Programs

SECOND EDITION

Carol Chase Thomas
University of North Carolina–Wilmington

Vivian Ivonne Correa
University of Florida

Catherine Voelker Morsink
Slippery Rock University of Pennsylvania

Merrill
an imprint of Prentice Hall
Englewood Cliffs, New Jersey   Columbus, Ohio

Library of Congress Cataloging-in-Publication Data

Thomas, Carol Chase.
    Interactive teaming : consultation and collaboration in special programs / Carol Chase
      Thomas, Vivian Ivonne Correa, Catherine Voelker Morsink.—2nd ed.
      p.   cm.
    Morsink's name appears first on the earlier edition.
    Includes bibliographical references and indexes.
    ISBN 0-02-420204-5
    1. Handicapped children—Education—United States. 2. Team learning approach
in education. 3. Communication in education—United States. 4. Group guidance in
education.   I. Correa, Vivian Ivonne.   II. Morsink, Catherine Voelker.   III. Title.
LC4031.T46   1995
371.91—dc20   94-28031
                                                  CIP

Cover art: Courtesy of Southeast School, Columbus, Ohio
Editor: Ann Castel Davis
Production Editor: Louise N. Sette
Text Designer: Jill E. Bonar
Cover Designer: Cathleen Carbery
Production Buyer: Deidra M. Schwartz
Electronic Text Management: Marilyn Wilson Phelps, Matthew Williams, Jane Lopez,
    Karen L. Bretz
Illustrations: Accurate Art

This book was set in ITC Garamond BT and Futura BT by Prentice Hall and was printed and
bound by R.R. Donnelley & Sons Company. The cover was printed by Phoenix Color Corp.

 © 1995 by Prentice-Hall, Inc.
A Simon & Schuster Company
Englewood Cliffs, New Jersey 07632

Earlier edition © 1991 by Macmillan Publishing Company

Photo credits: Daniel Floss/Prentice Hall and Merrill, 251; Barbara Schwartz/Prentice Hall and
Merrill, 69, 131, 161, 353; Anne Vega/Prentice Hall and Merrill, 37, 185, 217, 283, 311, 331, 377;
Tom Watson/Prentice Hall and Merrill, 5; and Todd Yarrington/Prentice Hall and Merrill, 103.

Printed in the United States of America

10 9 8 7 6 5 4 3 2 1

ISBN 0-02-420204-5

Prentice-Hall International (UK) Limited, *London*
Prentice-Hall of Australia Pty. Limited, *Sydney*
Prentice-Hall Canada Inc., *Toronto*
Prentice-Hall Hispanoamericana, S. A., *Mexico*
Prentice-Hall of India Private Limited, *New Delhi*
Prentice-Hall of Japan, Inc., *Tokyo*
Simon & Schuster Asia Pte. Ltd., *Singapore*
Editora Prentice-Hall do Brasil, Ltda., *Rio de Janeiro*

DEDICATION

*To my parents, John B. E. and Geraldine M. Chase;
sister, Janene E. Chase; and godmother, Ann R. Corley*

CAROL CHASE THOMAS

*To Dr. Everett Hill, Professor at Peabody College–Vanderbilt,
who passed away in March of 1994, for having been my
mentor and friend.*

*To my family for their continued love and support throughout
the years.*

VIVIAN IVONNE CORREA

To my children, Andrew Morsink and Kristin Morsink Young.

CATHERINE VOELKER MORSINK

Preface

Interactive teaming in special programs is a new concept of service delivery for school-age students who are currently placed in special education programs or are at risk for referral to such programs. The model proposed in this book is based on several assumptions:

◆ An increasing number of students are failing in the traditional public school program, both in general and in special education.

◆ The needs of individual students are too complex to be handled by a single professional working in isolation, and the needs of all of these groups of students are too diverse to be addressed by the knowledge base of a single profession.

◆ Increased diversity in cultural differences, both between professionals and families and among professionals from different cultures, further exacerbates the difficulty both of providing effective instructional programs and of developing effective communication systems.

◆ The time of trained professionals and the scarce resources of public education systems are too valuable to be wasted on uncoordinated or duplicated efforts that produce marginal results for special needs students.

The opening paragraph and items listed above were the beginning ideas of the preface to the first edition of *Interactive Teaming*, published in 1991. As the second edition goes to press three years later, the same assumptions are still present and the need for effective teaming models is even greater. The number of students served in special education programs continues to grow, and the cultural diversity of the population continues to expand. The time professionals have for collaboration and the resources of school systems seem to diminish instead of increase.

During this same time span, much attention has been given to organizational models or school restructuring efforts that call for skills in collaboration and teaming. Total Quality Management, school-based and site-based management, macro-system reform efforts, inclusion and transition models, and early childhood intervention programs all require collaboration and team decision making to be successful.

The interactive teaming model described in this text is based on transdisciplinary teaming and collaborative consultation models. The model focuses on two concepts:

1. *Consultation:* The sharing of knowledge by one professional with another.

2. *Collaboration:* Mutual efforts between professionals and parents to meet the special needs of children and young people.

The model includes key elements of total quality efforts, adult learning theories, and recognition of the importance of sensitivity to cultural differences.

This text is divided into three parts, each with several supporting chapters. Part 1 provides a foundation and overview of the contextual framework within which current and future programs for serving students who are disabled and at risk will need to be provided. The emergence of a new population of school-age students and the need for a new, coordinated model of implementing special services are highlighted. In Part 1 an outline of this model and comparisons with existing models are provided. The historical development of the new model includes a brief discussion of the models that preceded it: the medical model, the triadic model of consultation, the refinement of the triadic model to collaborative consultation, and the further extension to variations of the school-based and teacher assistance teams. Each represents a step closer to the interactive teaming model we propose here; the strengths and documented factors in the effectiveness of previous models have been incorporated into the new proposal.

In Part 2 we highlight the barriers to effective team functioning and outline the facilitating factors that make the teaming model work. These factors include understanding the roles and perspectives of team members, enhancing communication skills, considering cultural and linguistic diversity, developing service coordination skills, empowering team members through professional development, and supporting family involvement. We present each through a review of the relevant literature, with descriptions and examples of its application.

Part 3 features implementation of interactive teaming in four contexts—programs for (a) students from culturally and linguistically diverse backgrounds, (b) infants and preschoolers with disabilities, (c) students with mild disabilities, and (d) students with severe disabilities. We outline the necessary knowledge and skills of team members, both as direct service providers and as consultant-collaborators who provide indirect services.

Although the intervention strategies, team members, and their specific interactive processes differ by settings, all teams operate within the framework of problem identification, intervention, and evaluation of effectiveness. A concluding chapter features an extended case study showing how the whole model is applied, and provides guidelines for implications of interactive teaming for the future.

The guidelines by which the interactive team operates are modifications of those used in school-based management teams. The culture of the school—its values and rules—provides the contextual framework for establishing its goals. Teachers, parents, and other team members—rather than administrators and specialists—are empowered to analyze problems, make decisions, and evaluate programs designed to attain common goals. These goals are related to the provision of effective educational service programs for the students on whom the team focuses its efforts.

This book was developed by an interactive team, each member serving as consultant and collaborator to the two other members. In reality, each chapter has three co-authors. To avoid redundancy, however, the authorship of each chapter indicates only the person who was its primary developer. Carol Chase Thomas authored chapters 2, 3, 5, and 12; Vivian Correa authored chapters 6, 9, 10, 11, and 13; and Catherine Morsink authored chapters 1, 4, 7, 8, and 14.

Revising a textbook invariably turns out to be much more of a challenge than anticipated, especially when the authors are located in Florida, Pennsylvania, and North Carolina. We were fortunate in that we shared a common commitment to the goal of advancing the interactive teaming model, and that we had excellent supporters in this endeavor. We appreciate the constructive suggestions provided by the reviewers of the revision plan: Judith J. Ivarie, Eastern Illinois University; Mark P. Mostert, Moorhead State University; and Maria Lynn Nahmias, University of Arizona. Our students in undergraduate and graduate courses provided invaluable insights on how the text could be improved. We also wish to thank Mark Alford, Patty Lefever, Cheri Beverly, Tracey Hines, Linda Lenk, Robert Sattler, and Pamela Soeder for assistance in selecting and summarizing relevant research; and Helen Roll, JoAnne Santos, Cindy McCrery, Delores Daugherty, and Susan Eddy for their expertise and time spent editing, designing graphics, word processing, and formatting the various drafts. Ann Castel Davis and Carol Boll at Merrill were advocates of the text and supportive throughout the entire process.

As we worked on the revisions instead of the myriad other things we could have or should have been doing, a number of individuals provided continuous support and understanding: Robert Tyndall, Eleanor Wright, John Knight, Lilly Correa, Arnie Correa, Carly, and Cricket. A number of friends also were helpful and encouraging sounding boards: Kate Schlichting, Pat Leonard, Alma Lee Allen, and Linda Lowe.

CAROL CHASE THOMAS
VIVIAN IVONNE CORREA
CATHERINE VOELKER MORSINK

Contents

CHAPTER 7

Developing Service Coordination Skills   185

CHAPTER 8

Empowering Team Members Through Professional Development   217

CHAPTER 11

Implementation with Infants and Preschoolers with Disabilities   311

CHAPTER 12

Implementation for Students with Mild Disabilities   331

CHAPTER 13

Implementation for Students with Severe Disabilities   353

CHAPTER 14

Summary and Application of the Model in the Future   377

PART I

Context and Foundations

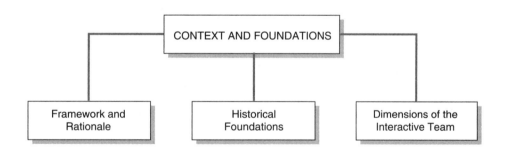

OVERVIEW

The first part of this text provides perspectives on historical, current, and future service delivery systems for students who are at risk or have special needs. In Chapter 1, the population for whom people on an interactive team will need to be concerned is described. The chapter also includes a review of past and current service delivery approaches and some of the problems inherent in the implementation of those systems. The chapter concludes with a summary of the research on effective schools, description of models that emphasize collegial problem solving among professionals, and common elements that contribute to interactive teaming.

Chapter 2 begins with a summary of the historical and legal foundations that have contributed to the development of consultation, collaboration, and teaming models. Selected consultation and teaming models are described, along with their impediments and positive features. In Chapter 3, the dimensions of the interactive team are identified and explained. The interactive teaming model is presented, and an application illustrating implementation of the model is provided.

CHAPTER 1

Framework and Rationale for Interactive Teaming

Definition of Interactive Teaming

Why Interactive Teaming Is Needed Now

Target Population
Increase in Students at Risk

When Interactive Teaming Can Be Used

Limitations of Current Approaches

Poor Quality of Instruction in Tracking and Pullout Programs
Marginal Professional and Parent Interactions

Promising New Practices

Effective Schools Research
Representative Models Using Collegial Problem Solving
Total Quality Management

The Common Elements Contributing to Interactive Teaming

Decision Points in Teaming

Application of Interactive Teaming

Summary

TOPICS IN THIS CHAPTER INCLUDE

◆ Definition of interactive teaming.

◆ Why interactive teaming is needed now.

◆ When interactive teaming is used.

◆ Limitations of current approaches.

◆ Promising new practices from which the components of interactive teaming are derived.

◆ An application providing an opportunity for structured observation of an interactive team.

Janice, a classroom teacher in a middle school, became a teacher because she wanted to make a difference in the world—to excite students about social issues and creative writing—to help young people learn, and discover, and grow. She is the kind of person who should be a teacher. She is bright, knowledgeable, enthusiastic, empathic, and optimistic about the future.

Yet, two years ago, Janice was on the verge of dropping out of the profession. She had been given more students than she thought she could handle, and when she tried to refer those with learning and behavior problems to the school's special programs, she was told these students would be placed on "the waiting list." The principal explained that the special programs were overloaded, because there were too many students with special needs in her suburban school: students whose parents had divorced, students addicted to drugs and stealing to support their habits, and students—barely more than children themselves—who were pregnant.

Janice felt discouraged and isolated. She and the other teachers in her building went into their classrooms and closed their doors, trying to cope single-handedly with their students' bored expressions, lack of ambition, and belligerence. Worst of all, Janice thought nobody else cared. Parents didn't come to PTA meetings; they didn't seem to care. The other teachers gathered in the faculty lounge only to gossip and collapse between classes; they didn't seem to care. But that was two years ago.

Today we see a new Janice. She is a member of an interactive team, consulting and collaborating with other professionals and with parents to design and carry out plans that make her special needs students' programs more effective. Sometimes the team is just two people—Janice and the special education teacher, for example. Sometimes, if a student has severe or multiple disabilities, a larger group is gathered to work as a team. Sometimes Janice is the consultant, the expert who knows more than the others about the specific subject area with which a student is having difficulty. At other times Janice is a collaborator, working with others to carry out the decisions made on the student's behalf by those who make up the team. She doesn't believe that teaming makes her job easier—quite the contrary, because she and her colleagues spend more time planning and working together than they would if each worked alone. However, she does consider her job more challenging and more rewarding, because she thinks the team makes better decisions than each person could make alone.

Janice, the teacher described in the vignette, has developed a new enthusiasm for teaching as a result of being part of a professional group—an interactive team—that shares responsibility for special needs students. In this chapter, *interactive teaming* is defined, and a rationale is presented for why interactive teaming is needed in today's schools and in the schools of the future. The times when interactive teaming is most appropriately used—those which involve decisions about a special needs student's program—are described. The limitations of current approaches are discussed, and the components of promising new practices from which the new interactive teaming model is derived are described.

DEFINITION OF INTERACTIVE TEAMING

The word *teaming* is used here to mean professional and parental sharing of information and expertise, in which two or more persons work together to meet a common goal. In this case, the goal is to provide the best possible educational program for a given special needs student. The *interactive team* is one on which there is mutual or reciprocal effort among and between members of the team to meet this goal.

It should be noted that interactive teams do not operate in isolation to serve exceptional or disabled students. Instead, they operate within the context of other macro-level teams. These include strategic planning teams, which guide decisions in partnerships across the boundaries of schools, businesses, and community agencies.

Macro-level teams also encompass districtwide teams focused on quality improvement. The interactive teams described in this text are micro-level versions of these larger teams, illustrative of school and business trends in collaboration.

Each team member may engage in *consultation,* any activity in which he or she is the expert who possesses more knowledge or skill than other team members about the issue being discussed. When the team member consults, she does this by sharing knowledge or skills, or by explaining or carrying out actions that demonstrate this knowledge. As a member of the interactive team, however, she shares knowledge in a reciprocal rather than an authoritarian manner. On an interactive team, the consultant is not always the same person; the person who consults possesses the necessary knowledge and expertise on a given topic at a particular time. The team member, such as Janice, may be a consultant on the academic subject of teaching creative writing; at the same time, Janice may also be the recipient of consultation from the school psychologist, who has more knowledge about behavior management. Similarly, the parent might be the consultant on the home behavior and history of the student, while being the recipient of the speech-language therapist's recommendations on language development.

The team member also engages in *collaboration,* a mutual effort to plan, implement, and evaluate the educational program for a given student. Collaboration is cooperative rather than competitive. It consists of joint or coordinated actions by team members to reach their common goal. For example, if Janice is a member of a team working with a gifted student who has cerebral palsy and requires an adapted computer for creative writing, she would collaborate with the special education teacher, the occupational therapist, the computer specialist, and the student's parents to plan, implement, and evaluate the student's special program. The features of interactive teaming—collaboration and consultation—are illustrated in Figure 1–1.

The whimsical story of the designing of a camel by a committee (Figure 1–2) illustrates the spirit and process that an interactive team displays as members shift between consultative and collaborative roles. Just as these specialists with diverse backgrounds and disparate vocabularies have functioned together to design a product for the desert that is superior to that which any one of them could have designed alone, so too can members of the interactive team respond to the demanding environment facing educators in the coming years. As we shall see, tomorrow's education and health-related professionals will not be facing stable, happy, eager students from the "grassy meadows" of affluent suburban schools. They will be largely placed in desolate rural areas or in urban blackboard deserts, where the majority of their students live in poverty, come from single-parent homes, speak another language or represent another culture, and have largely abandoned their hope that education is the key to a better future.

WHY INTERACTIVE TEAMING IS NEEDED NOW

This model of consistent consultation, collaboration, and team-based decision making is especially vital now because of the increase in the number of school-age students

Figure 1–1
Features of interactive teaming

who are disabled or at risk for school failure. Because there are so many students who experience difficulties, and because their difficulties are so complex, education, social services, and medical professionals working in isolation are unable to provide these students with appropriate educational programs.

Target Population

The target population served through interactive teaming practices is the group of school-age students who are currently placed in special education programs. It also includes students who are at risk for being placed in such programs and students experiencing school failure without placement.

Disabled Students in Special Education Programs.   Those students classified as disabled are defined by Public Law 94-142, The Education of All Handicapped Children Act, passed by the U.S. Congress in 1975, amended in 1990 as the Individuals with Disabilities Education Act (P.L. 101-476). The students include the following: learning disabled, speech impaired, mentally retarded, emotionally disturbed, deaf and hard of hearing, multihandicapped, orthopedically impaired, health impaired, visually handicapped, and deaf-blind. There were 4,817,503 disabled and at-risk children and youth, ages 0-21, served in special programs during the 1990–91 school year. The number of children and youth with disabilities has risen from 4.8% in 1976–77 to 7.1% in 1990–91. Students ages 6–21 were classified most often as learning disabled, speech impaired, mentally retarded, and seriously emotionally disturbed.

The Camel: A Horse Designed by a Committee

No doubt you have heard that a camel is a horse designed by a committee. Well, it's true. I know, because I was there. I'll tell you what took place. It was mid-morning on the 30th; the entire committee assembled and seated themselves.

"Acme Caravans Incorporated is opening a new market. They have the exclusive franchise for a trans-Sahara trade route and have invited our company to submit a proposal on an order for twenty horses to carry the trade goods, and forty more to carry the caravan's supplies and the pack horses' food and water. This committee is to develop our company's response."

"So they want sixty horses. Model 701B I suppose?"

"Maybe we should think about that. Remember, we used the 701B horse for that high-mountain job last winter, and it floundered when the snow was loose packed and powdery. The sand may be just as bad."

"You have a point there. The 701's small feet sank too deep. Maybe we need a model with a larger foot size."

"Yeah, make it about twice the diameter—maybe padded somewhat on the bottom so it will really spread out."

"Hey, that sounds good. Just like snow shoes—I mean, sand shoes."

"Anything else?"

"Well, yes. Two front toes would give a better grip than just one."

"OK. Let's make it two front toes on each foot. Got that?"

"I've read in the North Africa tour book about the extreme temperatures—135 degrees in the daytime and 40 degrees at night."

"What are you saying? Do you think we should increase the R rating of the exterior covering of the 701B?"

"Insulation pays off in the long run. And besides, don't you still get a tax break on weather-proofing?"

"How about an extra six inches of thick hair and fur on the back and head, and a couple of inches all around?"

"Not a bad idea. As for colors, mauve and taupe are really in this year."

"I don't know. I'm more inclined to the earth tones."

"Why don't we give some choices? Perhaps from a light sand beige to dark chocolate?"

"Is something bothering you?"

"Well, yes. The insulation is OK, but it may cause a real buildup of internal heat at maximum RPMs."

"I don't know. I thought we might gear it down to about two-and-a-half MPH as the cruising speed. At that rate we can keep the heat-loss/heat-gain pretty well balanced."

"We can still have a passing gear that can get its speed up to Mach point-oh-five when necessary."

"Sounds good. This fur will also protect the skin from the abrasion of the hard-blowing sand."

"Speaking of sand, do you remember the attempted helicopter rescue in Iran? That sand and dust really clogged up the choppers' air intake."

Figure 1–2

Decision making by the interactive process

Note: From "The Camel: A Horse Designed by a Committee" by Noojin Walker (March 1988). *The Clearing House, 61*(7), pp. 329–3 30, 1988. Reprinted with permission of the Helen Dwight Reid Educational Foundation. Published by Heldref Publications, 4000 Albemarle St., N.W., Washington, DC 20016. Copyright © 1988.

"Played heck with their vision, too."

"What we need is a way to keep the sand out of the system. Can we change the nostril of the 701B from an open hole to perhaps a slit that can open and close on demand?"

"Sure."

"And while we're at it, we can modify the eyelids and brow so that they are somewhat over-hanging."

"And increase the number and length of the eyelashes?"

"Definitely! You can't overestimate the value of keeping the vision protected."

"Neat! And these sand and wind protection features can also double as glare reducers. Man! That sun is bright!"

"Excuse me, but I have recalculated the heat-loss/heat-gain and the two-point-five MPH."

"So?"

"Well, we're going to have to lengthen the stride and cut down on the leg action if we are going to keep the heat from building up."

"OK, so what do you figure?"

"It needs a stride that will require legs that are eight meters tall."

"Wow! That would be one tall 701B! How would you ever get it loaded—with a crane?"

"Can't you adjust its thermostat? What's its operating temperature range anyhow?"

"Well, it's the usual plus-or-minus one degree tolerance."

"Let me figure—yeah, that's much better. If the internal temperature could vary 10 or 12 degrees with no burnout, it would let us shorten the stride some, and shorten the legs without increasing the leg action and RPMs."

"It would still be taller than the 701B, but we can program it so that it kneels down to be loaded or mounted."

"If it's going to kneel, do you think we should extend the insulation to the knees—maybe some fur pads there? That sand gets fiercely hot."

"Good idea."

"I don't know whether to mention this or not, but if we increase the operating temperature range to 12 degrees, this modified 701B won't need to sweat as much."

"What does this mean?"

"Sweating and its evaporation is a cooling mechanism. It's not going to need it."

"Well, what does that mean?"

"It's not going to lose as much water—not nearly as much."

"You know, if it doesn't lose much water by sweating, and if we were able to add the right kind of reserve water tank, it might be able to go a week or more without having to be refilled."

"These legs are long enough to let us hang a belly tank underneath just like the jet fighters."

"No good! No good! It would not leave enough height underneath to give good clearance over those rough bushes."

"And besides, when it knelt down to be loaded, it would be awfully uncomfortable—mashing all of that water."

"OK, then, let's put it on top."

"Hey, what's that going to look like—a big hump sitting up there?"

"Sure, but that's not all bad. It will be a good base to secure the loads to."

"Right. And the rider will have a much better field of vision."

"Should it have one hump or two?"

"Good question. Why don't we configure two models and let the buyer decide which one he wants?"

"Hmmm. A one-hump and a two-hump model. Marketing will like that."

"I don't know. How are we going to keep all of that water from sloshing around inside that hump as it gets empty? Do you plan to use tubes and baffles?"

"My suggestion is to make it somewhat collapsible. Fill the hump with fibrous connective tissues, sort of like your tubes and baffles. And pack the whole thing with fat. You know fat allows for a lot of water absorption. I figure it can carry 10 percent of the total body weight right there in that hump—or humps."

"I get it. As the fat and water are used the hump gets smaller. Sort of a built-in gauge to tell you how much is still left."

"Super plan! We could also modify the metabolic processes so that the water metabolized from the fat stays right inside the system."

"Sure. Any water that can be saved or recycled is just that much less that it will have to drink en route."

"Will that be a problem—I mean modifying the metabolism?"

"Not really. Our subcommittee has planned a truly rugged digestive system. So far, we can fuel this baby with any kind of desert vegetation—cactus, brush, and even those bitter thorny- bushes. And if necessary, it can digest dried fish, bones, leather, even a blanket."

"That's enough; we get your drift. So actually it can carry enough food and water in that hump to last for a week or more, and also eat almost anything along the way."

"Where are we with the payload?"

"Our calculations show that it will be able to carry about a half-ton, for a week or more, at a steady pace of 2-1/2 miles an hour."

"Is there any danger of overloading it?"

"Not much. We can build in a warning mechanism—groaning, followed by bellowing, and that sort of thing."

"Right on! And as the critical weight is approached, it can be programmed to spit at the loader to get his attention."

"Excellent proposals! With all of these warnings I figure we can load it to within one straw of breaking its back."

"Gee! This modification is really an improvement over the original 701B, at least in this terrain."

"But what is the cost?"

"Well, our cost subcommittee projects that if we use all natural materials and no plastics, the unit cost will be just a little more than the cost of the standard 701B horse. But because it doesn't require the exotic fuel, the extra water, and the support units to carry it all, we calculate that the total job will be about a 50 percent saving to Acme Caravan."

"Great!"

"OK, what about a name?"

"What do you think of CARAVAN MODEL ECONOMY LANDCRUISER?"

"Not bad. It's a little long, but. . . ."

"Group?"

"Sure. That's good. We can market it as CAMEL. It's easier to say. The ad group will love it."

"Good work. I guess that takes care of this business. Unless there is anything else, the committee is adjourned."

Figure 1–2, *continued*

These four categories represent almost 94% of the total number of children classified as disabled (U.S. Department of Education, 1992). Only those students who have been formally identified, placed in special programs, and labeled according to the procedures specified in P.L. 94-142, amended in 1990 as the Individuals with Disabilities Education Act (P.L. 101-476), are classified as "disabled." These are not, however, the only students in need of the services of the interactive team.

Students At Risk for School Failure.   The term *at risk* is defined by Reynolds (1989) as follows:

> The term *at risk* . . . refers to children who fall into various categories for which the base rate (or group frequency) for experiencing educational difficulties is relatively high (p. 129).

Reynolds (1989) further specifies that children who are either disabled or at risk are classified together as students with special needs:

> Special needs children show one or more of the following characteristics which have significance for educational planning: (a) they are not responding positively to the instruction offered to them in basic academic skills (usually reading); (b) their social behavior in school is unacceptable; (c) they are falling badly behind classmates in learning in academic subjects; (d) they have significant physical limitations or major health problems; (e) English is not their primary language (often associated with important cultural differences as well); or (f) they are extremely limited in experiences which provide background for formal education (p. 130).

Those students who meet the criteria in (d) of Reynolds's definition are likely to be labeled as disabled, whereas the others may or may not be currently placed in special education programs. The types of children and youth at risk for school failure include those who are homeless; who have been exposed prenatally to HIV, drugs, or alcohol; who were born prematurely; or who are victims of abuse or lead exposure (Stevens & Price, 1992).

It is becoming increasingly difficult to separate students who are labeled as disabled from those with characteristics that place them at risk for school failure. Hocutt, Cox, and Pelosi (1984) conducted a national study of special education placement issues and concluded that special education placement and program policies relate to funding patterns, as well as to laws. They point out that the number of students labeled as disabled in a given district is determined by the norms of the school district and that minority students are more often placed in special education programs if they are from families with low socioeconomic status.

A companion study by Pyecha, Kullgowski, and Wiegerink (1984) indicates that when the number of students identified as having one categorical label decreases, the number classified into another category is likely to increase. They show that recently the number of students in programs for the learning disabled has decreased (many states have mandated a "cap" or limit on such programs), while the number of those classified as emotionally disturbed or speech impaired has increased. The separation of students who are placed in special education programs from those who are at risk for future placement is extremely difficult. The classification issue is complicated by increases in poverty, family instability, substance abuse, and illegitimate births (Preston, 1984; Stevens & Price, 1992).

Increase in Students at Risk

Recently, the number of school-age students considered to be at risk has increased; the students include those with low academic achievement, poor task completion, and social maladjustment (Stevens & Price, 1992; Morsink & Lenk, 1992). Those who have studied this phenomenon have found a correlation between poor achievement and intense poverty. In schools with little poverty, low achievement averages 11.9%; in those with moderate poverty, it is 23.9%, and in schools with the highest poverty levels, 47.5% of the students have low achievement levels (Reeves, 1988). In addition, it has been shown that the newest groups of immigrant children and those with racial, cultural, and linguistic differences are at risk for school failure (First & Carrera, 1988; National Coalition of Advocates for Students, 1985). These demographic changes and related social problems have combined to create a large increase in the number of students who are disabled and at risk in the school population.

Although the number of students actually placed in special programs may remain stable or decline due to restricted funding, the numbers of those in need of special assistance are likely to increase. It is estimated that one in 500 to 600 newborns suffer from fetal alcohol syndrome and one in 300 to 350 have some fetal alcohol effects (Burgess & Streissguth, 1992). Between 15,000 to 30,000 children are affected with HIV (Stevens & Price, 1992). Each year 37,000 babies, born weighing less than 3½ pounds, live to experience significant learning difficulties (Bartel & Thurman, 1992). In addition, 7.5 million students have emotional problems severe enough for counseling; and 2.2 million are abused or neglected, according to Mernit (1990). The effect of lead poisoning, largely from ingestion of paint, is also a factor in the increase of children at risk for failure (Needleman, 1992). The implications of these conditions for increases in special programs are clear.

Demographic Changes.   Demographic changes that have taken place in the past 20 years have increased the number of risk factors that affect the learning of school-age children. Hodgkinson (1988) has summarized recent demographic changes and concluded that the schools of the future will be quite different from those of the past. Three demographic changes are occurring, all of which contribute to the increase in the number of school-age children who are at risk for failure:

1. The number of at-risk students has increased because of variations in the age of the population.
2. The number of children living in poverty is increasing as the gap widens between the rich and poor.
3. Fewer children have the emotional advantages of two-parent families and after-school care.

The number of at-risk students has increased because of variations in the age of the population. These data have been summarized in a special report in *Education Week* (Reeves, 1988).

Reeves shows that there is currently a larger proportion of young at-risk persons in the population due to the "baby boom," increased immigration, and longer life span. The median age is 30; in three decades it will be 40. In 1950 there were 17 workers for each retiree; in 1992 there were just 3 workers for each retiree, and by 2030, the ratio will be 2.2 to 1 (and 1 of the 2.2 may be on welfare).

Chandler and Stein (1987) say changes in the proportions of student groups changed dramatically between 1976 and 1984: While the number of white non-Hispanics declined, the percentage of Hispanic students increased by 28%, and the percentage of Asian students increased by 85%. Recently, in 23 of the 25 largest school districts, one third of the students are black or Hispanic (Lewis, 1985). Levin (1986) suggests that disadvantaged students in general represent 30% of the school population. Hodgkinson (1988) projects that by 2000, the majority of students enrolled in public schools will be from minority families.

More children are living in poverty as the gap between the rich and poor widens. According to the summary by Reeves (1988), the family income level in the United States increased by 20% between 1970 and 1986, but the median income for parents under the age of 25 dropped by 45%. For the poorest two-fifths of the population, the median income dropped by 12%, while for the richest two-fifths, the median income rose by 27%. Poverty encompasses one of every five children, and one in every four children under the age of 6.

Data from the 1990 Census support the earlier concerns, showing that family incomes are less than the poverty level of $13,000 for a family of four for 26.2 percent of all children living in large urban centers. These data also indicate that poverty levels have spread from large urban areas to smaller cities, and that some of the most extreme poverty exists in rural communities. Increases in poverty levels also intensify risk factors: poor nutrition and health care, neglect, abuse and violence (Fleischner & Van Acker, 1990).

Fewer children have the emotional advantages of a two-parent family with after-school care. According to Reeves (1988), fewer than 5% of the total number of households now consist of children living together with their two parents, an employed father and a homemaker mother. There are 95 million women raising children alone (36% of this number have no high school diploma and half are on welfare). In addition, it is predicted that 60% of the children born in 1983 will live in a single-parent family by the time they are 18 years old. Lewis (1985) states that the number of single-parent families has doubled since 1970; it is now 26% of all families, but for minority children it has risen to 49%. Seven-tenths of all American women age 17 to 44 are employed outside the home. Schmid (1988) says labor force participation for new mothers has reached 50.8%. Worsening economic problems could result in further changes in these data.

Related Social Problems in Secondary Students.   In addition to the dramatic changes in demography, school-age students face a number of social problems that increase the likelihood they will have school-related difficulties. These social problems have led to an increase in the number of secondary-level students with special needs, which place them at risk for school failure. These data have been summarized in a national report by the Education Commission of the States (Brown, 1985), and more recently in a study sponsored by the Carnegie Corporation (Hechinger, 1992). They include dramatic increases in teen-age pregnancy, crimes, and drug abuse, with an alarming increase in the incidence of violence. Homicides are now the third leading cause of death for people between 10 and 19 years of age in the United States. Adolescents in this country are at much higher risk of death than in other industrialized countries (Hechinger, 1992).

Ten million people in the United States are addicted to alcohol; 7 million children of these alcoholics are in the public schools, children with special needs and potential future problems (Leerhsen & Namuth, 1988); the incidence of problem drinking in high school seniors is up 300%; and it is estimated that 10% to 20% of our adolescents abuse alcohol (Brown, 1985).

The ECS also reported 700,000 high school dropouts and another 300,000 truants in 1984. The issue of high school dropouts is of major concern to the superintendents of our urban school districts (Superintendents, 1988). In addition, at least 3.4 million children in schools have a limited ability to use English, and even among those who graduate, the functional illiteracy rate is greater than 30% (Will, 1986).

In a policy report by the U.S. Department of Labor, it was found that these conditions will seriously affect the future of the work force. The Secretary's Commission on Achieving Necessary Skills (SCANS) estimates that more than half of our youth leave school without the knowledge and skills to acquire and retain a good job. This commission recommended that all students master the essential "workplace knowhow": basic skills, thinking skills, and personal qualities, plus five competencies, which enable them to use resources, interpersonal skills, information, technology, and systems in a productive manner (Secretary's Commission on Achieving Necessary Skills, 1991).

There is a high rate of discouragement and hopelessness among our youth. The report of the Education Commission of the States indicated that 10% to 15% of those ages 16–19 were alienated, disadvantaged, or both (Brown, 1985). These students, unless provided with assistance, are in danger of becoming a new "underclass". Eitzen (1992) suggests that ". . . some young people act in antisocial ways because they have lost their dreams" (p. 590). The real-life students behind these data are at risk for school failure; if they become parents, they are in danger of perpetuating the same conditions that will place their own children at risk.

WHEN INTERACTIVE TEAMING CAN BE USED

Given the demographic changes and the future needs of students in our schools, it seems apparent that professionals and parents need to work together as a cohesive group, an interactive team. Interactive teaming, which involves sharing of information among and between professionals and parents, is used most appropriately at the *decision points* that signal potential school failure and a resultant need for professional intervention in the student's educational program. Five of these basic types of decisions have been identified by Salvia and Ysseldyke (1988): *referral, screening, classification, instructional planning,* and *evaluation of pupil progress.*

Referral is the process of requesting assistance for a student with special needs. The first decision point has been modified, from referral to prereferral. Prereferral is the stage at which the observer recognizes that a student is at risk for school failure, and begins to document the difficulties, the attempted interventions, and their effectiveness.

Formal referral for a special program may or may not occur. If prereferral is successful, the team will not need to request the formalities required for referral and placement. Advocates of prereferral say these procedures can help teachers modify their instructional practices, not only helping a wide range of students and fostering teacher growth, but also reducing the number of referrals to special programs. From a major review of 96 such teams in seven states, Chalfant and Psych (1989) concluded that prereferral teacher assistance teams had an 88.7% rate of success in interventions and a 63.9% decline in the number of inappropriate referrals. These authors cite the need for additional staff time and training, as well as administrative support for the prereferral teams.

In screening, tests are administered and observations are made to determine whether the student qualifies to receive special services. Special services are provided only after the student has met the criteria to receive special services. After classification, professionals and parents meet to develop an educational plan, specifying the services the student will receive, the people who will provide the services, the learning objectives to be mastered, and the way the success of the program will be monitored.

Evaluation of pupil progress is the measurement of the degree to which the student has met the objectives listed in the educational plan. The five decision points originally proposed by Salvia and Ysseldyke (1988)—referral, screening, classification, instructional planning, and evaluation of pupil progress—have been modified to reflect the newer emphasis on prereferral and provision of services in interactive teaming. The contrasts between the traditional (special education referral and pullout) model, and the newer approach of interactive teaming are summarized in graphic form at the end of this chapter.

When a teacher such as Janice is concerned that a particular student in her class is not making satisfactory progress, she, either independently or in collaboration with another professional, should make a series of systematic observations of difficulties, then design, implement, and evaluate the effectiveness of the program changes designated. If changes result in satisfactory progress for the student, the teacher may conclude that there is no need for referral. If progress is not satisfactory, the teacher may refer the student for screening. If he or she qualifies for classification as disabled according to the definitions used in the school district, this student may be placed in a special education program. If there are other kinds of special needs (e.g., not a native speaker of English, or family's income below the poverty level), this student also may be eligible for other kinds of special services, such as bilingual or compensatory education. After classification and placement in a full-time or part-time special class, the student is provided with a special instructional program. Later, this program is evaluated to determine whether the student has made progress, or conversely, whether changes need to be made.

It should also be noted that interactive teaming will be used more frequently in a wide range of new settings. These include areas such as preschool, postschool, and related family service programs. All of these areas enable families to obtain a full range of health and human services, coordinated through a single point of contact. These will be described in detail in later chapters of the book. The team may consist of as few as two people during some phases in this process. For example, it is possible to involve only the classroom teacher and the child's parent during the early stages of prereferral. Later, the number of team members will increase if the student is tested by several professionals who need to have input into the planning of the program. The number of members on the team will also increase if the case is complex and the problem requires a wide range of expertise.

Once the program has been planned, its implementation and evaluation may involve only a few of the people who provided initial input; for example, it may be that only the school psychologist or special education teacher works with the classroom teacher or perhaps the parent in the design of specific methods to help a student learn to read, or to modify deviant behavior. In such cases, the interactive team should function in a dynamic way; that is, professionals and parents consulting and collaborating with each other as needed, based on the decisions to be made and the current needs of the child.

LIMITATIONS OF CURRENT APPROACHES

Interactive teaming represents a proposed alternative to the current programs serving students who are disabled and at risk, because it has been shown that these programs have limited effectiveness. Currently, services are delivered primarily through the individual efforts of regular and special education teachers who staff "lower tracks" or special pullout programs, and through social services personnel who provide a variety of related services that are frequently uncoordinated. All of these programs are limited in their effectiveness, and none has typically incorporated interactive teaming. The inability of special education teachers to provide consistently high-quality instruction and the presence of marginal professional and parent interactions and follow-up are among the major limitations in these current approaches.

Poor Quality of Instruction in Tracking and Pullout Programs

In an effort to provide for the educational needs of disabled and at-risk students, many schools have divided students into groups, or tracks, in which the more able learners are separated from those with learning difficulties. Oakes (1986) summarizes the history and effects of tracking, pointing out that it contributes to a mediocre education for more than 60% of our students, in addition to perpetuating social and economic inequality. Tracking offers advantages for only the top 40% of students. The curriculum for that top 40% is based on high-level content, while that of the lower track students consists of workbooks and ditto sheets; also, top-track students receive more of the teacher's instructional time and work in a more positive classroom climate. This structure, according to Oakes, appears to buy increased achievement for the few at the expense of apathy and mediocrity for the many students.

It appears also that it is extremely difficult for teachers in pullout programs to provide special students with adequate direct instruction or feedback. Although designed to provide additional individualized instruction for students with special needs, many programs in which remedial students are isolated and pulled out of the regular classroom are providing less actual instruction than that available in the mainstream classroom. Haynes and Jenkins (1986) found that disabled students in Washington state, placed in resource rooms for reading instruction, spent 52% of their time doing private seatwork without the teacher's assistance, and only 25% of their time actually reading. At the same time, their classroom teachers, assuming that these students were being provided with reading instruction in the resource room, provided them with no additional instruction in the classroom.

Allington (1987), who has studied a large number of remedial programs in New York, has also shown that students in these programs receive a low quality of instruction, and that they spend the majority of their time just sitting—staring at mounds of seatwork—and waiting for the teacher to come and help them. This unfortunate reality also has been observed in special education programs in Florida, where observations were made in nearly 100 classrooms over a two-year period (Algozzine, Morsink, & Algozzine, 1987; Fardig & Morsink, 1985). In Minnesota, it was found that remedial students received an average of only 45 minutes a day of active academic responding (Graden, Thurlow, & Ysseldyke, 1982).

It is equally unfortunate that these same students are often receiving inadequate instruction in the regular classroom. Anderson, Hiebert, Scott, and Wilkinson (1985) have suggested that students in the primary grades spend 50% to 70% of their time working independently. Rupley and Blair (1987), in observation of 12 primary teachers' monitoring of seatwork tasks in reading, have indicated that 50% of these teachers assigned seatwork before conducting reading instruction, that they assigned the same seatwork to the entire group, and that only 10% of these teachers modeled the task before asking students to complete it.

One of the major difficulties with the programs offered for students at risk is that they present repetitive content, using remedial drills that are not challenging. Knapp, Turnbull and Shields (1990) have summarized the difficulties of remedial programs, concluding that the traditional remedial curriculum may intensify student failure through delay of more interesting work or because it does not provide a meaningful context for learning activities. Levin (1986) has developed "accelerated learning" for students at risk, a curriculum similar to the high level, creative problem solving traditionally offered only to gifted students. This approach has been found to increase both the learning rate and the enthusiasm of students at risk.

Marginal Professional and Parent Interactions

One of the major limitations of the existing special programs is that they have not led to an increase in either professional or parent-professional interactions. Although intended to provide coordinated programs for students with special needs, many efforts have resulted in further fragmentation of special services. Johnston, Allington, and Afflerbach (1985) found that students who are taught in separate settings (mainstream and special class) often receive entirely different, conflicting approaches to reading instruction. They found the majority of specialists did not know what kind of instruction the child was receiving in the regular classroom, and only 8% of the classroom teachers could identify the materials used in the special class.

It has been found also that social services for high school students with mild to severe special needs are isolated and fragmented (Boone, 1990; Farrar & Hampel, 1987). In their on-site study of 15 urban high schools, Farrar and Hampel found that the relationships between and among a variety of social services professionals were ambiguous and informal, though appearing to be bureaucratic. These programs lacked department heads, had no systematic operating procedures, were flawed by little information about related community agencies, and were plagued by endless paperwork. Students with similar problems in these schools were provided with a variety of disparate services, while departments failed to share responsibilities.

These authors acknowledge that it is difficult to establish coordinated programs for students' problems in which the diagnosis is ambiguous (e.g., depression) or for which the prescription is controversial (e.g., teen pregnancy). They also point out that some of the social programs have changed in scope and responsibility, that the larger schools often have a totally differentiated staff of specialists, and that new programs come and go in response to fads and available funding. The result is that many existing social services lack continuity and coordination.

Current programs are also limited by a lack of meaningful parental participation in decision making. Pfeiffer (1980) has found that minimal parental involvement in the team decision-making process, particularly as it relates to the Individual Educational Program (IEP) conference, is one of the major problems in current special education programs. Boone (1990) has found that parental participation is also minimal in the Individual Transition Planning (ITP) conference that enables the adolescent to make the transition from school to the adult world. A low rate of participation is characteristic of parents who represent cultural and linguistic minorities (Boone, 1990; Lynch & Stein, 1987). Although intended to increase the level of parental participation, then, the new requirements of special education laws have not had this desired effect.

A number of groups (e.g., Coulter, 1987; Will, 1986) have supported alternative proposals designed to serve disabled and at-risk students more effectively. The proponents of these proposals believe they can provide special students with a higher quality of instruction by serving them in the regular classroom and/or by eliminating formal classification as a prerequisite to special services. The proposed alternatives include some interesting features, although none of them has incorporated mutual support, which is essential in interactive teaming.

More recently, professional groups have emphasized the need to provide a full continuum of services, with placement decisions made individually. Inclusion in the regular classroom and home school are preferred to the degree that this alternative meets the needs of the student and provides an appropriate education for all students in the class (Council of Administrators of Special Education, 1990). Others suggest that the concept of a continuum implies separate placement in environments with varying intensities of service. They suggest using a "constellation" of services that make a broad range of support and personnel available to any student without the requirement for placement in a special program (Thousand & Villa, 1990).

Limited Understanding of the Change Process.   New proposals offered without regard for the major factors that facilitate change are not likely to be implemented effectively (Cuban, 1988; Skrtic, 1987). Some proposals have been offered without an understanding of the structure of schools and in the absence of significant input from the people most affected by the changes—the classroom teachers.

The structure of schools is a major barrier to any proposed change. Classrooms in schools all over the nation are very much alike. In a recent study of 525 high school classrooms, researchers found that though classrooms had different "personalities"— climate, community, administration, relationships among staff—they were alike in their "deep structure" (Tye, 1987). Their curriculum, policies, and reliance on test scores as measures of success were similar. These classrooms had an average size, with students seated noninteractively in rows while teachers engaged in frontal teaching and demonstrated "safe" control over learning. These commonalities were found in urban, rural, and suburban schools, regardless of socioeconomic status.

Skrtic (1987) points out that "it has always been so" because schools are locked into patterns that dictate grades and commonality and separate rooms. He suggests that schools faced with new problems can add new programs or create new classes, but they cannot incorporate new structures. When forced to change, teachers may simply pretend to do so, while continuing to operate as usual behind closed doors. Cuban (1988) expresses the same concern about the structure of schools and their resistance to change, pointing out that we need to study previous effective changes to determine those that have succeeded, and to ask—before changing—about the effect of this change on the system and on society.

It has been pointed out that emphasis on excellence in the late 1980s was characterized by the establishment of new standards, which appeared exclusionary, and that the movement created high levels of polarization between professionals (Shaw, Biklen, Conlon, Dunn, Kramer & DeRoma-Wagner, 1990). The excellence movement also increased dropout rates of students at risk for failure (Tanner, 1989).

Current trends are more consistent with the recommendations of Shaw et al. (1990) for an inclusionary model that provides appropriate education for disabled students within the context of the total system. For example, recent trends in educational measurement encourage students to monitor the quality of their own work (Wiggins, 1991). Other proposals for reform in vocational education also have potential to benefit disabled and at-risk students. These include work in units with relevance beyond the classroom, which feature collaborative learning, use of resources outside the school, flexible use of time, and allowing students to express learning in their own language or in other creative ways (Newmann, 1991).

Because of marginal budgets and the high cost of education, there is also a growing interest in cost effectiveness. In a study of special education costs, Pyecha, Kullgowski, and Wiegerink (1984) studied the budgets of eight school districts in five states from 1980 through 1983. They found that personnel represented the greatest costs for special programs (64% to 92%) and that transportation costs had also increased. As a result, most school districts were forced to decrease their expenditures for professional development and materials, increase class size, place students in "least restrictive programs," and place students into categories with the maximum advantages in funding.

It appears, then, that a society in which the value system equates individual worth with economic productivity, and which classifies people according to a medical model of disability, is unlikely to respond to the need for change unless it can be shown that this change will have a positive economic effect.

PROMISING NEW PRACTICES

Some new practices, based on the concepts that underlie the model of interactive teaming, offer promise for program improvement. These practices are derived from the summary of research on effective schools, which focuses on teams that have been able to facilitate academic achievement and social adjustment in students who are at risk for school failure. These practices also appear to enhance the effectiveness and morale of the professionals who implement them.

Effective Schools Research

From a summary of the research on effective schools, it can be determined that schools in which there is a central mission, on which the school works as a team, are more effective than those in which there are individual teacher goals. In schools with a central mission, productivity, morale, and effectiveness increase (DeBevoise, 1984), and the teacher's sense of isolation is lessened (Ashton & Webb, 1986). According to Stedman (1985), these schools have several things in common: personal attention to students; skillful use of teachers; parental involvement; emphasis on ethnic studies; student responsibility for school affairs; and preventive teaching as opposed to remediation.

Ashton and Webb (1986), in an extensive study of a teacher's sense of efficacy, have shown that feeling a lack of efficacy is often related to the teacher's belief that he or she is isolated in the futile attempt to solve complex problems. This is particularly true in schools with a high concentration of students at risk (Olson & Rodman, 1988; Rosenholtz & Kyle, 1984). In an ethnographic study on the socialization of teachers, Blase (1985) has shown that beginning teachers become less creative and less involved with students over time, and that they need support systems from within to prevent them from becoming traditionalists or authoritarians who focus on low-order skills. The most effective schools are those in which the members of the staff are able to collaborate in the effort to improve the quality of their services to students. Thousand and Villa (1990) add that teachers who operate within adhocratic collaborative teams report high levels of morale and a sense of empowerment.

Representative Models Using Collegial Problem Solving

The demographic and social changes described so far have created a new population of students and a new set of circumstances that cannot be addressed by old mandates for school and program improvement. Successful reform needs to include provisions for collaborative activity at a collegial level (Cuttance, 1985; Purkey & Smith, 1983, 1985).

Currently Used Models.   Bell (1987) has reviewed the promising proposals for school improvement that involve *teacher empowerment* and collaborative effort. They include the following:

◆ *Quality circles:*   Small groups with similar jobs meet regularly to discuss and solve problems (Bonner, 1982). In quality circles, members have volunteered to participate, and they have no authority to implement their recommendations.

◆ *Self-management teams:*   An extension of quality circles, in which members are given some degree of authority for daily management of the organization's activities. The team includes all members and selects an internal leader, but the organization's manager appoints an external leader to coordinate or facilitate their activities (Bell, 1987).

◆ *Shared decision making:*   Teachers are involved in making schoolwide recommendations for improvement (Schneider, 1984). This has been used particularly in making decisions that involve professional development programs (Thompson & Cooley, 1984).

◆ *School-based management:*   A process through which decisions typically made by central district administrators are delegated to management groups in local schools (Marburger, 1985). Rather than involving everyone on the staff, management activities are conducted by a small group consisting of the principal, representative teachers, parents, and community members. The most effective groups begin by outlining their operating procedures, conducting a needs assessment, and establishing goals with measurable objectives.

Total Quality Management (TQM)

This special form of teaming was initially implemented and is used largely in business and industry settings (Lawler, 1993). It is viewed as a vehicle for the improvement of processes within the system. Most focus on ways to reduce errors in processes, making them more effective in providing services.

TQM, an innovation by Deming (1986) and also based on the concepts of Csikszentmihalyi (Schmoker & Wilson, 1993), was the catalyst for postwar economic recovery in Japan. It combines principles from psychology, leadership, and statistics into a systematic plan for continuous improvement of services.

TQM, which has begun to be used in school restructuring, incorporates the principles of interactive teaming, and is most often referred to as total quality education (TQE) in the school context. Schmoker and Wilson (1993), indicating that site-based management alone has not produced higher achievement in schools, have summarized the use of total quality principles and analyzed the factors that account for their success. Schmoker and Wilson (1993) note that, in business and industry, as in school applications, the appearance of TQM principles fails without willingness to empower workers and give them trust. Successful schools use these simple principles, without becoming rigid Deming disciples. They also caution that real improvement takes time—probably five years, though morale may improve sooner. Specific problems may be identified and solved, building on success. Continuous improvement through use of data and team analysis is a common element in all of the successful programs.

Schmoker and Wilson (1993) indicate that the Total Quality Management principles have been applied successfully in a variety of schools. They also note that it is important for implementers to ask questions, such as:

◆ Are employees working together on the most important problems?

◆ What data are used to determine priorities?

◆ Are we making progress? What works/doesn't work?

◆ How can we improve?

THE COMMON ELEMENTS CONTRIBUTING TO INTERACTIVE TEAMING

The most promising proposals for improving schools' responsiveness to the increased number of disabled or at-risk students are those that include the features of teacher empowerment, shared "ownership" of problems, and the common goal of providing each student with the best possible program. These same features are incorporated into interactive teaming. Goodlad (1984) has stressed that the common patterns of teacher isolation, with top-down mandates for change and improvement, lead only to superficial compliance. Stedman (1987) has pointed out that several factors involving collaboration account for the successes in the effective schools research, such as the emphasis on community participation and ownership, shared governance by teachers, and the emphasis on student responsibility. Wilson and Firestone (1987) have given examples of ways in which innovative leaders can work around the bureaucratic structures in schools to facilitate collaboration (e.g., help teachers network their skills, encourage a buddy system for parents, enhance the communications among constituents).

Among the successful attempts to encourage teaming in new teachers are those that provide mentors (Bunting, 1988) or involve coaching (Leggett & Hoyle, 1987). The practices that facilitate teacher collaboration include opportunities to develop lesson plans and units, to talk together about new ideas, and to observe each other in classrooms (Little, 1981). All these approaches involve some form of interactive teaming, although the implementers have not used that label.

The most encouraging thing about the use of interactive teaming is that it has been successful even in schools with the most difficult students. These are schools that have a large number of students who are disabled or at risk, particularly minority students who do not believe that school achievement is related to economic gain (Olson & Rodman, 1988). They are schools with the worst combination of poverty, low parental achievement, and racial and cultural isolation. The staff members are the newest and least-prepared teachers—those trained to work with an average and ideal student population that no longer exists.

Olson and Rodman (1988) point out that the old excuses for school failure—the poor home environments of a few students—are no longer valid when these limitations are representative of the majority of the student population. One of the successful team responses to school failure has been implemented in New Haven, Connecticut, by a team of Yale University, public school, mental health, and community personnel (Comer, 1989), and extended throughout the nation to several other school districts (Schmoker & Wilson, 1993). In this program, success has been attributed to the collaborative contributions of people with diverse areas of expertise. Comer has also been able to document improvement in the educational achievement of parents as well as their children.

Three school districts in Hammond, Indiana, have initiated a collaborative program to train new professionals to work in urban schools by designating one school in each district as an urban education center (Olson & Rodman, 1988). Task forces representing the teaching staff, administration, and community will reach consensus on the curriculum, entrance criteria, and implementation plan for the new program.

Maeroff (1993) describes some effective teams used to facilitate school change. First offered through leadership academies, such as those sponsored by the Rockefeller Foundation at the University of New Mexico and Michigan State University, these teams grew in strength as they developed the support of colleagues, learned new process skills, facilitated an academic excellence atmosphere, and forged new links with business and the community. According to Maeroff, some of the factors that increased the team's ability to succeed in making changes are as follows:

◆   Set important priorities for school.
◆   Model appropriate skills and interactions.
◆   Anticipate resistance, provide responses.
◆   Interact with peers in school and help community become involved.
◆   Keep sense of humor, positiveness; communication.
◆   Find time to work together.
◆   Maintain communication.

Maeroff indicates that teams may initially believe that their school's problems (lack of budget, time, clear mission, knowledge; temporary staff, unions) are so severe, the team cannot be of much help. It is important for the team to focus on the major problems of students, rather than seeming to deal with superficial issues.

Smith (1992) describes the common strengths of teams in which university and school partners have come together to agree on common goals for professional practice. In a survey of the 38 programs that won the Association of Teacher Educators (ATE) Distinguished Program in Teacher Education awards, 1977–89, it was found that there were common factors in award-winning programs. These included practical or clinical collaboration, which featured both learning how to teach and acquisition of interpersonal relationship skills for the participants. Most had a governance team with representatives from both partners, and a structure that allowed for the relationship of theory to practice. Characteristics that seemed to enable partnerships to survive over time included equality between partners, emphasis on significant school-based programs with collaboration in the settings where education occurs, and the assignment of responsibility based on participants' skills.

These successful teams—both micro teams that function within a school, and macro teams that extend to include school partnerships—have a common element: They are planned and implemented by representative, interactive participants, as opposed to being mandated by legislatures or district administrators. They follow the recommendations of the Carnegie Report for new governance structures, and they respond to the concerns of the Chief State School Officers that schools cannot help the most difficult students without providing a whole range of special services (Olson & Rodman, 1988). Teacher and related professional competence, combined with the belief that even the most difficult students can learn, are viewed as essential elements in the success of these teams. Sergiovanni (1987) stresses that successful schools in this age of diversity are those in which professionals believe that all students can succeed, and that they have a right to do so.

Decision Points in Teaming

Figure 1–3 illustrates the differences between the current system of serving students with special needs and the proposed system called *interactive teaming*. It follows the five decision points modified from the work of Salvia and Ysseldyke (1988), initially identified as referral, screening, classification, instructional planning, and evaluation of pupil progress.

At decision point 1 in the current system, referral is costly and time-consuming; there is often a backlog of referrals, and students may have to wait a long time before services can begin. In the interactive teaming model, a prereferral team meets to discuss the educational needs of a student even before a referral is made. At this stage, the team members might be able to resolve the problem and eliminate the need for costly referral.

Decision point 2 involves screening. In the current system, this means the student is tested by several isolated specialists and that the data from testing may not be well-integrated. Screening is most often followed by classification—the identification

Figure 1–3
Contrasts between the current system and the proposed model for interactive teaming.

of the student as disabled. Interactive teaming proposes joint problem solving by members of the team to ensure that multiple inputs are received before making the decision about classification.

Decision point 3, services, is most often characterized in the current system by the delivery of expert advice by consultants who tell the practitioner what to do with the student, and by the individual efforts of teachers to provide remedial instruction. In interactive teaming, "services" are characterized by coordinated consultation and collaboration among the members of the team.

Decision point 4 involves the development of an instructional plan. In the current system, the Individual Educational Program (IEP) is often written before the meeting and presented to parents for their signature. In interactive teaming, the IEP is written during the meeting, and represents the joint efforts of team members, including parents.

At decision point 5, evaluation, the child is currently given periodic tests focused on standardized measures of achievement to determine whether he or she has mastered the prescribed program content. In interactive teaming, the focus of evaluation is on the program; measurement is ongoing and the analysis is focused on ways in which the team can change the program to increase its effectiveness.

APPLICATION OF INTERACTIVE TEAMING

Working as an effective team member is much more difficult than working alone. The team members have differing perspectives; speak varying "languages"; and demonstrate a range of behaviors that result in both effective and ineffective use of power and authority.

One of the most useful ways to begin thinking about the strengths and problems inherent in teaming is to observe a team engaged in the process of information sharing and decision making. The exercise in Figure 1–4 is designed to guide the reader through this experience as a foundation for understanding the procedures in subsequent chapters of this text.

The exercise was designed by Mary K. Dykes of the University of Florida. She uses it to prepare future special education teachers to work effectively as team members, and is reprinted here with her permission.

SUMMARY

Educators and related professionals now experience intensified pressures to collaborate in the solution of increasing education-related problems, because:

◆ In the near future the majority of our students will have complex special needs.
◆ Current programs are ineffective in serving the increasing numbers of students with complex special needs.
◆ Proposed solutions that do not take into account the body of knowledge about the process of change will not be any more effective.

Those who have summarized the research on effective schools suggest that:

◆ Teachers in these schools are committed to a central mission.
◆ This mission is focused on maximizing the educational opportunities for students.
◆ Teachers in effective schools work together as a team to achieve this goal.

Observation Guide to be completed as you watch a real or taped meeting of a professional team in action. As you observe, complete this Observation Guide, "Power/Authority in Teaming (Dykes, 1987)." A sample of this activity, completed by Naomi Miller (1989) follows.

Note: Read this entire description before you begin.

Observe the team for 10 minutes to get an idea of who has the most authority, the nature of the authority (G = group given, S = self-proclaimed, D = declared by 3rd party, R = granted by rules or law). In a second 10-minute observation complete the following table. Identify the team member with the most power or group control at the end of each one minute period. Time each observation separately, take data and record on table. Then, begin next one-minute sample.

P = Power   S = Source

Minute	1	2	3	4	5	6	7	8	9	10
Team Members	P/S	P/S	P/S	P/S	P/S	P/S	P/S	P/S	P/S	P/S
1. Counselor	/S	/S	/S					/S		
2. Psychologist					/D	/D				
3. Sp. Ed. Teacher									/G	/G
4. Parent				/D			/D			
5.										
6.										
7.										

Source: G = Group
          S = Self-proclaimed
          D = Declared by role
          R = Rules/law

The chart is a record, showing team members who seemed to have the most power at the end of each one-minute sample during 10-minute observation.

Reprinted by permission

Responses by Miller, Naomi (1989) to form developed by Dykes, Mary Kay (1987). Observation Guide for Power/Authority in Teaming (assignment for EEX 6786, Fall, 1989). (Unpublished manuscript). Gainesville, FL: University of Florida.

		1	2	3
eg	C	/G		/S
	D		/R	

Figure 1–4
Power/authority in teaming

Upon completion and evaluation of your grid on the previous page, answer the following questions:

A) Did one person stay in a more authoritative role than others? Why?

Answer:

The counselor in this I.E.P. staffing attempted to exert more control than the other members. She appeared to be trying to prove her role in the team as she is the newest permanent member of the group.

B) Did the power figure change? If so, how did the new person gain power—usurp, demand, request, etc.?

Answer:

Power figures changed throughout the meeting. The main leader, the counselor, tended to usurp power that appeared to be resented by the other members of the group. The psychologist, an intern, requested control. She took her cue from the counselor but was received well. The special education teacher demanded control and she spoke from a strong knowledge base. Parent control was requested when the other members indicated a time for involvement.

C) Did individuals use authority (power) to benefit the group or were relations strained within the group? How do you know? (verbal or nonverbal)

Answer:

Relations between the counselor and the group appeared strained. The other members were not comfortable with the amount of attempted authority. She exhibited an over exerted trunk-lean, louder voice, and tenser actions. The other members related well together, eye-contact, posture, tone, and gestures all indicated good communication.

D) Were attempts made to get all members to contribute? Were the efforts usually made by the same person(s)? Explain. How were the efforts made (vocal, nonvocal, pause/eye contact, etc.)? Were efforts successful?

Answer:

The group functioned collectively. The counselor distributed control between members. First, they went over introductions and then the counselor gave control to the psychologist to go over psychological reports. At certain points throughout the conference, parent participation was invited. Finally, the counselor directed involvement to the I.E.P. formulation, and this is where the special education teacher took over. In the end, the special education representative tried to involve the parent through questions. Control was distributed from the counselor to the psychologist through verbal cues, whereas a gesture was made when the counselor directed the power to the special education teacher. Most other efforts were verbal.

Figure 1–4, *continued*

E) What, if any, relation did you observe between power and a team member's use of data? (If the individual brought actual assessment or observation data to conference were they viewed as high or low power? Why?)

Answer:

The psychologist produced data from the psychological report. She gained a high power control base when presenting the data and this was viewed as her knowledge power base. The parent was in agreement with the results of the data.

F) List observed and personal and/or professional characteristics of those who had (1) the most power and (2) the least power.

Answer:

	Most	Least
Personal:	Empathetic, calm, sincere, and understanding, good eye contact.	Demanding in nonverbal indicators. Overwhelming.
Professional:	Task-oriented, directly involved, invited involvement. Worked from experience.	Pushy on signing of papers. Tried to accept personal responsibility for student improvement.

G) List procedures a high–power team member used to facilitate the team efforts:

Answer:

Positive: The special education teacher was very confident with her position. She allowed the counselor and psychologist to take their positions also. She displayed verbal and nonverbal cues showing interest. She handled her "duties," explaining the program, I.E.P. formulation and getting signatures with ease. She explained her information in understandable terms and made the parent feel comfortable.

Negative: There were moments when her involvement could have directed conversation and eased tension rather than the counselor taking control of the situation. She ended the meeting somewhat abruptly by saying that she had to go to another appointment. No opportunities for future interaction were indicated.

H) Were some team members prepared but spoke only when specifically requested to do so? How could you handle such a situation?

Answer:

Yes, the psychologist took control when it was time to display the psychological reports. The situation will probably be resolved when she becomes more comfortable with the authoritative position she holds. It was her first I.E.P. conference and she was just testing her abilities.

I) What, if any, role did age, sex, years of experience, professional training, e.g., therapist, physician, educator, psychologist, have in determining who the team members perceived as the authority or power figure? Did you observe a professional or personal "pecking order?" Explain.

Answer:

As already mentioned, the special education teacher's experience at the position and in this location, enabled her to be very confident in her role. The lack of professional training of the school psychologist stood in the way of her performance. Finally, the counselor's fight for power inhibited her effectiveness. The only person who was involved in a "pecking order" was the counselor, the others ignored the undercurrents.

J) Identify the most effective team member. Identify the least effective team member.

Answer:

The most effective team member was the special education teacher. She was involved, prepared, and comfortable, which set the interaction at ease. She did not allow the meeting to stray from the topics, yet still allowed for parent and professional involvement.

The counselor was the least effective in this meeting. She was trying very hard, too hard it appeared. She was the one to greet the parent and pushed too hard to try and appear friendly. Her power–seeking behaviors undermined her effectiveness.

Observe each for three minutes—keep a running log of what each was doing (e.g., eye contact with, posture, attention, etc.). Contrast the two sets of behavior.

Answer:

Most effective: Attentive, eye contact maintained with person in control. She was in control after the first eight minutes while formulating the I.E.P. She had a relaxed confident posture along with an authoritative voice and tone.

Least effective: Once she was out of her "director" role, she began to slouch and look at her watch. She was writing on some other papers that she was working on. Her attention was minimal.

Figure 1–4, *continued*

The model proposed in this book—interactive teaming—is a response to the nation's increasingly complex problems in special needs programs, as it incorporates the features of teacher empowerment, community responsiveness, and professional collaboration, all of which characterize effective schools for disabled and at-risk students.

The interactive team is a group that functions at the highest level of professionalism, because it involves both consultation and collaboration. The interactive teaming model includes components that have been used previously to provide services to students with mild disabilities and in programs that provide educational, medical, and social services to students with severe disabilities. The historical foundations and specific dimensions of interactive teaming will be described in detail in the following two chapters.

ACTIVITIES

1. Observe interactive teaming in your own classroom or clinical program, or interview a person who teaches in such a program. How do the students in this program differ from those in your classes when you attended school? In what ways are the professionals in this program collaborating (or failing to collaborate) to provide effective educational and medical services for students with complex needs?

2. Describe your attitudes about or past experiences with activities in which you were asked to interact with other professionals to develop an educational product or program. In what ways did your experiences lead you to be optimistic about the benefits of interactive teaming? Pessimistic? What, in your opinion, has to happen if collaboration is to succeed?

3. Imagine that you have an unlimited budget and the power to implement any type of programs you choose that would serve the growing number of students with special needs. Describe the program(s) you would implement.

REFERENCES

Algozzine, K., Morsink, C., & Algozzine, B. (1987). In search of differentiated instruction: An analysis of teaching behaviors in self-contained special education classrooms. *Florida Journal of Teacher Education, 4,* 62–70.

Allington, R. (1984). Oral reading. In P. D. Pearson (Ed.), *Handbook of reading research*. New York: Longwood.

—. (1987, October). Current practice and future directions: Implementation of categorical programs: Reading instruction. In *The education of students with special needs: Gearing up to meet the challenges of the 1990s*. Symposium conducted at The Wingspread Conference, Racine, WI.

Anderson, R., Hiebert, E., Scott, H., & Wilkinson, I. (1985). *Becoming a nation of readers: The report of the commission on reading*. Washington, DC: National Institute of Education.

Ashton, P., & Webb, R. (1986). *Making a difference: Teachers' sense of efficacy and student achievement*. New York: Longman.

Bartel, N., & Thurman, K. (1992). Medical treatment and educational problems in children. *Phi Delta Kappan, 74*(1), 57–61.

Bell, J. (1987). *School-based management: An idea whose time has come.* Wilmington, NC: University of North Carolina-Wilmington, School of Education. Unpublished manuscript.

Blase, J. (1985). The socialization of teachers. *Urban Education, 20,* 235–256.

Bonner, J. S. (1982). Japanese quality circles: Can they work in education? *Phi Delta Kappan, 63,* 681.

Boone, R. (1990). *The development, implementation, and evaluation of a preconference training strategy for enhancing parental participation in and satisfaction with the individual transition conference.* (Doctoral dissertation, University of Florida, 1989) *Dissertation Abstracts International, 51*(3), 618A.

Brown, R. (1985). *Reconnecting youth: The next stage of reform.* Denver, CO: Business Advisory Commission, Education Commission of the States.

Bunting, C. (1988). University-public school collaboration in the preparation of teachers: The North Carolina model. *The Clearing House, 61,* 315–316.

Burgess, D., & Streissguth, A. (1992). Fetal alcohol syndrome and fetal alcohol effects: Principles for educators. *Phi Delta Kappan, 74*(1), 24–30.

Chalfant, J., & Psych, M. (1989). Teacher-assistance teams: Five descriptive studies on 96 teams. *Remedial and Special Education, 10*(60), 49–58.

Chandler, M., & Stein, J. (Eds.) (1987). *The condition of education* (Statistical Report). Washington, DC: U.S. Department of Education, Center for Educational Statistics.

Comer, J. (1989). Children can: An address on school improvement. In R. Webb & F. Parkay (Eds.), *Children can: An address on school improvement by Dr. James Comer with responses from Florida's Educational Community* (pp. 4–17). Gainesville, FL: University of Florida, College of Education Research & Development Center in collaboration with the Alachua County Mental Health Association.

Coulter, A. (1987). *Position statement: Advocacy for appropriate educational services for all children.* New Orleans: National Association of School Psychologists.

Council of Administrators of Special Education. (1990, Sept. 29). *Position paper on least restrictive environment.* Las Vegas: CASE Board of Directors.

Cuban, L. (1988). A fundamental puzzle of school reform. *Phi Delta Kappan, 69,* 341–344.

Cuttance, P. (1985). Frameworks for research on the effectiveness of schooling. *Studying school effectiveness.* Schaumburg, IL: Palmer Press.

DeBevoise, W. (1984). Synthesis of research on the principal as instructional leader. *Educational Leadership, 41*(5), 14–20.

Deming, W. E. (1986). *Out of the crisis.* Boston: MIT Center for Advanced Engineering Studies.

Dykes, M. K. (1987). Observation guide for power/authority in teaming. Unpublished manuscript. Gainesville, FL: University of Florida Department of Special Education.

Eitzen, S. (1992). Problem students: The sociocultural roots. *Phi Delta Kappan, 73,* 84–590.

Fardig, D., & Morsink, C. (1985). *Classroom observations of SLD, EH, and EMH teachers using the Florida Performance Measurement System.* Gainesville, FL: University of Florida, Department of Special Education.

Farrar, E., & Hampel, R. (1987). Social services in American high schools. *Phi Delta Kappan, 69,* 297–303.

First, J., & Carrera, J. (1988). *New voices: Immigrant students in U.S. public schools.* Boston, MA: National Coalition of Advocates for Students.

Fleischner, J., & Van Acker, R. (1990). Changes in the urban school population: Challenges in meeting the need for special education leadership and teacher preparation personnel. In L. M. Bullock and R. I. Simpson (Eds.), *Critical issues in special education: Implications for personnel preparation* (pp. 73–91). Denton: University of North Texas.

Goodlad, J. (1984). *A place called school: Prospects for the future.* New York: McGraw-Hill.

Graden, J., Thurlow, M., & Ysseldyke, J. (1982). *Instructional ecology and academic responding time for students at three levels of teacher-perceived behavioral competence* (Research Report No. 73). Minneapolis: University of Minnesota, Institute for Research on Learning Disabilities.

Haynes, M., & Jenkins, J. (1986). Reading instruction in special education resource rooms. *American Educational Research Journal, 23,* 161–190.

Hechinger, F. (1992). *Fateful choices: Healthy youth for the 21st century.* New York: Carnegie Corporation.

Hocutt, A., Cox, J., & Pelosi, J. (1984). *A policy-oriented study of special education's service delivery* system. Vol. I. An exploration of issues regarding the identification and placement of LD, MR, and ED students (RTI Report No. RTI/2706-06/OIFR). Research Triangle Park, NC: Research Triangle Institute, Center for Educational Studies.

Hodgkinson, H. (1988). The right schools for the right kids. *Educational Leadership, 45,* 10–15.

Johnston, P., Allington, R., & Afflerbach, P. (1985). The congruence of classroom and remedial reading instruction. *Elementary School Journal, 85,* 465–477.

Knapp, M., Turnbull, B., & Shields, P. (1990). New directions for educating the children of poverty. *Educational Leadership, 48,* (2), 4–8.

Lawler, J. (1993, April 2). Quality is a matter of teamwork. *USA Today,* p. 4–5B.

Leerhsen, C., & Namuth, T. (1988, January 18). Alcohol and the family. *Newsweek,* pp. 62–68.

Leggett, D., & Hoyle, S. (1987). Preparing teachers for collaboration. *Educational Leadership, 44,* 58–63.

___. (1985). *The educationally disadvantaged: A national crisis* (Working Paper No. 6). Philadelphia, PA: The State Youth Initiatives Project: Public/Private Ventures.

Levin, H. (1986). *Educational reform for disadvantaged students: An emerging crisis.* West Haven, CT: National Education Association Professional Library.

Lewis, A. (1985). Young and poor in America. *Phi Delta Kappan, 67,* 251–252.

Little, J. (1981). School success and staff development. In *The role of staff development in urban desegregated schools, executive summary.* Washington, DC: National Institute of Education.

Lynch, E., & Stein, R. (1987). Parent participation by ethnicity: A comparison of Hispanic, black, and Anglo families. *Exceptional Children, 54,* 105–111.

Maeroff, G. (1993). Building teams to rebuild schools. *Phi Delta Kappan, 74,* 512–519.

Marburger, C. L. (1985). *One school at a time: School based management: A process for change.* Columbia, MD: The National Committee for Citizens in Education.

Mernit, S. (1990). Kids today. *Instructor,* 35–43.

Miller, H. (1989). Sample responses to Dykes' *Power authority in teaming.* Unpublished manuscript. Gainesville, FL: University of Florida Department of Special Education.

Morsink, C. (1984). *Teaching special needs students in regular classrooms.* Boston: Little, Brown and Company.

Morsink, C., & Lenk, L. (1992). The delivery of special education programs. *Remedial and Special Education, 13*(6), 33–43.

National Coalition of Advocates for Students. (1985). *Barriers to excellence: Our children at risk.* Boston: Author.

Needleman, H. (1992). Childhood exposure to lead: A common cause of school failure. *Phi Delta Kappan, 74*(1), 35–37.

Newmann, F. (1991). Linking restructuring to authentic student achievement. *Phi Delta Kappan, 72,* 458–463.

Oakes, J. (1986). Keeping track, part 1: The policy and practice of curriculum inequality. *Phi Delta Kappan, 68,* 12–17.

Olson, L., & Rodman, B. (1988, June 22). The unfinished agenda, part II. *Education Week,* pp. 17–33.

Pfeiffer, S. (1980). The school-based interprofessional team: Recurring problems and some possible solutions. *Journal of School Psychology, 18,* 389–394.

Preston, S. (1984). Children and the elderly in the U.S. *Scientific American, 251,* 44–49.

Purkey, S., & Smith, M. (1983). Effective schools: A review. *The Elementary School Journal, 83,* 427–452.

___. (1985). School reform: The district policy implications of the effective schools literature. *The Elementary School Journal, 85,* 353–390.

Pyecha, J., Kullgowski, B., & Wiegerink, R. (1984). *Special education costs and funding trends and their relation to the provision of special education and related services.* Research Triangle Park, NC: Research Triangle Institute, Center for Educational Studies.

Reeves, M. S. (1988, April 27). Reform at 5: The unfinished agenda, part 1. *Education Week,* pp. 14–23.

Reschly, D. (1988). Minority MMR overrepresentation and special education reform. *Exceptional Children, 54,* 316–323.

Reynolds, M. (1989). Students with special needs. In M. C. Reynolds (Ed.), *Knowledge base for the beginning teacher* (pp. 129–142). Oxford, England: Pergamon Press.

Rosenholtz, S., & Kyle, S. (1984). Teacher isolation: Barrier to professionalism. *American Educator, 8,* 10–15.

Rupley, W., & Blair, T. (1987). Assignment and supervision of reading seatwork: Looking in on 12 primary teachers. *The Reading Teacher, 40,* 391–393.

Salvia, J., & Ysseldyke, J. (1988). *Assessment in special and remedial education* (4th ed.). Boston: Houghton Mifflin.

Schmid, R. (1988, June 16). Majority of new moms are reporting to work. *Gainesville Sun,* pp. 1A, 8A.

Schmoker, M., & Wilson, R. (1993). Transforming schools through total quality education. *Phi Delta Kappan, 74,* 389–395.

Schneider, G. (1984). Teacher involvement in decision making: Zones of acceptance, decision conditions, and job satisfaction. *Journal of Research and Development in Education, 18,* 25–32.

Secretary's Commission on Achieving Necessary Skills. (1991). *What work requires of schools: A SCANS report for America 2000.* Washington, DC: U.S. Department of Labor. (ERIC Document Reproduction Service No. ED 332 054).

Sergiovanni, T. (1987). *The principalship: A reflective practice perspective.* Newton, MA: Allyn and Bacon.

Shaw, S., Biklin, D., Conlon, Dunn, J., Kramer, J., & DeRoma-Watnger, V. (1990). Special education and school reform. In L. M. Bullock and R. L. Simpson (Eds.). *Critical issues in special education: Implications for personnel preparation.* Denton, TX: North Texas University.

Skrtic, T. (1987). *An organizational analysis of special education reform.* Washington, DC: The National Inquiry into the Future of Education for Students with Special Needs.

Smith, S. (1992). Professional partnerships and educational change: Effective collaboration over time. *Journal of Teacher Education, 43,* (4), 243–256.

Stedman, L. (1985). A new look at the effective schools literature. *Urban Education, 20,* 295–326.

___. (1987). It's time we changed the effective schools formula. *Phi Delta Kappan, 69,* 215–224.

Stevens, L., & Price, M. (1992). Meeting the challenge of educating children at risk. *Phi Delta Kappan, 74,* 18–23.

Superintendents. (1988). *Dealing with dropouts: The urban superintendents' call to action.* Washington, DC: U.S. Government Printing Office.

Tanner, C. (1989). Probable impacts of educational reform on at-risk students. *Journal of Research and Development in Education, 22*(2), 1–5.

Thompson, J., & Cooley, V. (1984). Improvement in leadership, curriculum, and staff development can lead to long–term gains. *NASSP Bulletin, 68,* 1–6.

Thousand, J., & Villa, R. (1990). Sharing expertise and responsibilities through teaching teams. In W. Stainback and S. Stainback (Eds.). *Support networks for inclusive schooling: Integrated interdependent education.* Baltimore: Paul H. Brookes, 151–166.

Tye, B. B. (1987). The deep structure of schooling. *Phi Delta Kappan, 69,* 281–283.

U.S. Department of Education (1992). *To assure the free appropriate public education of all children with disabilities.* Fourteenth Annual Report to Congress on the Implementation of The Individuals with Disabilities Education Act. Washington, DC: National Association of State Directors of Special Education.

Walker, N. (1988). The camel: A horse designed by a committee. *The Clearing House, 61*(7), 329–330.

Wiggins, G. (1991). Standards, not standardization: Evoking quality student work. *Educational Leadership, 48*(5), 18–25.

Will, M. (1986). *Educating students with learning problems: A shared responsibility.* Washington, DC: U.S. Department of Education, Office of Special Education and Rehabilitation Services.

Wilson, B., & Firestone, W. (1987). The principal and instruction: Combining bureaucratic and cultural linkages. *Educational Leadership, 45,* 18–23.

CHAPTER 2

Historical Foundations
of Consultation,
Collaboration, & Teaming

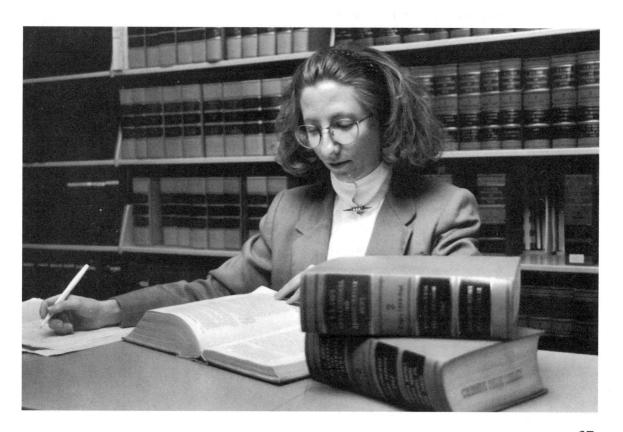

Historical and Legal Foundations

Professional Viewpoints: Early 1970s

Legal Influences: 1970s, 1980s, and 1990s

Expanding Applications: Late 1970s, 1980s, and 1990s

Consultation and Collaboration

Definitions

Models

Dimensions

Goals

Competencies

Process

Teaming

Definitions

Models

Dimensions

Goals

Competencies

Process

Impediments and Barriers

Consultation

Teaming

Positive Features

Application

Summary

TOPICS IN THIS CHAPTER INCLUDE

◆ Description of the historical and legal foundations of consultation, collaboration, and teaming.

◆ Definitions of consultation, collaboration, and teaming.

◆ Models of consultation, collaboration, and teaming.

◆ Dimensions and goals of consultation, collaboration, and teaming.

◆ Competencies and processes in consultation and teaming.

◆ Impediments and positive features of consultation and teaming.

◆ An application illustrating these approaches.

Dan Hayes, a school psychologist, is responsible for the assessment of students in three schools in the district. The district also expects its psychologists to serve as consultants and team members in their assigned schools. Dan has commented often on the variance in how well he believes he is able to meet that expectation in his three assigned schools.

At the meetings at Maxway Elementary, Dan feels primarily like a reporter. The assistant principal, Mrs. Payton, is in charge of all meetings to discuss students, and she prides herself on running brief and efficient meetings. The usual format is to have Dan and his colleagues present their assessment data and recommendations in round-robin fashion. However, questions and discussion are not encouraged because of the extra time involved, and Mrs. Payton says such talk among professionals usually only confuses the parents. After the professionals make their reports, Mrs. Payton provides a summary and a list of options to the parents. The parents usually are silent listeners until this point, and Dan thinks they often are intimidated by the number of professionals present and Mrs. Payton's businesslike approach. He has commented to his colleagues that more often than not, the parents select the first option presented and rarely ask questions. He has tried to talk to Mrs. Payton about various ways to enhance the input of the professionals, but the response always has been, "Why make things more complicated than they are? We've always done it this way, and I don't want to change now. Our meetings go quickly, so let's not do anything that might prolong them."

At Zion Primary School, Dan believes his role is more like that of a consultant, but he is uncomfortable with being introduced to the parents as the "expert" and viewed as the one whose recommendations should carry the most weight. Because the principal at Zion does not like to ask his staff to attend meetings regularly, Dan finds that he frequently has to attend several meetings to discuss the same issues on a single child because not all the personnel are willing or able to meet at the same time. In addition to the strains this places on his schedule, Dan is aware that trying to attend several meetings is a hardship for some parents.

In contrast to these two schools, when Dan attends meetings at Anderson Middle School, he feels like more of a team member. The principal, Mr. Gutierrez, has identified one day per week as a meeting day, and he encourages his staff to be available for meetings on students or curriculum matters. Mr. Gutierrez posts the schedule for the meetings on students and lists which teachers and professionals need to attend. Although he attends the meetings, he contributes as a team member rather than as team leader. The leadership role is rotated among Dan, a special educator, a regular classroom teacher, and the counselor based upon a schedule they designed at the beginning of the year.

Input from the parents is encouraged, and all the professionals value the exchanges and ideas among the team members. Team members frequently consult and collaborate with others outside of the group meetings, and any additional information or strategies obtained in those sessions are shared at the beginning of each team meeting. Dan thinks the situation at Anderson is advantageous to all of the people involved, and that the quality of the decisions made is much higher than at his other two schools.

This vignette illustrates various processes professionals and parents can engage in to share information on students. It also describes the effects the setting and attitudes can have upon what actually occurs and how well people are able to fulfill their roles. In this example, Dan was able to complete the assessment tasks expected of him in a similar way at all three schools. However, implementation of the aspects of his role that involved consulting and serving as a team member varied markedly among the three schools. This variance was due to the attitudes of the team members on what should be done by whom, who is considered the "expert," the leadership style implemented, the value placed on input from others, and a lack of willingness to change. However, at Anderson Middle, Dan was able to be a consultant, collaborator and team member—and his colleagues also were able to serve in those roles.

The interactive teaming model proposed in this text has been developed as an attempt to take into account the myriad factors affecting the provision of educational and other types of program services for students with special learning and behavioral needs. In addition, appropriate implementation of the model should reduce the discrepancies in how services are delivered and professionals and parents are able to interact.

The model is built upon components of various approaches and service delivery alternatives that have been presented and researched primarily in the fields of special education and school psychology. However, it is important to note at the outset that interactive teaming includes not only psychologists and special educators, but also parents and other professionals who are concerned with the welfare and education of children. These professionals include regular classroom teachers, physicians, social workers, counselors, physical and occupational therapists, adapted physical educators, speech/language clinicians, and other related services personnel.

This chapter includes a selected review of the literature on consultation, collaboration, and teaming models advanced in the past two decades. The models will be defined, and their characteristics will be delineated. Dimensions or characteristics of these models, programmatic goals, and competencies of personnel involved in implementation will be described. Finally, impediments or barriers and effective features of the models will be summarized.

HISTORICAL AND LEGAL FOUNDATIONS

Professional Viewpoints: Early 1970s

In the early 1970s, professionals in special education and school psychology began to comment on the changes needed in their fields to improve services to students with special needs and the professionals who were working with or teaching those students. Deno (1970) presented a model of service delivery for special education students that included consultation services as the first level above total regular classroom integration. Lilly (1971) stated that professionals needed to change how they viewed children with mild learning and behavior problems, and how they behaved toward those students. He suggested that rather than labeling the students as exceptional, the situation should be considered exceptional.

Instead of functioning in a direct service role with mildly disabled students, Lilly proposed that special educators serve in a support and training role for the regular classroom teachers who would have primary responsibility for educating the children. Fine and Tyler (1971) also commented on the idea of support for teachers from school psychologists. They called for psychologists to move away from the limited test-and-report approach to one that focused more on teacher consultation and the development of interpersonal functioning and helping relationships.

LEGAL INFLUENCES: 1970s, 1980s, AND 1990s

A legal impetus for teachers, psychologists, and others to work together on concerns about students with special needs appeared in 1975 in Public Law 94-142, The Education for All Handicapped Children Act. Although child study teams existed in some systems before this (Pryzwansky & Rzepski, 1983), certainly the law and its accompanying regulations served as a catalyst for professionals working together. Section 121 a. 532 (e) of P.L. 94-142 states: "The evaluation is made by a multidisciplinary team or group of persons, including at least one teacher, or other specialist, with knowledge in the area of suspected disability." The law also specified cooperation to "insure that the placement decision is made by a group of persons, including persons knowledgeable about the child, the meaning of the evaluation data, and the placement options." Kaiser and Woodman (1985) noted that this law removed the primary decision-making role on special education placement from the school psychologist to a team of people including parents, speech pathologists, teachers, school administrators, nurses, physicians, social workers, and counselors.

The passage of Public Law 99-457, amendments to the Education of the Handicapped Act of 1986, further strengthened the idea of professional collaboration or teaming, in this case to meet the needs of young children. Part H of this law requires states to "develop and implement a statewide comprehensive, coordinated, multidisciplinary, interagency program" for early intervention services. This legislation includes children from birth through age 2 who have been diagnosed as having a mental or physical condition that will likely result in a disability. At the discretion of a state agency, it can also include children who are considered at risk for developmental problems (Siders, Riall, Bennett, & Judd, 1987).

Public Law 94-142 was amended again in 1990 by Public Law 101-476, the Individuals with Disabilities Education Act. In this legislation, the exceptionalities of autism and traumatic brain injury were added, and references to "handicapped children" were changed to "children with disabilities". The law stipulates increased collaboration among special educators, classroom teachers, and related services personnel, and places more emphasis on transition services for students age 16 or older. The Americans with Disabilities Act of 1990 also provides strong legal and civil rights support for equality of opportunity and the value of individuality. Discrimination on the basis of disability is forbidden, and the barriers that prohibit people with disabilities from participating in activities in public locations must be removed. As businesses, public service agencies, and educational institutions have begun the process of implementing this act, consultation and teaming approaches among employees and employers have been used.

EXPANDING APPLICATIONS: LATE 1970s, 1980s, AND 1990s

In the late 1970s and the 1980s, consultation and teaming approaches began to receive attention beyond the original proposals for support and helping relationships and the legal requirements for identification and placement. Special issues on consultation appeared in such professional journals as *Behavioral Disorders* (Nelson, Neel, & Lilly, 1981) and *Teacher Education and Special Education* (1985), *Remedial and Special Education* (1988), and *Preventing School Failure* (1991).

Consultation received much support as:

◆ An effective way to reduce regular educators' referrals for special education services (Cantrell & Cantrell, 1976; Ritter, 1978; Sindelar, Griffin, Smith, & Watanabe, 1992).

◆ A way to diminish the need for labeling or providing differentiated services for mildly disabled students whose academic and behavioral needs are similar (Morsink & Lenk, 1992; Newcomer, 1977).

◆ A skill all teachers need to respond to changing school practices (e.g., Denemark, Morsink, & Thomas, 1980; President's Commission on Teacher Education, 1992).

◆ A viable service delivery alternative for mildly disabled students (cf. Friend, 1988; Reynolds & Birch, 1982).

◆ A requirement for the success of students in mainstreamed classrooms (Friend, 1984; Nelson & Stevens, 1981; Safran & Barcikowski, 1984; Salend, 1994; Simpson & Myles, 1990; Wood, 1992).

◆ An approach to dealing with the unique needs of secondary-level pupils (Huefner, 1988; Patriarca & Lamb, 1990; Tindal, Shinn, Walz, & Germann, 1987).

◆ An important element in infant and preschool programs (Hanline & Knowlton, 1988; Lowenthal, 1992).

◆ An area needing more research in the response to the Regular Education Initiative (Lloyd, Crowley, Kohler, & Strain, 1988).

◆ A model for transition planning (Sileo, Rude & Luckner, 1988).

In addition to the special issues of journals previously cited, a new journal focusing on consultation was initiated in 1990, *Journal of Educational and Psychological Consultation*. A number of new textbooks targeted for special educators, psychologists, and other related area professions also have been published on the topics of consultation, collaboration, and teaming in the late 1980s and 1990s. These texts include *Psychological Consultation* (Brown, Pryzwansky & Schulte, 1991); *Consultation, Collaboration, and Teamwork* (Dettmer, Thurston, & Dyck, 1993); *Interac-*

tions: Collaboration Skills for School Professionals (Friend & Cook, 1992); *Consultation Concepts and Practices* (Hansen, Himes, & Meier, 1990); *Collaborative Consultation* (Idol, Nevin & Paolucci-Whitcomb, 1994); *Effective School Consultation* (Sugai & Tindal, 1993), and *Collaboration in the Schools* (West, Idol, & Cannon, 1989).

Consultation also has been recognized and supported by professionals inside and outside special education settings, as well as in various other types of service delivery programs. In an article for school counselors, Umansky and Holloway (1984) commented on the changes in education that created the need for counselors to serve as consultants. Physical therapists are finding an increasing amount of their role descriptions to be consulting with teachers (cf. Lindsey, 1985). Physicians have supported the concept of consultation and collaboration, and they believe their input is necessary in treating all aspects of a child's functioning (cf. Brown, 1987; Marshall & Wuori, 1985). Alternative programs for young children, such as day-care and home-based programs, are utilizing consultation as a way to meet professional development needs (Jones & Meisels, 1987; Klein & Sheehan, 1987; Trohanis, 1981). Community-based programs for developmentally delayed people have implemented consultative services (e.g., Como & Hagner, 1986; Powers, 1986). In addition, consultation has been used to address the needs of physically disabled people who live in rural settings (e.g., Moore & Allen, 1986).

Examples of teaming approaches in a variety of settings also have been documented in the literature. Major journals have run topical issues on teaming, including *Teacher Education and Special Education* (Egan & Bluhm, 1981) and *School Psychology Review* (1983). Kaiser and Woodman (1985) noted that rehabilitation centers and mental health clinics have had ongoing integrated team services for their clients. Vocational and industrial educators have begun advocating a team approach for meeting the needs of special needs and at-risk students (Feichtner & Sarkees, 1987; Spencer-Dobson & Schultz, 1987). Transitional programs for preschoolers (Brown, 1987) and adults with special needs (Edgar, 1988) cite teaming as a key aspect. Ancillary personnel, such as physical and occupational therapists, support teaming as a way to fit into the total school system or program functioning (e.g., Lindsey, O'Neal, Haas, & Tewey, 1983; McAfee, 1987).

The Council for Exceptional Children supported the importance of consultation, collaboration, and teaming by inclusion of these areas in the *CEC Common Core of Knowledge and Skills Essential for All Beginning Special Education Teachers* (Swan & Sirvis, 1992). The *Common Core* is composed of 107 knowledge and skill statements in eight categories. Examples of statements and categories related to consultation and collaboration are listed below:

Skill #25. Collaboration with parents and other professionals involved in the assessment of students with individual learning needs.

Category VII. Communication and Collaborative Partnerships

Knowledge #85. Importance and benefits of communication and collaboration, which promotes interaction with students, parents, and school and community personnel.

Knowledge #87. Developing individual student programs working in collaboration with team members.

Skill #90. Use collaborative strategies in working with students, parents, and school and community personnel in various learning environments.

Skill #93. Encourage and assist families to become active participants in the educational team.

Skill #95. Collaborate with regular classroom teachers and other school and community personnel in integrating students into various learning environments.

The extensive support for consultation, collaboration, and teaming from a variety of viewpoints and service delivery options, along with legal mandates and support from key professional organizations, make further exploration of these approaches vital. The next sections will define consultation, collaboration, and teaming, discuss characteristics and processes, and delineate how aspects of these approaches are part of the foundation for interactive teaming.

CONSULTATION AND COLLABORATION

Definitions

The variety of definitions of consultation frequently is due to the differences in the philosophical views and professional roles of the authors. Based on their extensive review of the literature, West and Idol (1987) concluded that consultation has at least three general meanings: *medical,* in which a doctor calls upon the expertise of another physician for counsel; *organizational,* which involves change in a system; and *mental health,* where a consultant provides assistance to another professional on problems the latter may be experiencing with a client.

Tharp (1975) described consultation as a triadic process in which the consultant attempted to bring about changes in a target person through a consultee or mediator. Bergan's (1977) definition included two forms of consultation, depending on whether the goals were considered to be long-range (*developmental* consultation) or designed to remediate an immediate problem (*problem-centered* consultation). Brown, Wyne, Blackburn, and Powell (1979) noted that consultation is a process involving the establishment of trust and communication and "joint approaches to problem identification, the pooling of personal resources, to identify and select strategies that will have some probability of solving the problem that has been identified, and shared responsibility in the implementation and evaluation of the program or strategy that has been initiated" (p. 8). Idol-Maestas (1983) focused on the support regular classroom teachers can gain from consultants that will help them cope with students' academic and social behavior problems. Conoley and Conoley (1982) emphasized the voluntary and nonsupervisory design of a consultative relationship.

Medway's (1979) definition included the phrase *collaborative problem-solving* to describe the interaction that occurs among professionals. The collaborative nature of consultation has received much attention in the literature for school psychologists (cf. Gutkin & Curtis, 1982; Piersel, 1985). Hawryluk and Smallwood (1986) noted:

Regardless of theoretical orientation, school consultation is based on the premise that positive change in student behavior can be produced indirectly when a consultant engages with teachers or other school personnel in collaborative problem solving (p. 519).

Special educators also have advocated this collaborative approach. Idol, Paolucci-Whitcomb, and Nevin (1986) defined *collaborative consultation* as "an interactive process that enables people with diverse expertise to generate creative solutions to mutually defined problems. The outcome is enhanced, altered, and produces solutions that are different from those that the individual team members would produce independently. The major outcome of collaborative consultation is to provide comprehensive and effective programs for students with special needs within the most appropriate context, thereby enabling them to achieve maximum constructive interaction with their nonhandicapped peers" (p. 1).

In the second edition of their textbook, Idol and her colleagues (1994) noted: "The process creates synergy, with different outcomes that are better than the original solutions that any team member would produce independently" (p. xi).

Heron and Harris (1987) included the concept of professionals working together in consultation by stating:

It is a collaborative, voluntary, mutual problem-solving process that may or may not involve the achievement of several subordinate objectives and that leads to the prevention or resolution of identified problems (p. 3).

Friend and Cook (1992) also noted the importance of collaboration and defined it as:

A style for direct interaction between at least two co-equal parties voluntarily engaged in shared decision-making as they work toward a common goal (p. 6).

Dettmer, Thurston, and Dyck (1993) defined school consultation and the role of consultant as follows:

School consultation is activity in which professional educators and parents collaborate within the school context by communicating, cooperating and coordinating their efforts as a team to serve the learning and behavioral needs of students.

A school consultant is a facilitator of communication, cooperation, and coordination who consults, collaborates, and engages in teamwork with other educators to identify learning and behavioral needs, and plan, implement, and evaluate educational programs to meet those needs (p. 14).

Sugai and Tindal (1993) emphasize a behavior-analytic approach to consultation and collaboration. In the preface of their book, they state:

Consultation is defined as a structured series of problem-solving steps or interactions that occur between two or more individuals. We emphasize the development and modification of solutions from information that is systematically obtained and analyzed within the context of the immediate problem. We view collaboration as the outcome of a successful consultation in which educators engage in a coordinated or united effort to solve a problem (p. viii).

A final point in defining consultation is clarifying what it should *not* be. Pryzwansky (1974) stated that consultation should not be an "expert" providing some type of prescription. Gutkin and Curtis (1982) distinguished between the traditional medical model approach that focused on psychological problems as mental illnesses, and the current approach to consultation that is based primarily on behavioral psychology. West and Idol (1987) also pointed out the difference between consultation and counseling by stating that the former should be focused on issues, whereas the latter tends to be focused on individuals. Hansen, Himes, and Meier (1990) noted that consultation differs from collaboration, because collaborators carry joint responsibility for situations and in consultation the consultee retains ownership of the case or program.

Models

West and Idol (1987) identified 10 models of consultation from their examination of the literature in special education and school psychology. Three of the models they described will be discussed here because they are essential to an understanding of interactive teaming. Those models are *triadic* (and its relationship to collaborative), *organizational,* and *behavioral* consultation.

As previously indicated, *triadic consultation* (Tharp, 1975; Tharp & Wetzel, 1969) involves three people: consultant, mediator, and target. Tharp (1975) describes the roles of each person as follows:

◆ The *target* is the person with the problematic behavior, the change of which is the primary goal of the directed influence.

◆ The *mediator* is the person with the available means of social influence for effecting that goal.

◆ The *consultant* is the person with the knowledge to mobilize the mediator's influence (p. 138).

In the triadic model, the target may be a student or an adult in whom others believe a behavior change is desirable. The mediator is a parent, teacher, or other professional who will be attempting to bring about a behavior change in the target. The consultant can be a parent, teacher, administrator, or other professional who has expertise to share regarding strategies to change the behavior.

In the illustration of the triadic model in Figure 2–1, the existence of two dyads within the model is also shown in the bottom part of the box. The dyads are consultant-mediator and mediator-target. Each influences the other, and there is an indirect influence of the consultant on the target, as shown by the dotted line in the top diagram.

Figure 2–1

The triadic model

Note: From "The Triadic Model of Consultation: Current Considerations" by R. G. Tharp, 1975. In C. Parker (Ed.), *Psychological Consultation: Helping Teachers Meet Special Needs.* Reston, VA: The Council for Exceptional Children, p. 137. Adapted by permission.

Collaborative consultation (Idol, Paolucci-Whitcomb, & Nevin, 1986) is essentially an extension of the triadic model. Idol et al. specified that the target typically is a student with some type of problem, the mediator usually is a regular classroom teacher, and the consultant can be a special educator, speech therapist, principal, or the like. Although the authors commented that this model can result in collaboration and sharing among professionals with various types of expertise, implementation has primarily focused upon a triadic relationship among regular and special educators attempting to meet the needs of students with special characteristics.

Organizational consultation (e.g., Brown, Kiraly, & McKinnon, 1979; Gallessich, 1982) focuses on the process of change in the systems of an organization or group of people. The interactions among group members, interrelationships among subsystems, shared decision making, and communication skills are highlighted in this model. The consultant can be anyone within the system and is viewed primarily as a facilitator of the group process.

Behavioral consultation (Bergan, 1977) is based on social learning theory and the application of the principles of applied behavior analysis. The primary emphasis is on student behavior change, so it can be considered a client-centered and problem-solving approach (Piersel, 1985). Proponents of behavioral consultation, especially in recent years, also have indicated the importance of considering a child's interactions within a total environmental system to understand influences on behavior (Cipani, 1985; Friend, 1988; Hawryluk & Smallwood, 1986), and they have noted that some degree of change will occur in the consultee's behavior as a result of involvement in the consultative process (Gutkin, 1986).

The defining features of this consultation model are the use of direct observation methods resulting in problem definitions in observable and measurable terms, identification of target behaviors for change, and the use of data-based intervention and assessment methods (Hawryluk & Smallwood, 1986). Sugai and Tindal (1993) focus their behavior-analytic and best-practices approach to consultation on the learned nature and lawfulness of behavior and the potential for change by manipulating aspects of the environment.

Dimensions

The dimensions or characteristics of consultation can be affected by the emphasis or focus of the consultant. However, Gutkin and Curtis (1982) identified a set of core characteristics they believe are present in almost all the models they reviewed:

1. *Indirect service delivery:*   Working on a child's behavior through another professional rather than directly with the child.
2. *Consultant-consultee relationship:*   Establishment of an open and trusting relationship.
3. *Coordinate status:*   Viewing the consultee as an equal, rather than operating in a hierarchical power structure.
4. *Involvement of the consultee in the consultation process:*   Active participation of the consultee throughout the process.
5. *Consultee's right to reject consultant suggestions:*   The freedom to select among the options presented instead of being pressured to follow along with every recommendation.
6. *Voluntary nature of consultation:*   Participants are involved because they recognize a need and want some assistance, not because they are being forced to attend.
7. *Confidentiality:*   The information provided is not shared with others who are not involved in the consultation process.

The dimensions or elements of collaboration are similar to those of consultation listed above. Cook and Friend (1991) noted that collaboration is a voluntary endeavor. In addition, they commented that individuals who collaborate *share a common goal, share responsibility for decisions and accountability for outcomes,* and must believe in *parity*; that is, each participant has something valuable to contribute and the *contributions are valued by others.*

The critical elements of collaborative consultation were identified by Villa, Thousand, Paolucci-Whitcomb, and Nevin (1990). They stated that participants *value one another as possessors of unique expertise, distribute task and relationship functions* among members of the group, *hold one another accountable*, and *monitor and adjust emphasis on task and relationship behaviors.*

Goals

Some authors stress the *helping relationship* goal of consultation and collaboration (e.g., Fine & Tyler, 1971), whereas others focus more on the *training* or *teaching* of another professional such skills as assessment, programming, management, and monitoring (e.g., Idol-Maestas, 1983; Parker, 1975). West and Idol (1987) summarized aspects of the latter goal by noting that consultation can provide remedial services for presenting problems, as well as attempt to increase consultee skills to prevent— or more effectively respond to—future problems. In their review of six consultation service delivery models, Idol and West (1987) noted that they focused upon three types of outcomes: changes in students, changes in teachers, and changes in systems. Pugach and Johnson (1990) commented that consultants can provide the stimulus for general classroom teachers to change their instructional practices to "increase the likelihood that students with learning and behavior problems will be successful" (p. 240).

Brown, Wyne, Blackburn, and Powell (1979) presented a comprehensive list of goals for consultation that included (a) placing high priority on the psychological development of the student, (b) using parent and community resources to assist the student, (c) enhancing the skills of consultees, (d) facilitating communication among professionals, (e) improving human relations in the school, and (f) increasing educational achievement of students. Idol, Nevin, and Paolucci-Whitcomb (1994) described other possible positive outcomes of collaborative consultation: changes in the collaborators and changes in the organization. They stated that as a result of engaging in the collaborative process, the collaborators are expected to:

1. Increase their individual knowledge bases by learning from each other.
2. Improve their interpersonal skills (communication, group interaction, and problem solving).
3. Make cognitive and emotional shifts in their own intrapersonal attitudes toward how to be more effective team members and toward what the learning possibilities might be for learners who have special needs or who are currently experiencing school failure (p. xii).

Competencies

Studies in the area of competencies considered necessary for effective consultation have focused upon those needed by consultants as well as by consultees. The interactive and confidential nature of consultation makes empirical measures difficult to obtain, so the research has tended to take the form of recommendations, consensus ratings among professionals, or self-reports.

Special educators who serve as consultants typically are in the role of resource teacher. The consultant aspect of this role has been the topic of considerable debate since the mid-1980s in terms of whether (a) this is an appropriate expectation

(Brown, Kiraly, & McKinnon, 1979); (b) it is an important element for the success of mainstreaming (Speece & Mandell, 1980); (c) principals and regular classroom teachers see it as a vital part of the resource role (Evans, 1981); (d) special educators feel confident in the role (Aloia, 1983); and (e) it is an expectation or policy by the state departments of education (West & Brown, 1987).

Recommendations regarding competencies generally are similar to those presented by Haight (1984). She stated that the consultant role requires specific knowledge in a variety of areas; skills in analysis, problem solving, and synthesis; and the ability to promote human relations, communication, and skill development in others. Friend (1984) surveyed resource teachers, regular classroom teachers, and principals regarding their views on the skills needed for consultation. All three groups of educators indicated that the skills usually considered integral to a consultative role should be possessed by resource teachers. The results of the study led Friend to comment that resource teachers appear to be expected to be "super teachers" and to fulfill a lengthy list of job duties. West and Cannon (1988) conducted a study to identify the competencies needed by both regular and special educators in working in a collaborative consultation model. These authors used a Delphi method to survey 100 interdisciplinary experts in 47 states. The competencies that received the highest ratings were in the areas of personal characteristics, collaborative problem solving, and interactive communication.

The training to develop consultation competencies typically is included in programs for health and medical practitioners (Courtnage & Healy, 1984) and school psychologists and counselors, but such training is less often a part of the course of study for special educators (Salend & Salend, 1984) and even more limited—if present at all—for regular educators. Training programs have been described that use a variety of approaches, such as single-subject measurement designs (Idol-Maestas, 1983), interactive video (Evans, 1985), collaboration between university faculty and field-based teachers (Paolucci-Whitcomb & Nevin, 1985), and collaboration among post-doctoral-level personnel from various departments (McClellan & Wheatley, 1985). However, as Gable, Young, and Hendrickson (1987) noted, training in consultation competencies is still limited in most programs, and if it is available, it usually is at the graduate instead of the undergraduate level. A summary of programs designed to teach special educators skills in consultation may be found in Idol and West (1987). An inservice and preservice curriculum for teachers, support staff and administrators has been developed by West, Idol, and Cannon (1989).

Process

The process implemented in consultation is based upon the focus, type of problem, and the people involved. Although described in a variety of terms by different authors, the process generally includes the steps listed in Figure 2–2 (compiled from Brown, Pryzwansky, & Schulte, 1991; Cipani, 1985; Dettmer, Thurston, & Dyck, 1993; Gutkin, 1993; Heron & Harris, 1987; Idol, Paolucci-Whitcomb, & Nevin, 1986; Kampwirth, 1987; Kurpius, 1978; Sugai & Tindal, 1993).

1. *Establishing the relationship*—meeting and establishing trust with the consultee.
2. *Gathering information*—checking a variety of sources to get background on the problem.
3. *Identifying the problem*—determining the history and frequency of the problem, defining it in measurable terms.
4. *Stating the target behavior*—considering whether the behavior needs to be increased or decreased, and by what criteria the behavior is to be judged.
5. *Generating interventions*—discussing options to consider, selecting ones to try.
6. *Implementing the interventions*—putting the interventions into effect and collecting data on their success or failure.
7. *Evaluating the interventions*—determining whether the desired outcomes have been reached and modifying as necessary.
8. *Withdrawing from the consultative relationship*—ending the process when the goal has been reached or an agreement is made not to continue.

Figure 2–2
The process of consultation

TEAMING

Definitions

The definitions delineated in the literature on teaming frequently are very similar, although emphases may vary slightly depending on the model being defined. Pfeiffer (1980) noted that a team is an organized group of professionals from different disciplines who have unique skills and a common goal of *cooperative problem solving*. Abelson and Woodman (1983) commented on *interdependence* among team members, and the relationships and norms that help control team and individual behavior. Bailey (1984) observed that teams learn, grow, and change as they attempt to collaborate. Dettmer, Thurston, and Dyck (1993) stated that consultation, collaboration, and teaming share two characteristics: "engaging in interactive processes and using specialized content to achieve shared goals" (p. 16). They also noted that collaboration and teamwork allow participants the opportunity to build on the strengths of their colleagues.

Models

Three models of teams, as well as three types of committee approaches, have been identified. The teaming models will be described first: multidisciplinary, interdisciplinary, and transdisciplinary. These three models are illustrated in Figure 2–3.

Figure 2–3
Models of teams

Multidisciplinary team

Interdisciplinary team

Transdisciplinary team

Key:
PA = Parent
RC = Regular classroom teacher
SE = Special educator
SP = Speech/language clinician
SW = Social worker
PH = Physician
PT = Physical therapist
OT = Occupational therapist
APE = Adapted physical educator
PSY = Psychologist
CO = Counselor

The *multidisciplinary team* developed from the medical model as people with expertise in various fields shared their observations about a patient, and frequently those findings were reported to one person (Hart, 1977). Pfeiffer (1981) stated that the "key elements of a multidisciplinary team are a common purpose, cooperative problem solving by different professionals who possess skills and orientations, and a coordination of activities" (p. 330).

An *interdisciplinary team* may include the same members as the multidisciplinary team, but in this model the team members evaluate a child and then meet as a group to discuss their observations. Bailey, Helsel-DeWert, Thiele, and Ware (1983) described the interdisciplinary process by saying it "is at one level, the complex interaction of individual skills, professional and personal priorities, client needs, group dynamics, and institutional regulations. At its heart, however, is the individual participant and his or her ability to contribute in a way that facilitates meeting group goals" (p. 248).

The *transdisciplinary team* was developed to attempt to reduce the fragmentation of services that often occurred in the other two models (Hart, 1977). In this approach, interdisciplinary services may be used to make the initial assessment and develop an implementation plan. Golightly (1987) said the major factor that distinguishes transdisciplinary from the other models is the extension through the program implementation phase. Sailor and Guess (1983) stated, "The transdisciplinary approach is an education/treatment model that effectively integrates program goals and objectives from various disciplines and professions. The integration begins in the assessment process and extends through direct programming effort" (p. 207). Lyon and Lyon (1980) advocated the transdisciplinary approach over the other two because it promotes more efficient use of the expertise from various professionals. Gast and Wolery (1985) also supported the transdisciplinary approach because it would allow for multiple interventions to occur concurrently for a child. The model has been used most frequently with students with severe disabilities, but it also could be used with children who have other types of exceptionalities (Golightly, 1987). (See Orelove & Sobsey, 1991 for additional comparisons of the three models and implementation for children with multiple disabilities.)

Dimensions

The characteristics of the transdisciplinary approach apply most directly to the interactive teaming model, so they will be summarized here and examined in more detail in Chapter 3. Lyon and Lyon (1980) cited the following characteristics:

1. *Joint team focus*:   The various professionals involved in serving a child need to work together.

2. *Professional development approach*:   Each professional will need to share information and skills with other group members.

3. *Role release implementation*:   Roles and responsibilities must be accepted and shared among group members.

Orelove and Sobsey (1991) identified other characteristics of a transdisciplinary model, including the following:

1. *Indirect therapy approach:*   Team members serve as consultants to others rather than providing only direct service to students or clients.

2. *Multiple lines of communication:*   Regular team meetings are conducted to share information, knowledge, and skills among participants.

3. *Integration of services:*   Planning is based on a common set of goals, and therapies and services are integrated instead of delivered in isolation.

Goals

The two obvious goals for teaming approaches are similar to the ones described for consultation: *improvement in treatment or education for a child with special needs,* and the *training of professionals in skills beyond their own areas of expertise.* Other benefits espoused for teaming approaches include improved accuracy for assessment and placement decisions, a forum for sharing a variety of perspectives, the development and evaluation of programs, providing consultative services to parents and community members, and an extension of psychoeducational services into schools (cf. Kaiser & Woodman, 1985; Orelove & Sobsey, 1991; Pfeiffer, 1980, 1981; Reynolds, Gutkin, Elliott, & Witt, 1984). Pryzwansky and Rzepski (1983) cited the technical assistance, role enhancement, and professional development opportunities available through a school-based team approach. Siders, Riall, Bennett, and Judd (1987) noted that a transdisciplinary team model facilitated viewing the child and family as part of an ecological system. Stanwood (1988) also noted the importance of viewing the child as part of a "school-family systems orientation," and commented on how that perspective could contribute to improvements in the functioning of a school system administrative placement committee. Thomas (1986) suggested implementation of a team approach as a strategy to reduce the high school dropout rate.

Maher and Hawryluk (1983) recommended consideration of individual, group, and organizational needs, and they provided a set of questions to consider when attempting to identify the tasks or goals that might be appropriate for a team to address in school situations:

1. What educational services and programs are to be provided to individual, group, and organizational clients?

2. To provide appropriate programs to these clients, what educational service delivery tasks need to be accomplished?

3. Within what period of time must task accomplishment occur?

4. Given the tasks that have been identified, which ones might be effectively and efficiently carried out by means of one or more versions of a team approach?

5. What specific kinds of teams might be used? (pp. 181–182).

Competencies

Although special educators and psychologists, as well as those from other disciplines, have been expected through role descriptions and legal mandates such as P.L. 94-142 to participate as team members, the number of training programs designed to improve competencies in this area is limited. In their national survey of preservice teacher training programs, Courtnage and Smith-Davis (1987) found that of the 360 responses received from a possible 513 programs, only 52% of the respondents indicated that they had some degree of training on teaming. Moreover, only 34 of those institutions said the training was required in a separate course or practicum setting; the remainder indicated that the training was included in other courses or experiences.

The competencies that have been identified as important for teaming are typically included in articles about programs or coursework at various institutions. Three recent such descriptions will be briefly summarized. Additional information may be found in the 1981 special issue of *Teacher Education and Special Education* (Egan & Bluhm, 1981).

Courtnage and Healy (1984) described a preservice program at the University of Northern Iowa that was designed to assist prospective educators in developing skills in the referral, evaluation, and staffing processes in schools. The program is competency- and procedure-based, and includes coursework as well as a practicum experience. Siders, Riall, Bennett, and Judd (1987) outlined a model transdisciplinary graduate program at the University of Southern Mississippi at Hattiesburg. Their program is focused on developing leadership skills in professionals from various disciplines who will be working with disabled children. This program also is competency-based, and offers several options for field placement sites.

A third program description was provided by Hudson, Correa, Morsink, and Dykes (1987) of the University of Florida. This preservice program includes a course on transdisciplinary teaming that is taken concurrently with a field-based internship. The six competency areas developed in the program are interpersonal communication, collaborative consultation, case management, power and politics in schools, parent conferences, and awareness of cultural diversity. These competency areas are similar to the collaboration training curriculum for preservice and inservice educators developed by West, Idol, and Cannon (1989), which includes the following components: consultation theory/models; research on consultation theory, training, and practice; personal characteristics; interactive communication; collaborative problem solving; systems change; equity issues and values/belief systems; and evaluation of consultation effectiveness.

Process

The process or sequence of steps in teaming is determined by the type of need presented and the purpose—e.g., identification, IEP development, change in placement—of the meeting(s). Thus, if the purpose of a meeting is to develop an IEP, the sequence of steps might include the sharing of progress data and the establishment of annual goals by the parents and professionals. If the purpose is a change in placement, team members will need to present their data and justification for the change. One example of a detailed sequence of the major steps for a referral process was outlined by Courtnage and Healy (1984). The steps are displayed in Figure 2–4.

Major flow steps of the referral and interdisciplinary meeting process

1. Gather initial student information.
2. Complete initial checklist for identifying behaviors of concern.
3. Designate concerned behaviors and determine the need for data collection.
4. Determine procedures to collect additional data.
5. Collect additional data, analyze data, and formulate a referral decision.
6. Complete referral form.
7. Prepare the pupil for referral.
8. Describe the need for an evaluation meeting and give roles of participants.
9. Determine relevant student information needed for presentation at evaluation meeting.
10. Prepare for evaluation meeting.
11. Evaluate the evaluation meeting—procedures and affective domain.
12. Describe the need for an IEP meeting and give roles of participants.
13. Determine relevant student information needed for presentation at IEP meeting.
14. Prepare for IEP meeting.
15. Evaluate the IEP meeting—procedures and affective domain.
16. Describe the need for the re-evaluation meeting and give roles of participants.
17. Determine relevant student information needed for presentation at re-evaluation meeting.
18. Prepare for re-evaluation meeting.
19. Evaluate the re-evaluation meeting—procedures and affective domain.
20. Describe the need for referring special education students after placement.
21. Activate referral and staffing follow-up activities for those special education students who indicate: (a) unusual progress, (b) significant academic behavior problems, (c) a need for outside resources.

Figure 2-4

The process of teaming

Note: From "Interdisciplinary Team Training: A Competency- and Procedure-Based Approach" by L. Courtnage & H. Healy, 1984, *Teacher Education and Special Education, 7,* 3–11. Copyright © 1984 by Special Press. Reprinted with permission of Special Press and the Teacher Education Division of the Council for Exceptional Children.

Committee Approaches. Three additional examples of groups of professionals meeting to discuss children are *teacher assistance teams* (Chalfant, Pysh, & Moultrie, 1979), *school consultation committees* (McGlothlin, 1981), and the *prereferral intervention model* (Graden, Casey, & Christenson, 1985). All three approaches use many of the consultation strategies previously described, and they often are referred to as collaborative consultation models because the educators involved provide indirect services to students. Another similarity is that they all are designed to assist teachers in making appropriate referrals, as well as to support teachers who have mainstreamed students or students who do not qualify for special services. The committees could be considered interdisciplinary in composition, although they often are composed primarily of regular and special educators with occasional involvement from administrators and parents. As typically implemented, they would not be viewed as transdisciplinary because they are not involved in all of the procedures for a child from assessment to implementation; rather, they are designed to address day-to-day problems that may arise in a particular school or to serve as prereferral screening committees to determine if a student needs to be continued in the referral process and considered for placement in a special program.

Of the three approaches, the prereferral intervention model has been implemented most often by state and local school systems and has received increased attention from researchers. Graden (1989) stated a preference for the term *intervention assistance,* because she thought this more accurately reflected the component of collaboration, and noted that the use of a team in and of itself did not create problems; rather, the functioning of the team as collaborative or expert advice giving made the difference. Pugach and Johnson (1989a) described prereferral intervention as a progressive concept because it promotes interactions between general or regular educators and special educators, and results in sharing of problem-solving strategies for students who will not qualify for special services.

Several reviews of research have delineated the positive outcomes of prereferral intervention, including increases in abilities of teachers to meet a variety of needs, improvements in teachers' attitudes toward students with learning and behavior problems, decreases in overidentification of students as disabled, and positive changes in student achievement and behavior (cf. Morsink & Lenk, 1992; Nelson, Smith, Taylor, Dodd & Reavis, 1991; Sindelar, Griffin, Smith & Watanabe, 1992). However, several authors also have pointed out the problems with quality and validity of research on prereferral (Sindelar et al., 1992), the need for additional training on interventions and formative and summative evaluation procedures (Nelson et al., 1991), and the importance of striving to achieve parity between classroom teachers and specialists (Pugach & Johnson, 1989b).

IMPEDIMENTS AND BARRIERS

Consultation

The factors that can hinder the implementation of consultation result from a number of causes. The fact that professionals have existed as separate entities for such a long time—and frequently have established their own "language" and "turf"—often makes communication difficult (cf. Reppucci & Saunders, 1974). Differences in levels of skill and expertise, as well as the number and type of responsibilities, flexibility in working environment, and differing views of the status of one's position can present problems (Parker, 1975). The contrast between real and ideal time to do consultation often presents a challenge for the educators involved (Evans, 1980; Gerber, 1991). Consultants may find that even when the time is available, the consultees are resistant to their suggestions (Hughes & Falk, 1981; Idol-Maestas & Ritter, 1985), or the tendency to train specific interventions rather than a problem-solving approach weakens credibility for the process (Goodwin & Powell, 1981).

Other impediments include lack of the following: (a) role definition (Haight, 1984); (b) standardization of consultation (Kratochwill & Van Someren, 1985); (c) training for consultants and consultees and inservice programs (Idol & West, 1987; Johnston, 1990); and, (d) policies and leadership at the state level (West & Brown, 1987). Kampwirth (1987) cited two more barriers: The consultant attempting to be all things to all people and those involved in the process becoming discouraged when change is not immediately evident. Underfunding and faulty assumptions about program effectiveness were mentioned by Huefner (1988).

Lack of consistent implementation of consultation also has been problematic. As Lilly (1987) noted in an article 16 years after his original description of the concept, "consultation has been written about more than it has been practiced in special education" (p. 494). Friend (1988) called for conceptual clarity, professional preparation, and mature discussions of the aspects of various models. Johnson, Pugach, and Hammitte (1988) described pragmatic barriers (e.g., insufficient time, overwhelming caseloads) and conceptual barriers (e.g., differences in the thinking of special educators and classroom teachers, problems with hierarchies among education professionals).

As the 1980s ended, Greer (1989) commented that collaboration had "come to mean almost solely linkages structured for the sake of such institutional goals as cost-effectiveness, logistical expedience, and managerial convenience. It has come to be a sort of administrative axle grease used to reduce bureaucratic wear and tear" (p. 191). Hansen, Himes, and Meier (1990) pointed out the effect of cultural differences on the implementation of consultation and collaboration. Witt (1990) questioned whether a collaborative relationship could be established given the typical hierarchical nature of consultation being provided by "experts" in school settings. Phillips and McCullough (1990) called for the institutionalization of a collaborative ethic, use of ecologically sensitive standards for selection of program formats to be used, and delineation of specific implementation guidelines.

Teaming

A number of barriers to teaming have been cited in the literature. The lack of participation in team meetings, particularly that of regular educators, is a problem frequently identified by authors (e.g., Ysseldyke, Algozzine, & Allen, 1982). Quality of decisions made and ensuring shared decision making were two concerns cited by Pfeiffer (1980). Organizational barriers to focusing on school-family relationships were mentioned by Pfeiffer and Tittler (1983). Inadequate resources, including personnel, and lack of procedures to evaluate team functioning were mentioned by Maher and Hawryluk (1983).

Yoshida (1983) stated that teams frequently do not operate as participatory groups, but rather as forums for powerful people to develop support for their opinions. Fleming and Fleming (1983) noted that team members often do not make positive changes in team functioning when the process is not going well; instead, they blame problems on the perceived weaknesses of other members rather than taking responsibility for the team's effective operation. These authors also mentioned four challenges facing teams: reduction of stress, efficient use of time, developing the skills and knowledge base of all members, and assigning available resources appropriately. Problems cited by Abelson and Woodman (1983) were increased role ambiguity, duplication of effort, and confusion regarding the responsibility for decisions. Bailey (1984) attributed team dysfunctions to a lack of consideration of teams as developing and changing units composed of subsystems that need to function in a cohesive manner. Lack of training for team members was a frequently cited source of difficulty (e.g, Kaiser & Woodman, 1985).

Tindal, Shinn, and Rodden-Nord (1990) also commented on limitations of time as a barrier to developing joint relationships. They also cited impasses in consensus decision-making, differences in anticipated working relationships, and difficulties with program evaluation. In their discussion of transdisciplinary teams, Orelove and Sobsey (1991) grouped factors that hinder teams into three categories: (a) philosophical and professional challenges (differences in philosophy and orientation of team members, diminishment of professional status, and isolation of parents); (b) interpersonal challenges (threat of training others and threat of being trained, role conflict or ambiguity); and (c) administrative challenges (failure to understand the approach, resistance to change, concern about professional ethics and liability).

POSITIVE FEATURES

Although the barriers described in the preceding section have resulted in some implementation problems for consultation, collaboration, and teaming models, the approaches have several positive features that remain important for consideration. These features will be highlighted here and explored further in the next chapter in terms of their relationships to the interactive teaming model.

The first positive feature is the opportunity for the development of professional skills. Although consultation approaches often are viewed as one "expert" providing information to another, in the collaborative consultation models it is recognized that *all* parties have knowledge to share with others. In teaming approaches the range of possible interactions and knowledge exchange becomes even greater because of the number of people from various fields who are involved. In the transdisciplinary teaming model especially, the opportunities are enhanced because the team operates on a basis of professional sharing from the time of the initial assessment through the implementation phase. An additional benefit that should result from such professional interactions is an increase of collegiality among the people involved, rather than a feeling of individuals operating in isolated situations.

The second feature is the one of primary importance: the potential for improved services for students with special needs and at-risk children. Professionals meeting to share perspectives and knowledge and striving to provide a cohesive and comprehensive array of services will be much better able to address the variety of needs presented by such children than educators, health professionals, or social services operating independently. The results of several studies on consultation and teaming show positive gains for students, as well as improvements in skills and attitudes of teachers (cf. Adamson, Cox, & Schuller, 1989; Givens-Ogle, Christ, Colman, King-Streit, & Wilson, 1989; Idol-Maestas, 1983; Nelson & Stevens, 1981; Polsgrove & McNeil, 1989).

A third positive feature of consultation and teaming involves the legal support and mandates that exist for these two approaches. Most states have a continuum of service delivery alternatives that include some form of consultation or collaboration. Also, as mentioned earlier in the chapter, The Education for All Handicapped Children Act and subsequent amendments mandate team decision making for assessment, placement, and transition planning processes.

APPLICATION

What follows is an example of how consultation and teaming might be implemented in response to the referral of Peter, a child suspected of having a mild hearing loss. The case study illustrates the interaction and information that can be obtained from an individual who has certain areas of expertise (e.g., consulting), and shows how knowledge and strategies can be shared among a group of professionals (i.e., teaming).

Observation.   Peter is a fourth-grader whose teacher, Mr. Alford, has noted that he appears to be having difficulty hearing. In the past two weeks, Mr. Alford has observed that as he walks around the room dictating words for a spelling test, Peter turns in his seat so he is always facing the teacher. Mr. Alford also has noticed several times that if Peter was looking away when the directions for an assignment were given, as the other students began to work he would raise his hand and ask for an explanation of the task. Today Mr. Alford watched Peter on the playground. Whenever Peter's best friend Andrew would call to him, Peter would not respond unless he was looking at Andrew at the time. Several times Andrew had to run after his friend to get him to join in the activities.

Consultation.   Mr. Alford mentions his concerns about Peter to the school nurse, Ms. Schlichting. She asks Mr. Alford questions about Peter's background, such as any previous concerns being listed on the cumulative folder, any recent illnesses, any changes in his articulation of words, and so on. Because Mr. Alford is not aware of any previous concerns, illnesses, or speech changes, Ms. Schlichting suggests that a form be sent home to Peter's parents securing permission for her to do some basic auditory screening. After those results are obtained, she will decide whether to recommend that the parents consider taking Peter to a physician for an examination to determine a medical cause of the problem or to an audiologist for additional testing. She also describes the two major types of hearing loss, conductive and sensorineural, and the effects of each.

Teaming.   At the weekly team meeting, Mr. Alford describes his concerns about Peter to his colleagues. Ms. Roll, the speech-language clinician, asks questions about Peter's attentiveness and verbal responses to questions in class. Mr. Collins, the counselor, inquires about Peter's interactions with his friends and whether he appears to be withdrawn or aggressive. He also asks if Peter acts frustrated about being left out of activities because of his lack of response to conversations or invitations to play. Ms. Leonard describes the behaviors of a hearing-impaired student in her fifth-grade class and offers some suggestions to Mr. Alford on how to key in on Peter's facial expressions and actions to determine if he is following the discussions and explanations in class.

The special educator, Ms. Chandler, also offers some suggestions on how to emphasize key words and use the blackboard effectively so Peter can focus in on those cues. She recommends that Mr. Alford contact Peter's mother to inquire if she has noticed similar behaviors, and to suggest that Peter's hearing be tested either at school or by a physician. At the conclusion of the discussion, Mr. Alford agrees to call the mother, and he also has a list of other possible indicators of a hearing loss to consider as he observes Peter while waiting for the test results. In addition, he has strategies to help ensure that Peter is able to follow classroom activities.

SUMMARY

An examination of consultation, collaboration, and teaming reveals that:

◆ These approaches have been advocated by professionals from various disciplines for at least the past 25 years.

◆ A legal basis for the approaches exists in federal laws such as P.L. 94-142 and amendments to it, as well as in state and local education agency service delivery alternatives.

◆ A variety of models have been reviewed in the literature.

◆ Dimensions, goals, competencies, and processes are similar in many instances.

◆ The approaches have barriers that can interfere with successful implementation.

◆ Among the positive features for consultation, collaboration, and teaming are the documented gains for students and professionals.

◆ Several components of consultation and teaming approaches that have been described in this chapter are incorporated into the interactive teaming model proposed in this text. The specific dimensions of interactive teaming will be presented in the next chapter.

ACTIVITIES

1. Construct a table listing the benefits and disadvantages of consultation and teaming. Compare your list with those of your classmates or colleagues. What similarities or differences were noted? Were any of the differences due to professional training or role (e.g., special educator, psychologist, social worker)?

2. Interview an administrator and a parent about their preferences for consultation, collaboration, or teaming. List reasons they prefer one over the other or a combination of the two approaches. How were their preferences affected by previous experiences?

3. Explain how you think consultation, collaboration, and/or teaming could be incorporated into your role. Address such areas as how you would include time for these activities in your daily and weekly schedules, what groups of professionals you are likely to interact with, and what barriers you might encounter.

4. Describe the professional growth opportunities you believe you would gain from being involved in consultation, collaboration, and/or teaming approaches. How would your job change? Would you need additional training to feel that you could be an effective consultant, collaborator, or team member?

REFERENCES

Abelson, M. A., & Woodman, R. W. (1983). Review of research on team effectiveness: Implications for teams in schools. *School Psychology Review, 12,* 125–136.

Adamson, D. R., Cox, J., & Schuller, J. (1989). Collaboration/consultation: Bridging the gap from resource room to regular classroom. *Teacher Education and Special Education, 12,* 46–51.

Aloia, G. F. (1983). Special educators' perceptions of their roles as consultants. *Teacher Education and Special Education, 6,* 83–87.

Bailey, D. B. (1984). A triaxial model of the interdisciplinary team and group process. *Exceptional Children, 51,* 17–25.

Bailey, D. B., Helsel-DeWert, M. J., Thiele, J., & Ware, W. B. (1983). Measuring individual participation on the interdisciplinary team. *American Journal of Mental Deficiency, 88,* 247–254.

Bergan, J. R. (1977). *Behavioral consultation.* Columbus, OH: Merrill.

Brown, B., Pryzwansky, W. B., & Schulte, A. C. (1991). *Psychological consultation.* Boston: Allyn & Bacon.

Brown, D., Wyne, M. D., Blackburn, J. E., & Powell, W. C. (1979). *Consultation: Strategy for improving education.* Boston: Allyn & Bacon.

Brown, L. F., Kiraly, J., & McKinnon, A. (1979). Resource rooms: Some aspects for special educators to ponder. *Journal of Learning Disabilities, 12,* 56–58.

Brown, W. (1987). Rainbow connection instructional guide. *Techniques, 3,* 257–259.

Cantrell, R. P., & Cantrell, M. L. (1976). Preventive mainstreaming: Impact of a supportive service program on pupils. *Exceptional Children, 42,* 381–386.

Chalfant, J. C., Pysh, M. V., & Moultrie, R. (1979). Teacher assistance teams: A model for within-building problem solving. *Learning Disability Quarterly, 2,* 85–96.

Cipani, E. (1985). The three phases of behavioral consultation: Objectives, intervention, and quality assurance. *Teacher Education and Special Education, 8,* 144–152.

Como, P., & Hagner, D. (1986). *Community work development: A marketing model.* Stout, WI: Stout Vocational Rehabilitation Institute. (ERIC Document Reproduction Service No. ED 274 775)

Conoley, J. C., & Conoley, C. W. (1982). *School consultation: A guide to practice and training.* New York: Pergamon Press.

Cook, L., & Friend, M. (1991). Principles for the practice of collaboration in schools. *Preventing School Failure, 35*(4), 6–9.

Courtnage, L., & Healy, H. (1984). Interdisciplinary team training: A competency- and procedure-based approach. *Teacher Education and Special Education, 7,* 3–11.

Courtnage, L., & Smith-Davis, J. (1987). Interdisciplinary team training: A national survey of special education teacher training programs. *Exceptional Children, 53,* 451–458.

Denemark, G., Morsink, C. V., & Thomas, C. C. (1980). Accepting the challenge for change in teacher education. In M. C. Reynolds (Ed.), *A common body of practice for teachers: The challenge of Public Law 94-142 to teacher education.* Washington, DC: The American Association of Colleges of Teacher Education.

Deno, E. (1970). Special education as developmental capital. *Exceptional Children, 37,* 229–237.

Dettmer, P., Thurston, L. P., & Dyck, N. (1995). *Consultation, collaboration, and teamwork for students with special needs*. Boston: Allyn & Bacon.

Edgar, E. (1988). Transition from school to community: Promising programs. *Teaching Exceptional Children, 20,* 73–75.

Egan, M. W., & Bluhm, H. P. (1981). *Teacher Education and Special Education, 4*(1).

Evans, R. J. (1985). *Special education consultation: Interactive video simulation: Adults, teachers, and consultants*. (ERIC Document Reproduction Service No. ED 258 423)

Evans, S. (1980). The consultant role of the resource teacher. *Exceptional Children, 46,* 402–404.

___. (1981). Perceptions of classroom teachers, principals, and resource room teachers of actual and desired roles of the resource teacher. *Journal of Learning Disabilities, 14,* 600–603.

Feichtner, S., & Sarkees, M. (1987). Working together: The special needs team. *Vocational Education Journal, 62,* 22–24.

Fine, M. J., & Tyler, M. M. (1971). Concerns and directions in teacher consultation. *Journal of School Psychology, 9,* 436–444.

Fleming, D. C., & Fleming, E. R. (1983). Problems in implementation of the team approach: A practitioner's perspective. *School Psychology Review, 12,* 144–149.

Friend, M. (1984). Consultation skills for resource teachers. *Learning Disability Quarterly, 7,* 246–250.

___. (1988). Putting consultation into context: Historical and contemporary perspectives. *Remedial and Special Education, 9*(6), 7–13.

Friend, M., & Cook, L. (1992). *Interactions: Collaboration skills for school professionals*. New York: Longman Publishers.

Gable, R. A., Young, C. C., & Hendrickson, J. M. (1987). Content of special education teacher preparation. Are we headed in the right direction? *Teacher Education and Special Education, 10,* 135–139.

Gallessich, J. (1982). *The profession and practice of consultation*. San Francisco: Jossey-Bass.

Gast, D. L., & Wolery, M. (1985). Severe developmental disabilities. In W. H. Berdine & A. E. Blackhurst (Eds.), *An introduction to special education* (2nd ed.). Boston: Little, Brown and Company.

Gerber, S. (1991). Supporting the collaborative process. *Preventing School Failure, 35,* 48–52.

Givens-Ogle, L., Christ, B. A., Colman, M., King-Streit, S., & Wilson, L. (1989). Data-based consultation case study: Adaptations of researched best practices. *Teacher Education and Special Education, 12,* 46–51.

Golightly, C. J. (1987). Transdisciplinary training: A step forward in special education teacher preparation. *Teacher Education and Special Education, 10,* 126–130.

Goodwin, J., & Powell, T. H. (1981). Toward a more effective consulting teacher: Some strategies. *Education Unlimited, 3,* 14–16.

Graden, J. (1989). Redefining "Prereferral" intervention as intervention assistance: Collaboration between general and special education. *Exceptional Children, 56,* 227–231.

Graden, J. L., Casey, A., & Christenson, S. L. (1985). Implementing a prereferral intervention system: Part I. The model. *Exceptional Children, 51,* 377–384.

Greer, J. (1989). The prime factor in education. *Exceptional Children, 56,* 191–193.

Gutkin, T. B. (1993). Cognitive modeling: A means for achieving prevention in school-based consultation. *Journal of Educational and Psychological Consultation, 4,* 179–183.

___. (1986). Consultees' perceptions of variables relating to the outcomes of school-based consultation interactions. *School Psychology Review, 15,* 375–382.

Gutkin, T. B., & Curtis, M. J. (1982). School-based consultation. In C. R. Reynolds & T. B. Gutkin (Eds.), *The handbook of school psychology*. New York: Wiley.

Haight, S. L. (1984). Special education teacher consultant: Idealism versus realism. *Exceptional Children, 50,* 507–515.

Hansen, J. C., Himes, B. S., & Meier, S. (1990). *Consultation concepts and practices*. Englewood Cliffs, NJ: Prentice-Hall.

Hanline, M. F., & Knowlton, A. (1988). A collaborative model for providing support to parents during their child's transition from infant intervention to preschool special education public school programs. *Journal of the Division for Early Childhood, 12,* 116–125.

Hart, V. (1977). The use of many disciplines with the severely and profoundly handicapped. In E. Sontag, J. Smith, & N. Certo (Eds.), *Educational program-*

ming for the severely and profoundly handi-capped. Reston, VA: The Council for Exceptional Children, Division on Mental Retardation.

Hawryluk, M. K., & Smallwood, D. L. (1986). Assessing and addressing consultee variables in school-based behavioral consultation. *School Psychology Review, 15,* 519–528.

Heron, T. E., & Harris, K. C. (1987). *The educational consultant: Helping professionals, parents, and mainstreamed students* (2nd ed.). Austin, TX: Pro-Ed.

Hudson, P. J., Correa, V. I., Morsink, C. V., & Dykes, M. K. (1987). A new model for preservice training: Teacher as collaborator. *Teacher Education and Special Education, 10,* 191–193.

Huefner, D. S. (1988). The consulting teacher model: Risks and opportunities. *Exceptional Children, 54,* 403–414.

Hughes, J. N., & Falk, R. S. (1981). Resistance, reactance, and consultation. *Journal of School Psychology, 19,* 134–142.

Idol, L., Nevin, A., & Paolucci-Whitcomb, P. (1994). *Collaborative consultation* (2nd ed.). Austin, TX: Pro-Ed.

Idol, L., Paolucci-Whitcomb, P., & Nevin, A. (1986). *Collaborative consultation.* Rockville, MD: Aspen Systems Corporation.

Idol, L., & West, J. F. (1987). Consultation in special education (Part II): Training and practice. *Journal of Learning Disabilities, 20,* 474–494.

Idol-Maestas, L. (1983). *Special educator's consultation handbook.* Rockville, MD: Aspen Systems Corporation.

Idol-Maestas, L., & Ritter, S. (1985). A follow-up study of resource/consulting teachers: Factors that facilitate and inhibit teacher consultation. *Teacher Education and Special Education, 8,* 121–131.

Johnson, L. J., Pugach, M. C., & Hammitte, D. J. (1988). Barriers to effective special education consultation. *Remedial and Special Education, 9*(6), 41–47.

Johnston, N. S. (1990). School consultation: The training needs of teachers and school psychologists. *Psychology in the Schools, 27,* 51–56.

Jones, S. N., & Meisels, S. J. (1987). Training family day care providers to work with special needs children. *Topics in Early Childhood Special Education, 7,* 1–12.

Kaiser, S. M., & Woodman, R. W. (1985). Multidisciplinary teams and group decision-making techniques: Possible solutions to decision-making problems. *School Psychology Review, 14,* 457–470.

Kampwirth, T. J. (1987). Consultation: Strategy for dealing with children's behavior problems. *Techniques: A Journal for Remedial Education and Counseling, 3,* 117–120.

Klein, N., & Sheehan, R. (1987). Staff development: A key issue in meeting the needs of young handicapped children in day care settings. *Topics in Early Childhood Special Education, 7,* 13–27.

Kratochwill, T. R., & Van Someren, K. R. (1985). Barriers to treatment success in behavioral consultation: Current limitations and future directions. *Journal of School Psychology, 23,* 225–239.

Kurpius, D. J. (1978). Consultation theory and process: An integrated model. *Personnel and Guidance Journal, 56,* 335–339.

Lilly, M. S. (1971). A training based model for special education. *Exceptional Children, 37,* 745–749.

___. (1987). Response to "Consultation in special education" by Idol and West. *Journal of Learning Disabilities, 20,* 494–495.

Lindsey, D. (1985). A model performance appraisal instrument for school physical therapists. *Clinical Management, 6*(5), 20–26.

Lindsey, D., O'Neal, J., Haas, K., & Tewey, S. (1983). *A cooperative adventure: Physical therapy services in North Carolina's schools.* Raleigh, NC: State Department of Public Instruction.

Lloyd, J. W., Crowley, E. P., Kohler, F. W., & Strain, P. S. (1988). Redefining the applied research agenda: Cooperative learning, prereferral, teacher consultation, and peer-mediated interventions. *Journal of Learning Disabilities, 21,* 43–52.

Lowenthal, B. (1992). Collaborative training in the education of early childhood educators. *Teaching Exceptional Children, 24*(4), 25–29.

Lyon, S., & Lyon, G. (1980). Team functioning and staff development: A role release approach to providing integrated educational services for severely handicapped students. *Journal of the Association for the Severely Handicapped, 5,* 250–263.

Maher, C. A., & Hawryluk, M. K. (1983). Framework and guidelines for utilization of teams in schools. *School Psychology Review, 12,* 180–185.

Marshall, R. M., & Wuori, D. F. (1985). Medical and education literature on physician/teacher collaboration. *Journal of School Health, 55,* 62–65.

McAfee, J. K. (1987). Integrating therapy services in the school: A model for training educators, administrators, and therapists. *Topics in Early Childhood Special Education, 7,* 116–126.

McClellan, E., & Wheatley, W. (1985). Project RETOOL: Collaborative consultation training for post-doctoral leadership personnel. *Teacher Education and Special Education, 8,* 159–163.

McGlothlin, J. E. (1981). The school consultation committee: An approach to implementing a teacher consultation model. *Behavioral Disorders, 6,* 101–107.

Medway, F. J. (1979). How effective is school consultation? A review of recent research. *Journal of School Psychology, 17,* 275–282.

Moore, E., & Allen, D. (1986). *An outreach program: Addressing the needs of the physically impaired in rural communities.* (ERIC Document Reproduction Service No. ED 285 370)

Morsink, C. V., & Lenk, L. L. (1992). The delivery of special education programs and services. *Remedial and Special Education, 13*(6), 33–43.

Nelson, C. M., Neel, R. S., & Lilly, M. S. (1981). Consultation as a support system for behaviorally disordered pupils and their teachers. *Behavioral Disorders, 6*(2).

Nelson, C. M., & Stevens, K. B. (1981). An accountable model for mainstreaming behaviorally disordered children. *Behavioral Disorders, 6,* 82–91.

Nelson, J. R., Smith, D. J., Taylor, L., Dodd, J. M., & Reavis, K. (1991). Prereferral intervention: A review of the research. *Education and Treatment of Children, 14,* 243–253.

Newcomer, P. (1977). Special education for the mildly handicapped: Beyond a diagnostic and remedial model. *Journal of Special Education, 11,* 153–165.

Orelove, F. P., & Sobsey, D. (1991). *Educating children with multiple disabilities: A transdisciplinary approach.* (2nd ed.). Baltimore: Paul H. Brookes Publishing Co.

Patriarca, L. A., & Lamb, M. A. (1990). Preparing secondary special education teachers to be collaborative decision makers and reflective practitioners: A promising practicum model. *Teacher Education and Special Education, 13,* 228–232.

Paolucci-Whitcomb, P., & Nevin, A. (1985). Preparing consulting teachers through a collaborative approach between university faculty and field-based consulting teachers. *Teacher Education and Special Education, 8,* 132–143.

Parker, C. A. (1975). *Psychological consultation: Helping teachers meet special needs.* Reston, VA: The Council for Exceptional Children.

Pfeiffer, S. I. (1980). The school-based interprofessional team: Recurring problems and some possible solutions. *Journal of School Psychology, 18,* 388-394.

___. (1981). The problems facing multidisciplinary teams: As perceived by team members. *Psychology in the Schools, 18,* 330–333.

Pfeiffer, S. I., & Tittler, B. I. (1983). Utilizing the multidisciplinary team to facilitate a school-family systems orientation. *School Psychology Review, 12,* 168–173.

Phillips, V., & McCullough, L. (1990). Consultation-based programming: Instituting the collaborative ethic in schools. *Exceptional Children, 56,* 291–304.

Piersel, W. C. (1985). Behavioral consultation: An approach to problem solving in educational settings. In J. R. Bergan (Ed.), *School psychology in contemporary society: An introduction.* New York: Merrill/Macmillan.

Polsgrove, L., & McNeil, M. (1989). The consultation process: Research and practice. *Remedial and Special Education, 10*(1), 6–13, 20.

Powers, M. D. (1986). Promoting community-based services: Implications for program design, implementation, and public policy. *Journal of the Association for Persons With Severe Handicaps, 11,* 309–315.

President's Commission on Teacher Education. (1992). American Association of State Colleges and Universities.

Preventing School Failure. (1991). Vol. 35(4).

Pugach, M. C., & Johnson, L. J. (1989a). Prereferral intervention: Progress, problems, and challenges. *Exceptional Children, 56,* 217–226.

Pugach, M. C., & Johnson, L. J. (1989b). The challenge of implementing collaboration between general and special education. *Exceptional Children, 56,* 232–235.

Pugach, M. C., & Johnson, L. J. (1990). Fostering the continued democratization of consultation through action research. *Teacher Education and Special Education, 13,* 240–245.

Pryzwansky, W. B., & Rzepski, B. (1983). School-based teams: An untapped resource for consultation and technical assistance. *School Psychology Review, 12,* 174–179.

Pryzwansky, W. W. (1974). A reconsideration of the consultation model for delivery of school-based psychological services. *Journal of Orthopsychiatry, 44,* 579–583.

Remedial and Special Education. (1988). Vol. 9(6).

Reppucci, N. D., & Saunders, J. T. (1974). Social psychology of behavior modification: Problems of implementation in natural settings. *American Psychologist, 29,* 649–660.

Reynolds, C. R., Gutkin, T. B., Elliott, S. N., & Witt, J. C. (1984). *School psychology: Essentials of theory and practice.* New York: Wiley.

Reynolds, M. C., & Birch, J. W. (1982). *Teaching exceptional children in all America's schools* (rev. ed.). Reston, VA: The Council for Exceptional Children.

Ritter, D. R. (1978). Effects of a school consultation program upon referral patterns of teachers. *Psychology in the Schools, 15,* 239–243.

Safran, S. P., & Barcikowski, R. S. (1984). LD consultant information in mainstreaming: Help or hindrance? *Learning Disability Quarterly, 7,* 102–107.

Sailor, W., & Guess, D. (1983). *Severely handicapped students: An instructional design.* Boston: Houghton Mifflin.

Salend, S. J. (1994). *Effective mainstreaming: Creating inclusive classrooms* (2nd ed.). New York: Merrill.

Salend, S. J., & Salend, S. (1984). Consulting with the regular teacher: Guidelines for special educators. *The Pointer, 28,* 25–28.

School Psychology Review. (1983). Vol. 12(2).

Siders, J. Z., Riall, A., Bennett, T. C., & Judd, D. (1987). Training of leadership personnel in early intervention: A transdisciplinary approach. *Teacher Education and Special Education, 10,* 161–170.

Sileo, T. W., Rude, H. A., & Luckner, J. L. (1988). Collaborative consultation: A model for transition planning for handicapped youth. *Education and Training in Mental Retardation, 23,* 333–339.

Simpson, R. L., & Myles, B. S. (1990). The general education collaboration model: A model for successful mainstreaming. *Focus on Exceptional Children, 23*(4), 1–10.

Sindelar, P. T., Griffin, C. C., Smith, S. W., & Watanabe, A. K. (1992). Prereferral intervention: Encouraging notes on preliminary findings. *The Elementary School Journal, 92,* 245–259.

Speece, D. L., & Mandell, C. J. (1980). Resource room support services for regular teachers. *Learning Disability Quarterly, 3,* 49–53.

Spencer-Dobson, C. A., & Schultz, J. B. (1987). Utilization of multidisciplinary teams in educating special needs students. *Journal of Industrial Teacher Education, 25,* 68–78.

Stanwood, B. (1988). *Effective utilization of multidisciplinary teams.* Unpublished manuscript. Wilmington: University of North Carolina-Wilmington, School of Education.

Sugai, G. M., & Tindal, G. A. (1993). *Effective school consultation: An interactive approach.* Pacific Grove, CA: Brooks/Cole.

Swan, W. W., & Sirvis, B. (1992). The CEC common core of knowledge and skills essential for all beginning special education teachers. *Teaching Exceptional Children, 15*(1), 16–20.

Teacher Education and Special Education. (1985). Vol. 8(3).

Tharp, R. G. (1975). The triadic model of consultation: Current considerations. In C. A. Parker (Ed.), *Psychological consultation: Helping teachers meet special needs.* Reston, VA: The Council for Exceptional Children.

Tharp, R. G., & Wetzel, R. J. (1969). *Behavior modification in the natural environment.* New York: Academic Press.

Thomas, C. C. (1986, March). *Problem-solving strategies for school assistance teams.* Paper presented at the Region II Exceptional Children Administrators Staff Development Conference, Atlantic Beach, NC.

Tidal, G., Shinn, M. R., & Rodden-Nord, K. (1990). Contextually based school consultation: Influential variables. *Exceptional Children, 56,* 324–336.

Tindal, G., Shinn, M., Walz, L., & Germann, G. (1987). Mainstream consultation in secondary settings: The Pine County model. *Journal of Special Education, 21,* 94–106.

Trohanis, P. L. (1981). *Consultation and the TADS experience.* (Occasional Paper Number 1). Chapel Hill: The University of North Carolina. (ERIC Document Reproduction Service No. ED 224 227)

Umansky, D. L., & Holloway, E. L. (1984). The counselor as consultant: From model to practice. *School Counselor, 31,* 329–338.

Villa, R., Thousand, J., Paolucci-Whitcomb, P., & Nevin, A. (1990). In search of new paradigms for collaborative consultation. *Journal of Educational and Psychological Consultation, 1,* 279–292.

West, J. F., & Brown, P. A. (1987). State departments of education policies on consultation in special education: The state of the states. *Remedial and Special Education, 8*(3), 45–51.

West, J. F., & Cannon, G. S. (1988). Essential collaborative consultation competencies for regular and special educators. *Journal of Learning Disabilities, 21,* 28, 56–63.

West, J. F., & Idol, L. (1987). School consultation (Part I): An interdisciplinary perspective on theory, models, and research. *Journal of Learning Disabilities, 20,* 388–408.

West, J. F., Idol, L., & Cannon, G. (1989). *Collaboration in the schools: An inservice and preservice curriculum for teachers, support staff, and administrators.* Austin, TX: Pro-Ed.

Witt, J. (1990). Collaboration in school-based consultation: Myth in need of data. *Journal of Educational and Psychological Consultation, 11,* 367–370.

Wood, J. W. (1992). *Adapting instruction for mainstreamed and at-risk students* (2nd ed.). New York: Macmillan.

Yoshida, R. K. (1983). Are multidisciplinary teams worth the investment? *School Psychology Review, 12,* 137–143.

Ysseldyke, J., Algozzine, B., & Allen, D. (1982). Participation of regular education teachers in special education team decision making. *Exceptional Children, 48,* 365–366.

Dimensions of the Interactive Team

TOPICS IN THIS CHAPTER INCLUDE

◆ Discussion of the bases for the team's work.

◆ A model of an interactive team.

◆ Descriptions of the aspects of team membership and leadership.

◆ Procedures for implementing the interactive teaming process.

◆ An application illustrating the contrast between a successful and unsuccessful team meeting.

When the McMillans' son, Antwaun, was 4 years old, he became seriously ill in the middle of the night. Hearing her son crying, Mrs. McMillan checked on Antwaun and found him to have a very high fever. She awakened her husband, and they took the boy to the emergency room. On the way to the hospital, Antwaun had a seizure.

The pediatrician at the hospital diagnosed the problem as a severe ear infection and said the seizure was caused by the high fever. He prescribed a baby-aspirin substitute and an antibiotic and assured them that Antwaun would be much improved in 24 hours when the medication began to take effect. The McMillans took Antwaun home feeling optimistic that their son would soon be back to his talkative, happy-go-lucky self.

Two days later, however, Antwaun was still listless and unresponsive. His mother called their family pediatrician, who said to give the medication one more day, and if he still was not improved to bring him in for an appointment. The next day Antwaun did not talk at all when his mother awakened him. She immediately dressed him and took him to the pediatrician. Dr. Corley examined Antwaun and noted that the infection had caused a fluid build-up in his middle ear. She prescribed another medication and suggested that he not return to his preschool program for at least another week.

Mr. McMillan worked a swing shift and was on the "graveyard" schedule that week, so he stayed home with his son while his wife returned to work. He noted that Antwaun seemed reluctant to talk or play and began staring into space for long periods of time, but he thought this was because of the medication.

After a week, Antwaun seemed better, so his parents sent him back to his preschool program. At the end of the first day, his teacher called. She said Antwaun was withdrawn and that during playtime the recreation specialist had commented that he displayed autistic-like behaviors, such as twirling and flapping his hands. The public nurse had visited the program that day to conduct a presentation on food groups, and she had commented to the teacher that perhaps Antwaun had a hearing loss because he was so inattentive. Alarmed by this information, the McMillans made another appointment with Dr. Corley.

She assured them that Antwaun's behavior was due to the fact that his ears were still infected, and she said that tubes might be necessary to drain off the excess fluid. Antwaun returned to preschool but still acted listless and inattentive. Two weeks later, the director of the preschool called. He said that Antwaun seemed to have lost some of his language skills and that he was striking out at peers when they approached him. He inquired whether Antwaun could have suffered brain damage or emotional trauma from the fever and suggested that they might want to consider moving Antwaun to a preschool for disabled children. Now extremely concerned and confused, Mrs. McMillan called Dr. Corley again and suggested that she talk with the people at the preschool about how the ear infection could be affecting Antwaun's behavior. Mrs. McMillan said she was feeling like a "go-between," trying to relay all the messages from one person to the next, and she stated that she would like everyone involved to meet together to share their observations, discuss possible causes, and suggest what needed to be done. Dr. Corley agreed to come to a meeting the following week.

The McMillans contacted the preschool personnel, who also agreed to attend a meeting. They suggested including an audiologist who had worked with some of the students the previous year. The audiologist said she would come to provide insights on how a hearing loss, even a temporary one, can affect a child's behavior and language.

At the meeting, all the professionals shared their observations about Antwaun, and his parents commented on his behavior at home. Although at first they were quite defensive, eventually the educators agreed they might have been hasty in labeling some of Antwaun's behaviors as autistic or brain-damaged, and they also commented that some additional inservice on hearing impairments might be worthwhile for the entire staff. The parents learned some strategies for interacting with Antwaun at home. Everyone agreed to meet again in three weeks to discuss any changes or improvements that might occur after all of the medication had been taken and Antwaun's ears were less congested. His parents also agreed to take him for an audiological examination before the next meeting, so those results would be available for review.

The effects of professionals and parents operating in "separate worlds" are illustrated at the beginning of this vignette. When no one is in charge, everyone functions as a separate entity, even though each individual is concerned with the same child. Consequently, communication does not occur and the results often are fragmented services for a child and confusion for adults. After the McMillans were able to get the professionals to communicate, the situation improved, but much time and energy could have been saved if the people involved had been able to operate within a team framework from the beginning.

In Chapter 1, *interactive teaming* was defined as a mutual or reciprocal effort among and between members of a team to provide the best possible educational program for a student. The strength of this approach is the potential for effective, comprehensive, and cohesive services when all the people involved work together instead of functioning as separate individuals or disciplines. As stated in Chapter 2, interactive teaming includes features from the collaborative consultation and transdisciplinary teaming models used primarily in special education and school psychology. In addition, interactive teaming incorporates components identified in recent research on effective schools and school-based management (e.g., David, 1989; Lezotte, 1989), decision-making processes, adult learning, and Total Quality Management (Berry, 1991; Deming, 1986) recognizing that all the components and factors must be implemented within the context of a school or institutional program for at-risk students or those with identified special needs. In addition, barriers that have interfered with the implementation of other models described in the previous chapter must be addressed.

This chapter includes an explanation of the dimensions of interactive teaming. Incorporated in the dimensions are the purposes and objectives of the model, description of the competencies of team members, and processes and procedures for implementation. Some of the barriers and limitations of other approaches that were cited in chapters 1 and 2, including the absence of decision-making processes and dissimilar goals, are discussed as part of the explanation of the dimensions. Part 2 of the text, Facilitating Factors, provides additional information on how to address potential barriers to interactive teaming, such as a lack of understanding of the roles, the process of change, miscommunication, ineffective leadership, insensitivity to cultural diversity, and limited family involvement.

Recent literature on collaboration, effective schools, total quality management, leadership, and teaming models contains several factors, parameters, or dimensions identified as necessary for the success of the students and the satisfaction of the professionals involved. Wangemann (cited in Wangemann, Ingram, & Muse, 1989) reviewed the literature on successful collaborations and noted that the following "ingredients" are essential:

1. Clarity of purpose.
2. Complementary dissimilarity between the partners.
3. Overlapping self-interests.
4. Sufficient time to build bridges of communication and trust.
5. Clarification and coordination of roles and responsibilities within the partnership.
6. Shared ownership.
7. Emphasis on action rather than structure building.
8. Adequate resources.
9. Leadership from key administrators.
10. Institutional commitment to the satisfying of mutual self-interests.
11. An ongoing system for research and evaluation.
12. An understanding of each institution's culture.

Harrison, Killion, and Mitchell (1989) reported on their attempts to implement site-based management in a school district in Colorado. They said the lessons learned from their mistakes included recognition of the following needs: (a) clarification of concepts and terms at the beginning, (b) definition of roles and then support and modeling of the new role expectations, (c) provision of training for school personnel and on-site support for administrators, and (d) preparation for the process of change and implications resulting from change.

Phillips and McCullough (1990) identified five key requirements for developing and implementing school-based collaborative approaches. The first is that administrative support must progress from a primarily managerial and facilitative focus to action-oriented participation. The second requirement is that systematic program development, multilevel planning and decision making must occur. Third, membership on the team must be composed primarily of people from the consumer group (i.e., regular classroom teachers) rather than specialists. This factor will help people develop ownership and commitment to the goals. Fourth, feasibility must be considered in choosing interventions and formats to be used. Finally, they pointed out that resistance to collaboration and teaming can be reduced through practical and specific professional development.

Laycock, Gable, and Korinek (1991) noted the following considerations for selecting collaborative structures: (a) process of program planning should be collaborative,

(b) underlying philosophical assumptions should guide choices made, (c) structures should be compatible with existing collaborative structures, (d) alternatives can be combined to enhance the delivery of services, (e) planning teams should adapt models to fit current needs, and (f) program adjustments should be based on evaluation data.

Characteristics that maximize effectiveness of teams were described by Elliott and Sheridan (1992). They noted the importance of shared leadership and ensuring that the group used problem-solving guidelines. They also stated the necessity of planning activities, agenda setting, clarifying communication, participation of group members, use of conflict management strategies, and review of group processes.

Recent literature on leadership and Total Quality Management also stresses certain aspects designed to enhance team functioning. Covey (1991) emphasized the significance of shared values or governing principles, and said strategies, structures, systems, skills, and styles will flow from these values. Blankstein (1992) endorsed the philosophy of Deming (1986) as a framework within which to integrate developments such as teacher participation and site-based management. This philosophy endorses the idea that the role of management or leadership is to improve the system or organization so that individuals can work together. Several of Deming's (1986) principles are especially relevant to teaming models: (a) create constancy of purpose for improvement of product and service, (b) adopt and institute leadership, (c) break down barriers between staff areas, (d) institute a vigorous program of education and self-improvement for everyone, and (e) put everybody in the organization to work to accomplish the transformation.

Based on the research of these authors and others who have been involved in the study or implementation of models that contain components similar to interactive teaming, 10 dimensions have been identified that are considered essential for effective implementation:

1.   Legitimacy and autonomy.
2.   Purpose and objectives.
3.   Competencies of team members and clarity of their roles.
4.   Role release and role transitions.
5.   Awareness of the individuality of team members.
6.   Process of team building.
7.   Attention to factors that affect team functioning.
8.   Leadership styles.
9.   Implementation procedures.
10.   Commitment to common goals.

Each of these dimensions is examined in more detail in the remainder of this chapter.

BASES FOR INTERACTIVE TEAMING

Legitimacy and Autonomy

To be successful, any group must have a reason to exist and the freedom to operate. Team decision making and consultation with families are stipulated by Public Laws 94-142, 99-457, and 101-476; therefore, the legitimacy of a framework such as interactive teaming is supported by law, as well as by a recognition of the need to collaborate by professionals in various fields. However, even if a legal basis exists and teaming is endorsed by individuals, the team and its decisions must be valued by organizations, administrators, and staff to be effective (Maher & Hawryluk, 1983; Phillips & McCullough, 1990).

A second consideration is the necessity of autonomy and the support for this concept. Time and support personnel must be provided for team members to be able to plan and reflect together, and to be responsive to the accountability measures that often accompany increased autonomy (Pugach, 1988). In addition, team members and others in organizations should recognize that the composition of a team may differ at various times due to the specific needs of a child (Golightly, 1987; Orelove & Sobsey, 1991) and the culture and priorities of a district or school (cf. Orlich, 1989).

Given these considerations, part of team autonomy is realizing that the "constellation" of people involved may change over time, depending upon the purpose of the information sharing (e.g., assessment results) or decision making (e.g., placement, intervention design) about a student or client. As a result, all members of a team may not be involved in every interaction. Consultation and collaboration between individuals or among subgroups should be viewed as enhancing the overall effectiveness of a team and contributing to team consistency and cohesiveness. The Interactive Teaming Model and illustrations of how consultation and collaboration can occur among members are shown in Figure 3–1.

Purpose and Objectives

A team needs an identified purpose and objectives around which decisions can be made. The major purpose for interactive teaming is to share information and expertise to ensure that the best possible decisions are made and effective programs are implemented. The types of decisions an interactive team can be involved in include those identified by Salvia and Ysseldyke (1988): referral, screening, classification, instructional planning, and evaluation of pupil progress. (See Chapter 1 for definitions of these terms.) Specific objectives will be derived from the decisions made and the roles people will play in implementing those decisions. For example, a social worker may participate in an interactive team meeting at which the decision is made to place a child in a special education program. She is aware of a community program that offers free tutoring for economically disadvantaged students, and she thinks this child would qualify. Her objectives are to determine eligibility, make the necessary contacts if the child is eligible, and then assist with communication with the child's grandmother, who is acting as guardian.

Figure 3–1
The interactive teaming
model

Note: Not all of these persons will need to be present at every meeting.

Key:
PA = Parent
RC = Regular classroom teacher
SE = Special educator
SP = Speech/language clinician
SW = Social worker
PH = Physician
PT = Physical therapist
OT = Occupational therapist
APE = Adapted physical educator
PSY = Psychologist
NU = Nurse

CO = Counselor
PR = Principal
DI = Dietician
CS = Computer specialist
ESL = English as a second language
VO = Vocational specialist
ME = Migrant educator

ASPECTS OF TEAM FUNCTIONING

Competencies of Team Members and Clarity of Their Roles

Team members should first be able to demonstrate competencies in their own disciplines before they are expected to acquire knowledge in other areas (Siders, Riall, Bennett, & Judd, 1987). In addition to the discipline-specific competencies, they will need to be competent in the areas previously described as essential for consultants and team members: collaborative problem solving, interactive communication, leadership, awareness of cultural diversity, referral, and evaluation (cf. Courtnage & Healy, 1984; Hudson, Correa, Morsink, & Dykes, 1987; Siders, Riall, Bennett, & Judd, 1987; West & Cannon, 1988). Maher and Hawryluk (1983) cited several other considerations for selection of team members: (a) a willingness to receive training in other areas, (b) the ability to participate in a problem-solving situation, (c) possession of enough time to contribute to team processes, and (d) the potential for implementing their own tasks as identified by the team.

Along with attainment of individual competencies, team members must be accurate in their perceptions of the competencies and roles of others (Orelove & Sobsey, 1991). At times members may be unclear about the expertise of people from different disciplines or the roles those people should play in a team situation. Clarity of roles and expertise is essential and will be explored further in Chapter 4.

Role Release and Role Transitions

In addition to understanding the roles and recognizing the competencies of others, team members must be able to "release" their own knowledge and share it with others. *Role release* has been defined by Lyon and Lyon (1980) as referring "to three levels of sharing between two or more members of an educational team: general information, informational skills, and performance competencies" (pp. 253–254). They described the first level as sharing knowledge about basic procedures or practices; for example, a special educator explaining to the principal the behavior management system he is using in his classroom. Informational skills include teaching others to make judgments; for example, an adaptive physical educator teaching a regular classroom teacher how to determine if a child is using a correct skipping motion in a game. The third level, performance competencies, includes training another person to perform specified skills, such as an occupational therapist teaching a parent how to use an adaptive feeding device with a severely disabled child.

A similar conception of sharing roles and expertise was presented in a publication by the United Cerebral Palsy Association and cited by Golightly (1987). She described the six "role transitions" as follows:

> First, role extension entails designing and implementing instructional objectives within one's own discipline. Second, role enrichment involves designing instructional objectives to include strategies from other disciplines. Third, role expansion involves deriving information from the deliberate pooling of knowledge and skills among team members. Fourth, role exchange permits carrying out the intervention strategies learned from other team members. Fifth, role release involves effectively imparting disciplinary skills to others and providing follow through to ensure appropriate application. Sixth, role support, used in complex interventions, entails using consultative back-up when extensive disciplinary expertise is needed. (p. 128)

An example of how role release was realized in a preschool program involving teachers and physical and occupational therapists was presented by Mather and Weinstein (1988). These authors noted that when the sharing of expertise began, mutual trust was established and the professionals became committed to designing the best program for the students, instead of being concerned with protecting their own "turf."

Awareness of the Individuality of Team Members

Research in the areas of adult learning and professional growth has implications for interactive teaming, because not only will team members represent different disciplines, but they also may be at different points in their own professional development. Three models useful for understanding these differences are Professional Stages, Career Cycles, and Conceptual Levels. Awareness of these potential differences may enhance a team member's ability to understand another individual's responses and behaviors in certain situations.

Peryon (1982) paralleled the *Professional Stages* of teachers with the phases of adulthood described by Sheehy (1977). Peryon identified these stages:

1. New teachers: They strive to become the ideal and use what they have been taught; they need support, encouragement, and recognition as professionals.
2. Teachers with 5 to 10 years of experience: They have confidence and know what works for them; they need to be recognized as competent.
3. Middle period of teaching: They often are rethinking old ideas and analyzing their professional goals for the future; they need to be given a chance to grow and be reinforced for new achievements.
4. Mature period of teaching: They have reached self-actualization in terms of their careers; they need to be recognized as top professionals and to be needed by others.

Burke, Christensen, and Fessler (1984) presented the concept of *Career Cycles*. Their model is similar in some ways to the stages described by Peryon; however, it includes induction and both career wind-down and exit. It also incorporates more of a systems view because factors in the personal and organizational environments are included. The Career Cycles are illustrated in Figure 3–2 and described more fully in Figure 3–3. It is important to note that teachers or other professionals do not necessarily proceed through these cycles sequentially according to years of experience, and in fact they may be in two cycles at the same time. Examples of the latter point are beginning professionals (induction) who are competent and growing, or beginners who are experiencing career frustration.

The third approach to be discussed is the *Conceptual Stages* of adults identified by Hunt (1981) and further developed by Sprinthall and Thies-Sprinthall (1983). These researchers contend that adults develop a mode of responding to complex situations such as teaching. Their behaviors and verbal comments may be affected by the conceptual stage at which they are functioning. These stages are not necessarily correlated to years of experience or intelligence; rather they illustrate how a person may respond in a given situation. The Conceptual Stages are presented in Figure 3–4 on page 81.

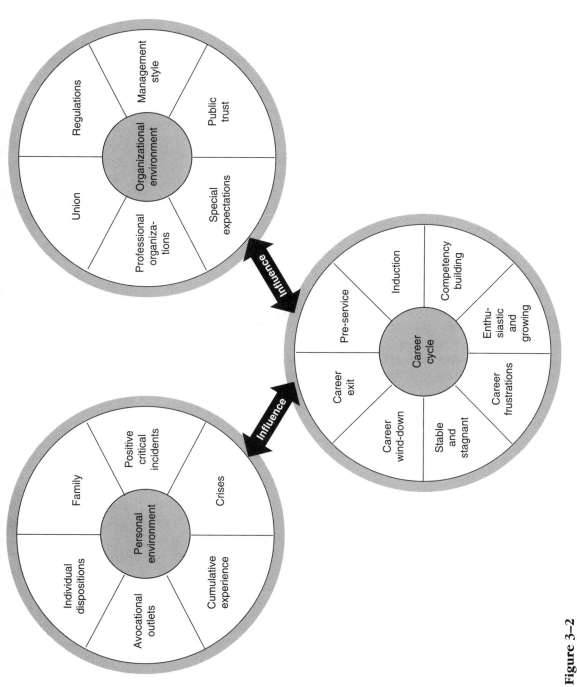

Figure 3–2

A model of the stages of the teacher career cycle and the environmental factors that affect it

Note: From *Teacher Career Stages: Implications for Staff Development* by P. S. Burke, J. C. Christensen, and R. Fessler, 1984, Bloomington, IN: Phi Delta Kappa Foundation. Reprinted by permission.

The stages of the Career Cycle can be characterized by the following descriptors:

1. **Preservice**
   Preparing initially in a college or university
   Retraining for a new role or assignment through coursework or inservice

2. **Induction**
   Teaching during the first few years
   Shifting to another position, building, or system
   Socializing into the system
   Striving for acceptance by students, peers, supervisors
   Attempting to achieve comfort in dealing with everyday occurrences

3. **Competency Building**
   Improving teaching skills and abilities
   Seeking new materials, methods, and strategies
   Demonstrating receptiveness to new ideas
   Attending workshops and conferences willingly
   Enrolling in college coursework through own initiative

4. **Enthusiastic and Growing**
   Exhibiting high level of competence
   Progressing as professional
   Experiencing high job satisfaction
   Enjoying going to work and interacting with students
   Seeking new ways to enrich teaching
   Helping to identify appropriate staff development activities

5. **Career Frustration**
   Feeling frustration and disillusionment with teaching
   Experiencing waning job satisfaction
   Questioning worth of work
   Feeling "burnout"
   Experienced usually at midpoint of career, but also with new teachers

6. **Stable but Stagnant**
   Putting in "a fair day's work for a fair day's pay"
   Doing only what is expected
   Doing an acceptable job, but not committed to excellence
   Participating only at surface level
   Being a passive consumer of staff development

7. **Career Wind-Down**
   Preparing to leave profession
   Reflecting on positive experiences and looking forward to retirement
   Resenting forced job termination or anxious to get out of unrewarding job

8. **Career Exit**
   Retiring or leaving job for other circumstances
   Being unemployed after involuntary or elective job termination
   Exiting temporarily for child rearing
   Exploring career alternative such as moving to a nonteaching position

Figure 3–3

Descriptors of career cycles

Note: From *Teacher Career Stages: Implications for Staff Development* by P. S. Burke, J. C. Christensen, and R. Fessler, 1984, Bloomington, IN: Phi Delta Kappa Foundation. Reprinted by permission.

Stage A

Strong evidence of concrete thinking

Knowledge seen as fixed

Employs a singular "tried–and–true" method

Exhibits compliance as a learner and expects the same from pupils

Low on self-direction and initiative. Needs detailed instructions

Doesn't distinguish between theory and facts

Almost an exclusive reliance on advance organizers

Teaching is "filling the students up with facts"

Stays at Bloom's Level One and Two regardless of student level

Enjoys highly structured activities for self and for pupils

Uncomfortable with ambiguous assignments

Does not question authority

Follows a curriculum guide as if it were carved in stone

Verbalizes feelings at a limited level. Has difficulty recognizing feelings in pupils

Reluctant to talk about own inadequacies; blames pupils exclusively

Stage B

Growing awareness of difference between concrete vs. abstract thinking

Separates facts, opinions, and theories about teaching and learning

Employs some different teaching models in accord with student differences

Evidence of teaching for generalization as well as skills

Some evidence of systematic "matching and mismatching"; can vary structure

Some openness to innovations and can make some appropriate adaptations

Shows sensitivity to pupil's emotional needs

Enjoys some level of autonomy; self-directed learning a goal for self and for the pupils

Employs Bloom's Taxonomy, Levels One through Four, when appropriate

Evaluations are appropriate to assignments

Stage C

Understands knowledge as a process of successive approximations

Shows evidence of originality in adapting innovations to the classroom

Comfortable in applying all appropriate teaching models

Most articulate in analyzing one's own teaching in both content and feeling

High tolerance for ambiguity and frustration. Can stay on task in spite of major distractions

Does not automatically comply with directions—asks examiner's reasons.

Fosters an intensive questioning approach with students

Can use all six levels of Bloom when appropriate

Responds appropriately to the emotional needs of all pupils

Can "match and mismatch" with expert flexibility

Exhibits careful evaluations based on objective criteria according to level of assignment

Figure 3–4

Descriptions of Hunt's conceptual stages—teachers' attitudes toward learning and teaching

Note: From "Teachers' Adaptation: 'Reading' and 'Flexing' to Students" by D. E. Hunt, 1981. In B. Joyce, C. Brown, and L. Peck (Eds.), *Flexibility In Teaching,* New York: Longman. Reprinted by permission.

The Process of Team Building

One frustration often voiced by members on a newly formed team is, "Things aren't happening quickly enough." Two important considerations for interactive team members to recognize are that teams comprise individuals, and those individuals must have time to develop as a unit (cf. Bailey, 1984). Abelson and Woodman (1983) described a model of team building based on the work of Tuckman and Jensen (1977). This model consists of five stages that an interactive team may go through in the process of becoming established:

1. *Forming*: Individuals become oriented to the team; communication networks are started.

2. *Storming*: Conflict and polarization may occur; leadership may be tested.

3. *Norming*: Role relationships are redefined; team goals are established; leadership is defined and accepted.

4. *Performing*: Members work to accomplish the task.

5. *Adjourning*: Members deal with changes in relationships and feelings about self-esteem, depending on whether the task was satisfactorily completed.

Considering that teams need time to build and for individuals to adjust, team members can understand that immediate efficiency is not always possible. Also, it is useful to remember that people who have served on teams before will usually adapt much more quickly than those who are new to this type of unit.

Attention to Factors that Affect Team Functioning

Three areas frequently mentioned as problematic to team functioning are a lack of involvement of all team members, an increase in interprofessional rivalry instead of collaboration or "boundary crossing," and a lack of structure in decision making (cf. Epstein, 1988; Kabler & Genshaft, 1983; Kaiser & Woodman, 1985; Yoshida, 1983). The implications of those areas for interactive teams will be considered in terms of the factors of goal structures, communication climates, roles in meetings, and consensus-building strategies.

Goal Structures.   Johnson, Johnson, and Holubec (1986) described three types of goal structures that may be held by participants in a group situation. The structures are *cooperative,* in which group members seek outcomes that are beneficial for all members of the group; *competitive,* in which the goals of the participants are linked so that each can win only if the others fail; and *individualistic,* in which no correlation exists between the goals of the group and the individuals. In the cooperative goal structure, the one most advantageous to interactive teams, all members of the group contribute to the design of a common solution to a problem. In the competitive structure, each member strives to win independently. In the individual goal structure, members may work side by side but alone, because they are working to accomplish their own goals.

In their review of the three types of goal structures on the professional self-esteem, achievement, positive interpersonal relationships, and social support of adults, Johnson and Johnson (1987) found the cooperative structure to be superior in all areas. These effects are illustrated in Figure 3–5.

Communication Climates.   Two distinctly different climates of teams in which interactions may take place have been identified by Gibb (1961), both of which can be readily identified by the behaviors of the participants. In a *defensive climate,* participants may attempt to evaluate the ideas of another in a judgmental manner. In a *supportive climate,* they encourage others to describe events and situations, and they in turn attempt to describe what other speakers have said. In the defensive mode, the participant attempts to control the discussion by dominating or lecturing; in the supportive mode, the person asks others to assist in identifying the problem and possible solutions.

In a defensive climate, team members may enter a meeting with a predetermined strategy designed to manipulate the others into a decision. In a supportive climate,

Figure 3–5

Outcomes of collegial learning

Note: From "Research Shows the Benefits of Adult Cooperation" by D. W. Johnson and R. T. Johnson, 1987, *Educational Leadership, 45*(3), pp. 27-30. Copyright 1987 by the Association for Supervision and Curriculum Development. Reprinted with permission of the Association for Supervision and Curriculum Development, David W. Johnson, and Roger T. Johnson. All rights reserved.

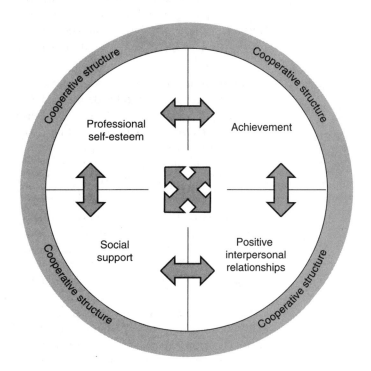

team members have engaged in planning, but their reactions are more spontaneous, depending on the needs of other group members and the situation. They allow others to express concerns and ideas that may not be on "their lists."

In a defensive mode, participants may be neutral, stating, "It doesn't matter to me," or "I don't care—whatever you want is fine." The neutrality of suggesting that anything others want is acceptable indicates this person is defensive by virtue of being uninvolved and unconcerned. In contrast, the supportive team member expresses empathy by restating and attempting to clarify feelings and ideas that may affect the problem.

Superiority is descriptive of the defensive climate, and equality is representative of supportive interactions. The school psychologist who acts as if she knows more than the others in the group, or the special educator who behaves as if regular educators are "unspecial" and have nothing to contribute is expressing superiority. In contrast, the principal who tells a parent that her observations of the child at home are important is emphasizing equality. Each participant is acknowledged as having a contribution to make to understanding the problem; in this case, the mother's expertise in the child's developmental history and home behaviors is given recognition.

Considering the various types of goal structures and communication climates is important for interactive team members who wish to interact effectively with others on the team. The individual who is cooperative—who wants the group goals to be facilitated, as opposed to having his or her own agenda—is more successful in working with others. The individual who is supportive rather than defensive is better able to assist the group in achieving and maintaining a problem-solving focus.

Roles in Team Meetings.   A classic study on the roles members can play in team meetings was conducted by Benne and Sheats (1948). They noted that group participation can be divided into three categories of roles: *task, maintenance,* and *negative.* These roles can be played by both leaders and group members, and all can play several roles during the course of a meeting. Task and maintenance roles are the ones most facilitating to the process of interactive teaming. A summary of the roles adapted from the work by Hybels and Weaver (1986) is included in Figure 3–6.

Consensus Building.   In addition to the goal structures, communication climates, and roles that members can play during meetings, the *decision-making processes* used to reach consensus will affect the team's functioning. If a process is not used, members tend to become frustrated and believe the team is not accomplishing anything, or that their thoughts and ideas are not valued by other team members.

In interactive teaming, participants should strive to work as a team and reach consensus decisions whenever possible. For consensus to be reached, team members must be aware of the needs of all involved and agree on a process for determining team decisions. An example of considering the needs of others was provided by Bailey (1987), who identified five areas of importance when working with families:

Task Roles

These people help get the task done, assist in coming up with new ideas, and aid in collecting and organizing information:

- *Initiators-expediters* suggest ideas and help keep the group on task.
- *Information givers and seekers* will track down information and enhance the quality of the discussion.
- *Critics-analyzers* look at the good and the bad in the data, detect points that need additional elaboration, discover information that has been left out, and model organized behavior.

Maintenance Roles

The people fulfilling these roles focus on the emotional tone of the meeting and also help keep the meeting going:

- *Encouragers* praise others for their contributions and the group's progress, are active listeners, and help others feel good about what is happening.
- *Harmonizers-compromisers* help resolve conflicts and determine solutions that are acceptable to everyone. They also remind others that group goals are more important than individual agendas.
- *Observers* help further group cohesiveness, and are sensitive and aware of the needs of each person.

Negative Roles

The individuals who are playing these roles slow the group down and interfere with progress:

- *Aggressors-resistors* attack others to make themselves look superior.
- *Recognition-seekers* and *self-confessors* call attention to themselves and make contributions that are off-task or lengthy.
- *Help seekers* join groups to meet their own needs and use the group to further their own agendas.
- *Withdrawers* make no contributions and may appear bored or shy.

Figure 3–6

Roles in team meetings

Note: From *Communicating Effectively* (pp. 240-244) by S. Hybels and R. L. Weaver, 1986, New York: McGraw-Hill. Adapted by permission of McGraw-Hill, Inc.

The ability to (1) view a family from a systems perspective; (2) systematically assess relevant family needs; (3) use effective listening and interviewing techniques; (4) negotiate values and priorities to reach a joint solution; and (5) act as "quality advisors" in helping families match needs with available community resources (p. 64).

A number of decision-making processes have been identified in the literature. The challenge for team members is selecting the most appropriate one for their situation. Most are similar to the sequence suggested by Doyle and Strauss (1976) and further developed by Margolis and Brannigan (1987). These authors recommended the following steps: (a) Define the problem, (b) analyze the problem and any factors that could be contributing to it, (c) generate possible alternatives, (d) establish and agree on criteria for selecting solutions, and (e) select and evaluate possible solutions.

Two examples of decision-making processes are *Problem Resolution Through Communication* by Fine, Grantham, and Wright (1979), and the *Nominal Group Technique* developed by Delbecq, Van de Ven, and Gustafson (1975) and summarized by Kaiser and Woodman (1985). Problem Resolution Through Communication stresses listening and communication skills, and it includes considerations of feelings and taking another's point of view (Figure 3–7). Nominal Group Technique is especially useful in ensuring that all team members participate in the decision-making process and that the decision reflects a consensus of the group. The steps in the Nominal Group Technique are listed in Figure 3–8.

Leadership Styles

Leadership behaviors, styles, and beliefs are integral to the success of an interactive team. As will be explained in Chapter 7, any member of the team can serve as the leader, but someone must assume that role for the team's work to be completed.

Administrators such as principals, directors, or division heads do not have to function as team leaders in interactive teaming situations, but they can assist the team's work in other ways. Gerber (1991) noted that administrators need to provide program advocacy and promote the goals of collaborative efforts. He also stated that they should visibly participate, because this enhances credibility, and they should provide support for maintenance and durability of collaboration.

Leadership styles affect how team meetings are conducted and the views others may have toward the person in the role of leader. The beliefs leaders have about what they consider to be the "rules of the game" also will affect the functioning of the team.

Hybels and Weaver (1986) identified three leadership styles in conducting team meetings: authoritarian, democratic, and laissez-faire. The *authoritarian* leader is definitely in charge and controls who talks and what they discuss. Under this type of leadership, individuals may not feel free to contribute or to share their honest opinions. The *democratic* leader ensures that all points of view are recognized and that all members are involved in contributing to a decision. This type of leadership generally results in increased motivation for team members and more creativity in decisions generated. The *laissez-faire* leader does not require or actually assume a responsibility for leading the group. As a result, typically very little is accomplished. The type of leadership style most appropriate for interactive teaming is the democratic style; however, if time for decision making is limited, the authoritarian style may have to be implemented on a short-term basis, but contributions from all members should still be encouraged. The laissez-faire style would not be suitable unless the purpose of the meeting is simply interaction without the necessity of accomplishing a task or making a decision.

Phase	Purpose	Considerations
Initiation • door opening • active listening • "I" statements	• Establish rapport • Tentative ident. of problem • Stimulate discussion	Who has the problem? What are the child's feelings?
Information processing • door opening • active listening	• Gather data • Elicit perceptions • Identify issues • Ventilation	What is reality? What are issues? Tolerate some overdetailing & generalization
Constructive confrontation • "I" statements • reflecting • discrepancies	• Mutualize reality • Establish teacher's position • Ident. of issues	• Activate other person • Avoid generalizations • Avoid overdetailing • Avoid tangents

Review options
• what are options?
• what are outcomes?
• what else is involved?
	• Focus on solutions
	• Identify outcomes of
	  options
	• Consider self-other
	  situation
		• Consider several options
		  not just the "best"
		• Avoid overdetailing and
		  tangents

Structuring for change
• what, who, how,
  where, when, why?
	• Select viable options
	• Plan change program
	• Consider contingencies
		• Should be concrete, specific
		• Should consider
		  involvement of self-other
		  situation
		• How much structure is
		  needed?

Evaluation
• what happened?
• how do we know?
• what now?
	• To determine what
	  changes occurred
	• To consider any new issues
	• To decide what happens now
		• Be aware of limit-testing
		• Be prepared to revisit
		  earlier phase

Return to an earlier phase if an impasse occurs

Figure 3–7

Problem resolution through communication

Note: From "Personal Variables That Facilitate or Impede Consultation" by M. J. Fine, V. L. Grantham, and J. G. Wright, 1979, *Psychology in the Schools, 16,* p. 537. Reprinted by permission of the publisher.

Step 1—Silent generation of ideas in writing. Each member is asked to write down key ideas related to the issue under consideration silently and independently. The benefits of this step are that members can think/reflect freely, interruptions are avoided; undue focusing on a particular idea or content area is minimized; competition, status pressure, and conformity are avoided; the group remains problem-centered; and the group avoids selecting a choice prematurely.

Step 2—Round-robin recording of ideas. Each member is asked sequentially to provide one idea until all ideas are processed. The group leader records each item on a blackboard or flip chart. Benefits include: equal participation, increase in problem-mindedness, depersonalization—the separation of ideas from personalities, an increase in the ability to deal with a larger number of ideas, tolerance for conflicting ideas, encouragement of hitchhiking (generating new ideas from presented ideas), and the development of a written record.

Step 3—Serial discussion for clarification. Each idea is discussed in turn. During this process, each item can potentially receive adequate discussion/clarification, logic can be provided behind arguments and disagreements, and differences of opinion can be recorded without undue argumentation. It is important to stress here that steps 2 and 3 are solely for idea generation and clarification and not evaluation.

Step 4—Preliminary vote on item importance. Each member independently rank orders, in his or her opinion, the most salient items. Typically, a limit is placed (e.g., each member's top five). Independent listing minimizes status, personality characteristics, and conformity pressures. From the total list, the most salient items emerge, ranked in order, based on the total frequency of each item.

Step 5—Discussion of the preliminary vote—(optional). Each member is allowed a brief period to comment on the selected items. This allows the group to examine inconsistent voting patterns and also allows for discussion of items that received unusually high or low rankings.

Step 6—Final vote. The group combines individual judgment into a group decision using a mathematical procedure. This allows for a sense of closure, accomplishment, and documentation. It is important to note that the mathematical resolution may take the form of a rank ordering, a system of rating each item, or the selection of a single best item based on the frequency of votes for each item. The procedure should fit the group's needs.

Figure 3–8

Nominal group technique

Note: From "Multidisciplinary Teams and Group Decision-Making Techniques: Possible Solutions to Decision-Making Problems" by S. M. Kaiser and R. W. Woodman, 1985, *School Psychology Review, 14,* pp. 464-465. Reprinted by permission of the publisher.

Beliefs about the "rules of the game" when serving as a team leader will affect how one fulfills the role. The rules listed in Figure 3–9 are derived from literature, interviews with leaders, and personal experiences. Some are stated humorously, not because they should be taken lightly, but rather because "many a truth is stated in jest."

IMPLEMENTATION OF INTERACTIVE TEAMING

Implementation Procedures

The actual procedures involved in implementing the interactive teaming process should and will vary depending on such factors as the age of the child, severity of the problem, and types of professionals available. The steps presented in Figure 3–10 on pages 92–93 are generic ones that will need to be adapted to specific situations. (Additional information on implementing these procedures for different types of students is provided in chapters 10-13 and the Case Study at the end of the text.)

Guidelines to remember when implementing the steps are (a) encourage everyone to contribute during the discussion, including the person presenting the situation; (b) reach consensus on the definition of the problem before discussing possible interventions; and (c) consider all factors that could be relevant to the problem or possible interventions. These factors could include materials, teaching techniques, antecedents and consequences of behaviors, criterion level of performance expected, classroom and home environments, and mastery of prerequisite skills.

Commitment to Common Goals

The final dimension necessary for an interactive team to be a successful and effective operating unit is shared commitment to common goals. The primary goal is to meet the needs of students. To accomplish this within an interactive teaming framework, team members must believe that collaboration, teaming, and integrating services are viable and vital ways to meet students' needs. Along with this belief, those involved must recognize that the "whole is greater than the sum of the parts"—that is, professionals and parents can achieve better results working together than when they operate as individuals or separate disciplines (Dunn, 1989; Pugach, 1988). The services provided will be more comprehensive and less fragmented, multiple interventions can be implemented simultaneously, and the chances of behaviors being learned and generalized are greatly increased (Adamson, Cox, & Schuller, 1989; Golightly, 1987; Idol, Nevin, & Paolucci-Whitcomb, 1994).

A secondary goal, which follows from the first, is the support of the concepts of professional development and role release. Professionals and parents must be willing to share ideas and techniques with others, and support their fellow team members in

1. **Always do right. This will gratify some people and astonish the rest.**
   This rule can seldom be violated, even by those with established power. *Right* is defined in different ways by various societies and cultures, so it is essential that the leader learn the values of the culture or society. An entry-level leader must project and possess absolute integrity in the conduct of all affairs, and must understand that the standards are applied more rigorously to his or her conduct than to the conduct of others

2. **Rose-colored glasses never come in bifocals.**
   This is another way of saying that there are no knights in shining armor who go around righting all wrongs with a stroke of the sword. The behaviors of a leader are often less than "perfect" in the judgement of others who do not have the total perspective that would enable them to understand the rationale for decision making. Sometimes a leader may have to struggle with what is "right" and balance it with what is essential to help someone save face or to comply with political realities that will allow a different "right" to occur in the future.

3. **If you mess up, 'fess up!**
   Everyone makes errors. Experienced leaders who don't admit and learn from their mistakes are bound to repeat them. Potential leaders who don't admit and learn from their mistakes will not be given an opportunity to repeat them. Successful leaders try to anticipate and prevent errors; when they have erred, they make sure they don't repeat them. They do this by rehearsing and planning, so that possible events are anticipated whenever possible.

4. **Criticism is a compliment.**
   The inability to accept and to profit from constructive criticism often prevents people from becoming successful leaders. Using the comments of others to one's own benefit can help a person grow in a role and be able to fulfill self- and others' expectations.

5. **If you yell at the umpire, you get thrown out of the game.**
   Experienced leaders know that you should not confront authority figures in public or cause them to lose face in front of others, even if they are wrong. They know that when you have an honest disagreement with the authority person, you should go to that person's office and close the door for your discussion. When you emerge, you should support the commonly agreed upon position.

Figure 3–9
Rules of the game

implementing what has been learned. Such sharing may require "paradigm shifts" to better understand one another (Lopez, Dalal, & Yoshida, 1993), and taking responsibility for one's own learning as well as the learning of others (Skrtic, 1991).

If the commitment to students rather than "turf" or the commitment to assisting fellow team members is missing, the team concept will not succeed. If the commitment and the other dimensions are present, the interactive team can be effective. As illustrated in Figure 3–11 on page 94, the effective team is unified in working toward a shared goal, and the ineffective team is bogged down.

6. **Don't go off half-cocked until you have all the facts.**
   Overreaction is a common error, particularly among first-time leaders who might think they need to assert their authority. It can be costly, particularly if an action is taken before the whole picture is assessed.

7. **If I didn't laugh, my heart would break.**
   If the role of leader is taken seriously all the time, it is easy to become tense and discouraged and eventually become ineffective. Sometimes the best way to deal with a situation is to laugh and relieve some of the tension.

8. **Follow the invisible leader—the common purpose.**
   The most effective leaders have learned how to generate group support for their ideas by instilling within the group a sense of "ownership" for the ideas. They begin by listening carefully to what others have to say and by analyzing the effect of a particular plan on other team members.

9. **Speak softly but carry a big stick.**
   Some people who aspire to become leaders or who find themselves in leadership roles think they have to prove they are powerful by being pushy. This behavior usually has the opposite effect of turning people away from their leadership. Those who are successful have learned the value of using a soft, polite tone rather than acting every role as if they were starring in a tough-guy movie.

10. **It ain't over 'til it's over.**
    Going back into the game to try again, even in the face of an apparent defeat, is the mark of a champion. All experienced leaders know that you win some and you lose some. It isn't important, or possible, to win them all. Keeping your perspective is a matter of understanding that the score at the end of the game is more important than the score at the half, and that the win/loss record at the end of the season is the record that counts. Effective leaders are persistent in the face of obstacles. When they fail to win their points, they come back to pursue the issue in a different way or at another time.

APPLICATION

Let us examine two descriptions of a team meeting, one unsuccessful and the other successful. In the first example, the leader does not seem aware of the necessary dimensions of teaming. He is not aware of the individuality of team members, does not attend to the process of team building, uses an inappropriate sequence of procedures, and exhibits an ineffective leadership style. Note how these factors interplay to produce an unsuccessful, dysfunctional teaming session.

Unsuccessful teaming: At the beginning of the first meeting of the team, the leader stated that this session needed to be "short and sweet" because he had a more

The following steps need to be adapted to specific situations, including whether this is a first meeting, a follow-up meeting, or a meeting to make a specific decision such as determination of placement.

1. The person designated as leader or chairperson should *notify the other members* of a meeting time and place, and distribute any available background information to be read before the discussion.

2. At the beginning of the meeting, the leader should make sure everyone has met the others and *state the purpose* and agenda items.

3. The person who requested the meeting should *describe the problem(s).* Other group members should ask questions for clarification, if necessary, and also contribute their own observations to corroborate or contrast with the problem being described.

4. The group should reach consensus on a specific, measureable, and observable *definition of the problem.* (For example, if the problem presented is "Gerry has a bad attitude about school," group members should ask questions and discuss the situation to determine if this means she does not start assignments when directions are given, is not making passing grades on tests, is not submitting her homework, or has been truant.)

5. If more than one problem is identified, each should be discussed, and then all should be *prioritized in terms of importance* to child's and adult's well-being, *and in terms of severity levels.* The desired level of performance (e.g., 75% or better on tests, no more than two absences per month) also should be determined.

6. The *history and frequency* of the problem should be determined (e.g., the problem has occurred 17 times in the last four weeks).

7. Any *previous interventions attempted* should be discussed, and their success or lack of success should be presented. This is an important step to keep from continually suggesting ideas that have been attempted, and it is also an opportunity to build on strategies that have proved effective.

Figure 3–10
Implementation procedures

important meeting to attend in 30 minutes. The foster mother for Angelina was immediately angered by the comment. She emphatically stated that she was not interested in participating in a meeting that people did not consider important. The social worker tried to calm her down, and suggested that the meeting proceed but that they could schedule additional time if needed. The leader then said, "Well, we all know that Angelina has been abused, and her biological mother is a crack cocaine addict. Now who has some ideas on what can be done?" The psychologist said he would like to share test results, but the special educator broke in and said she needed to know how to handle this child in her classroom tomorrow, because she had displayed very aggressive behaviors for the past two days. The foster mother began to describe how

8. All team members should *brainstorm possible interventions.* Consensus should be reached on which interventions should be attempted in which order and by whom. Consistency in applying reinforcers and consequences should be a primary consideration. If consensus is not readily obtainable, one of the strategies described in Chapter 5 on communication skills, such as the Nominal Group Technique, should be used.

9. Procedures for *collecting data* should be established. It is important to have a data collection system and to implement it to be able to decide on the effectiveness or failure of an intervention. The major criteria for the data collection system are that it measures the target behavior accurately, is easy to implement, and does not interfere with teaching (cf. Tawney & Gast, 1984; Wolery, Bailey, & Sugai, 1988).

10. The *data decision rules* should be determined (i.e., how long will an intervention be attempted before switching to another one). An important consideration is that the intervention needs to be applied consistently and on consecutive days for at least three to five days before a decision can be made on whether it is having the desired effect. An additional consideration is that for some behaviors such as talk-outs, an intervention that involves removal of attention (e.g., ignoring) may result in the behavior getting worse before it gets better.

11. The *responsibilities* for each team member should be clarified. If one or more members are going to provide information or materials, conduct additional observations, consult with others, or serve as reinforcers or people who will deliver negative consequences, these expectations should be clear to everyone.

12. A *timeline for activities* and a follow-up meeting to assess progress should be scheduled.

13. The team should meet regularly to *evaluate the interventions* to determine if changes or modifications need to be made.

14. Members of the team should meet as needed to provide *consultative and collaborative* assistance to each other.

15. Team members should *evaluate team effectiveness* periodically and determine if any changes need to be made in operating procedures, team composition, or other areas.

she used timeout at home, but the leader said, "I'm sorry to interrupt, but I really must leave for my next meeting. When would you like to meet again?"

In the second example, the leader ensures that the competencies of team members are recognized and their roles are clear. He allows time for the team to build and follows a sequence of steps to lead the group through the meeting. He also promotes the concept of role release. Notice how these factors promote successful teaming.

Successful teaming: At the beginning of the first meeting of the team, the leader asked all the members to introduce themselves and describe their roles and relationships to Angelina. After this was accomplished, the leader suggested that each person share any observations or assessment data that had been completed at the time. He

AN EFFECTIVE TEAM	AN INEFFECTIVE TEAM
A team is a unified group of people who join in a cooperative problem-solving process to reach a shared goal.	• Goals are unclear • Members are unprepared • Leadership is poor • Commitment to task is lacking

EFFECTIVE	INEFFECTIVE
Participation and leadership are distributed among all members.	Participation is unequal, leadership is delegated and based on authority.
Goals are cooperatively formed to meet individual and group needs.	Members accept imposed goals.
Ability and information determine influence and power.	Position determines influence; obedience to authority is stressed.
Two-way communication.	Communication about ideas is one-way; feelings are ignored.
Decision-making steps are matched with situation; consensus is sought for important decisions.	Decisions are made by highest authority with minimal member involvement.
Conflict is brought out and resolved.	Conflict is ignored, avoided, or denied.

Figure 3–11

Characteristics of effective and ineffective teams

Note: From "An Inservice Program for Improving Team Participation in Educational Decision-Making" by L. S. Anderlini, 1983, *School Psychology Review, 12*, p. 163. Reprinted by permission of the publisher.

also encouraged team members to ask questions as each individual gave his or her report. Next, he asked everyone to identify what he or she considered to be the primary problems in this case.

After a discussion that included the history and frequency of the problems, the group was able to reach consensus that the two top-priority problems were Angelina's kicking others and hitting herself on the head. The leader asked if anyone had identified interventions that were successful for either of these behaviors. The foster mother described how she had used timeout, and the special educator discussed how she had used selective attention and praised Angelina when she interacted appropriately. The counselor suggested including Angelina in a peer group that she conducted for abused and acting-out students. The adapted physical educator discussed games he could share with the special educator that developed cooperation skills.

The leader recommended closing the meeting and scheduling the next meeting in two weeks to discuss Angelina's progress and how the interventions of timeout and selective attention were working in the other settings. He also recommended that individual group members continue their discussions in the intervening time so information on particular strategies could be shared. The counselor agreed to contact the foster mother about the groups, and the special educator and adapted physical educator agreed to meet the next day to continue their discussion on cooperative games.

SUMMARY

Consideration of the research of models and programs with components of interactive teaming suggests that 10 dimensions must be present for the model to be effective:

◆ Legitimacy and autonomy.

◆ Purpose and objectives.

◆ Competencies of team members and clarity of their roles.

◆ Role release and role transitions.

◆ Awareness of the individuality of team members.

◆ Process of team building.

◆ Attention to factors that affect team functioning.

◆ Leadership styles.

◆ Implementation procedures.

◆ Commitment to common goals.

Factors considered to be possible barriers to interactive teaming—such as a lack of role understanding and communication skills, leadership problems, and a lack of awareness of cultural and family considerations—are addressed in the next section of this text.

ACTIVITIES

1. Interview a professional involved in service delivery to at-risk children or students with special needs. Ask how role release is accomplished in his or her job. Also ask which aspects of the role are difficult to release, and which aspects should not be attempted by someone who does not have professional training in that area.

2. Identify your Professional Stage, Career Cycle, and Conceptual Stage. How are they alike and how are they different? Which experiences and educational opportunities do you think have contributed to your cycle and stages?

3. Observe a team meeting and analyze the *goal structures, communication climates,* and *roles* that occur. What contributed to each? Were people consistent or did they change during the course of the meeting?

4. Interview four professionals who have been on teams. Ask them how the team was established and maintained. Also ask them to identify the decision-making processes and implementation procedures used by their teams. Finally, ask them to classify the leadership style of the person in charge of the team as authoritarian, democratic, or laissez-faire.

REFERENCES

Abelson, M. A., & Woodman, R. W. (1983). Review of research on team effectiveness: Implications for teams in schools. *School Psychology Review, 12,* 125–136.

Adamson, D. R., Cox, J., & Schuller, J. (1989). Collaboration/consultation: Bridging the gap from resource room to regular classroom. *Teacher Education and Special Education, 12,* 46–51.

Anderlini, L. S. (1983). An inservice program for improving team participation in educational decision-making. *School Psychology Review, 12,* 160–167.

Bailey, D. B. (1984). A triaxial model of the interdisciplinary team and group process. *Exceptional Children, 51,* 17–25.

___. (1987). Collaborative goal-setting with families: Resolving differences in values and priorities for services. *Topics in Early Childhood Special Education, 7*(2), 59–71.

Benne, K. D., & Sheats, P. (1948). Functional roles of group members. *Journal of Social Issues, 4,* 41–49.

Berry, T. H. (1991). *Managing the total quality transformation.* New York: McGraw-Hill.

Blankstein, A. M. (1992). Lessons from enlightened corporations. *Educational Leadership, 49,* 71–74.

Burke, P. S., Christensen, J. C., & Fessler, R. (1984). *Teacher career stages: Implications for staff development.* Bloomington, IN: Phi Delta Kappa Foundation.

Courtnage, L., & Healy, H. (1984). Interdisciplinary team training: A competency- and procedure-based approach. *Teacher Education and Special Education, 7,* 3–11.

Covey, S. R. (1991). *Principle-centered leadership.* New York: Simon & Schuster.

David, J. L. (1989). Synthesis of research on school-based management. *Educational Leadership, 46*(8), 45–58.

Delbecq, A. L., Van de Ven, A. H., & Gustafson, D. H. (1975). *Group techniques for program planning: A guide to nominal group and delphi processes.* Glenview, IL: Scott, Foresman.

Deming, W. E. (1986). *Out of the crisis.* Boston: MIT Center for Advanced Engineering Studies.

Doyle, M., & Strauss, D. (1976). *How to make meetings work: The new interaction method.* Chicago: Playboy Press.

Dunn, W. (1989). Integrated related services for preschoolers with neurological impairments: Issues and strategies. *Remedial and Special Education, 10*(3), 31–39.

Elliot, S. N., & Sheridan, S. M. (1992). Consultation and teaming: Problem solving among educators, parents, and support personnel. *The Elementary School Journal, 92,* 315–338.

Epstein, L. (1988). *Helping people: The task centered approach*. New York: Merrill/Macmillan.

Fine, M. J., Grantham, V. L., & Wright, J. G. (1979). Personal variables that facilitate or impede consultation. *Psychology in the Schools, 16,* 533–539.

Gerber, S. (1991). Supporting the collaborative process. *Preventing School Failure, 35*(4), 48–52.

Gibb, J. R. (1961). Defensive communication. *Journal of Communication, 11,* 141–148.

Golightly, C. J. (1987). Transdisciplinary training: A step forward in special education teacher preparation. *Teacher Education and Special Education, 10,* 126–130.

Harrison, C. R., Killion, J. P., & Mitchell, J. E. (1989). Site-based management: The realities of implementation. *Educational Leadership, 46*(8), 55–58.

Hudson, P. J., Correa, V. I., Morsink, C. V., & Dykes, M. K. (1987). A new model for preservice training: Teacher as collaborator. *Teacher Education and Special Education, 10,* 191–193.

Hunt, D. E. (1981). Teachers' adaptation: "Reading" and "flexing" to students. In B. Joyce, C. Brown, & L. Peck (Eds.), *Flexibility in teaching*. New York: Longman Publishers.

Hybels, S., & Weaver, R. L. (1986). *Communicating effectively*. New York: Random House.

Idol, L., Nevin, A., & Paolucci-Whitcomb, P. (1994). *Collaborative consultation* (2nd ed.). Austin, TX: Pro-Ed.

Johnson, D. W., & Johnson, R. T. (1987). Research shows the benefits of adult cooperation. *Educational Leadership, 45*(3), 27–30.

Johnson, D. W., Johnson, R. T., & Holubec, E. (1986). *Circles of learning: Cooperation in the classroom* (rev. ed.). Edina, MN: Interaction Book Company.

Kabler, M. L., & Genshaft, J. L. (1983). Structuring decision-making in multidisciplinary teams. *School Psychology Review, 12,* 150–159.

Kaiser, S. M., & Woodman, R. W. (1985). Multidisciplinary teams and group decision-making techniques: Possible solutions to decision-making problems. *School Psychology Review, 14,* 457–470.

Laycock, V. K., Gable, R. A., & Korinek, L. (1991). Alternative structures for collaboration in the delivery of special services. *Preventing School Failure, 35*(4), 15–18.

Lezotte, L. W. (1989). School improvement based on the effective schools research. In D. K. Lipsky & A. Gartner (Eds.), *Beyond separate education: Quality education for all*. Baltimore: Paul H. Brookes.

Lopez, E. C., Dalal, S. M., & Yoshida, R. K. (1993). An examination of professional cultures: Implications for the collaborative consultation model. *Journal of Educational and Psychological Consultation, 4,* 197–213.

Lyon, S., & Lyon, G. (1980). Team functioning and staff development: A role release approach to providing integrated educational services for severely handicapped students. *Journal of the Association for the Severely Handicapped, 5,* 250–263.

Maher, C. A., & Hawryluk, M. K. (1983). Framework and guidelines for utilization of teams in schools. *School Psychology Review, 12,* 180–185.

Margolis, H., & Brannigan, G. G. (1987). Problem solving with parents. *Academic Therapy, 22,* 423–425.

Mather, J., & Weinstein, E. (1988). Teachers and therapists: Evolution of a partnership in early intervention. *Topics in Early Childhood Special Education, 7,* 1–9.

Orelove, F. P., & Sobsey, D. (1991). *Educating children with multiple disabilities: A transdisciplinary approach* (2nd ed.). Baltimore: Paul H. Brookes.

Orlich, D. C. (1989). Education reforms: Mistakes, misconceptions, miscues. *Phi Delta Kappan, 70,* 512–517.

Peryon, C. D. (1982). Systematic development of special educators as facilitators of mainstreaming. *Journal of Special Education Technology, 5*(3), 31–36.

Phillips, V., & McCullough, L. (1990). Consultation-based programming: Instituting the collaborative ethic in schools. *Exceptional Children, 56,* 291–304.

Pugach, M. C. (1988). Restructuring teaching. *Teaching Exceptional Children, 21,* 47–50.

Salvia, J., & Ysseldyke, J. E. (1988). *Assessment in special and remedial education* (4th ed.). Boston: Houghton Mifflin.

Sheehy, G. (1977). *Passages—Predictable crises in adult life*. New York: Bantam Books.

Siders, J. A., Riall, A., Bennett, T. C., & Judd, D. (1987). Training of leadership personnel in early intervention: A transdisciplinary approach. *Teacher Education and Special Education, 10*(4), 161–170.

Skrtic, T. M. (1991). The special education paradox: Equity as the way to excellence. *Harvard Educational Review, 61,* 148–191.

Sprinthall, N. A., & Thies-Sprinthall, L. (1983). The teacher as an adult learner: A cognitive-developmental view. *National Society for the Study of Education, 82nd Yearbook*. Chicago: The University of Chicago Press.

Tawney, J. W., & Gast, D. L. (1984). *Single subject research in special education*. New York: Merrill/Macmillan.

Tuckman, B. W., & Jensen, M. A. C. (1977). Stages of small group development revisited. *Group and Organization Studies, 2,* 419–427.

United Cerebral Palsy Association. (1976). *Staff development handbook: A resource for the transdisciplinary process*. New York: Author.

Wangemann, P., Ingram, C. F., & Muse, I. D. (1989). A successful university-public school collaboration: The union of theory and practice. *Teacher Education and Special Education, 12,* 61–64.

West, J. F., & Cannon, G. S. (1988). Essential collaborative consultation competencies for regular and special educators. *Journal of Learning Disabilities, 21*(28), 56–63.

Wolery, M., Bailey, D. B., & Sugai, G. M. (1988). *Effective teaching: Principles and procedures of applied behavior analysis with exceptional students*. Boston: Allyn & Bacon.

Yoshida, R. K. (1983). Are multidisciplinary teams worth the investment? *School Psychology Review, 12,* 137–143.

PART II

Facilitating Factors

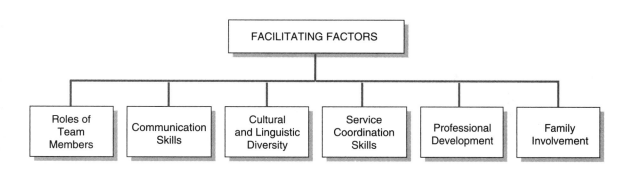

OVERVIEW

The chapters in this part describe the facilitating factors that contribute to effective team functioning. Chapter 4 on the roles of team members provides descriptions of the roles of professionals, paraprofessionals, and parents. The chapter also illustrates how team members can provide direct services and serve as collaborators. In Chapter 5 communication is defined, and factors to consider in communication are explained. The verbal and nonverbal forms of communication are described, and strategies for managing conflict and resistance are presented.

Chapter 6 includes a definition of *culture* and an examination of the effects of cultural and linguistic diversity on students, families, schools, and team members. In Chapter 7, service coordination skills, essential parameters for the leadership of professionals, are identified and guidelines for the procedures that team leaders should implement are explained. Chapter 8 includes a description of power and empowerment, and illustrates three types of professional development. The final chapter in this part, Chapter 9, contains descriptions of factors that have influenced changes in attitudes about family involvement and outlines how family members can assist in providing services to their children as they fulfill vital roles as interactive team members.

4

Understanding Roles and Perspectives of Team Members

TOPICS IN THIS CHAPTER INCLUDE

◆ Overview of the problems and promises of teaming with professionals who have different goals, training, and perspectives.

◆ Description of the changes in the composition and functions of the team, as determined by the complexity of the problem and the type of facility within which it operates.

◆ Descriptions of the roles of each team member, both as direct service provider and as collaborator or consultant, and discussion of the overlapping functions of certain roles.

◆ Application of the interactive teaming model to a case in which the special education teacher and speech-language therapist collaborate to help a special student with language development.

 Darrell, a 12-year-old middle school student who had been classified as Trainable Mentally Handicapped, was the subject of the team meeting to plan his instructional program. Darrell was an African-American who went to live with his maternal grandmother after his mother died in childbirth. He was placed in a compensatory education program when he entered school as a 6-year-old, then placed in a full-time special education classroom a year later. In the current meeting to plan his instructional program, the team was to focus on moving Darrell into the special education resource room part time, while continuing the support he and his family were receiving in the form of speech-language therapy, behavior modification, and nutritional counseling. His grandmother, who was elderly and unemployed, was receiving public assistance for herself and for Darrell.

The school psychologist said, "Darrell is functioning within the range of moderate mental retardation. His academic achievement scores, according to the WRAT, are significantly below his grade level but consistent with expectations given his mental age. He exhibits passive-aggressive behavior with adults, while becoming more openly hostile with his peers."

The speech-language therapist said, "His primary disability is a severe developmental delay in language acquisition, which impedes his social and academic functioning. I need to conduct a current language assessment, with particular emphasis on his MLU."

The dietitian said, "His nutritional intake may be a contributing factor to his attention deficit disorder. I suggest that he receive a more balanced diet, emphasizing complex carbohydrates, while limiting the number of exchanges in saturated fats and synthetic sugars."

The social worker said, "He is eligible for related special services such as speech therapy and nutritional counseling, which could be supported by third-party payments."

Darrell's grandmother, who was totally confused, simply nodded her head and smiled.

Darrell's case illustrates dramatically the differences in the roles, perspectives, and vocabularies of professionals on the interactive team. Because each person is a highly trained professional, he or she has specialized knowledge to contribute to the solution of problems. This professional training can be a major asset to the functioning of the team when the professional's knowledge is recognized and translated in a meaningful way. Or it can become a barrier, leading to misunderstanding, territoriality, and conflict.

In this chapter, the differences in the roles and perspectives of team members are described. The changes in the composition and functions of the team are explained according to the context in which it operates—the program for culturally different, mildly disabled, or severely disabled students. The contributions of each team member, both as a service provider and as a collaborator, are defined. Finally, the interactive teaming model is applied to Darrell's case, described above, in an example showing consultation and collaboration between two members of the team, the special education teacher and the speech-language therapist.

ROLES AND PERSPECTIVES OF TEAM MEMBERS

The first major task in establishing interactions among team members is recognizing that these individuals have widely disparate roles, vocabularies, and perspectives as a result of their highly specialized professional training. These differences, however, can be viewed as potential strengths if they are respected by all members of the team and used appropriately by the leader.

Collaboration among professionals is particularly difficult when it involves members of the education and the allied health professions. Eggers (1983) described their difficulties as follows:

> Imagine a sporting event with doctors, nurses, therapists and other health professionals competing against educators and developmental psychologists. Each team insists that the game be played on their field by their rules—impossible conditions for productive, organized competition. . . . the silliness of the image fades and is replaced by an image of a child being pulled in multiple directions by different types of professionals while bewildered, frustrated parents pace the sidelines. (p. 2)

The differences among members of the health-related and education professions are real. In health-related professions, specialists call the people they serve "patients" or "clients"; they provide "treatment" as short-term health care, usually in response to a crisis. Education-related professionals call the people they serve "students" and they provide "treatment" as long-term instruction from a developmental perspective.

In addition, the range and nature of the advocacy groups, organizations, and regulations with which each group must deal are different. While educators function within organizations dependent upon public funds and regulated by legislative mandates, health professionals often receive reimbursement from third parties such as insurance companies, Medicaid, and the Social Security system, each having its own set of forms and payment schedules. Each group of professionals has its own perspective, as well as multiple layers of subspecialties. Collaboration becomes increasingly difficult as the layers of subspecialties increase.

TEAM COMPOSITION AND FUNCTIONS

The team's composition and functions are affected by new trends in service delivery, which have increased the number of programs available at the preschool and postschool level. Changes in the composition and functions of the team are also due to the fact that the number of persons on the team is variable, depending on the nature of the problems it addresses.

TRENDS: PRESCHOOL AND POSTSCHOOL SERVICE DELIVERY

Two trends in service delivery for special needs students have implications for team composition and functions. These trends are the expansion of educational programs into preschool and postschool settings.

In both cases, this expansion increases the need for professionals to interact with others outside the traditional school setting. This interaction frequently extends into the related professions of human and social services, making coordination both more important and more complicated. Professionals across agencies will be required to advocate for children and help the families of these children negotiate the multiple bureaucracies that provide service delivery (Davenport, 1990).

Although it is difficult to work across these boundaries, preliminary data indicate that such efforts can be productive. Yale researchers, summarizing the results of 72 collaborative programs for children and their families, have concluded that interagency linkages have provided both program quality and cost effectiveness (Kagan & Rivera, 1990). They cited (a) training for caregivers and teachers, (b) consistent regulations based on joint planning, and (c) parental involvement among the practices they identified as promising.

New preschool programs reflect the growing emphasis on early intervention for children who are disabled or at risk. Team members will need to be aware that it is especially important to promote active social interactions between children, particularly in situations that can facilitate improved play behaviors (Esposito & Koorland, 1989; Guralnick & Groom, 1988).

Increased family involvement will also be essential in preschool programs. Successful service delivery will be based on understanding of new family styles, diversity, and their adverse conditions (Vincent & Salisbury, 1988). Team members will need to include parents as full partners in decision-making, de-emphasizing traditional views of "dominant and submissive" roles (Darling, 1989). They will also need to remain sensitive to the family's needs for privacy (Krauss, 1990).

Preschool services will also extend to the provision of services for infants as required by P.L. 99-457. Larger numbers of infants will survive as medical science advances and many of them will require special education services (Bartel & Thurmond, 1992; Odom & Warren, 1988). Team members will need to consider services for these infants and toddlers as noncategorical (Mack, 1988). Decision-makers will also need to consider the new research findings, which indicate that with intensive, high quality instruction, a low student-teacher ratio, and establishment of a predictable environment, it is possible that even drug-exposed babies can score normally on developmental tests by the age of 2 (Bellisimo, 1990; Rist, 1990). Effective programs, however, will require collaborative planning among agencies.

Team members will also need to function in designing programs for post-school students, in transition between traditional schooling and employment. Among the issues these teams will confront are the following:

◆ More people with disabilities will be employed in the future. There is increasing employer awareness that disabled workers, as a group, are above average in dependability and job stability (Chamberlain, 1988). New regulations in the Americans with Disabilities Act (ADA) require employers to analyze the essential functions of jobs and to make necessary modifications for disabled workers.

◆ Transition teams will design and coordinate training that enables students to succeed in the work force. These training factors have been identified through research (Roessler, Brolin & Johnson, 1990). A need has been identified for curriculum change (Halloran & Ward, 1988), placement in community-based programs (McDonnell, Hardman & Hightower, 1989), and supported employment (Gemmel & Peterson, 1989) to facilitate transition to adult life.

◆ Collaborative, interagency planning will be among the most important factors in the success of transition programs (Sileo, Rude & Luckner, 1988).

CHANGES IN TEAM COMPOSITION AND FUNCTIONS

As indicated in Chapter 1, an interactive team can consist of as few as two members or as many as are required to provide the specialized knowledge and skills for the student in question. The number of people on the team increases with the complexity and nature of the problem. Not all members are present at every meeting, and not every meeting of the team is formal. Professionals may interact informally as required to maintain communication and provide follow-up for the decisions made by the larger group.

It should also be pointed out that each team member has two functions: to provide direct services and to serve as a collaborator. *Direct services* are offered as individual "hands-on" activities with the special needs student and family. *Collaboration* falls under *indirect services,* that is, consultation on subjects in which he or she has expert knowledge, or team efforts to plan, implement, and evaluate the student's program.

Effective use of the specialized knowledge and skills of each member of the team requires an understanding of the knowledge and skills that other individuals have acquired through their professional training. It also requires appropriate application of these skills to the tasks for which the team has responsibility: planning, implementation, and evaluation of the special needs student's program.

The knowledge and skills of persons most often found on interactive teams will be highlighted briefly. In addition to the special educator, these teams may include family members, an administrator, classroom teacher, school psychologist, counselor, social worker, speech-language therapist, ESL or bilingual education specialist, migrant or compensatory education teacher, school nurse, physical therapist, occupational therapist, and other health-related professionals.

Team members may also interact with specialists in computer education, adaptive physical education, and vocational or transition education, and they may be responsible for the supervision of paraprofessionals. As indicated earlier, the number of people on a given team is dependent upon the nature and complexity of the student's problems. In addition, the number of people available and the degree to which they serve as specialists or as generalists depends on factors such as the size of the school district or clinical facility and whether it is in a rural, suburban, or urban area. These factors can affect a district's or facility's financial resources and availability of specialized personnel.

ROLES OF SPECIAL EDUCATORS

The role of the primary service provider—the special educator—changes according to the context in which service is offered. Services may be provided for students who are culturally different, mildly disabled, or severely disabled. The roles of the special educator in each of these three contexts are outlined as follows and presented in greater detail in chapters 11, 12 and 13, while trends and issues in infant and preschool programs are presented in Chapter 11.

Role When Serving Culturally Different Students

The special or remedial educator who serves culturally different students interacts primarily with the student's family members, with the school administrator and classroom teachers, and with professionals trained in teaching bilingual education or English as a second language. In this capacity, the special educator is both a service provider and a collaborator.

Role as Service Provider.   The knowledge and skills needed by the special educator who works with this population of students have been specified in detail by Fradd, Weismantel, Correa, and Algozzine (1988) and by Fox, Kuhlman, and Sales (1988). It is generally agreed that this professional should be aware of the problems inherent in teaching culturally different students and should demonstrate knowledge about cultural differences, as well as the ability to apply this knowledge in the instructional setting (Fox, Kuhlman, & Sales, 1988). It is further recognized that the teacher of culturally different students needs some knowledge about language development, language assessment, and multicultural education systems (Fradd, Weismantel, Correa, & Algozzine, 1988).

Role as Collaborator.   The team member who works with culturally different students also needs to be an effective collaborator. The understanding of one's own culture and cultural biases is an important step in the development of the flexibility and open-mindedness that characterize effective collaborators. Specific guidelines for these skills are presented in greater detail in Chapter 11 on cultural diversity.

Role When Serving Students with Mild Disabilities

The special or remedial educator who serves students with mild disabilities—those who are classified as learning disabled, educably mentally handicapped or developmentally delayed, behaviorally disordered, or mildly disabled in some physical or sensory capacity—deals largely with the student's parents and with other members of the education profession. These people include the school administrator, school psychologist, counselor or social worker, speech-language therapist, classroom teacher, adaptive physical educator, and paraprofessional.

Role as Service Provider. The special or remedial educator who works with students with mild disabilities most often functions in a school-based setting, operating a resource, itinerant, or team-teaching program to provide part-time intervention for students with specific academic and behavioral difficulties. The primary functions of this role are student assessment, program evaluation, and the provision of instruction.

For the student who has had difficulties, the special educator may conduct an educational assessment, administering a series of tests to determine the student's current levels of functioning and specific deficits in academic areas such as reading, math, and study skills. The special educator may also observe the student in the regular classroom or evaluate the student's behavioral characteristics, using checklists and interviews with parents and teachers to collect data related to program eligibility and placement.

When the mildly disabled student's educational program is planned by the team, the special educator presents the data that were obtained. The special educator may also discuss the difficulties that typically characterize students in the specific category for which this student is being considered and present program placement options that seem most appropriate. This may happen less formally during prereferral discussions.

When the instructional program has been implemented, the special educator measures the effectiveness of the program that has been designed, using continuous measurement techniques. These procedures enable the specialist to chart the student's performance on specific academic and behavioral objectives, and to obtain data that are useful both in making appropriate modifications and in communicating with other members of the team (Deno & Mirkin, 1977; Wesson, Fuchs, Tindal, Mirkin, & Deno, 1986).

The special educator's primary responsibility is to provide instructional services in an intensive (one-to-one or small group) short-term program. This program is sometimes conducted outside of the regular classroom, part time during the school day (see Morsink, 1984). More recently, this student receives services within the context of the regular classroom, frequently from the classroom teacher (Morsink & Lenk, 1992). The competencies needed by special educators of mildly disabled students have been studied in depth and will be summarized in Chapter 12.

Role as Collaborator. In addition to providing direct services to the student, the special educator has an important role as a collaborator on the related services team. The special educator provides information about the special student's learning needs and characteristics, and about special strategies and materials that have been found to be effective for students with certain difficulties. When providing this information, the special educator is a consultant to others.

The special educator also often functions collaboratively with others to collect additional data on the child's needs, during pre-referral or before placement in a special program. The most common format for this collaboration is the *teacher assistance team,* which functions to identify educational problems and develop interventions to be implemented by the referring classroom teacher. (Campbell, 1987b). Teacher assistance teams have worked effectively to help teachers implement interventions for students with academic or behavior problems (Chalfant, 1989; Chalfant, Pysh, & Moultrie, 1979), and they have been discussed in Chapter 2.

Similarly, a prereferral intervention model based on an indirect, consultative model of service delivery, has been successful in preventing future student problems. In the prereferral intervention model, the regular classroom teacher and special education consultant work together to increase the teacher's ability to individualize instruction for heterogeneous groups of students (Graden, Casey, & Christenson, 1985). Additional information on this topic is presented in Chapter 12.

Role When Serving Students with Severe Disabilities

The special educator who serves students with severe disabilities also fulfills the dual roles of service provider and collaborator. The service provided is—on a continuum—more nearly that of developmental/medical than educational/remedial assistance. The special education collaborator, in this case, is more closely aligned with members of the allied health professions than with classroom teachers and other general education personnel.

Role as Service Provider.   The student with severe disabilities often has multiple handicapping conditions. These include physical and sensory handicaps, in addition to some degree of mental retardation or neurological impairment. Also, these students may have manifestations of behavior disorders with a resultant need for behavior modification. And, because this student may take medications, suffer from seizures, or have special needs for medical equipment such as tracheostomy tubes or catheters, the special educator should have knowledge about the safe and legal use of procedures that may be required. Specialized competencies for teachers of students with physical and multiple disabilities have been studied in depth by Dykes, Brenner, and Lee (1985) and are presented in greater detail in Chapter 13. These generic techniques are required so that special education teachers are able to position, lift, and transport disabled students; monitor use of medications and prosthetic devices; manage seizures; and modify aberrant behaviors.

The major function of the special educator who serves severely disabled students is to teach them and to synthesize their special related services. Because of the multiple disabilities involving related services of a medical nature, however, the teaching function may appear to be of secondary importance. The special educator plans, implements, and monitors an instructional program based on the student's current educational-developmental level. This program is most often based on the student's development of functional skills such as self-care, daily living, communications, and vocational skills. It should not, however, be based on the assumption of need for custodial care; instead, it should focus on the development of skills that maximize the student's opportunities for full participation in society, with consideration for the quality of life. Some programs that serve severely disabled students are in special classrooms or center schools; for students who require a continuous level of special instruction and an integrated educational/medical program, this type of placement may be appropriate. For others, however, placement in regular schools may be workable and beneficial (Biklen, 1988).

Regardless of the setting in which the student with severe disabilities is placed, the role of the special educator also includes teaching students the skills of "normalization"—how to act and speak "normally" (Wolfensberger, 1972). Normalization strategies have been used to gain community acceptance of group homes for the retarded (Heal, Haney, & Novak Amado, 1988). Similarly, it has been found that the same strategy—emphasizing the disabled student's abilities and developing behaviors valued by the norm group—is instrumental in gaining acceptance for severely disabled students in the mainstream of education (Biklen, 1988; Littlejohn, 1989). Recent reports of the longitudinal work by Lovaas (1987) indicate that extensive individual and family therapy can modify even the aberrant behaviors of students classified as autistic. As a result of implementing this "normalization" treatment at the preschool level, the majority of targeted students in Lovaas's study were able to participate more fully in general education programs when they reached school age.

Finally, the teacher of severely disabled students will want to become familiar with and seek resources for the implementation of new technology, particularly that related to computer use (Burkhead, Sampson, & McMahon, 1986; Morsink, 1984), which may enable disabled individuals to function independently and to participate more fully in the new information/service society (Naisbitt, 1982).

Role as Collaborator.   The special educator often functions as a collaborator in the position of team leader or "*educational synthesizer*" (Campbell, 1987a, p. 107). In this leadership position, the teacher uses an accepted functional curriculum to identify the content to be mastered by the student. Then the special educator coordinates the activities of related services professionals who design assessment and instructional procedures to accommodate the student's movement, vision, hearing, and postural limitations. The team leader coordinates the educational program through group meetings and review of the student's performance data, collected by the professionals who implement various aspects of the program. After reviewing these data, the coordinator determines whether the student is acquiring targeted skills and then communicates these findings to various team members, who subsequently make appropriate adjustments in the program.

The special educator who serves students with severe disabilities is often confronted with the need for *role release* (Bailey, 1984), as described in Chapter 3, in which team members share expertise and often more than one person on the team performs the same function. The professional development function is also important on the interactive team. At times this involves sharing information from one's own discipline with others who need to understand it to implement their component of the program effectively; at other times it requires the ability to respect and accept the consultation of parents and other professionals who are specialists in various aspects of the student's care program (Bailey, 1984).

ROLE DESCRIPTIONS OF OTHER TEAM MEMBERS

As indicated earlier, the number of people on a team will vary, as determined both by the nature and severity of the student's problem, and by the size and resources available in the school district or clinical program. The roles of other team members are described in clusters, which include those with related or overlapping functions. These include the following: the program administrator; the classroom teacher; the school psychologist, counselor, or social worker; the speech-language therapist, the teacher of bilingual education or English as a second language; the physical therapist, occupational therapist, adaptive physical educator, and computer specialist; the vocational or transition specialist; the teacher of migrant or Chapter 1 programs; the school nurse, and other health-related professionals. The roles of family members and paraprofessionals are presented separately, in chapters 9 and 7, respectively.

Program Administrator

The contributions and specialized knowledge of the administrator are considered first because it is important to emphasize that the person with this title is not ordinarily the team leader. The organization's administrator, recognizing the team's value, delegates responsibility for its coordination to a team leader. The role of the leader will be described in more detail in Chapter 7. It should be noted that, although the administrator is not ordinarily the team's leader, it is essential that the administrator support the concept of teaming, and see the team's function as supportive of the organization's overall mission.

Those who have implemented school-based teacher assistance teams have learned that the administrator, who typically is responsible for teacher evaluation, often is not the best person to serve as the team leader because team members may be reluctant to share concerns about their effectiveness with the person who will evaluate them. The role of the administrator, therefore, is proposed as that of overall management of the school or clinic and its programs—but as a member rather than leader of the interactive team.

The administrator is charged with overall fiscal, legal, and programmatic responsibility for the unit in which the team functions. This unit is usually a school, and its administrator is a principal when the team serves students from culturally diverse backgrounds or those with mild disabilities. It may be a clinic or specialized organization with a director when the team serves students with severe disabilities. Because the administrator has overall responsibility for the unit, she must give permission for the team to function as a decision-making body, as well as provide it with the necessary information and support to implement its decisions. Also, because the administrator has overall responsibility for the unit, she must balance the budget and see that all legal mandates and protections are observed while attending to the needs of all constituencies. The administrator's priority is the welfare of the entire unit, rather than serving as a personal advocate for the special needs of any one student or program.

The specialized areas of knowledge of the administrator or director include but are not limited to the following: leadership and change; professional development and relations; planning and evaluation; public and community relations; personnel management; and knowledge about budgets, law, educational and medical programs, resources, and facilities. In some cases, the school administrator is the instructional leader for the unit, although observations of what elementary and secondary principals actually do seem to suggest that this activity represents less than 20% to 30% of their time (Howell, 1981). And, in clinical settings, it is unlikely that the director is trained in both education and the allied health professions in addition to having expertise in administration.

For the team to function effectively, however, it is particularly important for the administrator to understand and convey to the public that she values this team and has delegated to it decision-making authority for the programs of special needs students. It is equally important for the administrator to provide the members of the team with information about the legal policies and procedures within which they are authorized to operate, and to provide them with information about the fiscal and instructional resources available to them in program implementation. After having established the team, however, the administrator steps down from the direct leadership role and delegates responsibility for the team's functioning to the team itself.

Classroom Teacher

The classroom teacher has unique skills and knowledge that may be applied to the development, evaluation, and implementation of the special student's instructional program. The classroom teacher is more often involved when the student is culturally different or mildly disabled, although in some cases the severely or multiply disabled student may also be served part time in the regular school program.

The classroom teacher has been trained as a specialist in "normal" human growth and development. This team member is therefore in an excellent position to observe the special needs student's interactions with peers who demonstrate age- and grade-appropriate behaviors. Such observations are not possible in the special classroom, where this student is separated from peers who set the *norms* for age-appropriate learning and behavior. The classroom teacher who observes a first-grader reversing letters knows that other "normal" 6-year-olds sometimes do the same thing. The classroom teacher who observes a moody, hostile adolescent recognizes that all adolescents are moody and may occasionally appear to be hostile or withdrawn. The classroom teacher, by comparing the individual's behavior with the group norms, is also able to determine that a 9-year-old who frequently reverses letters or an adolescent who is consistently hostile or withdrawn may have special needs. It is of primary importance that the classroom teacher make data-based observations of these behaviors, comparing the target student's performance with that of others in the group, to determine the nature and severity of the problem. In making such observations, the teacher should take care to define the behavior precisely, specify the conditions for observation, and ensure that the observations are made under consistent environmental conditions (Haring & Phillips, 1972; Morsink, 1984). Classroom teachers who make such observations will be much more effective members of the team because they are able to communicate the precise nature of the student's problems in coping with the school curriculum and the classroom environment.

The classroom teacher is also a specialist in the academic subject matter or scope and sequence of the curriculum for particular grade levels or subjects. This team member's primary responsibility is to implement the academic curriculum in the classroom. Peterson (1988) has pointed out that the role of the teacher is now viewed primarily as that of a "thoughtful professional," one who understands the relationship between teaching and learning and is able to enhance the student's cognitive functioning in a specific academic area. Others (Gensante & Matgouranis, 1989; Ross, 1989) have referred to effective teachers as those who use "reflective teaching," describing what they do and its effect on learners, and using this information to improve their instruction.

The classroom teacher's most important role with the special student, both before and after referral (if the student is placed), focuses on the provision of appropriate learning experiences. Nevin and Thousand (1986) and Villa and Thousand (1988) have summarized a number of strategies that have been found effective in accommodating the special student in the classroom environment. These include outcomes-based strategies such as peer tutoring, cooperative learning, mastery learning, and applied behavior analysis. In addition, it is important for the classroom teacher to establish an effective environment in which the special student can learn: one that has a positive classroom climate and that includes teacher-directed instruction, followed by opportunities for students to practice their skills under supervision, with teacher feedback (Larrivee, 1985; Morsink, Thomas, & Smith-Davis, 1987; Rosenshine & Stevens, 1986).

It should be understood by other members of the team that classroom teachers are trained to accommodate students in groups, rather than to tutor them individually. It is the classroom teacher's primary responsibility to provide academic instruction for all members of the group, not only to enhance the learning of individuals with special needs. This professional is in the best position to assist the special needs student in working with the group, learning to follow routines and complying with accepted standards of group behavior. The classroom teacher, however, is not as effective as the special educator in providing intensive one-on-one or small-group instruction on specific academic skills or behavior management. The same characteristics that enhance the teacher's effectiveness in whole-group instruction may limit the ability to deal with individuals who have diverse needs, particularly when teachers lack the technological and human support to implement simultaneously a variety of diverse teaching strategies (Gerber, 1988). In addition, the classroom teacher, even if willing and well trained, often finds that clinical tutoring in the classroom environment may intensify the student's difficulties by calling attention to them in the presence of peers (Morsink, 1984).

School Psychologist, Counselor, or Social Worker

Because the roles of these three professionals often overlap, the descriptions of their roles will be clustered. Large, affluent school districts are likely to have all three of these individuals in every school, but those that are smaller or sparsely populated may have only one per school or per district.

Psychologist.   The person trained as a school psychologist is a psychoeducational specialist certified to administer formal tests of intellectual and interpersonal functioning. The school psychologist is also trained in the selection, administration, and interpretation of certain standardized and informal tests used to determine the student's eligibility for special programs and to assist in planning those programs (Frisbee, 1988; Larsen, 1984). In small districts, the psychologist may conduct the entire assessment, whereas in larger districts, other specialists may be part of the assessment team as necessary for individual cases—physicians or audiologists for evaluating hearing, physicians or vision specialists for conducting an assessment of visual functioning, and so on. Because assessment is of such importance in the referral and placement of the special student, it is particularly important that the school psychologist select instruments that are relatively free from bias and are administered in the student's own language, with adaptations for physical and sensory disabilities, and according to legally approved procedures (Larsen, 1984; Reid, 1987).

Counselor.   The school counselor may also conduct observations or collect assessment data during the referral stage of program decision making, although this professional is more highly trained in the assessment of social and emotional skills than in the measurement of cognitive functioning. The counselor frequently consults with teachers and parents to design individual and group programs that assist students in developing their interpersonal skills and in coping with their emotions (Tobias, 1988). Frequently in secondary and middle schools, the counselor is also responsible for designing and coordinating the student's class schedule, and assisting students with making decisions about their future plans for higher education or vocational careers. Often, especially in small districts that do not have a social worker, the counselor also functions as a liaison with personnel from a variety of community agencies.

Social Worker.   The social worker is the professional who collects information about the student's home background and history. This person is familiar with the variety of community resources and related services that may be used to help the special needs student and the family, and serves as the liaison with professionals in these agencies. A school social worker may be involved as a person who can interface with the public assistance and justice systems for students in foster homes or who may be the recipients of social security or welfare funds. The social worker may also conduct observations of the student in the home or classroom, and may administer assessment instruments or implement programs to assist the teacher, the student, and the family in coping with the behavior of difficult students (Ryberg & Sebastian, 1981).

Overlapping Functions.   Either the psychologist, counselor, or social worker may collect information from the student's home, locate resources, or serve as a liaison with community agencies (Ryberg & Sebastian, 1981). The psychologist, social worker, and counselor are all trained to observe the student in the classroom and then consult with teachers, parents, and other personnel in the design of programs to manage the student's behavior or to enhance learning ability. This team member is often trained in child advocacy, counseling, group process skills, and consultation. Recently, the professional organizations for school psychologists and counselors have urged that their members expand their roles beyond the assessment of problems to their prevention (AACD, 1984; NASP, 1974).

In larger districts, the psychologist, social worker, or counselor may be able to provide follow-up consultation, conduct group or individual counseling sessions, or work with parents. Some larger districts have been able, for example, to offer group counseling sessions in areas such as substance abuse, divorce, and test anxiety, which help prevent the increase in referrals for special programs (Bernstein & Simon, 1988). In small districts this team member may be serving several schools; fragmentation in job location may limit the position's functions to the administration and interpretation of psychological tests. In some instances, small districts are not able to employ a psychologist, counselor, or social worker. The person who serves as a psychologist may be employed by a social services agency, working under contract with the school district.

The psychologist, social worker, and counselor are heavily involved in the delivery of sensitive information, and they are often required to explain technical terms or to make suggestions for change in the status quo. In this role, it is particularly important that they use terminology that is clear, understandable, and inoffensive (Courtnage & Healy, 1984; Larsen, 1984; Tobias, 1988). These professionals' explanations should include information about the limitations of test data and of classification procedures. These explanations should also emphasize findings derived from multiple sources of information, as opposed to conclusions based on a single data point, such as the numerical score on a particular test.

The professional in this role frequently has the perspective of *child advocacy* as a first priority (Sigmon, 1987). The perspective of child advocate may appear, at times, to conflict with the perspective of the administrator or classroom teacher, and it may not seem to be compatible with the overall goals of the organization or the particular needs of the child's family. This possibility of conflict in perspective is also one to which team members need to remain sensitive.

Speech-Language Therapist and ESL or Bilingual Specialist

The people who assume these three roles have some functions and characteristics in common, yet their training is also highly specialized. Both their specializations and their common functions are presented.

Speech-Language Therapist.   The person trained as a speech-language therapist is an educational-medical professional certified by the American Speech-Language and Hearing Association (ASHA). For the student whose difficulties include speech or language development, the speech-language therapist (SLT) is an essential member of the professional team. The SLT is trained to diagnose and remediate expressive and receptive communication disorders to ensure the development of communication skills that are the foundation of all language-related learning (Morsink, 1983). This team member is in the best position to evaluate and treat a student who has difficulty with the content and form of language, or with the way language is transmitted through sounds (phonology), words (morphology), or word order (syntax), according to Bloom and Lahey (1978). This student is often one whose speech is immature or difficult to understand, and who has apparent inability to understand directions or difficulty expressing ideas verbally (Culatta, Page, & Culatta, 1981).

One of the most important functions of the SLT is to administer a series of formal and informal tests to determine the nature and extent of the language difficulty. The therapist might, for example, administer one or more tests of concept development, language production, and articulation. One of the most commonly used, and most practical measures of the student's language ability is the language sample, through which the SLT obtains the student's *mean length of utterance* (MLU), the average number of words per sentence or sentence fragment. For the mildly disabled student, the SLT may be particularly interested in obtaining a language sample to determine the way this student uses language in everyday situations. For the severely disabled student, the language assessment may focus on the student's ability to use and interpret gestures and to make basic needs understood.

When the student is from a culturally different background, it is particularly important for the SLT to determine whether the student's language is simply different as a result of culturally determined patterns or whether it is deficient (Westby, 1985). The SLT may be asked to assist when the student's oral reading performance is characterized by numerous dialect differences, indicative of common language patterns that occur in Black English or in students for whom another language (e.g., Spanish) is the first language. It is important for all who work with the student to recognize these patterns and distinguish them from language deficits (Spache & Spache, 1986).

ESL or Bilingual Specialist.   When English is the second language for the student, the SLT should collaborate with a specialist in that language. Large districts may have specialists in English as a Second Language (ESL) or in bilingual education. In small districts, it may be necessary to seek assistance from a community volunteer or a professional at a nearby university who is a native speaker of the language.

Overlapping Functions.   There are five areas in which it is particularly important for the SLT and bilingual teacher or foreign language specialist to collaborate; these have been summarized by Fradd and Weismantel (1988):

1. *Student identification.* Data combined from both specialists can be used to confirm or refute a label, such as "learning disability," as determined by the language assessment.

2. *Assessment and diagnosis.* Language dominance needs to be established, and the label "disabled" is applied only when the student is deficient in measures of intelligence, academics, or social behavior, as measured in the dominant language.

3. *Placement.* It is desirable to place the student in an integrated group, including both bilingual and general education students when possible.

4. *Instructional planning.* For the bilingual student, this includes a dual language plan for instruction in the academic and social skills, as well as a model for providing these services.

5. *Achievement review.* The annual review should include new language samples and work samples from the academic areas being remediated, as well as progress in the direction of mainstreaming.

To avoid conflicts, gaps, or overlapping functions, it may be useful to further delineate the specific training and roles of the ESL and bilingual education resource teachers. These have been specified in detail by Fradd and Weismantel (1988). The ESL teacher provides instruction focused on whole language and cognition including grammar and linguistics. The bilingual teacher provides instruction first in the non-English language and culture; the sequence of this instruction begins with affective skills and progresses to cognition and finally to academics. In large districts, there may be specialists in both ESL and SLT, whereas in smaller districts, these functions may be filled by the same individual or contracted by the school to an external specialist.

When the student's major difficulty is language development and use, it is of greatest importance for all adults to provide consistent models and to have common expectations. For the severely disabled, culturally different learner, it may be more important to communicate in the student's native language and in gestures or universal signs, because it is often not feasible to provide instruction in the use of English as a second language. The SLT and the ESL or bilingual specialist are the people on the team who can best provide information on the type of program that is most appropriate for a given student.

Physical Therapist, Adaptive Physical Educator, Occupational Therapist, and Computer Specialist

There are some commonalities and some differences between and among the functions and training of these professionals. Their roles will be presented separately, and the overlapping functions will be discussed.

Physical Therapist.   The physical therapist (PT) is a link between medicine and education, because the PT understands students' medical problems as well as the importance of movement in learning (Morsink, 1983). This specialist intervenes when education alone cannot fulfill the needs of the client because there is an inability to move, a discontinuity in the normal growth process, or a physical rather than a cognitive barrier to learning. The specific contributions of the physical therapist at differing points in the client's lifetime are expressed by Eggers (1983), as follows:

> For infants, the therapist can effect changes in potential for development, through good therapy and intervention, since the young child is adaptable even with severe damage. With preschool and young children, the therapist can intervene to prevent irreversible change. During the school years, the physical therapist can help the teacher to provide carry-over and generalization activities in the classroom, and can make the learning environment more conducive to learning by assisting with correct positioning and the use of adaptive equipment. (p. 5)

The physical therapist works to develop a program of assessment and intervention after the physician has referred the client for these services. Assessment of the disability includes a determination of the strength and range of movement, and the relationship between the movement and the individual's ability to learn or to perform learning-related functions. Because it is important to continue the physical therapy program on a regular basis, the PT often works collaboratively with the special educator, classroom teacher, and parents, who are responsible for carrying out some of the program in the therapist's absence. The nature and type of program designed for the more severely disabled student may include assistance with basic functional skills, such as feeding, self-care, and walking.

Adaptive Physical Educator.   This professional is trained in physical education, exercise physiology, and in the special needs of students with mild or severe disabilities. Those providing adapted physical education are trained to provide remediation in the areas of physical and motor fitness, psychomotor skills, leisure and recreation skills, and affective development. In addition, the adaptive physical educator can collaborate with other team members in designing cooperative games and motor development activities that enhance the child's physical skills, self-concept, and interactions with peers. Sometimes this professional works with community agencies to design special physical education programs, such as horseback riding or swimming for students with physical, emotional, or sensory limitations.

Occupational Therapist.   The occupational therapist (OT) assists the client, family, and team members in the design of specialized equipment and the retraining of skills that will enable the special needs student to function in the classroom or on the job. The role of the OT is described by Barker (in Morsink, 1983), as follows:

> . . . to facilitate, promote and maintain optimum independence of the student through adaptive skills and effective functioning in the school and social environments. The OT, utilizing a medical knowledge base, evaluates and plans goal-directed, developmentally sequenced activities as treatment for the correction of perceptual, sensory, psychosocial, motor or self-care deficits. (p. 6)

The OT is often engaged in the creation or modification of special devices to assist the person with physical or sensory disabilities in sitting, walking, eating, writing, reading, and so on. These include, for example, special devices to enable the person with poor motor skills to grip a pencil, or the amputee to drive a car.

Computer Specialist.   In the computer-based society, the adaptations required for full functioning may be those that enable the disabled person to use new technology, such as computers. Some computer specialists are trained to develop computer hardware and software that can be used by individuals with disabilities. Computers may be modified so they can be operated by an individual using a stick attached to the forehead or foot; they may also be programmed to synthesize speech or to translate speech into print or Braille. Computer specialists are also highly trained in the selection and design of software, which emphasizes programmed or errorless learning, to enable the student with learning difficulties to practice and master complex skills. Their skills are valuable to the team that serves students with mild disabilities, as well as those with severe disabilities.

Overlapping Functions.   Although the physical therapist, occupational therapist, and adaptive physical educator may all provide assistance with the development and use of motor skills, the PT is the only one whose assistance requires referral from a physician. The PT is more concerned with the development of basic motor skills, whereas the OT is more often concerned with the use of these skills in classroom and vocational settings. Both the PT and the adaptive physical educator are concerned with motor development; however, the PT works with clients individually and the adaptive physical educator also works with students in groups. Both the OT and the computer specialist may have the training to design adaptive equipment for use with computers; the OT, however, usually does not have training in the development of programmed software for use with computer-assisted instruction. These individuals may work together in large districts; in smaller, remote areas, one of these individuals may perform several functions if the team does not have access to all types of specialists.

Vocational or Transition Specialist

The professional who is a vocational educator is specially trained in preparing students for specific types of vocations, which include a variety of careers related to service industries in agriculture, food services, manufacturing, installation, and repair. Each vocational specialist is a professional trained in a highly specific area, who teaches this specialty in high schools or vocational schools. Although the vocational educator is knowledgeable in his or her area of training, this person does not always have training in adapting the vocational training program to the special needs of disabled students.

The transition specialist is more often an individual with generic training in vocational education and specialized knowledge in the training needs of disabled adolescents and adults. This professional assists the student, the family, and the school personnel in making the transition from the world of school to work. The transition specialist helps the team plan for the student's continuing vocational/educational training, home and community participation (e.g., where to live, how to obtain transportation), family relationships, financial support, recreation and leisure, as well as physical and emotional health (Boone, 1990). Planning for transition into the adult world is more difficult than planning for school-related programs, because there is no single agency to coordinate all aspects of the student's services.

Either the vocational educator or the transition specialist, or both, may work with the school and related community agencies to assess the skills of the student and match them with the requirements of a particular job. These professionals may be responsible for providing the special needs student with prevocational training and for conducting on-the-job support services such as job coaching, which ensure that the student will have the communications and interpersonal abilities, as well as the vocational skills, to succeed in the world of work (Bell, 1989).

Migrant Education or Chapter 1 Teacher

School districts and communities that have a large number of people classified as migrant workers or as having incomes below the poverty level may have one or more specialists in migrant or remedial education. The specialist in migrant education has acquired knowledge about the particular problems of the migrant worker's family, including residential instability and educational discontinuity.

The teacher in a Chapter 1 program serves the children of families whose incomes are below the poverty level. These are the children whose caregivers are eligible for aid to dependent children. Often, they are from single-parent families. The Chapter 1 specialist is trained to provide enrichment activities and remedial training to students who are not achieving well in school and who have low levels of motivation or low expectation for success. Federal programs now provide additional funding for whole schools with a high percentage of students who qualify for Chapter 1 funding. This Fund for the Improvement and Reform of Schools and Teaching (FIRST) Program (1989) enables the entire school to engage in collaborative efforts to effect school improvement.

School Nurse and Other Health-Related Professionals

In larger school systems, or in cases that involve clients with severe or multiple disabilities, there may be a school nurse or other health-related professionals on the team. When there is a medical problem, a physician will be involved in the diagnosis and in consultation or making recommendations for treatment, although the physician ordinarily interacts with the student's parents or other health-related professionals, rather than serving as a regular team member at school-based meetings.

School Nurse.   The school nurse may assist others in planning for educational programs that involve wellness, substance abuse, and prevention of disease. The nurse takes on an increasingly important function in the implementation of a program for a student who suffers from AIDS (Reed, 1988). In some districts, school policies or bargaining agreements require that the nurse oversee particular health-related procedures, such as dispensing medications. Each member of the team should request information regarding these policies.

Dietitian.   A dietitian or nutritional specialist may function as a consultant for students who, because of diabetes or other metabolic disorders, need assistance in planning and monitoring their diets. This specialist evaluates the individual's diet and nutritional status to determine the overall nutritional intake, as well as special needs such as those related to lower caloric intake or the reduction of sugar or sodium. The dietitian may work with the student's family, in addition to consulting with school and related services personnel, and may advise the team about special devices to assist with feeding or to monitor the intake of particular elements.

Other health-related professionals may serve as consultants or collaborators on the team, as needed. In every case, each of these specialists has particular knowledge in an area that may be of primary importance to the student's treatment.

Physician's Role As Consultant

The physician contributes to the interactive team largely as a consultant. It is unlikely that, unless the student has severe and multiple disabilities, the physician will be directly involved in the educational program. The role of the physician has been addressed in detail by Ross (1984), who outlines the procedures for conducting an evaluation of the student. This evaluation focuses on a case history, including a description of the current illness, past history, review of systems, and family or social history. When appropriate, the physician may also conduct a neurological or sensory examination. Students are most often referred to the physician because of symptoms such as hyperactivity, hearing loss, or seizures. When the physician's diagnosis is a condition such as epilepsy, cerebral palsy, muscular dystrophy, or mental retardation, the team will need to develop a complete plan that extends over a lifetime and allows such individuals to develop to their fullest potential. Input from the physician is provided most often in the form of a written report, detailing the medical findings of an examination and making recommendations that may be implemented by others on the team.

Roles of Family Members and Paraprofessionals

Family members often have perspectives that differ from those of the other team members, particularly when they represent different cultural backgrounds. Their role, knowledge, and perspectives are discussed in chapters 6 and 9. Chapter 9 presents the new emphasis on family systems and on the role of the parent or other family member as an equal member of the team.

The roles of paraprofessionals will be presented in Chapter 7; these individuals are subordinate to the other team members, and their duties are delegated and monitored by others.

APPLICATION

This application is based on the original work of Beach (1985) and is used here with her permission. Jean Beach is the special educator (SE) who works with Darrell, the student presented in the vignette at the beginning of this chapter, in the middle school special education resource room. Jean has made some observations of Darrell's language functioning in the resource room, and she is concerned that he has speech and language difficulties that are out of her area of expertise. She arranges for an *informational interview* with a team member, the speech-language therapist (SLT) who assists other students at the middle school. Jean is interested in observing the speech and language development program, in obtaining information about the referral process and screening/testing procedures, and in learning how to help Darrell and other students in her classroom who exhibit problems in language development.

She arranges to observe the SLT's language development class, which includes three other students from the special education resource room, during her planning period. Jean observes as the SLT directs activities in which the students learn analogies (e.g., "Pine trees have pine cones; apple trees have. . . . Trucks have wheels, dogs have. . . ."). Then she watches the SLT work with the group on articulating sounds in the initial, middle, and ending positions, using visual images presented as picture cards. Finally, she observes as the SLT administers a language test to another student, to determine his difficulties in phonology, syntax, semantics, memory, word finding, and retrieval. Jean makes notes on her observations, organizes the data she has collected on her observations of Darrell in the special education resource room, and arranges to meet with the SLT the next day to discuss what she has seen and request assistance with Darrell.

The conference begins with small talk about the school and their common training at the university where they both obtained their degrees, and it continues with Jean thanking the SLT for letting her observe the language development class and testing session the previous day. Then Jean addresses her concerns about Darrell's language difficulties.

SE: I have a student named Darrell in my resource room, who seems to have a lot of difficulties in language development. According to his cumulative folder, he was in the speech program once before—he has a structural deficit (some sort of hole in the speech mechanism itself)—but he received help in articulation and then was dismissed. He isn't having articulation problems like those of the other students I observed yesterday, but he certainly would have trouble with the analogies. I believe he has a more general language deficit, and I'm interested in referral to you for further testing. How do I proceed?

SLT: Here is a simple form. You just put the student's name and the date on the top line; then add a one-line description of your reason for the referral. I do testing one day a week. I would start with a screening test to determine if there is a need for further testing, and then—if more testing is necessary—we would get parent permission for a complete evaluation, including articulation, language development, voice, and fluency. After testing, I would meet with you and the parents to give you the results of what has been done and to make suggestions for future programming.

SE: I wasn't sure about the district's policy on testing. Do we need parent permission for screening?

SLT: No, but we would need permission for a complete evaluation, and, of course, for placement if that is needed.

SE: When I observed your group yesterday, I saw that another student in my resource room, who is paired with Darrell for some language activities, was having a lot of trouble with the analogies. Both of these students read at the preprimer level, although they're in sixth grade. I find that a tape recorder is quite helpful in working with them on their reading vocabulary words. If you think the recorder would help with some of the other language development activities in my classroom, I could help you put words on tape, and then both of these students could listen to them to get a little more practice.

SLT: That's a really good idea. It is much more meaningful to students receiving special help if they can do some of the same language development activities in their own classroom. The coordination and repetition makes the special program more effective.

SE: When I work with both of these students in their reading series, I use an approach that features modified phonetics. Right now they are practicing the *sh* digraph in the initial position of words, such as *ship, show, shine,* and so on. Their words are pronounced on tape, while the student circles the picture showing the correct sound, given a choice of two pictures. I've been correcting their papers for the past two weeks and I've picked up certain consistent errors which I've charted on graph paper. Would you be interested in seeing the graph?

SLT: Oh, yes! That would be very helpful. If we're both picking up the same error patterns, then we can work together more effectively to help the students.

SE: I also work with Darrell in a general language arts class, and I notice that it is really difficult for him to respond appropriately during group activities. I know what he is trying to say, but it comes out wrong. He'll say "ain't got no" or something, and then the group laughs. How can I help him?

SLT: When you ask him to make a verbal response, do you use picture cards or some other kind of visual cues? Or do you just use words?

SE: I would be using a lecture format, with verbal questions and answers.

SLT: It may be that he needs some additional visual cues to get the answers right. I have some syntax programs on picture cards; I'd be happy to let you borrow them to see if they might help.

SE: That would be great! I'll try that for a week or so and let you know how it works out. Listen, I know your planning period is over, and so is mine. But thanks again for letting me watch your groups yesterday and letting me watch you give the clinical evaluation of the language functions test that you might use with Darrell if needed. You've been really helpful in assisting me in working with him.

SLT: Thank you for giving me such precise data and descriptions of his problems. It will really help me in determining whether or not he needs additional testing and assistance. Since the copy machine is right next to my office and you use it a lot, maybe we can catch each other for a few minutes at a time to share information about Darrell and other students.

This conference between team members was highly productive for several reasons. Each acknowledged and respected the specialized training of the other. Both came together with the attitude that they shared a common goal of providing a better program for a student. Both shared and respected each other's expertise, showed a genuine interest in the other's program, and both expressed a willingness to continue the dialogue. Although the initial meetings were time consuming—the meetings lasted between 20 and 30 minutes—subsequent meetings could be brief, and each team member could make the other's job easier by sharing materials and expertise focused on their common goal.

SUMMARY

Members of the interactive team are highly trained professionals, each with specialized knowledge and skills that may contribute to the joint solution of problems. The team may consist of as few as two persons or it may be much larger; the team's size depends on the following:

◆ The nature and complexity of the student's problems.

◆ The size and resources of the facility.

New trends in preschool and postschool service delivery have been summarized. The roles of team members have been described; for the special educator, the roles differ somewhat, according to:

◆ The type of student: culturally different, mildly disabled, or severely multiply disabled.

◆ The SE's function as service provider or as collaborator.

The roles of other team members have been described, clustered by common and sometimes overlapping functions:

◆ The program administrator.

◆ The classroom teacher.

◆ The school psychologist, counselor, or social worker.

◆ The speech-language therapist, English as second language or bilingual specialist.

◆ The physical therapist, adaptive physical educator, occupational therapist, and computer specialist.

◆ The vocational or transition specialist.

◆ The migrant education or Chapter 1 teacher.

◆ The school nurse and other health-related professionals.

◆ The physician, as a consultant to the team.

The interactive team functions most effectively when each member understands and respects the expertise of others, and when all work together to accomplish their common goal: provision of the best possible program for a given special needs student. The communication skills needed by diverse professionals in reaching their common goal are presented in the next chapter.

ACTIVITIES

1. Imagine you are a member of a team. Conduct an informational interview with one of the professionals on the special education team, using the guidelines presented below.

   a. Plan for the meeting by collecting data and writing down the questions you want to ask the other team member.

   b. Start the meeting by establishing rapport and finding areas of common interest or understanding.

   c. State the purpose of your meeting.

   d. Share the information you have collected for the other team member.

   e. Ask the questions you have prepared to elicit specific information.

   f. Summarize what you have accomplished and make plans for follow-up meetings in the future.

2. Write a series of questions to present to members of a panel who represent the professionals identified in this chapter. You might, for example, want to ask about their specialized training, previous experiences with other professionals, or suggestions for working together more effectively.

3. Construct a table summarizing the major role each direct service provider plays and describing the collaborative contributions that could be made by each professional on the team.

REFERENCES

American Association for Counseling and Development. (1984). Primary prevention in schools [Special issue]. *The Personnel and Guidance Journal, 62,* 443–495.

Bailey, D. (1984). A triaxial model of the interdisciplinary team and group process. *Exceptional Children, 51,* 17–26.

Bartel, N., & Thurmond, K. (1992). Medical treatment and educational problems in children. *Phi Delta Kappan, 74,* 57–61.

Beach, J. (1985). *Interaction with speech-language therapist.* Unpublished paper, University of Florida, Department of Special Education, Gainesville.

Bell, F. (1989). *Potential training sites for severely handicapped persons in Alachua County.* Unpublished master's thesis, University of Florida, Gainesville.

Bellisimo, Y. (1990). Crack babies: The schools' new high risk students. *Thrust, 19,* 23–26.

Bernstein, R., & Simon, D. (1988). A stitch in time: The role of the school psychologist. *Counterpoint, 8*(4), 6–7.

Biklen, D. (1988). *Regular lives.* Washington, DC: WETA-TV Department of Educational Activities.

Bloom, L., & Lahey, M. (1978). *Language development and language disorders.* New York: Wiley.

Boone, R. (1990). The development, implementation, and evaluation of a preconference training strategy for enhancing parental participation in and satisfaction with the individual transition conference. (Doctoral dissertation, University of Florida, 1989). *Dissertation Abstracts International, 51*(3), 618-A.

Burkhead, E., Sampson, J., & McMahon, B. (1986). The liberation of disabled persons in a technological society: Access to computer technology. *Rehabilitation Literature, 47*(7), 162–168.

Campbell, P. (1987a). The integrated programming team: An approach for coordinating professionals of various disciplines in programs for students with severe and multiple handicaps. *Journal of Association for Persons with Severe Handicaps, 12*(2), 10 7-116.

—. (1987b). Teacher assistance teams. In B. Algozzine (Ed.), *Behavior problem management: Educator's resource service*. Rockville, MD: Aspen Publishers.

Chalfant, J. (1989). Learning disability policy issues and promising approaches. In F. Horowitz & M. O'Brien (Eds.), Knowledge base, research agenda, and social policy application [Special issue]. *American Psychologist, 44*(2), 392–398.

Chalfant, J., Pysh, M., & Moultrie, R. (1979). Teacher assistance teams: A model for within-building problem solving. *Learning Disabilities Quarterly, 2*(3), 85–97.

Chamberlain, M. (1988). Employer's ranking of factors judged critical to job success for individuals with severe disabilities. *Career Development for Exceptional Individuals, 11*(2), 141–147.

Courtnage, L., & Healy, H. (1984). *A model in team building*. Cedar Falls, IA: University of Northern Iowa College of Education.

Culatta, B., Page, J., & Culatta, R. (1981). *Improving language functioning: A manual for language clinicians and teachers working in regular education settings*. Lexington, KY: University of Kentucky Dean's Grant Project.

Darling, R. (1989). Using the social system perspective in early intervention: The value of a sociological approach. *Journal of Early Intervention, 13*(91), 24–35.

Davenport, S. (1990). The child with multiple congenital anomalies. *Pediatric Annals, 19*(1), 23–33.

Deno, S., & Mirkin, P. (1977). *Data-based program modification: A manual*. Minneapolis: University of Minnesota Leadership Training Institute.

Dykes, M. K., Brenner, J., & Lee, J. (1985). *Consensus study on motor disabilities competencies*. Unpublished manuscript, University of Florida, Department of Special Education, Gainesville.

Eggers, N. (1983, November). In C. V. Morsink (Ed.), Context for generic guidelines for allied health and education professionals who serve persons with disabilities. *Synthesis of proceedings, "Training Alliances in Health and Education," Meeting of the American Society of Allied Health Professionals* (USDOE, OSERS, Grant # G008301774). Philadelphia: American Society of Allied Health Professionals.

Esposito, B., & Koorland, M. (1989). Play behavior of hearing impaired children: Integrated and segregated settings. *Exceptional Children, 55*, 412–419.

Fox, C., Kuhlman, N., & Sales, T. (1988). Cross-cultural concerns: What's missing from special education training programs? *Teacher Education and Special Education, 11*, 155–161.

Fradd, S., & Weismantel, J. (1988). Developing and evaluating the program. In S. Fradd & J. Weismantel (Eds.), *Meeting the needs of linguistically and culturally different students: A handbook for educational leaders*. Boston: Little, Brown.

Fradd, S., Weismantel, J., Correa, V., & Algozzine, B. (1988). Developing a personnel training model for meeting the needs of handicapped and at-risk language-minority students. *Teacher Education and Special Education, 11*, 30–38.

Frisbee, C. (1988). *The role of the school psychologist with handicapped and at-risk students*. Unpublished manuscript, University of Florida, College of Education, Gainesville.

Fund for Improvement and Reform of Teaching (FIRST). (1989, May 2). *Federal Register, 54*(83). (CFDA No. 84. 211A)

Gemmel, S., & Peterson, M. (1989). Supported employment and provision of on-going support services: A pilot project. *Career Development for Exceptional Individuals, 12*, 123–128.

Gensante, L., & Matgouranis, E. (1989). The more I see, the better I teach. *Educational Leadership, 46*(8), 28.

Gerber, M. (1988). Tolerance and technology of instruction: Implications for special education reform. *Exceptional Children, 54*, 309–314.

Graden, J., Casey, A., & Christenson, J. (1985). Implementing a pre-referral intervention system: Part I, the model. *Exceptional Children, 51*, 377–384.

Guralnick, M., & Groom, J. (1988). Peer interactions in mainstreamed and specialized classrooms: A comparative analysis. *Exceptional Children, 54*, 415–425.

Halloran, W., & Ward, M. (1988). Improving transition programming: Changing special education's focus. *The Pointer, 32*(2), 43–46.

Haring, N., & Phillips, E. (1972). *Analysis and modification of classroom behavior*. Englewood Cliffs, NJ: Prentice-Hall.

Heal, L., Haney, J., & Novak Amado, A. (1988). *Integration of developmentally disabled individuals into the community* (2nd ed.). Baltimore: Paul H. Brookes.

Howell, B. (1981). Profile of the principalship. *Educational Leadership, 39,* 333–336.

Kagan, S., & Rivera, M. (1990). *Collaborations in action: Reshaping services for young children and their families.* New Haven, CT: Yale University, Bush Center in Child Development and Social Policy.

Krauss, M. (1990). New precedent in family policy: Individualized family service plan. *Exceptional Children, 56,* 388–395.

Larrivee, B. (1985). *Effective teaching for successful mainstreaming.* New York: Longman Publishers.

Larsen, J. (1984). The school psychologist and the teacher. In C. V. Morsink (Ed.), *Teaching special needs students in regular classrooms* (pp. 72–74) Boston: Little, Brown and Company.

Littlejohn, B. (1989). *A change strategy for mainstreaming severely handicapped students into the regular classroom.* Unpublished paper, University of Florida, Department of Special Education, Gainesville.

Lovass, I. (1987). Behavioral treatment and normal educational and intellectual functioning in young autistic children. *Journal of Consulting and Clinical Psychology, 55,* 3–9.

Mack, F. (1988). Future trends in early childhood special education. *Reading Improvement, 25,* 132–145.

McDonnell, J., Hardman, M., & Hightower, J. (1989). Employment preparation for high school students with severe handicaps. *Mental Retardation, 27,* 396–404.

Morsink, C. V. (Ed.). (1983, November). (With contributors E. Ellis, N. Eggers, J. Wittenmyer, G. Meyer, T. Barker, H. Johnson, J. Anderson, B. Stone, H. Garner, B. Gellman, B. Simon, & C. Del Polito). Context for generic guidelines for allied health and education professionals who serve persons with disabilities. *Synthesis of proceedings, "Training Alliances in Health and Education," Meeting of the American Society of Allied Health Professionals* (USDOE, OSERS, Grant # G008301774). Philadelphia, PA: American Society of Allied Health Professionals.

——. (1984). *Teaching special needs students in regular classrooms.* Boston: Little, Brown and Company.

Morsink, C. V., Thomas, C., & Smith-Davis, J. (1987). Noncategorical special education programs:

Process and outcomes. In M. Wang, M. Reynolds, & H. Walberg (Eds.), *Handbook of special education: Research and practice Vol. 1* (pp. 287–312). Oxford, England: Pergamon.

Morsink, C. V., & Lenk, L. (1992). The delivery of special education programs. *Remedial and Special Education, 13*(6), 33–43.

Naisbitt, J. (1982). *Megatrends.* New York: Warner Books.

National Association of School Psychologists. (1974). The changing role of the school psychologist: Primary prevention. *School Psychology Digest, 3*(4), 4–25.

Nevin, A., & Thousand, J. (1986). What the research says about limiting or avoiding referrals to special education. *Teacher Education and Special Education, 9,* 149–161.

Odom, S., & Warren, S. (1988). Early childhood special education in the year 2000. *Journal of the Division of Early Childhood, 12,* 263–271.

Peterson, P. (1988). Teachers' and students' cognitional knowledge for classroom teaching and learning. *Educational Researcher, 17*(5), 5–14.

Reed, S. (1988). Children with AIDS: How schools are handling the crisis [Special report]. *Phi Delta Kappan, 69,* K1–K12.

Reid, W. (1987). *Assessment and the Hispanic American.* Gainesville, FL: University of Florida Project on Bilingual Special Education.

Rist, M. (1990, January). The shadow children. *The American School Board,* 19–24.

Roessler, R., Brolin, D., & Johnson, J. (1990). Factors affecting employment success and quality of life: A one year follow-up of students in special education. *Career Development for Exceptional Individuals, 13*(2), 95–107.

Rosenshine, B., & Stevens, R. (1986). Teaching functions. In M. C. Wittrock (Ed.), *Handbook of research on teaching* (3rd ed., pp. 376–391). New York: Macmillan.

Ross, D. (1989). First steps in developing a reflective approach. *Journal of Teacher Education, 40*(2), 22–30.

Ross, J. (1984). The physician and the teacher. In C. V. Morsink (Ed.), *Teaching special needs students in regular classrooms* (pp. 77–83). Boston: Little, Brown and Company

Ryberg, S., & Sebastian, J. (1981). The multidisciplinary team. In M. Hardman, M. Egan, & E. Landau (Eds.),

What will we do in the morning? (pp. 12–29). Dubuque, IA: Wm. C. Brown.

Sigmon, S. (1987). Present roles and future objectives for school psychology. *Journal of Social Behavior and Personality, 2,* 379–382.

Sileo, T., Rude, H., & Luckner, J. (1988). Collaborative consultation: A model for transition planning for handicapped youth. *Education and Training in Mental Retardation, 23,* 333–339.

Spache, G., & Spache, E. (1986). *Reading in the elementary school* (5th ed.). Boston: Allyn & Bacon.

Tobias, A. (1988). *The role of the school counselor with handicapped and at-risk students.* Unpublished paper, University of Florida, College of Education, Gainesville.

Villa, R., & Thousand, J. (1988). Enhancing success in heterogeneous classrooms and schools: The powers of partnership. *Teacher Education and Special Education, 11,* 144–154.

Vincent, L., & Salisbury, C. (1988). Changing economic and social influences on family involvement. *Topics in Early Childhood Special Education, 8*(1), 48–59.

Wesson, C., Fuchs, L., Tindal, G., Mirkin, P., & Deno, S. (1986). Facilitating the efficacy of ongoing curriculum-based measurement. *Teacher Education and Special Education, 9,* 166–172.

Westby, C. (1985). Learning to talk—talking to learn: Oral-literature language differences. In *Communication skills and classroom success, Vol. 1* (pp. 181–213). San Diego: College Hill Press.

Wolfensberger, W. (1972). *The principal of normalization in human services.* Toronto: National Institute on Mental Retardation.

CHAPTER 5

Enhancing Communication Skills

Components of the Process of Communication

Definition of Communication

Elements of the Communication Process

Characteristics of Effective Communication in Interactive Teaming

Factors to Consider in Communication

Personal Factors

Attitudinal and Experiential Factors

Backup Support Factors

Context or Situational Factors

Forms of Communication

Nonverbal Behaviors

Listening

Verbal Behaviors

Using and Misusing Forms of Communication

Managing Conflict

Conflicts Within the Group

Dealing with Resistance

Application of Communication Strategies

Summary

TOPICS IN THIS CHAPTER INCLUDE

◆ Description of a model of communication.

◆ Characteristics of communication in interactive teaming.

◆ Factors to consider in communication.

◆ Forms of communication.

◆ Strategies for managing conflict.

◆ An application illustrating effective and ineffective communication.

 Principals and central office personnel have circulated the following example of what can happen as people try to communicate with each other. The original source of this communique is not known.

Halley's Comet

A school superintendent told the assistant superintendent the following: "Next Thursday at 10:30 a.m. Halley's Comet will appear over this area. This is an event that occurs only once every 75 years. Call the school principals and have them assemble their teachers and classes on their athletic fields and explain this phenomenon to them. If it rains, cancel the day's observation and have the classes meet in the auditorium to see a film about the comet."

The memo from the assistant superintendent to the principals stated: "By order of the superintendent of schools, next Thursday at 10:30 Halley's Comet will appear over your athletic field. If it rains, then cancel the day's classes and report to the auditorium with your teachers and students. You will be shown films, a phenomenal event which occurs only once every 75 years."

The principals announced to the teachers: "By order of the phenomenal superintendent of schools, at 10:30 next Thursday Halley's Comet will appear in the auditorium. In case of rain over the athletic field, the superintendent will give another order—something which occurs once every 75 years."

Teachers told their students: "Next Thursday at 10:30 the superintendent of schools will appear in our auditorium with Halley's Comet, something which occurs every 75 years. If it rains, the superintendent will cancel the comet and order us all out to our phenomenal athletic field."

Students reported to their parents: "When it rains next Thursday at 10:30 over the school athletic field, the phenomenal 75-year-old superintendent will cancel all classes and appear before the whole school in the auditorium accompanied by Bill Halley and the Comets."

In Chapter 4, the roles of parents and various professionals were described. Interactions among people who may have different perspectives in a team or consultative setting are affected by how well those involved are able to use a variety of communication skills to share and receive information and to resolve conflicts. The humorous Halley's Comet example illustrates how important accuracy and clarity are in preventing misunderstandings that may result when people in different roles attempt to communicate with one another.

The importance of communication skills for consultants and team members has been strongly supported in the literature. In fact, many people believe expertise in communication may be the most vital skill the individual can possess. Gutkin and Curtis (1982) stated:

> At the heart of all consultation methodology is the consultant's ability to establish a helping relationship and communicate effectively with the consultee. At its most basic level, consultation is an interpersonal exchange. As such, the consultant's success is going to hinge largely on his or her communication and relationship skills (p. 822).

Communication skills also have been identified through research studies and inclusion in training programs as required areas for development and expertise. In her study on the consultation skills needed by resource teachers, Friend (1984) surveyed principals, regular classroom teachers, and resource teachers. The educators said they placed much importance on such skills as establishing a climate of trust, explaining perceptions of a problem, defining problems, interviewing, resolving conflicts by using strategies to minimize hard feelings, and using specific strategies to facilitate interpersonal communication.

Similar results were obtained by West and Cannon (1988) in their study of collaborative consultation strategies needed by regular and special educators. Their results included the description of competency statements in the areas of personal characteristics, interactive communication, and collaborative problem solving—all of which relate to communication as a facilitating factor in interactive teaming. Finally, teacher education programs designed to teach teaming skills, such as the ones described by Hudson, Correa, Morsink, and Dykes (1987), Siders, Riall, Bennett, and Judd (1987), and West, Idol, and Cannon (1989) include development of communication and problem-solving skills as important competencies.

This chapter includes a description of a communication model and a discussion of vital characteristics of communication involved in interactive teaming. Factors to consider in communication are explained. The nonverbal, listening, and verbal forms of communication are described, along with skills to be developed and barriers that can be present. The final section of the chapter deals with procedures for managing conflict and resistance.

COMPONENTS OF THE PROCESS OF COMMUNICATION

Definition of Communication

Communication can be defined as a dynamic and ongoing process in which people share ideas, information, and feelings. The skills involved in communication are "not ends in themselves, but means or instruments that must be placed at the service of helping outcomes in order to be meaningful" (Egan, 1986, p. 73).

ELEMENTS OF THE COMMUNICATION PROCESS

The communication process comprises several elements, as shown in Figure 5–1. Hybels and Weaver (1986) described these elements as follows: *Senders-receivers* are the people who are sending and receiving the messages. Typically, people are senders and receivers at the same time because they are both initiating communication and receiving another's responses simultaneously. The *message* is composed of the ideas and thoughts being transmitted through verbal and nonverbal forms of communication. The *channel* is the route traveled by the message, which typically involves both sound and sight because we look at people's facial expressions as well as hear their words. *Feedback* is the response of the senders-receivers to each other, and as in the message, feedback can be both verbal and nonverbal. Feedback enables the sender to gauge whether or not the receiver understood the message as it was intended. *Noise* is the physical (e.g., loud voices, truck passing) or psychological (e.g., daydreaming, planning a trip) interference that prevents the message from being accurately comprehended. The *setting* is the location where the communication is taking place. Because settings can be formal (e.g., office or auditorium) or informal (e.g., comfortable room, restaurant), they can affect the feelings people have while they are com-

Figure 5–1

Elements of the communication process

Note: From *Communicating Effectively* (p. 13) by S. Hybels and R. L. Weaver, 1986, New York: McGraw-Hill. Reprinted by permission of McGraw-Hill, Inc.

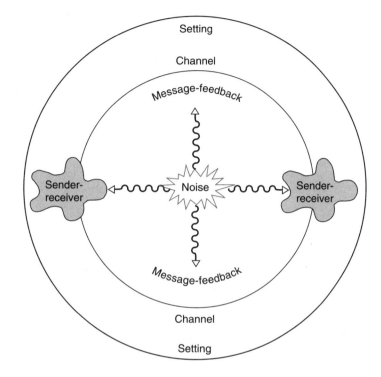

municating. Another variable to consider is whether the location represents someone's "territory," such as the director or principal's office, and whether that location intentionally or unintentionally intimidates the others involved in the communication (Dettmer, Thurston, & Dyck, 1993; Idol, Paolucci-Whitcomb, & Nevin, 1986).

CHARACTERISTICS OF EFFECTIVE COMMUNICATION IN INTERACTIVE TEAMING

In addition to being cognizant of the various elements of communication, team members need to be sensitive to the characteristics of effective interactions. Lang, Quick, and Johnson (1981) noted that good communication is *purposeful,* with an intent clear to all parties; *planned,* in terms of thinking through what should be transmitted; *personalized,* according to the receiver's background; *open,* in terms of people's being able to express feelings; and *clear,* in that the words used are part of the other's language. On the latter point of clarity, Ehly and Eliason (1983) cautioned professionals in the fields of education and psychology to be aware of their use of jargon and "psychobabble" (e.g., IEP, BEH, PDP, CAT testing), which can interfere with understanding.

Turnbull and Turnbull (1986) identified two prerequisites to effective communication that are vital to the teaming process: *knowing ourselves* and *developing respect and trust*. Gaining and maintaining the respect of others are obviously vital to the success of interactive team members. Establishing rapport can be accomplished by being willing to share information and learn from others (i.e., role release), treating others with respect, sharing credit for ideas, participating in activities beyond the scope of one's job (e.g., extracurricular and social functions), and demonstrating credibility by being aware of the domains of team members, such as showing an understanding of the dynamics of a regular classroom (Heron & Harris, 1987; Idol, Paolucci-Whitcomb, & Nevin, 1986; Lopez, Dalal, & Yoshida, 1993; Spodek, 1982).

Two final characteristics of communication required in teaming have been described previously in this text, but they merit repetition because of their importance: *confidentiality* and *sensitivity to cultural differences*. The willingness to protect the confidentiality of information shared in the collaboration and consultation of teaming interactions is vital. A person involved in such situations has only to be let down once by a consultant's or team member's breaking a confidence for him or her to be reluctant to participate again. Similarly, people from various cultures who receive adverse feedback on their communication skills or who are rebuffed by people who are unaware or uncaring about communication norms in their culture may learn to be defensive or unresponsive as a coping strategy.

FACTORS TO CONSIDER IN COMMUNICATION

Several factors affect the communication process as it occurs in the consultation and collaboration of teaming. These factors are related to personal characteristics, attitudes and experiences; the existence of backup support, such as data; and context and situational variables. Each of the factors will be described in the following sections.

Personal Factors

The qualities identified by Rogers (1961) as most important for people in helping roles were empathy, genuineness, and unconditional positive regard. *Empathy* is the ability to understand the world of others by "walking a mile in their shoes." Empathy is not the same as sympathy, which involves feeling sorry for someone; rather, it is placing oneself in the situation to examine how that person feels (Egan, 1986). In his review of the literature, Gladstein (1983) noted that two forms of empathy were described: emotional empathy, or the ability to be affected by someone else's emotional feelings; and role-taking empathy, which involves the ability to understand another's frame of reference or point of view.

Genuineness is the ability to be "real" in caring for others, instead of dealing with them in a superficial manner. Gutkin and Curtis (1982) referred to genuineness as the "cardinal rule" of effective communication, though as Turnbull and Turnbull (1986) recognized, this level of caring is not always as easy as it may appear: "On the contrary, many go through life seeking to develop this quality in themselves. It requires hard work to awaken this quality in ourselves and inspire it in others" (p. 114).

Unconditional positive regard is the ability to accept others without prejudice or bias, and to realize that they are entitled to their opinions.

Two other qualities named by Hybels and Weaver (1986) as contributing to or detracting from communication are initiative and assertiveness. *Initiative* involves taking the lead, as appropriate, to facilitate the process. *Assertiveness* is the ability to stand up confidently for what one thinks or feels. Assertiveness is often confused with aggressiveness, but the latter refers to an attempt to establish power and control even at the expense of the feelings of others. An aggressive team member may speak and act as though he is not concerned with the emotions or positions of other members, and this may set up a confrontational relationship. In her study of the contrasting behaviors of assertiveness, nonassertiveness, and aggressiveness, Arab (1985) noted that those who are assertive are effective collaborators, whereas those who exhibit characteristics of the other two behaviors are not.

Fine, Grantham, and Wright (1979) compiled another set of personal factors that can play a role in the effectiveness of people in collaborative or consultative roles. These factors are predominantly concerned with how the person in a helping role attends to his or her own needs and how that process facilitates or impedes consultation. They cited the following considerations:

1. The consultant's identity remains the same; that is, his/her own orientation and feelings about life and self cannot be separated from the consultation process.

2. The consultant needs to adhere to his or her own needs to be able to help others; that is, stress management and rejuvenation are vital to be able to continue to give to others.

3. The problem belongs to the consultee, not to the consultant; that is, consultants should be facilitators and assist in problem solving, but they should not "own" the problem.

4. The consultant must be willing to let go of feelings about "the way it is supposed to be"; that is, remember the purpose is to help another person grow and develop skills, rather than force him or her to follow a certain program or become a "clone."

5. Lack of closure in this process is acceptable; the problems to be resolved will take time and cannot be forced or speeded up.

6. The consultant should not try to carry the burden alone; others in the system should be called upon to share their expertise.

7. The perceptions and expectations of all concerned should be made explicit; that is, people in helping positions should clarify roles and responsibilities.

8. Alternatives should be offered to the consultee; that is, when a person is willing to try different interventions that have been suggested, the consultant should permit the person to select the one that seems most viable, and then support him or her in attempts to implement.

9. People involved should view this as a problem-solving process; the solutions will take time, rather than being immediate answers. Also, a number of problem-solving approaches can be used.

10. A broad skill repertoire is essential; that is, people in helping roles must be familiar with a variety of strategies and techniques.

11. Success must be considered as a value judgment; that is, all possible outcomes of the helping process—such as changes in the child, system, parents, and other professionals—must be considered, rather than determining success or failure based on one indicator.

Attitudinal and Experiential Factors

Closely linked with personal qualities are attitudinal and experiential factors that are the result of how team members feel about themselves, others, and the consultation or teaming process based on the experiences they have had. The factors can be examined individually from every team member's perspective, but for brevity's sake, in this chapter they will be described from the viewpoints of the consultant, consultee, and parents, because team members tend to fit into one of these three categories.

Weissenburger, Fine, and Poggio (1982) conducted a study on consultant and teacher characteristics as they related to the outcomes of consultation. They cited six teacher attitudes that may interfere with interventions suggested by a consultant (based on the work of Grieger, 1972). Those attitudes were "(a) the child needs fixing, (b) it is wrong to express negative feelings, (c) children must not be frustrated, (d) children 'should-ought' to behave in certain ways, (e) children are blameworthy for their misdeeds, and (f) the child 'makes me' feel that way" (p. 263).

The study by Weissenburger et al. yielded several other attitudes that can affect communication and the teaming process. They found that consultant facilitativeness as perceived by teachers was positively related to problem resolution, as well as teacher attitudes of "I'm OK—You're OK." Teacher dogmatism, or holding tightly to one's own beliefs rather than trying to learn from others, was found to hinder the desired outcomes of consultation.

Parents' attitudes also are affected by their previous experiences. Turnbull and Turnbull (1986) cited the following areas that can positively or negatively affect communication: parents' past experiences in dealing with professionals, personalities and values, and expectations and stereotypes. In addition, Bailey (1987) noted that often parents and professionals' priorities for education or treatment are different. He also commented that parents may appear to lack motivation if they do not understand the relevance of requests, or they may lack the time, skill, energy, or resources to follow up on recommendations. Professionals may not understand the needs of the family or may be unable to motivate family members, all of which contribute to the attitudes of both sides regarding future communication (Bailey, 1987).

Additional attitudinal considerations related to how perceptions can "color one's vision" are concerned with how parents may be categorized by professionals. Sonnenschien (1984) described how professionals can view parents in negative ways and thereby diminish effective communication. Sonnenschien stated that professionals can consider parents as vulnerable clients, patients, the cause of the problem, adversaries, less observant, hostile, less intelligent, resistant, denying, or anxious. Any of these views may have a negative effect on expectations for success or the development of a productive relationship with parents.

Two final considerations are the use of emotion-laden words and the lack of common experiences. On the former point, it is important to realize that parents will be particularly sensitive to words that describe their child in terms such as *retarded, handicapped,* or *disturbed.* Although it may be necessary to use these labels in program placement, professionals should take care to explain their meanings, as well as their tentative status and limitations. Also, the negative effect may be softened if professionals introduce such terms to parents in a private setting, rather than using them first in a team meeting (Losen & Losen, 1985).

The lack of common experiences is particularly evident in cases such as a childless professional who cannot understand the fatigue experienced by a working single parent who is asked to implement speech and physical therapy follow-up with a multiply disabled child every night and weekend. The parent may lack the professional's understanding of the importance of this follow-up in successful therapy. Open communication on the part of both parties can help bridge this gap. Interactive team members should remember to treat each situation individually and, as much as possible, to avoid stereotyping parents and other professionals based on previous experiences.

Backup Support Factors

A source of backup support for communication interactions is the existence of data. Each team member will be able to provide different types of data depending on the area of expertise. For example:

◆ Parents will be able to describe developmental milestones and home behaviors.

◆ Regular classroom teachers can contribute data on curriculum, achievement tests, and group teaching strategies.

◆ Psychologists can delineate the interpretation of intelligence tests.

◆ Special educators can outline teaching techniques and strategies for individualizing.

◆ Adaptive physical educators and physical therapists can demonstrate movement limitations and modifications.

◆ Counselors and social workers can share perspectives on emotional factors.

To provide these different types of data, team members will use observation as well as appropriate data collection strategies unique to their professional fields, such as single subject designs (Tawney & Gast, 1984; Zirpoli & Melloy, 1993), achievement and intelligence tests (Salvia & Ysseldyke, 1988; Venn, 1994), or statistical interpretations of other types of tests (Kerlinger, 1986).

One strategy for collecting and sharing data that is useful at the beginning of a team or consultative process is the *informational interview* (Hudson, 1987), which was illustrated in the Application section of Chapter 4. Any team member can use this strategy to establish rapport and share information with another. The six steps in the informational interview are these: (a) preplanning, (b) establishing rapport, (c) stating the purpose, (d) providing information, (e) using specific questions to obtain information, and (f) summarizing and planning a follow-up. These steps are illustrated in Figure 5–2.

Data collection is particularly important for the team as members attempt to identify problems, determine appropriate interventions, and evaluate the effectiveness of strategies that have been implemented. Team members will need to take the initiative in gathering appropriate data, organizing the data, and then sharing the results with others in an understandable manner.

Context or Situational Factors

The final set of factors that can affect communication are those related to the context or situation in which the interactions will occur. Hudson (1987) described two types of situations: proactive and reactive. In a *proactive* situation, parents and professionals meet to establish a positive relationship and share information. In this context they can be more relaxed, because they are meeting to anticipate and prevent problems. In a *reactive* situation, the team is meeting as a result of a problem's being manifested, and therefore members may be more emotional. In a reactive context, the emphasis in communication must shift from information sharing to listening, supporting, and discussing possible interventions.

FORMS OF COMMUNICATION

All the factors previously described can affect both forms of communication—nonverbal and verbal—and listening, which is a "bridge" between the two forms. *Nonverbal* behaviors include attending to what is being said and encompass what is commonly referred to as "body language." *Listening* involves understanding the message and indicating that understanding to the sender. *Verbal* behaviors include such strategies as descriptive statements, paraphrasing, and questioning. Each set of skills is now described in more detail.

Nonverbal Behaviors

Most communication messages are transmitted in ways other than the use of words alone. In fact, it has been suggested that up to 90% of the content of a message may be transmitted through nonverbal behaviors and vocal inflections.

Body Language and Attending Skills.   *Body language* often is the transmitter of silent messages, such as when a speaker diverts his eyes or covers part of his face (Nierenberg & Calero, 1971). Closely related to body language are *attending skills*. These behaviors indicate that the listener or receiver is psychologically and emotionally present and listening. Egan (1986) summarized five attending behaviors: (a) fac-

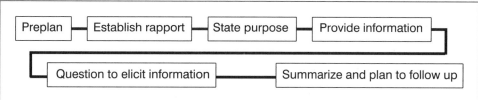

Steps:

1. *Preplan*—formalize an appointment, review any background material, and decide on questions to be asked.

2. *Establish rapport*—at the beginning of the meeting, talk briefly about nonprofessional interests that people may have in common. In Hawaii, this is called "talk story." On the mainland, it is often called "small talk."

3. *State purpose*—clarify the purpose of the meeting by stating that you are attempting to establish some common ground and to get to know each other in ways that will enable you to work together more productively.

4. *Provide information*—discuss yourself as a professional. Talk about your "philosophy" of education if you are talking with another educator. You may have a diagnostic-prescriptive philosophy that emphasizes the importance of individual differences which may be in contrast with the mainstream teacher's focus on group learning approaches. Or you may have an educational, as contrasted to a medical, orientation to treatment which differs from that of some health-related professionals. Share your ideas in a way that suggests you are trying to identify areas of commonality. Share samples of the child's work or some supportive data if you are talking with a parent.

5. *Use specific questions to elicit information*—ask questions about the other person's role, background, and philosophy. The focus here should be on ways in which you can work together. Search for commonalities in comparing what this person tells you and the information you provided to them.

6. *Summarize and plan to follow up*—stress the idea that this is the first step in what you hope will be a long and productive relationship. Thank the other person for their time and effort and indicate that you will be contacting them again. If you have a specific time or purpose, state it and try to arrange a common meeting time.

Figure 5–2

Informational interview

Note: From *Proactive and Reactive Consultation: A Model for Preservice Training* by P. Hudson, 1987, unpublished manuscript, University of Florida, Department of Special Education, Gainesville. Adapted by permission.

ing the person squarely or turning toward the person to whom you are communicating, (b) having an open posture instead of crossing arms and legs, (c) leaning toward the other person at times to indicate attentiveness, (d) maintaining eye contact, and (e) appearing relaxed and interested instead of fidgeting or looking at your watch. He cited the following advantages to the effective use of attending behaviors: (a) they let people know you are "with them" instead of thinking about or responding to other things in the environment, (b) the behaviors assist in establishing and maintaining good rapport, and (c) using these strategies puts the person in the position of being an effective listener.

Interpreting Nonverbal Messages.   Egan (1986) noted that nonverbal messages can modify a verbal message in the following ways: confirm, deny, confuse, emphasize, or control. In certain situations, however, "negative" nonverbal signals can be sent to understanding or familiar listeners without penalty. If certain team members appear to be bored, when in reality they are simply tired, it is probable that the understanding listener will forgive them. In contrast, if they send the same signal to a team leader who is sensitive to the need for respect, inattentiveness may be interpreted as rudeness or hostility. It is permissible for the team member to assume a relaxed posture—leaning back, with hands clasped behind neck—with an old friend, but the team member who portrays this nonverbal image to a parent or a newly introduced professional peer risks being thought of as uninterested and unwilling to modify professional beliefs. Obviously, the danger of misinterpretation of nonverbal signals is more acute at the beginning of a relationship than after it has been established and people know how to "read" others' signals.

There are two important reasons for team members to be able to pick up on nonverbal signals. First, they can avoid sending messages that may hinder communication in the sense that they are perceived negatively by the receiver. Second, people who are able to accurately "read" their listeners' nonverbal behaviors can use this feedback to enhance their communications. When receivers send negative signals, the perceptive sender changes the verbal or nonverbal message being sent. Ignoring the signals can have disastrous consequences, whereas reading them and responding accordingly can have great benefits (Losen & Losen, 1985).

Considerations.   Nonverbal communication behaviors may differ among cultures. For example, in the mainstream culture of the United States, it is considered important for the sender and receiver to receive feedback by looking at each other's eyes. However, this may not be true in every culture; in many Asian cultures, too much direct eye contact is a signal of disrespect, particularly when given by a person in a position of lower status. The appropriateness of touch and physical proximity also varies according to cultural standards, with people in Hispanic cultures tending to touch more and stand closer than those in Asian cultures. Smiling, which usually signals happiness and acceptance in the dominant cultural groups in the United States, may reflect embarrassment or even anger in some Asian cultures. In high context cultures, such as African-American, there is less reliance on verbal communication, so nonverbal communication and interpretation are very important (Miranda, 1993).

For the successful team member, it is also important to remember that the word *culture* can have a very general meaning. In the broadest sense, a culture is any group that has a history and comes together around a set of common goals, standards, and language. The teaching profession is a culture, and it is different from the cultures of physical therapy and social work. Each school or agency often has its own culture, just as each family has its own set of standards and customs. The team member who is not aware of those nonverbal behaviors that are expected in a particular professional culture is well advised to behave conservatively; for example, be careful about invading another's personal space or using extended direct eye contact. This sensitivity to nonverbal communication differences is especially important for all team members at the early stages of their interactions in a new group.

Listening

Listening can be considered a "bridge" between the nonverbal and verbal forms of communication because it incorporates elements of both and affects both. Listening also is a way to understand thoughts and needs as well as to demonstrate empathy. As Covey (1989) stated: "Seek first to understand, then to be understood" (p. 235).

Egan (1986) said:

The art of listening has three parts: (1) listening to and understanding nonverbal behavior; (2) listening to and understanding verbal messages; and (3) listening to and understanding the person. (p. 79)

Importance of Listening.   According to Hybels and Weaver (1986), listening makes up more than half of the time devoted to the various communications skills (see Figure 5–3). Despite its importance, however, Bolton (1979) commented that very few people are truly good listeners. Based on the research available, he found that even at the purely informational level it is estimated that 75% of what is heard is ignored, misunderstood, or quickly forgotten.

Figure 5–3
Percentage of time devoted to various communication skills

Note: From *Communicating Effectively* (p. 53) by S. Hybels and R. L. Weaver, 1986, New York: McGraw-Hill. Reprinted by permission of McGraw-Hill, Inc.

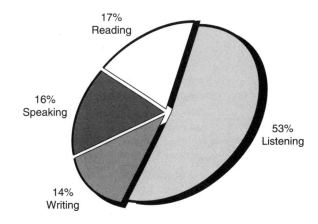

17% Reading

16% Speaking

53% Listening

14% Writing

Styles of Listening.   Gordon (1970) described two styles of listeners: active and passive. Turnbull and Turnbull (1986) stated that most people tend to prefer one style or another, but effective listeners use both styles depending on the situation. *Passive listeners* often are silent, but they remain involved in the interaction by demonstrating attending behaviors and giving words of encouragement. This style of listening is particularly appropriate when a team member needs to "vent" and share emotions.

In *active listening* the receiver is much more involved and animated. The listener frequently makes comments, asks questions, and shares his or her own experiences (Turnbull & Turnbull, 1986). Gordon (1970) believed this style of listening encourages people to express thoughts, assists in building relationships, and helps in finding solutions to problems. Active listening also communicates to other team members basic attitudes about how a receiver or listener feels toward and may react to another person. Gordon (1970) delineated these attitudes as follows:

1. You must *want* to hear what the other person has to say.
2. You must sincerely want to help the person with his/her problem.
3. You must genuinely be able to accept the other person's feelings, no matter how different they are from your own.
4. You must trust the other person's capacity to handle, work through, and find solutions to his/her own problems.
5. You must realize and appreciate that feelings are transitory in nature; consequently you need not fear them.
6. You must view the other person as separate from yourself with alternative ways of perceiving the world. (As summarized in Turnbull & Turnbull, 1986, p. 131.)

Listening Skills.   In implementing active listening, Gordon (1974) recommended the following three steps:

1. The receiver should listen carefully to what is being said.
2. After hearing the expression of strong feelings, the receiver should restate the feelings.
3. After restating those feelings, the receiver should infer the reason for the feelings. The statement is, "You feel . . . (angry) because. . . ."

This strategy can be used effectively in conversations among good friends or between a therapist and a client in a private meeting. There is, however, a certain amount of risk in using the "you" message in a team meeting, because the statement that one individual knows how and why another feels a certain way may be considered arrogant or rude. The suggested modification for use by team members is to soften the inference about feelings and to eliminate the use of the word *because*. This type of feedback is more appropriately used in a group discussion, particularly one in which the participants are relatively unknown to each other. The empathy statement in this case would be, "It sounds as if you are angry about this . . ."

Other skills to indicate a person is listening and to clarify what has been heard have been described by Brammer (1988). *Paraphrasing* involves responding to basic messages being sent by another person. *Clarifying* includes restating points or requesting restatements to ensure understanding. *Perception checking* is a strategy to determine the accuracy of the feelings or emotions detected. These skills, along with examples to illustrate how they can be used, are summarized with verbal skills in Figure 5–4 on page 148.

Verbal Behaviors

Like nonverbal and listening skills, verbal signals are critical for team members who wish to send and receive messages accurately. The elements of verbal skills to be discussed are paralanguage, content-level sequences, verbal skills, and roadblocks.

Paralanguage.   The way people say things is referred to as *paralanguage.* Hybels and Weaver (1986) identified the components of paralanguage as *rate* (speed), *pitch* (high or low), *volume* (loudness), and *quality* (pleasing or unpleasing). Each of these components can affect the meaning and interpretation of what is being said.

Another important component of paralanguage is *intonation.* Often intonation (i.e., *how* it is said rather than *what* is said) is a more powerful and more primitive conveyor of meaning than are words. The intonations in language convey warmth or disapproval to an infant, even before there is an understanding of words. When used by speakers of a foreign language, intonation also is effective in communicating meanings in the absence of specific word comprehension. The effective receiver or listener uses verbal intonation in a way similar to a handwriting analysis—to determine deeper meanings. Eisenhardt (1972) developed a series of examples that illustrate the point. She asked how many different ways can the word *please* be said and have it mean something different each time? A teacher might say "please!" to a child tapping his pencil annoyingly. A friend says "please" to another friend when begging for a favor. In each example the word remains the same, but the elements of intonation convey different meanings. Those elements are *stress, pitch,* and *juncture* (pause).

The three elements of intonation can be used effectively by team members to communicate assertiveness, neutrality, or empathy, depending on the situation and the previous responses of others in the group. For example, suppose the team member assuming the role of leader needs to communicate emphatically that the group will not make a decision on the basis of a single, biased test. The intonation of the message would communicate assertively, "We will not violate this child's right to a multidimensional assessment, nor to the parent's right to due process!" The words "not" and "right" would receive stress; a pause for emphasis would be placed between the words "assessment" and "nor," and the pitch would be lowered decisively at the end of the sentence. Conversely, the team member who had just been told by a divorced mother that her ex-husband had refused to pay child support would use a different intonation to convey empathy. The response, "Things must be really tough for you right now" would be characterized by softer inflections: a wavy pitch without distinct juncture, and stress on either the word "tough" or "you," depending on the focus of the conversation.

Content-Level Sequence. Fong (1986) has shown that there are different levels in the emotional content of verbal messages, each of which is appropriate at a different point in the sequence of developing a relationship with another person. It is possible to share feelings with a close associate, but not with a stranger; it is easier to criticize a friend than an enemy. Each of these situations illustrates the importance of using the appropriate level of emotional content in communication. According to Fong (1986), there are four levels: (a) small talk; (b) communicating an interest in common work or other experiences; (c) sharing some information about self; and (d) intimacy, the "you and I" relationship and feelings.

The first level, *small talk,* is characterized by impersonal contact, such as might be used with a total stranger in the supermarket. The topics of conversation that would be appropriate to use with a person standing in the checkout line include the weather, prices, and headlines. All of these are impersonal topics that can be shared superficially with someone sharing a temporary environment. If the comments are too lengthy or personal, the listener likely will turn away in discomfort. On first meeting, to tell another person about a death in the family is the verbal counterpart of throwing one's arms around a total stranger. This may seem an extreme and unlikely example, but consider an IEP conference at which a school psychologist begins the meeting by telling a father—who is a total stranger—that his third-grade son cannot read and is being considered for placement in a class called "learning disabilities." In the absence of prior conversations in which these two people have built some type of relationship, this statement would be totally out of sequence and could have long-term effects on future interactions.

At the second level, the two communicators *discuss common interests* that have to do with their work environments or past experiences. The communication begins with some impersonal questioning, in which one or both people try to find out something that is shared. One person may say, "Where did you go to school?" The other answers, "I went to the University of Kentucky." The first rejoins, "No kidding, my brother went there, too. Are you as big a basketball fan as he is?" If it turns out that there is a link, the communication will continue, and a higher level of communication can be established.

In level three, *sharing information about self,* the communicators attempt to exchange some thoughts, but not feelings. The initiator of the conversation would share his or her thoughts first, and solicit feedback on similar thoughts from the receiver. For example, a special education teacher and a regular classroom teacher are conversing in the lounge. The classroom teacher says, "Jose seems to be having some trouble hearing in my class. Does he have that same problem when he works with you?" The response would remain on the informational/thought level, with the objective of common problem solving. There are no feelings expressed, but there is a sharing of a high level of thought. A conversation at this level would be much more difficult and less productive, however, for two individuals who had not shared the first two levels, "Isn't this weather great?" and "I enjoy camping, too."

At the highest level, *intimacy,* team members find it possible to share feelings that have to do with the "I" and "you" relationship. Conversations at this level are concerned with impressions, the way people feel about one another, and their reactions. At this level it is advisable to be cautious, even when people think they know each other well. Feeling-level conversations between people of the opposite sex or from different cultural backgrounds are particularly difficult, because they can be easily misunderstood or misinterpreted.

In any event, conversations at this level should not be attempted prematurely. After their relationship was well established through the three previous levels, two team members who were having difficulty might approach each other at this level. For example, a speech therapist had designed an outstanding program in language development for a child, but the program was not succeeding because the special education teacher was not providing follow-up in the resource room. The speech therapist could say, "I feel so discouraged by my efforts to teach Charles to speak in complete sentences. I'm getting the impression that this is an intervention program you do not support. Since I only have Charles for 30 minutes a week, the follow-up in your room is very important." Notice the use of "I" messages rather than "you" messages as an attempt to keep the other person from becoming immediately defensive and to better the chances for an open discussion.

Verbal Skills.   Brammer (1988) described four sets of verbal communication skills, in addition to the listening skills that have been discussed. Those sets of skills are leading, reflecting, summarizing, and informing. *Leading skills* include direct and indirect leads, focusing, and questioning. The purposes of leading skills are to encourage the persons involved to get a conversation going, keep it on track, and encourage elaboration. *Reflecting skills* involve "mirroring" back feelings and content to the sender to communicate an understanding of one's frame of reference and feelings. *Summarizing skills* are designed to pull ideas together and ensure a common understanding of items that have been discussed and agreed upon. *Informing skills* provide information based on experience, knowledge, and background. The two types of informing skills are advising and informing. The latter is preferable in most instances, because some people are insulted when they are given "advice" by another. These skills and corresponding examples are described in more detail in Figure 5–4.

One other important set of verbal skills relates to statements designed to provide feedback. These statements can be phrased as descriptive or judgmental. *Descriptive* statements are based on data. Whenever possible, the descriptive statement should indicate a measured quantity and time frame, and it also should indicate the source of the data. For example, after observing in a teacher's classroom, the counselor might

1. **Listening Skills**

   Paraphrasing—responding to basic messages
   "You are feeling positive about this intervention, but you are confused as to the best way to implement it."
   Clarifying—restating a point or requesting restatement to ensure understanding.
   "I'm confused about this. Let me try to state what I think you have said."
   Perception checking—determining accuracy of feeling or emotion detected
   "I was wondering if the plan you chose is really the one you want. It seems to me that you expressed some doubt; did I hear correctly?"

2. **Leading Skills**

   Indirect leading—getting a conversation started
   "Let's start with you describing how things are going with the first strategy."
   Direct leading—encouraging and elaborating discussion
   "What do you mean when you say there is no improvement? Give me a recent example of an incident in class."
   Focusing—controlling confusion, diffusion, and vagueness
   "You have been discussing several problems with Tommy's behavior in class. Which of these is most important to you? To Tommy?"
   Questioning—inquiring about specific procedures in an open-ended way
   "Please explain the behavior management system you are currently using" not "Do you have any type of management system?"

3. **Reflecting Skills**

   Reflecting feelings—responding to the emotions expressed
   "It sounds as if you are feeling very frustrated with this situation."
   Reflecting content—repeating ideas in new words for emphasis
   "His behavior is making you wonder about your effectiveness as a teacher."

4. **Summarizing Skills**

   Summarizing—pulling themes together
   "Let's take a look at what we have decided thus far. We have agreed to try peer tutoring and a different reinforcement system."

5. **Informing Skills**

   Advising—giving suggestions and opinions based on experience
   "Based on my 14 years as a teacher, I can tell you that idea will not work!"
   Informing—giving information based on expertise, research, training
   "I attended a workshop on the jigsaw technique. Perhaps that strategy would help make the groups in your room more effective."

Figure 5–4

Communication skills

Note: From *The Helping Relationship: Process & Skills,* 4th ed. (pp. 66–67) by L. M. Brammer, 1988, Englewood Cliffs, NJ: Prentice-Hall. Adapted by permission of Prentice-Hall, Inc.

say, "I noticed that John and Jennifer responded to five out of the eight questions you asked during the 20 minutes I was in your room yesterday." This type of statement described exactly what was seen, when, for how long, and where the observation took place. *Judgmental* statements are based on feelings, which can come across positively or negatively. The same situation could be described in a judgmental way as, "It seemed to me that John and Jennifer answered most of the questions yesterday." This statement could be interpreted positively that John and Jennifer are doing well in class, but it also could be interpreted negatively if the implication was that the teacher primarily called on John and Jennifer because they knew the answers and that the teacher ignored the other students. As a rule, team members should use descriptive statements to avoid the chance that the message will be interpreted in a negative way.

Barriers.   Gordon (1974) identified a number of "roadblocks" to effective verbal communication. These *roadblocks* are barriers to interactions among individuals or in team situations. Examples of roadblocks are provided in Figure 5–5.

USING AND MISUSING FORMS OF COMMUNICATION

As team members use nonverbal, listening, and verbal skills, there are several considerations to keep in mind:

1. The verbal and nonverbal signals should match; otherwise, the message may be misinterpreted. Usually the nonverbal message will be interpreted more strongly and will have the greater impact. For example, the team member who says to another, "Tell me how that intervention is going" and then looks at her watch is adding the message, "I am interested if you can give me your answer very quickly, because I have somewhere else to go."

2. Listeners should respond to the signals and paralanguage of others and modify behaviors as necessary. This includes being sensitive to cultural differences (e.g., Miranda, 1993) and gender differences (c.f. Tannen, 1990).

3. Team members should be sensitive to the context and change roles accordingly (e.g., from leader to listener).

4. The verbal levels of communication should be implemented in the proper sequence so that respect is given to the extent or depth of the relationship, and familiarity is not rushed or assumed.

5. Consideration must be given to using the appropriate verbal skills without injecting roadblocks, employing stereotyped responses (e.g., using paraphrasing repeatedly), or jumping in with too many strategies too soon.

6. Team members should be sensitive to the real intent of a message (i.e., hearing what is really meant). Several tongue-in-cheek examples of statements and their "real" meanings are contained in Figure 5–6 on page 152.

1. **Ordering, Commanding**
   Can produce fear or active resistance.
   Invites "testing."
   Promotes rebellious behavior, retaliation.
   "You must . . ."; "You have to . . ."; "You will. . . ."

2. **Warning, Threatening**
   Can produce fear, submissiveness.
   Invites "testing" of threatened consequences.
   Can cause resentment, anger, rebellion.
   "If you don't, then . . ."; "You'd better, or. . . ."

3. **Moralizing, Preaching**
   Creates "obligation" or guilt feelings.
   Can cause others to "dig in" and defend their positions even more ("Who says?").
   Communicates lack of trust in other's sense of responsibility.
   "You should . . ."; "You ought to . . ."; "It is your responsibility. . . ."

4. **Advising, Giving Solutions**
   Can imply other is not able to solve own problems.
   Prevents other from thinking through a problem, considering alternative solutions and trying them out for reality.
   Can cause dependency, or resistance.
   "What I would do is . . ."; "Why don't you . . ."; "Let me suggest. . . ."

5. **Persuading with Logic, Arguing**
   Provokes defensive position and counterarguments.
   Often causes other to "turn off," to quit listening.
   Can cause other to feel inferior, inadequate.
   "Here is why you are wrong . . ."; "The facts are . . ."; "Yes, but. . . ."

6. **Judging, Criticizing, Blaming**
   Implies incompetency, stupidity, poor judgment.
   Cuts off communication over fear of negative judgment or "bawling out."
   Child often accepts judgments as true ("I am bad"); or retaliates ("You're not so great yourself!").
   "You are not thinking maturely . . ."; "You are lazy. . . ."

Figure 5–5

Roadblocks to communication

Note: From *Teacher Effectiveness Training* by T. Gordon, 1974, New York: David McKay Co. Adapted by permission.

MANAGING CONFLICT

Even when decision-making processes are being implemented, factors are being considered, and appropriate communication behaviors are being used, conflicts may still arise. Two important considerations regarding conflict are that it is a naturally occurring phenomenon in groups or organizations, and that it may actually result in improved functioning in the system. Owens (1987) made several comments related to the former point that have implications for interactive teams:

7. **Name-Calling, Ridiculing**
Can cause other to feel unworthy, unloved.
Can have devastating effect on self-image of other.
Often provokes verbal retaliation.
"Crybaby"; "Okay, Mr. Smarty. . . ."

8. **Analyzing, Diagnosing**
Can be threatening and frustrating.
Other can feel trapped, exposed, or not believed.
Stops other from communicating for fear of distortion or exposure.
"What's wrong with you is . . ."; "You're just tired"; "You don't really mean that."

9. **Reassuring, Sympathizing**
Causes other to feel misunderstood.
Evokes strong feelings of hostility ("That's easy for you to say!").
Other often picks up messages such as, "It's not all right for you to feel bad."

10. **Praising, Agreeing**
Implies high expectations as well as surveillance of other's "toeing the mark."
Can be seen as patronizing or as a manipulative effort to encourage desired behavior.
Can cause anxiety when other's perception of self doesn't match praise.
"Well, I think you're doing a great job!"; "You're right—that teacher sounds awful!"

11. **Probing, Questioning**
Because answering questions often results in getting subsequent criticisms or solutions, others often learn to reply with nonanswers, avoidance, half-truths, or lies.
Because questions often are unclear as to what the questioner is driving at, the other may become anxious and fearful.
Other can lose sight of his or her problem while answering questions spawned by concerns.
"Why . . ."; "Who . . ."; "What did you . . ."; "How. . . ."

12. **Diverting, Sarcasm, Withdrawal**
Implies that life's difficulties are to be avoided rather than dealt with.
Can imply other's problems are unimportant, petty, or invalid.
Stops openness when a person is experiencing a difficulty.
"Let's talk about pleasant things . . ."; "Why don't you try running the world!" Remaining silent; turning away.

Conflict in organizations is now seen as inevitable, endemic, and often legitimate. This is because the individuals and groups within the human social system are interdependent and constantly engaged in the dynamic processes of defining and redefining the nature and extent of their interdependence. Important to the dynamics of this social process is the fact that the environment in which it occurs is, itself, constantly changing. (p. 246)

The benefits of conflict that may result in improvements in the organization have been cited by Filley (1975) and Owens (1987). Filley pointed out that conflicts often stimulate the search for new solutions or facts, thus resulting in an improvement in group cohesion and performance. Owens noted that if a positive response is made to

Judith Martin, who writes about manners, points out some of the meanings behind metatalk:

How do you do? How are you? Both of these mean *Hello.* The correct question, when you want to know how someone's digestion or divorce is getting along, is *Tell me, how have you really been?*

Call me. This can mean *Don't bother me now—let's discuss it on office time,* or *I would accept if you asked me out* or *I can't discuss this here* or *Don't go so fast.*

I'll call you. This has opposite meanings, and you have to judge by the delivery. One is *Let's start something* and the other is *Don't call me.*

Let's have lunch. Among social acquaintances, this means *If you ever have nothing to do on a day I have nothing to do, let's get together.* Among business acquaintances, it means *If you have something useful to say to me I'll listen.*

Let's have dinner. Among social acquaintances, it means *Let's advance this friendship.* Among business acquaintances, it means *Let's turn this into a friendship.*

Please stop by some time and see me. Said to someone who lives in the same area, it means *Call me if you'd like to visit me.* Genuine dropping in disappeared with the telephone, so if you want to encourage that, you have to say *I'm always home in the mornings. Don't bother to call; just drop by.*

Please come and stay with me. Said to someone from another area, this means *I would consider extending an invitation at your convenience if it coincides with my convenience.*

We must get together. Watch out here, because there are several similar expressions. This one means *I like you but I'm too busy now to take on more friendship.*

We really must see more of each other. One of the tricky ones, this actually means *I can't make the time to see you.*

We must do this more often. Another variation. This one is really *This was surprisingly enjoyable, but it's still going to happen infrequently.*

Yours truly, Yours sincerely. The first is business, the second distant social. Both mean *Well I guess that's all I've got to say so I'll close now.*

Is all that clear? Oh, one last thing. People who say *I only say what I really mean,* really mean *I am about to insult you.*

Figure 5–6
Metatalk

Note: From *Miss Manners' Guide to Excruciatingly Correct Behavior* by J. Martin, 1982, New York: Atheneum Publishers, an imprint of Macmillan Publishing Company. Copyright © 1979, 1980, 1981, 1982 by United Features Syndicate, Inc. Reprinted with permission.

the conflict, people may be encouraged to search out effective ways of dealing with it, and improved organizational functioning (e.g., clarified relationships and clearer problem solving) may result. This cycle is illustrated in Figure 5–7. Note that the professionals are using active listening when communicating with other team members.

Conflict also may result in negative consequences, such as hostility and destructiveness on the part of group members (Owens, 1987). In such cases, team members may have to deal with a subset of the group or single individuals who are being resistant or defensive. Following are strategies for each of these types of situations.

Figure 5–7

Benefits of conflict

Note: From *Organizational Behavior in Education,* 3rd ed. (p. 249) by R. G. Owens, 1987. Englewood Cliffs, NJ: Prentice-Hall. Copyright © 1987 by Prentice Hall, Inc. Reprinted by permission.

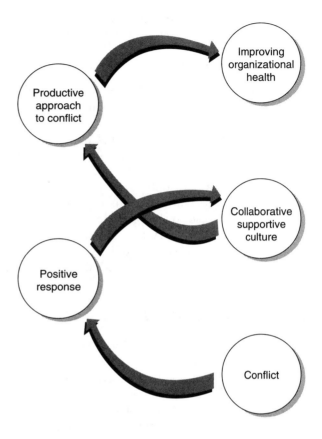

CONFLICTS WITHIN THE GROUP

When conflicts occur within a team or group, the people involved need to remind themselves to consider problems from a systems perspective (i.e., the whole child or organization) and not to focus on or attempt to change individual members (Turnbull & Turnbull, 1986).

Weider-Hatfield (1981) suggested a process that may be useful:

1. Examine the problem intrapersonally and ask, "Why am I feeling this way? Why are the others feeling differently?"
2. Try to get an interpersonal and common definition of the problem and differences other group members perceive.
3. Discuss the goals everyone shares.
4. Generate possible resolutions collaboratively.
5. Weigh goals against resolutions.
6. Evaluate the resolutions after time has passed.

The outcomes of conflicts within a group can be classified in three ways, depending on the results. Filley (1975) described these outcomes as:

1. *Win/lose:* Some group members win, while others believe they have lost.
2. *Lose/lose*: Both groups are disappointed in the outcomes.
3. *Win/win*: All members are satisfied with the outcomes.

Filley stated that win/win outcomes can be achieved through a process known as *integrative decision making (IDM)*. In IDM, participants consider relationships, perceptions, and attitudes that may be affecting the situation. They discuss and agree on a definition of the problem, and then generate possible solutions. The final step is reaching consensus or at least majority agreement on the best alternative(s) to resolve the problem. Another strategy for negotiating agreement was described by Fisher, Ury, and Patton (1991). They listed the following considerations: (a) separate the people from the problem; (b) focus on interests, not positions; (c) invent options for mutual gain; and (d) insist on using objective criteria.

DEALING WITH RESISTANCE

Karp (1984) defined *resistance* as "the ability to avoid what is not wanted from the environment" (p. 69). Piersel (1985) said that resistance can occur for a number of reasons: The person may not know what to do or expect; the person may have different expectations about what should be occurring; or the person may have no intent or need to problem solve due to previous unsuccessful results, an inability to recognize alternatives, or a need to avoid failure or the appearance of being unsuccessful or incompetent.

Nine types of resistance have been identified by Karp (1984). They are the *block, rollover, stall, reverse, sidestep, projected threat, press, guilt trip,* and *tradition.* The general considerations in dealing with resistance presented by Karp include allowing it to come to the surface by asking people for their feelings, showing that the resistance is honored by making eye contact and restating points, openly exploring the resistance by identifying how people feel, and rechecking with the people involved to make sure the understanding is accurate. Karp also recommended asking "what" or "how" questions rather than "why" questions, because the latter type tends to put people on the defensive. Another suggestion was to use "I" statements rather than "you" statements, because these also tend to make people respond defensively. Examples and strategies for dealing with the nine types of resistance are illustrated in Table 5–1 on pages 156–157.

Final considerations in dealing with people who are resistant are concerned with the behaviors team members demonstrate in the situation. As Turnbull and Turnbull (1986) stated, individuals who want to help others cease being resistant must demonstrate a willingness and openness to accept a mutual commitment toward resolving the problem. Brammer (1988) and Piersel (1985) both noted that a consultant must model, shape, and reinforce problem solving and reduction of resistance. The importance of these strategies was reiterated by Fine, Grantham, and Wright (1979) when they said, "If we are asking teachers to be nondefensive, to consider different facets of a situation, and to risk making choices without complete data, then our best ally may be the behavior we model for them" (p. 539).

APPLICATION OF COMMUNICATION STRATEGIES

In Table 5-2, on page 158, two illustrations of ineffective communication and desired communication in interactive teaming are provided. In the first example, the psychologist is using several acronyms (e.g., CAT, EMH, BEH) that the parent may not be familiar with. In addition, several emotionally laden words such as "obvious reading and language deficits" are used but not explained. In the desired communication column, the psychologist tries to explain testing results and provides examples of questions. In addition, she asks for the parent's comments about a placement instead of presenting it as a decision that has been made without the parent's input.

In the second example, the program administrator presents a decision based on numbers rather than on what individual students need. In describing a program for Jackie, he does not state whether a high school placement is in the best interest of the child's overall development, nor does he request the parents or special educator's input into the decision. Jargon such as "augmentative," "functional," and "APE" are used without explanation. In the desired communication column, the administrator presents a possibility for a placement, describes the potential benefits, and asks for ideas from the special educator and parents.

SUMMARY

An understanding of communication skills is an essential facilitating factor in interactive teaming. The areas encompassed in this understanding include the following:

◆ Awareness of a communication model that includes senders-receivers, messages, channels, feedback, noise, and setting.

◆ Sensitivity to characteristics of communication in interactive teaming.

◆ Consideration of personal, attitudinal, and experiential factors; backup support factors; and context or situational factors.

◆ Implementation of effective nonverbal, listening, and verbal skills.

◆ Knowledge of ways to manage conflicts in groups and strategies for dealing with resistant people.

The next chapter describes considerations for interacting with people from different cultures. The strategies contained in Chapter 6 are vital when serving on an interactive team with people from diverse professional and family backgrounds and cultures.

Table 5–1

Karp's Strategies for Dealing with Resistance

Type of Resistance	Example	Explanation	Possible Response
THE BLOCK	"I don't want to" or "I'd rather not!"	Most obvious form of authentic resistance. Easiest to work with. The resister is clear about what the demander wants.	"What are some of your objections?"
THE ROLLOVER (passive resistance)	"Tell me exactly what you want me to do."	Least common and one of the most difficult to identify and work with. Frequently the resister does not know role, what he/she is resisting. Expressed by minimal compliance with the letter of the demand and no compliance with the spirit of the demand.	"Are you clear about what is being asked of you?" "How do you think this will change your role?"
THE STALL	"I'll get on it first thing Thursday," or "I'll try to rearrange my schedule for that."	Difficult to distinguish between a stall and an honest response to present conditions. A knowledge of how a person usually responds to requests or demands will make the distinction.	"What things may prevent you from starting this tomorrow or in the near future?"
THE REVERSE	"Wow! What a great idea!"	A very subtle form of resistance and is practically impossible to identify without knowing the resister well. Occurs as a statement of enthusiastic support when what you were expecting from this individual was a hard time. The resister tells you what you want to hear—and then immediately forgets about it.	"I'm pleased with your response. What aspects do you like best?"
THE SIDESTEP	"Let Sally try it first; then I'll try it."	Expressed as a counterdemand to get someone else to do the desired thing. The appeal is to your sense of fairness. "How come you didn't tell Pam she had to do this?" This then puts you on the defensive to justify your choice.	"I understand your concern; what can I expect from you?"

Note: From "Working with Resistance" by H. Karp, 1984, *Training and Development Journal, 38*(3), pp. 69–73. Adapted by permission.

Type of Resistance	Example	Explanation	Possible Response
THE PROJECTED THREAT	"The (teachers) won't like it."	The resistance expressed here is in terms of an implied threat that someone else with some power won't approve of your demand. The third party's view may or may not be positive.	"I appreciate your concern and will check it with the others. In the meantime, what are your plans for . . .?"
THE PRESS	"You owe me one."	An authentic resistance. The resister does not want to cooperate and is calling in an old debt to get off the hook. It is your decision whether this is an appropriate time to pay back a debt.	"I realize I may owe you one; however, what are you planning on doing to implement . . .?"
THE GUILT TRIP	"See what you are making me do."	Guilt is a common tactic in shaping behavior. The resister's problem with what you want is his/her problem, not yours. It's good to work with the problem but not to shoulder it.	"I'm sorry this is a problem for you; however, what do you plan on doing . . .?"
THE TRADITION	"But we've always done it this way."	The most time-honored/traditional approach. This approach really is an appeal to safety, not effectiveness. Most who rely on this approach are those who are unwilling to take risks and have a low opinion of their own creativity and resourcefulness.	"I agree that the old approach has merits, but what could we do to adapt it to this new approach?"

Table 5–2
Contrasting Communication Strategies

Ineffective Communication	Desired Communication in Interactive Teaming
1. **Psychologist to parent:** "On the CAT your son was in the 10th percentile for his grade level. We think a placement in EMH class with an appropriate IEP would meet his needs. He has obvious reading and language deficits and his communication development is delayed. We suspect that he may also have BEH tendencies due to the frustration he has experienced in academic settings."	"I would like to explain the results of recent testing to you. Your son took a test in the areas of reading, language, and math. This chart illustrates how he did compared with others of his grade level. The types of questions he was responding to included (examples given). The results show that he has difficulty with reading comprehension, or understanding the meaning of what he has read. Have you noticed similar patterns as you read with him at home? Given this performance, what do you think would be the best plan for your child?"
2. **Program administrator to special educator and parents:** "The numbers in our programs for multi-disabled are low this coming year so we can't really justify having two classes at the elementary level. Therefore, we have decided to place the 15-year-old child at the high school level and move the other students into other classes. Jackie is verbal and does not need an augmentative communication system, so she does not need to be placed in the elementary nonverbal class. We want her to learn vocational and functional skills and continue to work on range of motion in PT. In addition, we do not think she needs APE any longer; instead we can have her work on computer literacy with the specialist and the OT."	"We are considering the best placements for our students with multiple disabilities for next year and wanted your input. One possibility is placing Jackie at a middle or high school level. This will enable her to have access to the computer lab and the classes on homemaking and work skills. What are your ideas on this?"

ACTIVITIES

1. Observe an interaction between a professional and a parent. Were respect and trust evident or missing? Was rapport established and maintained? Were cultural differences understood and accepted? Did verbal and nonverbal messages match?

2. Observe a team meeting among professionals. Was the situation proactive or reactive? What content-level sequences were used? Was jargon explained? Which verbal and listening skills were implemented? Were any judgmental statements or roadblocks evident? If so, what were the responses to them? If a conflict arose, how was it handled?

3. Conduct an informational interview with a parent or professional. Write your overall assessment of the interview. Also write an analysis of your use and the interviewee's use of effective communication strategies.

4. Design a checklist or rating scale of the behaviors you think are necessary for effective communication. Evaluate yourself on the behaviors. Observe a meeting and consider how the participants interact. If you think some people in the meeting are better at communicating than others, identify what behaviors or skills you think give them an advantage.

REFERENCES

Arab, C. (1985, May). *Getting what you deserve: Assertive, aggressive, and non-assertive behavior.* Paper presented at the Florida Academy of School Leaders, Daytona Beach.

Bailey, D. B. (1987). Collaborative goal-setting with families: Resolving differences in values and priorities for services. *Topics in Early Childhood Special Education, 7*(2), 59–71.

Bolton, R. (1979). *People skills.* Englewood Cliffs, NJ: Prentice-Hall.

Brammer, L. M. (1988). *The helping relationship: Process and skills* (4th ed.). Englewood Cliffs, NJ: Prentice-Hall.

Covey, S. R. (1989). *The 7 habits of highly effective people: Powerful lessons in personal change.* New York: Simon & Schuster.

Dettmer, P., Thurston, L. P., & Dyck, N. (1993). *Consultation, collaboration, and teamwork for students with special needs.* Boston: Allyn & Bacon.

Egan, G. (1986). *The skilled helper: A systematic approach to effective helping.* Monterey, CA: Brooks/Cole.

Ehly, S. W., & Eliason, M. (1983). Communicating for understanding: Some problems in psychology and education. *Journal for Special Educators, 19*(3), v–ix.

Eisenhardt, C. (1972). *Applying linguistics to the teaching of reading and the language arts.* Columbus, OH: Merrill.

Filley, A. C. (1975). *Interpersonal conflict resolution.* Glenview, IL: Scott, Foresman.

Fine, M. J., Grantham, V. L., & Wright, J. G. (1979). Personal variables that facilitate or impede consultation. *Psychology in the Schools, 16,* 533–539.

Fisher, R., Ury, W., & Patton, B. (1991). *Getting to yes: Negotiating agreement without giving in.* New York: Penguin Books.

Fong, M. (1986). *The levels of communication in personal relationships.* Unpublished manuscript, University of Florida, Department of Counselor Education, Gainesville.

Friend, M. (1984). Consultation skills for resource teachers. *Learning Disability Quarterly, 7,* 246–250.

Gladstein, G. A. (1983). Understanding empathy: Integrating counseling, developmental, and social psychology perspectives. *Journal of Counseling Psychology, 30,* 467–482.

Gordon, T. (1970). *Parent effectiveness training.* New York: Wyden.

—. (1974). *Teacher effectiveness training.* New York: David McKay.

Grieger, R. M. (1972). Teacher attitudes as a variable in behavior modification consultation. *Journal of School Psychology, 10,* 279–287.

Gutkin, T. B., & Curtis, M. J. (1982). School-based consultation: Theory and techniques. In C. R. Reynolds & T. B. Gutkin (Eds.), *The handbook of school psychology*. New York: Wiley.

Heron, T. E., & Harris, K. C. (1987). *The educational consultant: Helping professionals, parents, and mainstreamed students*. Austin, TX: Pro-Ed.

Hudson, P. (1987). *Proactive and reactive consultation: A model for preservice training*. Unpublished manuscript, University of Florida, Department of Special Education, Gainesville.

Hudson, P. J., Correa, V. I., Morsink, C. V., & Dykes, M. K. (1987). A new model for preservice training: Teacher as collaborator. *Teacher Education and Special Education, 10*(4), 191–193.

Hybels, S., & Weaver, R. L. (1986). *Communicating effectively*. New York: McGraw-Hill

Idol, L., Paolucci-Whitcomb, P., & Nevin, A. (1986). *Collaborative consultation*. Rockville, MD: Aspen.

Karp, H. (1984). Working with resistance. *Training and Development Journal, 38*(3), 69–73.

Kerlinger, F. N. (1986). *Foundations of behavioral research* (3rd ed.). New York: Holt, Rinehart and Winston.

Lang, D. C., Quick, A. F., & Johnson, J. A. (1981). *A partnership for the supervision of student teachers*. DeKalb, IL: Creative Educational Materials.

Lopez, E. C., Dalal, S. M., & Yoshida, R. K. (1993). An examination of professional cultures: Implications for the collaborative consultation model. *Journal of Educational and Psychological Consultation, 4,* 197–213.

Losen, S. M., & Losen, J. G. (1985). *The special education team*. Boston: Allyn & Bacon.

Miranda, A. H. (1993). Consultation with culturally diverse families. *Journal of Educational and Psychological Consultation, 4,* 89–93.

Nierenberg, G., & Calero, H. (1971). *How to read a person like a book*. New York: Hawthorn Books.

Owens, R. B. (1987). *Organizational behavior in education* (3rd ed.). Englewood Cliffs, NJ: Prentice-Hall.

Piersel, W. C. (1985). Behavioral consultation: An approach to problem solving in educational settings. In J. R. Bergan, *School psychology in contemporary society: An introduction*. Columbus, OH: Merrill.

Rogers, C. R. (1961). *On becoming a person: A therapist's view of psychotherapy*. Boston: Houghton-Mifflin.

Salvia, J., & Ysseldyke, J. E. (1988). *Assessment in special and remedial education* (4th ed.). Boston: Houghton-Mifflin.

Siders, J. Z., Riall, A., Bennett, T. C., & Judd, D. (1987). Training of leadership personnel in early intervention: A transdisciplinary approach. *Teacher Education and Special Education, 10*(4), 161–170.

Sonnenschien, P. (1984). Parents and professionals: An uneasy relationship. In M. L. Henniger & E. M. Nesselroad (Eds.), *Working with parents of handicapped children: A book of readings for school personnel*. Lanham, MD: University Press of America.

Spodek, B. (1982). What special educators need to know about regular classrooms. *Educational Forum, 46,* 295–307.

Tannen, D. (1990). *You just don't understand: Women and men in conversation*. New York: Ballantine Books.

Tawney, J. W., & Gast, D. L. (1984). *Single subject research in special education*. New York: Merrill/Macmillan.

Turnbull, A. P., & Turnbull, H. R. (1990). *Families, professionals, and exceptionality: A special partnership* (2nd ed.). New York: Merrill/Macmillan.

Venn, J. (1994). *Assessment of students with special needs*. New York: Merrill/Macmillan.

Weider-Hatfield, D. (1981). A unit in conflict management communication skills. *Communication Education, 30,* 265–273.

Weissenburger, J. W., Fine, M. J., & Poggio, J. P. (1982). The relationship of selected consultant/teacher characteristics to consultation outcomes. *Journal of School Psychology, 20*(4), 263–270.

West, J. F., & Cannon, G. S. (1988). Essential collaborative consultation competencies for regular and special educators. *Journal of Learning Disabilities, 21*(1), 56–63, 28.

West, J. F., Idol, L., & Cannon, G. (1989). *Collaboration in the schools: An inservice and preservice curriculum for teachers, support staff, and administrators*. Austin, TX: Pro-Ed.

Zirpoli, T. J., & Melloy, K. J. (1993). *Behavior management: Applications for teachers and parents*. New York: Merrill/Macmillan.

CHAPTER **6**

Considering Cultural and Linguistic Diversity

Definition of Culture

Importance of Cultural Competence

Recognition of Cultural Norms

Recognition of Language Differences

Understanding the Effects of Culture Context

Effect on the Student

Effect on the Family

Effect on the School

Effect on Team Members

Application

Summary

TOPICS IN THIS CHAPTER INCLUDE

◆ Definitions of culture within a broad context.

◆ Descriptions of cultural norms.

◆ Examples of language differences.

◆ Effects of culture context on students, families, schools, and team members.

 Robertito, a 7-year-old blind immigrant child from the Dominican Republic, and his mother, Maria, attended a four-day summer camp program for students with visual impairments and their families in Florida. One goal of this camp experience was to bring together parents of students with visual disabilities to share support and information on raising a young child with disabilities. Additionally, the camp was to provide parents with hands-on skills for working with their own children.

On the second evening of camp, all the families were eating dinner in the cafeteria. Maria was assigned to work with the occupational therapist (OT) on teaching Robertito to feed himself and eat a wider variety of foods. Because Maria did not speak English, an interpreter attended the session. The OT was firm with Maria regarding Robertito. The OT told Maria that if her son was to learn how to feed himself and eat a variety of foods, she was going to have to stop feeding him baby food or pureed home-cooked meals. Maria said she understood Robertito was a difficult child to feed, but "as long as his grandmother or she fed him his favorite foods, he would eat fine." The OT insisted that Maria not give in to her son. She asked the mother not to feed him any food that evening and let him go to bed hungry, in hopes of motivating him to eat the next morning. Through hand-on-hand guidance, she then forced Robertito to take some food from his plate and place it in his mouth. Robertito became agitated; then he began to resist and finally started to cry.

Maria's eyes filled; she swallowed hard but refrained from saying anything. She allowed the OT to continue. Eventually, the OT's insistence that Robertito feed himself visibly upset Maria. Watching her child throw a tantrum and spit out his food, Maria began to weep. Between sobs she cried to the interpreter that "her poor son was not able to handle the task, and that if his grandmother found out what they were doing to him, she would be extremely upset." The interpreter did not want to translate Maria's words.

At this point, the OT became frustrated with Maria and pointed out that other mothers in the group were not having any problems with teaching self-feeding. She told Maria that she was going to have to stop spoiling and overprotecting Robertito. The interpreter tried to soften this message, but Maria reacted angrily to the OT's tone of voice and curt mannerisms.

Working with parents and professionals from linguistically and culturally different backgrounds requires the majority-culture professional to demonstrate extraordinary skills and sensitivity in understanding those differences. The occupational therapist in this vignette lacked sensitivity to the Hispanic mother's inability to put her son through any suffering. Also, the OT failed to give adequate instructions to the interpreter: The objective of self-feeding is not negotiable, but the way the OT deals with meeting that objective must be adjusted to the fact that the mother and grandmother are from the Dominican Republic. Also, the OT must work through the interpreter, who frequently is a community volunteer. The OT thinks and acts within a professional context, in which even the meaning of words may differ from the meanings understood by the volunteer. Responsibility for integrating the volunteer into the professional context through training lies with the OT.

This chapter presents the issue of cultural differences and the effect of these differences on the interactive team members. The first part is a description of the differences between the mainstream and minority cultures in terms of rules, language patterns, and values. The rules, language patterns, and values of the mainstream members of the existing power structure are represented in the contexts in which professionals work. Members of minority cultures are often confused by the ways of the mainstream, which can reinforce their feelings of powerlessness.

The second part of the discussion of cultural differences is a description of the ways in which the culture for each organization (home, school, agency, institution) sets the context for that organization's mission. People from cultures that differ from those in which they must operate as interactive team members may be less effective if they do not recognize that they must work within the cultural context of their organization. They may feel conflict between the expectations placed on them as leaders in multicultural situations and the goals and objectives they have as trained professionals working within the structure of a particular organization.

The complexity of the multifaceted role of the modern professional who works with multicultural children with disabilities can be seen in the occupational therapist's situation. The OT works with a number of cultures: Anglos, Hispanic, professional therapist, volunteer, and parent/family. An important element of understanding the complexity of the role is understanding cultural diversity.

DEFINITION OF CULTURE

The word *culture* is used here in its broadest sense. It includes any group of people with a common set of values and a language. "Culture represents the encompassing expression of a person's life . . . that subsumes racial and ethnic rituals, symbols, language, and general ways of behaving" (Dilworth-Anderson, Burton, & Johnson, 1993, p. 628). For each child, the culture transmits a sense of ethnicity. *Ethnicity* is defined by Longstreet (1978) as "that portion of cultural development that occurs before the individual is in complete command of his or her abstract intellectual powers and that is formed primarily through the individual's early contacts with family, neighbors, friends, teachers, and others, as well as with his or her immediate environment of home and neighborhood" (p. 19). Dilworth-Anderson et al. (1993) add that ethnicity is part of our "sense of peoplehood and a shared community with others who are members of the same group" (p. 628).

Some might assume that any discussion about *cultural diversity* relates to Hispanic, African-American, Native American, or Asian (the groups most often given the term *minority*). But for purposes of this chapter, cultural diversity can encompass groups such as the Amish, Mormons, Appalachians, Jews, armed forces, homosexuals, the homeless, and the poor. These groups often are underrepresented in discussions of diversity. Although some of these groups may experience less economic or political subordination and may be more assimilated to the dominant culture (Ogbu, 1985; Tharp, 1989), they still possess distinct group identity and should be respected for their diversity. Overlooking the influences culture has on students and families who are not of color, have not immigrated to the United States, do not have an ethnic surname, or do not speak a native language other than English is an error in understanding cultural diversity. The following vignette illustrates this error.

Patrick, a 15-year-old Caucasian student with learning disabilities was participating in a class discussion on home and community in his social studies class. The teacher asked students to find their homes on a city map and write the street address and zip code on the board. Patrick became uncomfortable and turned his attention to the world globe in the classroom. In an effort to get Patrick back on task, the teacher asked him to take his turn at locating his home on the city map. Patrick became giddy and began to laugh, saying that he didn't want to do it. The teacher insisted and Patrick yelled, "No!" He was asked to leave the group and sit quietly in the reading corner. Later the teacher asked Patrick why he did not respond. He said he was embarrassed because he and his mother live in the local homeless shelter. The teacher apologized and revised her lesson the following day so that the students located the addresses of community libraries instead.

All students and families have a culture. Those cultural and linguistic characteristics affect almost all children's learning and families' beliefs. Educators must be sensitive to hidden or overlooked aspects of culture in students who do not outwardly appear to come from a more discernible group.

As we enter the 21st century, it is clear that educators are faced with a multitude of diverse students, families, and professionals. Immigration to the United States can be seen in all regions of the country, with Asian and Pacific immigrants entering the West, Latin Americans entering the South and Southwest, and Middle Easterners and Africans immigrating to the South and East coasts. The immigration of Eastern and Western Europeans and Canadians continues in the Eastern and Northeastern United States (*Modern Maturity,* 1992).

Lynch and Hanson (1992) wrote:

> The American landscape is now a kaleidoscope of cultures, and the changing patterns of color, customs, and language have introduced new energy, new concepts, and new concerns. One of the greatest concerns associated with increasing diversity is how human services agencies and programs can respond sensitively and effectively to families whose language, experience, and needs differ from those of the dominant culture in the United States. Defining, creating, and maintaining caring, responsive services is one of the most challenging tasks that face agencies and interventionists at the threshold of the 21st Century. (p. 355)

Unfortunately, students from diverse backgrounds are at risk for school failure (Cooper, 1990; Ogbu, 1985; Tharp, 1989). According to Williams (1992), "a number of predictors of school failure correlate directly with minority status, including poverty, family characteristics, parent education, and language minority status" (p. 157). The educational system is greatly challenged by these factors and must respond with effective education strategies that meet the diverse needs of all students.

With a broader definition of *diversity,* educators can understand that the educational system is a culture in and of itself and within that culture exists more diversity. The cultural diversity among members of different professional groups has been illustrated in the Chapter 4 discussion of these groups and their roles. According to the definition of *culture,* each community, each school or clinical program, each classroom, and each family has its own culture. The differences in values and language systems used as illustrations in this chapter show the need for people from all cultures to develop an understanding that their values and language systems may differ from those of people with whom they work.

IMPORTANCE OF CULTURAL COMPETENCE

 Jose is a 10-year-old student from Nicaragua. He arrived in the United States three months ago and was placed in a bilingual classroom with other limited English proficient students. However, in the past few weeks his teacher, Mr. Stein, has noticed that Jose is extremely aggressive and does not enjoy socializing with his peers. On two occasions, Jose became upset with his school work and began to cry. Mr. Stein referred Jose to a special education classroom for children with emotional distur-bances in a neighboring school. The special education teacher, Mrs. Lamb, has asked Mr. Stein to consider the fact that aggressive behavior may be a secondary reaction to acquisition of a new language.

The student from a different culture who is limited English proficient presents the educational system with a tremendous challenge. Jose may not be a candidate for special education, but professionals lacking knowledge and sensitivity to cultural and linguistic differences might proceed with this referral.

Developing cultural competence begins by first understanding one's own culture (Lynch & Hanson, 1992). Self-awareness of one's heritage, values, beliefs, customs, and behaviors is often the first step in understanding the culture of different groups of people. Professionals must further understand that they hold cultural assumptions about groups of people. Those assumptions often influence the interactions and judg-ments they have about culturally different individuals (Harry, 1992c). Table 6–1 includes an activity that can assist professionals in self-evaluation of their own cultural heritage, beliefs, biases, and behaviors.

RECOGNITION OF CULTURAL NORMS

The second step to becoming culturally competent involves understanding and learn-ing about the characteristics and norms of other cultural groups. This learning can take place through readings, interactions, and involvement with the culture one is studying (Lynch & Hanson, 1992).

The primary differences in cultural norms among diverse ethnic groups have been identified by Hallman, Bryant, Campbell, McGuire, and Bowman (1983), who indicated that the dimensions of these differences include how individuals perceive self, family, religion, sex roles, society, human nature, nature, and the supernatural. To some degree, ethnic groups retain the characteristics that mark them as culturally dif-ferent. For example, some ethnic groups are known by dress and foods; others, by religion and language.

Both professional teams and student or consumer groups include members with diverse cultural norms. If not recognized, these differences may create conflicts among professionals and between professionals and the families they serve. The fol-lowing are a few examples of cultural values that differ from the traditional middle-class white Anglo Saxon values on which most educational and social services pro-grams are based.

The cultural patterns of various Native American tribes have been studied in detail. Warren (1981) has described some of the anthropological studies that provide insight into cultural differences and the accompanying conflicts. Warren cited the con-flict between home and school or the larger society for the Cree (Mistassini) Indian people. At home the Cree are expected to be self-reliant, cooperative, nonaggressive,

Table 6–1
A Cultural Journey

Culture is not just something that someone else has. All of us have a cultural, ethnic, and linguistic heritage that influences our beliefs, values, and behaviors. To learn a little more about your own heritage, take this simple cultural journey.

Origins

1. When you think about your roots, what country(ies) other than the United States do you identify as a place of origin for you or your family?

2. Have you ever heard any stories about how your family or your ancestors came to the United States? Briefly, what was the story?

3. Are there any foods that you or someone else prepare that are traditional for your country(ies) of origin? What are they?

4. Are there any celebrations, ceremonies, rituals, holidays that your family celebrates that reflect your country(ies) of origin? What are they? How are they celebrated?

5. Do you or anyone in your family speak a language other than English because of your origins? If so, what language?

6. Can you think of one piece of advice that has been handed down through your family that reflects the values held by your ancestors in the country(ies) of origin? What is it?

Beliefs, Biases, and Behaviors

1. Have you ever heard anyone make a negative comment about people from your country(ies) of origin? If so, what was it?

2. As you were growing up, do you remember discovering that your family did anything differently than other families that you were exposed to because of your culture, religion, or ethnicity? Name something you remember that was different.

3. Have you ever been with someone in a work situation who did something because of his or her culture, religion, ethnicity that seemed unusual to you? What was it? Why did it seem unusual?

4. Have you ever felt shocked, upset, or appalled by something that you saw when you were traveling in another part of the world? If so, what was it? How did it make you feel? Pick some descriptive words to explain your feelings. How did you react? In retrospect, how do you wish you would have reacted?

5. Have you ever done anything you think was culturally inappropriate when you have been in another country or with someone from a different culture? In other words, have you ever done something you think might have been upsetting or embarrassing to another person? What was it? What did you do to try to improve the situation?

Imagine

1. If you could be from another culture or ethnic group, what culture would it be? Why?

2. What is one value from that culture or ethnic group that attracts you to it?

3. Is there anything about that culture or ethnic group that concerns or frightens you? What is it?

4. Name one concrete way in which you think your life would be different if you were from that culture or ethnic group.

and emotionally close to kin; at school and in the larger society, they are required to be independent, competitive, aggressive, and to establish shallow social contacts with a large group. Pepper (1976) discussed the perception of time held by some American Indian people. For them, time is present-oriented; it has to do with this day, this week; there is a resistance to future-oriented planning. For the Anglo-dominant society, time is regarded as a way of planning for the future; time is "saved" through planning.

Different socialization experiences within cultures may cause children to develop different cognitive or behavioral styles. Children from some Hispanic and some Pacific Island groups may be motivated more by the need for affiliation than for achievement. Some cultures engender a sense of fatalism that decreases motivation (Lynch & Hanson, 1992; Henderson, 1982). Smalley (1984) and Johnson and Johnson (1988) have also pointed out that poor black children are likely to have learned to use body language as a way of asserting their dominance over others, in an attempt to intimidate. These types of cognitive styles and social behaviors are different from those expected of children in the traditional classroom.

Tharp (1989) discussed differences in social organization, sociolinguistic, cognition, and motivation variables in Chicano, black, and white children. Although he found significant differences across the ethnic groups, he also noted differences within ethnic groups, particularly related to social status. He concluded that two areas should be addressed in classrooms with underachieving minority students. First, classrooms should focus on language development using "visual and holistic methods for the teaching of literacy, numeracy, and science" (p. 355). Second, he recommends that teachers provide contextualized instruction drawn from the everyday world of the students. Instruction can be contextualized by including students' personal experiences, expanding community-based instruction, and advocating for contextualization of the school itself through community and family collaboration.

RECOGNITION OF LANGUAGE DIFFERENCES

Language defines the speaker and the cultural group to which he or she belongs. It affirms solidarity or conveys social distance. Attitudes toward language are one of the greatest problems in *cross-cultural communication* (Edelsky & Hudelson, 1980, 1982). Professionals may be influenced by dialect and foreign accents; they may also misunderstand the underlying language structure. English, the language of instruction in American schools is characterized by the use of logic and linear presentation. The native languages of various cultural groups may be more circular or parallel in their construction or discourse style (Kaplan, 1966). To a speaker of English, an indirect style of discourse may appear rambling or disconnected.

According to Briggs (1982), language is primarily speech; its written form is secondary. All languages have complex sets of rules for combining sounds, ordering words, and using intonation, rules that enable people to convey meanings. Language form is based on general acceptance by members of a speech community of such a set of rules. Languages change in response to many factors. Variations occur according to rules or trends that are identifiable by linguists.

Variations of the accepted rules of any language occur within particular communities. These variations may be the result of borrowing words from one language for adapted use in another, when people speaking different languages live in the same area and wish to communicate. Variations also occur when speakers invent new uses for words, such as the use of the verb *go* in the space-age phrase *all systems are go*. Limited versions of any language may develop for use in a specialized setting, such as in a trade or professional society (jargon) or in a social clique (slang), and many varieties of any given language may exist at the same time (dialects). These variations make it difficult for people from different subgroups, even within the same "language group," to communicate with one another.

The discourse patterns of individuals—the ways they talk, write, read, and listen—are often specific to their own culture (Gomes, 1983). Summarizing the work of Scollon and Scollon (1981), Gomes pointed out that the way people present themselves (tone of voice, topics, attitudes) to others is influenced by the beliefs and customs of the culture in which they were reared. For example, the role of the child speaking to an adult may vary from a belief that silence communicates respect to a belief that silence communicates defiance. In another example, Briggs (1982) showed how people from the Aymara culture would find it inappropriate to make direct statements based on secondhand knowledge. The speaker of this language might be reluctant to ask for a glass of water without saying, "Let's both have a glass of water. I'm thirsty." Such linguistic differences, based on cultural perceptions of manners and appropriateness, can be confusing to people from another background.

In the discourse patterns in American schools, the teacher initiates the interaction, to which the child is expected to respond; then the teacher clarifies, corrects, or reinforces. The middle-class Anglo child is prepared to participate in these interactions at an early age, when he or she is asked to label objects or tell "how many," and then is praised or corrected. Later, this child is taught how to sit quietly and listen to a story, or is encouraged to tell stories, which are expected to be fictional or imaginative. Gomes (1983) cites the example of a rural southern child in whose culture people talked about life events in a poetic type of monologue. This child did poorly in the early school years, when he was required to answer specific questions with discrete bits of information; yet he excelled in the intermediate grades, when he was asked to deal with analogies or to draw inferences.

There is also a subtle linkage established between the dominant language and the status of speakers, in the sense that bilingual speakers use the preferred language because its use confers status. Edelsky and Hudelson (1982, 1989) have discussed language in the sense that it is used as the preferred language of a particular institution or group. They have discussed the fact that Chicano children preferred to speak English, the language with political and social status, rather than Spanish, which was native to them. The Anglo children laughed at the Chicano children who spoke Spanish, and the Anglo children refused to learn Spanish, even when it was taught to them.

Special services professionals who are representatives of the nondominant culture are sensitive to these subtleties. A. Pando (personal communication, May 1987) indicated that the Cuban American teachers in Miami who are most successful with their Cuban American students are those who use English in the classroom, but Spanish on the playground and in informal, personal conversations. S. Smalley (personal communication, October 1986) reported that black principals would be severely criticized for speaking Black English in a professional meeting. They are able to communicate effectively with reticent, black children with behavior disorders, however, by ignoring the Anglo script that suggests they ask the child to describe his point of view. They say instead, "Hey man, what it is?" Understanding of such linguistic subtleties is acquired usually through living in the cultural context in which the language is heard.

UNDERSTANDING THE EFFECTS OF CULTURAL CONTEXT

It is important to delineate how culture affects the following subsystems: students, families, schools, and team members. Figure 6–1 illustrates an interactive system that can be influenced by cultural diversity not common to the system. For example, the school subsystem has certain values and beliefs that can be adversely affected by the high enrollment of culturally diverse students. According to systems theory (Minuchin, 1974), the multicultural students' presence may cause distressing situations for professionals when they try to integrate these students into the mainstream school system. The following vignette helps illustrate this point.

Figure 6–1
Effects of cultural context
on various systems

Mr. Barbier, a Haitian high school teacher, has asked to meet with his principal regarding the attitudes of the other teachers in the high school. Mr. Barbier explains to the principal that he has witnessed, on more than one occasion, a grave lack of respect and understanding by other teachers toward the Haitian students attending his bilingual mathematics and science classes. On one occasion a teacher verbally reprimanded a student for dancing and singing between classes, and stated that the student should not have come to the United States if he was going to behave like he lived in the jungles of Haiti. Furthermore, Mr. Barbier says, many of the students are being overreferred to the principal's office for seemingly aggressive behavior toward their peers. Mr. Barbier explains that in the Haitian culture young boys tease each other by hitting and calling each other names.

The professional working with these Haitian students must respect and value the uniqueness and inherent strengths of different cultures (Harry, 1992b; Kumabe, Nishida, & Hepworth, 1985; Lynch & Hanson, 1992) to keep harmony within the school subsystem. Each of the four subsystems (i.e., students, families, schools, and team members) is changed to some degree when a different set of cultural rules, beliefs, and values is infused. Not accommodating the differences can result in negative effects: inappropriate programming for students, lack of sensitivity toward families, and outright discriminatory behavior toward students. In the following sections the effect of culture context on each of the subsystems is described.

Effect on the Student

The consequences are predictable when a large discrepancy exists between the dominant cultural expectations of the school and the nondominant cultural expectations demonstrated by the child's behavior. Insensitivity to these cultural and linguistic differences can result in either the provision of ineffective programs or the misplacement of students into special education classrooms. The special services team has a responsibility for both aspects of this problem.

Warren (1981), who reported on instructors' reactions to children's verbal and nonverbal styles, noted that teachers and aides attended to Caucasian children more than to Navajo children. Warren described the Navajo child as teacher-oriented, and the Caucasian child as peer-oriented. Warren also raised a question about the effects on the Navajo children of the teacher's relative lack of attention.

Another study, conducted by the Civil Rights Commission (1975), also showed how children may differ in their experiences with teachers in schools. This study, conducted in California, New Mexico, and Texas, was based on observations with the Flanders Interaction Analysis System, which measures interactions between the teacher and class, and between the teacher and each student. The researchers identified significant differences in 6 of the 12 variables in teachers' interactions with Anglo as compared with Chicano students: teacher praising, teacher acceptance or use of student ideas, teacher questioning, positive teacher response (warmth, approval), all noncriticizing teacher talk, and all student speaking were higher for the Anglo than for the Chicano students (Mexican American Education Study, 1973). Further, Rosenthal and Jacobson (1968) and Good and Brophy (1972) showed that teachers' attitudes and expectations toward particular groups will affect their behavior towards these groups and may also influence students' performance. Sergiovanni (1987) extended this line of thinking to the expectation that *all* schools hold for the success of *all* students.

In the general literature on effective schools, the academic achievement of the average student is used as a measure of effectiveness, and the no-nonsense, subject-matter oriented teacher who gives whole-group presentations followed by directed recitation is considered the model. This type of instructional environment is not, however, conducive to the highest academic growth among poor urban students (Hilliard, 1992; Stedman, 1985). Brophy (1979) concluded that students of low socioeconomic status seemed to respond better to teachers who were warm and encouraging, gave praise, and minimized criticism, than they did to teachers who were "businesslike and demanding" (p. 737). Cazden, John, and Hymes (1972) documented the importance of the teacher's understanding of linguistic differences as a vehicle for enabling teachers to "hear through" children's language and to listen for their meanings rather than their "errors."

Westby and Rouse (1985) discussed cultural minority children as coming from a *high-context culture,* which requires a less individually competitive environment; conversely, students from a *low-context culture,* usually the Anglo-American culture, respond better to a school environment that is structured and competitive. Westby and Rouse (1985) have summarized a number of the common differences between the norms of the Anglo (low context) and the minority (high context) cultures. The Anglo culture is characterized by these features:

◆ Individual functioning.

◆ One person in control.

◆ Precise, explicit messages.

◆ "Education leads to advancement".

◆ Sacrifice "now" for the future.

◆ Time consists of single events.

◆ Activities are scheduled.

◆ Talking and planning for the future.

◆ Emphasis on time and success.

The minority culture, according to Westby and Rouse, is more likely to be characterized by these features:

◆ Group functioning (member is part of group).

◆ No attempt for an individual to control.

◆ Unresponsive to structure.

◆ Language has a "now" purpose.

◆ Response to immediate (now) payoff.

◆ Time consists of several events at once.

◆ Not responsive to schedules, time limits.

If a team is composed of members with such differences in norms, misunderstandings and conflicts may arise. Educators who are sensitive to the needs of culturally and linguistically diverse students should provide opportunities throughout the school day that support the child's cultural learning style. For example, high-context activities, such as art, music, and home economics, which involve group participation and less structure, may be more effective for students from some cultures than are seatwork and programmed instruction.

Similarly, Gilbert and Gay (1987) reported that poor black children prefer activities that involve group sharing and nondirective teacher intervention. Additionally, the authors mentioned that poor black children evidence *stage-setting* behaviors, such as sharpening pencils, asking for repeated directions, and checking with peers as to instructions, before beginning a task. Stage-setting behavior is often punished by teachers, who tend to be time-oriented. But completion of a task within a time allocation is not as important to these children as is attempting to do the task. Recognition for effort is expected by the students, although teachers often praise them only when they have completed the task. Gilbert and Gay suggested that professionals who understand these differences in learning and behavioral styles do not need to compromise the school's objectives for quality performance in their provision of learning environments and activities that more appropriately match the needs of minority students.

Perhaps the conflict between what an individual's culture values and the behaviors expected by the system's dominant culture can never be satisfactorily resolved: those who refuse to conform do not succeed in places like school; those who conform have denied their heritage (Benevides, 1980). On the other hand, Hale-Benson (1986) suggested that black students who eventually achieve are those who refuse to accept a demeaning relationship with their teachers.

Tharp (1989) concludes "there is evidence that when cultural differences in social organization, sociolinguistic, cognition, and motivation are reflected in compatible classroom practices, such compatibility makes for classrooms that are endorsed by culture members and students of those cultures and are associated with greater child participation and enjoyment and better school achievement" (p.355). Harry (1992b) states that cultural incongruity in instruction and curriculum is what puts a child at risk for failure. She defines cultural incongruity as a mismatch of one's teaching style with the child's learning style. There is ample research that supports the notion that mainstream American classrooms emphasize analytical and verbal skills with a highly competitive and behavioristic orientation. Yet, Harry observed that children from culturally and linguistically diverse backgrounds learn best in an environment that is more imaginative, highly contextual, and less adult-directed.

Certain teacher behaviors have been observed which better match the learning styles of culturally and linguistically diverse children including "slower pacing of verbal exchanges during lessons, less teacher-directed and more peer-directed cooperative activity, greater self-determination of students' behavior, and a low-keyed style that does not 'spotlight' individual students" (Harry, 1991b, p. 76). The specific strategies for implementing educational programs for students from culturally and linguistically diverse groups will be discussed in Chapter 10. More detailed information on the limited English proficient student's characteristics and educational needs will be included.

Effect on the Family

Mrs. Sonyo, a Filipino mother of a 5-year-old child with developmental delays, was referred by the special education teacher to the school social worker because of the mothers' inability to follow through on toilet-training programs implemented in school. The social worker made a home visit. She discovered that the 5-year-old boy was allowed to be without underwear and was punished for urinating only by being removed from the area. The social worker told Mrs. Sonyo that if she did not intervene with her son's problem, she would have to report her to the Department of Child Protective Services.

In this scenario, the professional must understand the cultural values and beliefs of families from this nondominant cultural group to avoid an insensitive scene. Often professionals working with culturally and linguistically diverse families of children with disabilities view the family's child-rearing customs as faulty and make erroneous judgments as to the family's coping strategies. In fact, the opposite is often true. Some ethnic family child-rearing beliefs are actually strengths for coping with the child with disabilities. For example, Mrs. Sonyo believes her child is a gift from God and that he brings good luck and blessings to the family. In the Filipino culture, young children are given much attention and are allowed to mature without excessive external intervention (Kumabe, Nishida, & Hepworth, 1985).

Professionals need to understand the influences of culture on the family's beliefs and customs. Comprehending the acculturation process of families from diverse ethnic groups is a prerequisite to working effectively with those families in a collaborative partnership. For example, a family's religion and spirituality have traditionally been overlooked by professionals, yet many families report that their faith provides them significant support (Hanson & Lynch, 1992). Thus, religious practice becomes an area professionals need to understand as well. Hanson, Lynch, and Wayman (1990) provide valuable strategies for gathering information from families in the areas of childrearing practices, views of disabilities, views of special education intervention, views of family roles, and communication styles. The following questions can guide professionals in becoming knowledgeable about the family's cultural beliefs:

◆ How many years has the family been in the United States?

◆ What were the family's living conditions in their native country?

◆ Was the family exposed to war or turmoil in their native country?

◆ Does the family accept English as a second language in the home?

◆ Is the family literate in their native language?

◆ Do extended family members play a role in the family system?

◆ Does the family live in a community that is made up predominantly of persons from their same culture?

◆ Does the family have respect for elders and people in authority?

◆ How do the culturally and linguistically diverse family members feel about their child's disabilities?

◆ What does the family believe caused the child's disabilities?

◆ Does the family accept Western values of scientific medicine and technological basis for health care?

◆ Does the family believe in having their child with disabilities go to religious healers, curanderos, witch doctors, elders, and so on?

The answers to these questions will provide the professional with some measure of the level of acculturation of the family to the dominant culture. Conflicts are found especially in families who are recent immigrants into a new culture. The conflicts may result in alienation from the original culture, in family instability, and in *intergenerational differences* (Harry, 1992c; Santisteban, 1980; Szapocznik, Perez-Vidal, Kurtines, & Hervis, 1986). People in a state of cultural transition may experience a high degree of psychological distress (Hernandez, 1982). The profiles that can be generated from informal methods of assessing family values and cultural beliefs vary within cultural groups such as Asians, Hispanics, and blacks. For example, there is a wide range of *intracultural and linguistic differences* among Cubans, Puerto Ricans, Central and South Americans, Spaniards, and Mexicans (Harry, 1992a; Isaacs, 1986; Mardiros, 1989). Professionals must not overgeneralize information on cultural groups and inadvertently fall into stereotyping behavior.

Effect on the School

The school professional's behavior is influenced by the cultural context within which that organization operates. Sims (1980), in his analysis of the reasons for difficulty in the integration of culturally different children with disabilities into the schools, has suggested that the difficulties in integration stem from three Western European ideas:

> (1) a disposition to regard anything short of perfection as unacceptable; (2) an intense emphasis on respect for authority, obedience to family, and loyalty to God; (3) a perception that those who are culturally or radically different are inferior. (p. 36)

To further illustrate the source of cultural conflict existing in schools today, Carlson (1964) labeled organizations as *domesticated* or *wild*, in terms of the control of both the organization and the client over their relationship. A private university, for example, is wild because of its control over admissions and its clients' voluntary enrollment. A public high school, which must accept all students and operates on compulsory attendance, is domesticated. The team leader who operates within the culture of a public school (or clinical program) will need to understand at least three major limitations imposed upon domesticated programs: the slowness in acceptance of innovations, the limited ability to encourage improved performance, and the difficulty of establishing common goals.

Because wild organizations depend on competition for survival, they are more likely to encourage innovation. Domesticated organizations, on the other hand, are protected from competition and need not perform at a high level to survive. They are, however, burdened by numerous public regulations. This cultural variable—the absence of competition as an organizational value—may prevent educational leaders from moving ahead quickly in the implementation of innovations.

For organizations that compete, innovations that lead to an increase in sales or demand for services are the major measures of success. Reinforcement is transmitted by the administrator to those most responsible for innovations that result in product or service improvement. Regulations that impede improvement are discarded and risk taking is encouraged (Peters & Austin, 1985). In noncompetitive organizational cultures, there is no direct relationship between performance and reward. This lack of clear mechanisms for rewarding desired behavior may make it more difficult for the leader to modify the individual staff member's behavior.

Additionally, it is more difficult for professionals in schools than for CEOs in private industries to establish common goals. Although it is more difficult, it is not impossible for the professional to accomplish goal setting. Staff collaboration has been identified as the norm in effective schools (Purkey & Smith, 1985; Snyder & Johnson, 1985), and researchers have emphasized the importance of each school's staff in analyzing its own particular culture and mission. DeBevoise (1984) stressed the importance of basing the focus of school improvement on the specific needs of the community from which the mission was derived. Stedman (1985) pointed out that the school's contextual variables were particularly important in urban schools, because in these schools the mission may be broader than the traditional focus on academic achievement as measured by standardized tests. This contextual variable may make it more difficult for school leaders to identify the common goals upon which a school's mission should be based.

The complexities of cultural differences make it difficult for professionals in educational organizations to succeed. However, the professional who takes these variables into account can be ultimately more successful than the professional who does not. People from "powerless" groups who aspire to team leadership positions may start with an advantage: They already know that differences in culture and in context exist, and they have learned to adjust to these differences. However, it is important to note that professionals who come from a minority culture are not always automatically sensitive to the conflicts that others in their culture experience in adjusting to the mainstream.

Effect on Team Members

As previously stated, the team member's behavior is influenced by the values and standards of the culture in which the organization exists. For public schools, the school's constituent groups may be predominantly middle class and Anglo. For example, Christensen (1992) reported from a study that although 53% of the children and families served by early intervention program were of color, only 17% of the staff represented people of color. Williams (1992) noted an absence of racial diversity within teachers' ranks, where 90% are Caucasian, 7% are African-American, and the remaining 3% come from other nonwhite backgrounds. Similarly, predictions of the number of African-American teachers will drop to barely 5% by the year 2000 (Ford, 1992).

Although clearly in the minority, people from the school's nondominant culture who aspire to become effective team members will experience some conflicts as they encounter the differences between what they value and the behaviors expected of entry-level professionals in positions for potential leadership. Blacks may be troubled, for instance, by the thought that they have to become "Uncle Toms" to be accepted and to succeed.

People who wish to facilitate organizational change do need to understand the organization's rules and to work constructively within the system. This does not mean, however, that they must abandon their own values. Rather, they practice *strategic compliance*. One of the most fascinating ironies is that, though the same quiet, obedient, cooperative behavior is expected of neophyte leaders as is expected of school children, those who ultimately achieve high-level positions of leadership are allowed to be dominant and encouraged to be decisive. For those who survive, there is ultimately hope that they will be able to reaffirm their individuality. The following vignette further illustrates the dilemma encountered by a team member from a nondominant culture with the dominant school culture.

Ms. Gonzales is a teacher of students with learning disabilities. She is a native of Nicaragua and currently is having problems with her principal. Mr. Jones, an Anglo-American, is her principal and has given her unsatisfactory evaluations on her teaching performance. Mr. Jones reports that Ms. Gonzales "babies" the students in her class and provides them with little discipline. He states that she is not demanding enough of her students, and that they are not moving through the curriculum as quickly as he would like. Ms. Gonzales has responded to conferences with Mr. Jones on her poor evaluations in an aggressive manner, threatening Mr. Jones with a grievance and discrimination.

Meanwhile, the students in Ms. Gonzales's program are making minimal progress. Ms. Alvarez, a Puerto Rican special education supervisor, has been included in the conferences in hopes of mediating between the two professionals. Her analysis of the situation is that Ms. Gonzales strongly believes, like many Hispanic women, that children should be indulged and taken care of in a mothering manner. Ms. Gonzales believes that children with disabilities are special children from God and that they should be pampered, due to the suffering they are experiencing as children with disabilities.

Collaboration among these professionals requires an awareness and respect for the other's beliefs and values. Examples of these have been presented earlier in this chapter. Both Mr. Jones and Ms. Gonzales must come to an understanding of each other's perspectives and respect each other's point of view. Ms. Gonzales's nurturing behavior does not necessarily have to be perceived as negative or as a weakness. However, Ms. Gonzales must be held accountable for the students' Individual Educational Plan (IEP) objectives and structured classroom activities. She must understand that Mr. Jones expects his students to perform in school and to progress through the curriculum adopted by the school district. Ms. Alvarez, the supervisor, may be able to serve as a *culture broker* in this situation (Correa, 1989). The culture broker provides each professional with an understanding of one another's perspective. In this case, Ms. Alvarez was the culture broker, blending both the school-culture perspective and the Hispanic-culture perspective into the problem-solving team process.

People from the nondominant culture who aspire to become professionals in special services programs will confront some conflicts as they encounter the differences between what they value and the behaviors expected of good students and families in traditional schools in the United States. It may take more time, energy, and commitment on the part of professionals from different cultural backgrounds to develop a level of shared understanding and common knowledge that will provide them with a basis for collaboration. Intercultural collaboration of professionals with families allows all members of the team to contribute to the construction of effective instructional programs for students of diverse backgrounds. Quality programming for multicultural students with disabilities is worth the time and energy of team members.

APPLICATION

A school district in a major metropolitan city is preparing for the start of a new school year and teacher preplanning inservices. The assistant principal of a local elementary school, Ms. Roledo, is in charge of providing the new teachers with an orientation to the school. This year the school will have a student population composed of about 70% Mexican-Americans, 20% Native American, and 10% Anglo students. The new teachers are mostly Anglo-American, and they are in need of understanding of the cultural background of their Mexican-American students. Ms. Roledo arranges the following action plan for implementing an inservice titled "Understanding Mexican-American Students and Their Families".

Step 1. Consultation with Mexican-American School Personnel. Ms. Roledo arranges a meeting of the faculty members who are Mexican-Americans. She asks them for their input on the issues that should be raised in the inservice. She asks them to outline any problems they may have encountered with faculty or staff members who were not sensitive to the Mexican-American population.

Step 2. Consultation with Target Mexican-American Families. Ms. Roledo contacts a few Mexican-American families who have been active in the school program during the past year. She asks them to talk openly about what they would like teachers to know about the Mexican-American culture. Ms. Roledo also asks about any problems the families encountered with teachers at the school.

Step 3. Consultation with Mexican-American High School Students. Ms. Roledo meets with a few Mexican-American students who have been at the school for at least a year. She gathers information from them on what they think teachers should know about Mexican-American values and culture. She asks what problems they have encountered in school that might have been related to conflicts arising from different understandings of cultural backgrounds.

Step 4. Setting up a Panel Discussion. Ms. Roledo invites three Mexican-Americans—a faculty member, a parent, and a student—to serve on a panel for an inservice presentation. She gives them each topical areas that will be discussed during the panel discussion and spends some time listening to them practice their responses to the questions. She uses the information as a basis for preparing a brief handbook on awareness of the culture of Mexican-American students and their families.

Step 5. Compiling Information. Ms. Roledo contacts the local Mexican-American church and invites the priest to visit. She asks for his reactions to the information gathered from the other consultations. He reviews the handbook.

Step 6. Presentation of Inservice. During the first week of preplanning, Ms. Roledo presents an inservice workshop. Each member of the school staff receives the handbook, along with particular information about the Mexican-American students currently enrolled. The panel discussion group members then make their comments. Time is allowed for interaction between panel members and school staff. The inservice is geared to the culture of Mexican-Americans in general, while encompassing the particular "lived culture" of Mexican-Americans in the school community. Ms. Roledo hopes that hereafter Mexican-American students will not be overreferred for special services on the basis of their culturally determined behaviors.

SUMMARY

The following delineate the critical needs for cultural competence when working with interactive teaming:

◆ It is important for special services professionals to first learn to understand their own cultural identity and then to accept cultural diversity and understand its dimensions.

◆ Although understanding cultural and linguistic diversity results in the improvement of educational and related services programs for all students, the consequences of a lack of this understanding are erroneous labeling of students as disabled and misplacement in special education programs.

◆ Be realistic. Schools are societal institutions designed to transmit the culture of the dominant society. Integration may be difficult if the dominant society views the culturally or linguistically different person as inferior or undesirable.

◆ It is equally as important to be realistic about the difficulties of domesticated organizations in encouraging innovations and defining common goals. Public programs are domesticated organizations, and the interactive team is one that seeks innovation based on the establishment of common goals.

◆ Effective educational services for ethnic minority students and their families require more than just an understanding of cultural values, beliefs, and customs. Sensitization to cultural differences must be followed by action and implementation. Collaboration with families and professionals from diverse cultural backgrounds can be an enriching experience for all involved.

In this chapter the focus has been on the consideration of cultural differences—both those that arise from the cultural differences among team members and the people they serve, and those that originate within the context of the organization. A variety of cultural and linguistic differences have been presented as examples in need of understanding, but not as stereotypes for which prescriptions can be written. This understanding of cultural differences is presented as a facilitating factor for the work of the interactive team: the planning, implementation, and evaluation of the culturally and linguistically diverse student's program.

ACTIVITIES

1. Play a cultural simulation game such as *BaFá BaFá* (Shirts, 1977). Help the class acknowledge the diverse feeling of interacting with a different culture. Transcribe their feelings on transparencies as they are discussed.

2. Facilitate a cultural journey (Hanson & Lynch, 1992). Ask students to describe their own culture, beliefs, traditions, foods, and holidays. Have students describe family stories depicting their families' experiences in the United States. Ask students if they have ever experienced discrimination due to their cultural background.

3. Discuss culturally diverse experiences among class participants. What countries have the participants visited? What cultural groups did they interact with? What

were the cultural norms experienced by the participants? Were their experiences positive or negative, or both?

4. Observe a local bilingual education program. What were the students like? How did the teachers and others interact with the students?

REFERENCES

Benevides, A. (1980). Cultural awareness training for the exceptional teacher. *Teaching Exceptional Children, 13,* 8–11.

Briggs, L. (1982). Understanding the role of language in bilingual education. In M. Montero (Ed.), *Bilingual education teacher handbook* (pp. 13–36). Cambridge, MA: Evaluation, Dissemination, and Assessment Center for Bilingual Education.

Brophy, J. (1979). Teacher behavior and its effects. *Journal of Educational Psychology, 71,* 733–750.

Carlson, R. (1964). Environmental constraints and organizational consequences: The public school and its clients. In D. Griffiths (Ed.), *Behavioral science and educational administration: The Thirty-sixth yearbook of the NSSE* (pp. 262–278). Chicago: University of Chicago Press.

Cazden, C., John, V., & Hymes, P. (Eds.). (1972). *Functions of language in the classroom.* New York: Teachers College Press.

Christensen, C. M. (1992). Multicultural competencies in early intervention: Training professionals for a pluralistic society. *Infants and Young Children, 4,* 49–83.

Cooper, A. M. (1990). Fallacy of a single model for school achievement: Considerations for ethnicity. *Sociological Perspectives, 33,* 159–184.

Correa, V. C. (1989). Involving culturally diverse families in the education of their limited English proficient handicapped and at risk children. In S. Fradd & M. J. Weismantel (Eds.), *Meeting the needs of culturally and linguistically different students: A handbook for educators* (pp. 130–144). San Diego: College-Hill Press.

DeBevoise, W. (1984). Synthesis of research on the principal as instructional leader. *Educational Leadership, 41*(5), 14–20.

Dilworth-Anderson, P., Burton, L., & Johnson, B. (1993). Reframing theories for understanding race, ethnicity, and families. In P. G. Boss, W. J. Doherty, R. LaRoss, W. R. Schumm, & S. K. Steinmetz (Eds.), *Sourcebook of family theories and methods: A contextual approach* (pp. 627–649). New York: Plenum.

Edelsky, C., & Hudelson, S. (1982). Reversing the roles of Chicano and Anglo children in the bilingual classroom: On the communicative competence of the helper. In J. A. Fishman & G. D. Keller (Eds.), *Bilingual education for Hispanic students in the United States.* New York: Teachers College.

Edelsky, C., & Hudelson, S. (1989). *Contextual complexities: Written language policies for bilingual programs.* Washington, DC: Office of Educational Research and Improvement. ERIC Document No. ED 314943.

Ford, B. A. (1992). Multicultural education training for special educators working with African-American youth. *Exceptional Children, 59,* 107–114.

Gilbert, S., & Gay, G. (1987). Improving the success in school of poor black children. *Phi Delta Kappan, 67,* 133–137.

Gomes, B. (1983). Discourse patterns. In J. Gelatt & M. P. Anderson (Eds.), *Bilingual language learning system.* Rockville, MD: American Speech-Language-Hearing Association. OSERS/DPR Grant #G0081101996.

Good, T., & Brophy, J. (1972). Behavioral expressions of teacher attitudes. *Journal of Educational Psychology, 63,* 618–624.

Hale-Benson, J. (1986). *Black-children: Their roots, culture and learning styles.* Baltimore, MD: Johns Hopkins University Press.

Hallman, C. L., Bryant, W. W., Campbell, A., McGuire, J., & Bowman, K. (1983). *U.S. American value orientations* (Cultural Monograph No. 4). Gainesville: University of Florida, College of Education, Bilingual Multicultural Education Training Project.

Hanson, M. J., & Lynch, E. W. (1992). Family diversity: Implications for policy and practice. *Topics in Early Childhood Special Education, 12*, 283–306.

Hanson, M. J., Lynch, E. W., & Wayman, K. I. (1990). Honoring the cultural diversity of families when gathering data. *Topics in Early Childhood Special Education, 10*, 112–131.

Harry, B. (1992a). An ethnographic study of cross-cultural communication with Puerto Rican-American families in the special education system. *American Educational Research Journal, 29*, 471–494.

Harry, B. (1992b). *Cultural diversity, families, and the special education system: Communication and empowerment*. New York: Teachers College Press.

Harry, B. (1992c). Developing cultural self-awareness: The first step in value clarification for early interventionists. *Topics in Early Childhood Special Education, 12, 333–350.*

Henderson, R. (1982). *Teacher relations with minority students and their families*. Washington, DC: American Association of Colleges for Teacher Education. OSERS/DPP Grant #OEG007902045.

Hernandez, C. (1982). Acculturation of Cuban mothers and children's adjustment. (Doctoral dissertation, Hofstra University, 1983). Dissertation Abstracts International, 43, 4148B.

Hilliard, A. G. (1992). Behavioral style, culture, and teaching and learning. *Journal of Negro Education, 61,* 370–377.

Isaacs, M. (1986). *Developing mental health programs for minority youth and their families: A summary of conference proceedings*. Georgetown, MD: Georgetown University CASSP Technical Assistance Center.

Johnson, S., & Johnson, V. (1988). *Motivating minority students: Strategies that work*. Springfield, IL: Charles C. Thomas.

Kumabe, K., Nishida, C., & Hepworth, D. (1985). *Bridging ethnocultural diversity in social work and health*. Honolulu: University of Hawaii, School of Social Work.

Longstreet, W. S. (1978). *Aspects of ethnicity*. New York: Teachers College Press.

Lynch, E. W., & Hanson, M. J. (1992). *Developing cross-cultural competence: A guide for working with young children and their families*. Baltimore: Paul H. Brookes.

Mardiros, M. (1989). Conception of childhood disability among Mexican-American parents. *Medical Anthropology, 12,* 55–68.

Mexican American Education Study. (1973, March). *Teachers and Students*. Washington, DC: U.S. Civil Rights Commission.

Minuchin, S. (1974). *Families and family therapy*. Cambridge, MA: Harvard University Press.

Ogbu, J. U. (1985). Research currents: Cultural-ecological influences on minority school learning. *Language Arts, 62,* 860–869.

Pepper, F. C. (1976). Teaching the American Indian child in mainstream settings. In R. L. Jones (Ed.), *Mainstreaming and the minority child* (pp. 133–158). Minneapolis, MN: The Council for Exceptional Children.

Peters, T., & Austin, N. (1985). *A passion for excellence: The leadership difference*. New York: Warner Books.

Purkey, S., & Smith, M. (1985). School reform: The district policy implications of the effective school's literature. *Elementary School Journal, 85,* 353–390.

Rosenthal, R., & Jacobson, L. (1986). *Pygmalion in the classroom: Teacher expectation and pupils' intellectual development*. New York: Holt, Rinehart, and Winston.

Santisteban, D. (1980). *Acculturation, assimilation, and psychological stress* [Review of *Narrative, literacy, and face in interethnic communication*, by R. Scollon & S. Scollon]. Norwood, NJ: Ablex Press.

Scollon, R., & Scollon, S. (1981). *Narrative, literacy, and face in interethnic communication*. Norwood, NJ: Ablex Press.

Sergiovanni, T. (1987). *The principalship: A reflective practice perspective*. Boston: Allyn & Bacon.

Shirts, G. (1977). *Bafá Bafá: A cross cultural simulation*. Del Mar, CA: Simille II.

Sims, W. (1980). Humanizing education for handicapped and culturally different students. *The Journal of Professional Studies, 5,* 35–48.

Smalley, S. (1984). Cultural differences. In C. Morsink (Ed.), *Teaching special needs students in regular classrooms* (pp. 54–59). Boston: Little, Brown and Company.

Snyder, K., & Johnson, W. (1985). Retraining principals for productive school management. *Educational Research Quarterly, 9*(3), 19–27.

Stedman, L. (1985). A new look at the effective schools literature. *Urban Education, 20,* 295–326.

Szapocznik, J., Rio, A., Perez-Vidal, A., Kurtines, W., & Hervis, O. (1986). Bicultural effectiveness training: An experimental test of intervention modality for families experiencing intergenerational/intercultural conflict. *Hispanic Journal of Behavioral Sciences, 8,* 303–330.

Tharp, R. G. (1989). Psychocultural variables and constants: Effects on teaching and learning in schools. *American Psychologist, 44,* 349-359.

United States Commission on Civil Rights. (1975). *A better chance to learn: Bilingual/bicultural education.* Washington, DC: U.S. Government Printing Office.

Warren, R. (1981). Values, cultural diversity, and classroom practice: The dilemma of unfulfilled expectations. In C. C. Thomas (Ed.), *Toward a research base for the least restrictive environment: A collection of papers* (pp. 159–167). Lexington: University of Kentucky, Dean's Grant Project. (OSERS/DPP Grant #G007801072).

We the people. *Modern Maturity,* June–July, 1992, 30–34.

Westby, C. E., & Rouse, G. R. (1985). Culture in education and the instruction of language learning-disabled students. *Topics in Language Disorders, 5*(4), 15–28.

Williams, B. F. (1992). Changing demographics: Challenges for educators. *Intervention in School and Clinic, 3,* 157–163.

CHAPTER 7

Developing Service Coordination Skills

Essential Skills for Leadership of Professionals

Research on Leadership
Summary of Skills for Team Leaders

Initial Tasks of the Team Leader

Setting up the Team
Identifying Resources
Establishing Operating Procedures

Service Coordination Procedures for Quality Advisors

Coordinating Needed Services
Delegating Responsibility
Providing Follow-Up
Guiding Paraprofessionals and Volunteers

Application

Summary

TOPICS IN THIS CHAPTER INCLUDE

◆ Discussion of essential skills for leadership of professionals.

◆ Description of the initial tasks of the team leader.

◆ Guidelines for procedures needed by subsequent team leaders, who serve as quality advisors: coordinating services, delegating responsibility, providing follow-up, and guiding paraprofessionals or volunteers.

◆ Application of the interactive teaming model to a situation in which the quality advisor delegates to and provides follow-up with a paraprofessional.

At their first meeting, the team discussed the educational and social needs and placement options for Juan, an 11-year-old Hispanic boy with diabetes, who was having difficulties in reading achievement and social adjustment. The first meeting was attended by Juan's mother, his sixth-grade teacher, the special educator (an LD resource teacher), the speech-language therapist, and the school nurse; it was chaired by the school counselor. After hearing the parent and teacher's descriptions of Juan's reading difficulties, the counselor noted that it was late and recommended gathering more information about Juan's diet, his classroom behavior, and his language abilities in English, his second language. When the team met again two weeks later, the LD teacher was the only person who had gathered additional information.

As the counselor attempted to initiate problem solving at the second meeting, he was puzzled by the group's reactions. He first noted that Juan's mother was not participating, even when she was asked to speak. Then he noted that the sixth-grade teacher responded with hostility to the report on classroom observations by the LD teacher, while the nurse and speech-language therapist completed unrelated paperwork. The second meeting ended as the first one had, with the counselor suggesting that the group still needed additional information. The parent walked quietly away, while several other participants muttered protests about wasted time.

This team had no goals and no operating procedures. The team suffered from a lack of direction, because the counselor was viewed only as a facilitator who convened the meeting and encouraged the discussion. Everybody was assumed to be working together but nobody was "in charge." The leader neither delegated responsibility nor conducted follow-up activities. The special educator, who took nondelegated initiative for conducting a classroom observation, was viewed by the classroom teacher as an intruder. Juan's mother, who had assumed that she was to be the hostess for a social visit from the school nurse, had not been contacted. The counselor, who did not understand the essential skills and procedures for team leadership, had apparently assumed that everyone on the team would just "collaborate."

In this chapter, the essential skills for team leaders are presented from the perspective that they involve the management of tasks rather than people. The initial tasks of the team leader are described, and the procedures used subsequently by the leader in service coordination are discussed in detail. To avoid confusion, we will call the subsequent leaders who coordinate services the "quality advisors." Finally, the interactive teaming model is applied to the procedures for leadership in service coordination through an example of how a team leader can delegate to and provide follow-up on the activities of a paraprofessional.

ESSENTIAL SKILLS FOR LEADERSHIP OF PROFESSIONALS

For an interactive team to function effectively, it needs a special kind of leadership. Drucker (1969) pointed out long ago that the management of professionals (such as those who make up the interactive team) is much more complex than the management of workers. It is collegial rather than directive and needs to occur within an organization that is performance-oriented rather than authority-oriented.

In the interactive teaming model, the role of leader can be filled by any member of the team. The leader is selected by the program administrator, who delegates responsibility for coordination of services to this leader. The team leader is a service coordinator who maintains the continuity of the team over time and across meetings that focus on the special needs of individual students. For each individual student, the team also uses as its quality advisor the person with greatest knowledge of the services or content expertise about the case. While the advisor changes with each case, the leader remains constant.

To be effective, the leader needs to be supportive of others as they carry out their tasks and must assume accountability for the overall effectiveness of the program.

The team leader is aware of the different roles and perspectives of team members as described previously, and is able to select, from among the expertise presented by members of the team, the best person(s) to whom to delegate responsibility for coordinating a particular student's program. The leader needs to demonstrate all the skills, attributes, and behaviors of effective leaders in organizations. These skills, attributes, and behaviors are now summarized as a synthesis of the research on effective leadership.

Research on Leadership

Effective leaders can help professionals with different backgrounds and vocabularies to focus on a common set of future goals (Hempfill, 1958; Kaplan, 1985; Lipham, 1964; Deming, 1986; Juran, 1992).

Investigators observing leaders in diverse contexts have identified two broad dimensions of leadership. They have determined that the effective leader needs to initiate *structure* and demonstrate *consideration*. To initiate structure is to establish patterns, methods, and procedures for accomplishing tasks. To demonstrate consideration is to develop trust, warmth, and respect with the staff (Covey, 1990; Halpin & Winer, 1957; Hempfill & Coons, 1957).

Some early students of leadership described leaders as either task-oriented or relationship-oriented (McGregor, 1960), although Hersey and Blanchard (1974) were among those who questioned the dichotomous view. In their categorization of styles, Hersey and Blanchard suggested also that the effective leader had a range of styles and that the ability to adapt style to the situation was an important dimension of effectiveness. Further expansion of the concept of adaptation in leadership was proposed by Bennis (1989) and Covey (1990).

The extension of Hersey and Blanchard's work into studies of effective school principals showed that these school leaders had a variety of styles, but all demonstrated that they were able to encourage staff collaboration and develop innovative practices (DeBevoise, 1984; Hall, Rutherford, Hord, & Huling, 1984). According to the research of Clifton and his associates (SRI, 1980), the effective school leader develops positive relationships with colleagues and is capable of creating an open, supportive environment. Covey (1990) emphasizes that caring and integrity must be genuine and integral to the leader's being, as opposed to superficially acquired techniques. Sergiovanni (1992) views school leadership as a form of stewardship: relating to individuals, honoring their values. He terms this a "servant leadership" based on trust and mutual respect.

The concept of *power* has also been widely discussed as a dimension of leadership. Effective leaders are able to use power for organizational good, as opposed to personal gain (McClelland, 1975). The most productive exercise of power in the leadership of professionals comes through participatory management, which empowers others (Powers & Powers, 1983). This concept is discussed further in Chapter 8. These leadership concepts, inherent in Deming's (1986) Total Quality Management (TQM), were originally initiated in business and industry. The TQM leadership concepts are based on teamwork, and focus on team members as participants in decisions that seek continuous improvement in response to feedback from "customers", clients, or constituents. These concepts have been extended to applications in educational institutions by Tribus (1992) and Bonstingl (1992). The TQM principles have been applied also to school restructuring as it relates to programs for special students by Audette and Algozzine (1992).

The team leader should keep in mind that the team's goal is continuous improvement. Deming (1986), who emphasized the importance of "constancy of purpose," indicated that the critical steps in the continuous improvement cycle are (a) plan, (b) do, (c) check, and (d) act. He suggests that improvement of the system, or process, is the way to obtain results. This point of view enables team members to focus on a common goal, and to identify and eliminate barriers to achieving this goal. A mind set for long-range planning, with continuous improvement, is essential for the team leader, who can then encourage flexibility, risk-taking, and innovation.

Wilson (1993) summarizes several studies of characteristics and behaviors of empowered teacher-leaders, which are similar to those ascribed to effective leaders in general. They are hard-working and creative; they collaborate with others to provide assistance. In defining the characteristics of effective teacher-leaders, Wilson also cites the work of Kouzes and Posner (1990), who conducted a major study of managers in public and private organizations. Their research supports earlier conclusions of others in regard to effective leadership that empowers team members: Leaders take risks, challenge the existing system, communicate the shared vision, engage in teamwork, and support and inspire others. Effective leaders coach and encourage their teams, while serving as role-models and planners. These teacher-leaders are more comparable to the team leaders described in this text. They do not seek full "leadership" roles as administrators; instead, they function as team leaders in collegial settings.

Summary of Skills for Team Leaders

In summary, leadership has been defined as behavior that facilitates change. It has a dimension of power, which focuses on the strength necessary to accomplish goals that are believed to promote the common good. Effective leadership includes both an emphasis on fulfilling the organization's mission and on the development of trust and respect between the leader and group. From a synthesis of the behaviors, skills, and attributes found in the leaders of organizations that meet the criteria of excellence, six generic constructs that describe the effective leadership of professionals are proposed. Their definitions are presented in Figure 7–1.

As can be seen in Figure 7–1, the leader of professionals needs special skills to maintain the careful balance between directing the activities of the group and allowing competent professionals the autonomy they require to function effectively. As indicated earlier, in reaching this balance, it is important for the leader to understand his or her role as the management of tasks, rather than the management of people. Finally, the team leader should understand that complexity, conflict, and ambiguity are to be expected. Bennis (1989) emphasizes that "sooner or later, each of us has to accept the fact that complexity is here to stay and that order begins in chaos" (p. 113).

1. **Initiating Structure**

   This is the leader's task-oriented behavior of stating the organization's purpose, establishing the mechanisms and procedures, and defining the roles of members, through which the organization may fulfill its mission (Halpin, 1959; Lazarsfeld, 1963; Gersten, Carnine, & Green (1982). It has a "power" dimension, focused on the use of power for corporate as opposed to personal uses (McClelland, 1975; Covey, 1990; Deming, 1986), and for the educational leader, it includes a personal commitment to a cause that can benefit others (SRI, 1980).

2. **Facilitating Goal Achievement**

   These are the leader's acts of implementation that enable the team members to collaborate in the fulfillment of their common purpose (Lazarsfeld, 1963; SRI, 1980; Bennis, 1989; Senge, 1990). These acts include translating the organization's mission into specific goal statements, delegating tasks, and reinforcing excellence (Blanchard & Johnson, 1982; Gersten et al., 1982).

3. **Demonstrating Consideration**

   This is the leader's relationship-oriented behavior, which emphasizes the social and personal aspects of working with people in the organization and building positive, supportive relationships with team members (SRI, 1980). It focuses heavily on providing the work group with support and demonstrating to them that they are respected, trusted, and valued (Halpin, 1959; Lazarsfeld, 1963; Covey, 1990).

4. **Showing Adaptability**

   This is the leader's proactive and reactive behavior that may be classified as situational. It is based in part on Hersey and Blanchard's (1974) concept that leaders have not only a dominant style, which is essentially task-oriented or relationship-oriented, but that effective leaders also have a range of supporting styles from which they can select, depending on the situation.

5. **Using Direct Feedback**

   This is the behavior of listening and being available that shows the leader believes the organization's mission, its workers, and its constituents are important (Peters & Austin, 1985). It includes the leader's assessment of the actions, needs, and viewpoints of patrons, faculty, and students, and the use of this insight in decision making (SRI, 1980; Deming, 1986; Scholtes, 1988; Juran, 1992).

6. **Encouraging Innovations**

   This is the behavior through which the leader builds in provisions for growth, change, and development (Lazarsfeld, 1963). As emphasized by Peters and Austin (1985), Bennis (1989), Covey (1990), and Tribus (1992), it includes support of risk taking to encourage the development of a better service or product. For the leader of the interactive team, this service or product is related to the program developed for the special needs student.

Figure 7–1

Summary of essential skills for leaders of professionals

INITIAL TASKS OF THE TEAM LEADER

The team leader's initial tasks set the stage for effective collaboration. These activities include (a) setting up the team, (b) identifying resources, and (c) establishing operating procedures. Each of these tasks is described briefly.

Setting up the Team

The interactive team is a new and flexible group that is not a part of the established administrative structure within the school or clinical program. In Chapter 4's discussion of the role of the administrator, it was pointed out that the administrator has overall fiscal and legal responsibility for the unit's program. This administrator—the principal or program director—does not usually function as the team leader and therefore needs to *delegate* to the team leader the authority to plan, implement, and evaluate programs for special needs students. This is how the administrator gives the team its legitimacy and autonomy, as described in Chapter 3. It is also another way of showing that the team leader has the administrator's "permission" to accomplish the team's tasks, an essential part of delegating responsibility, described later in this chapter.

Glatthorn and Newberg (1984), in their discussion of the team approach for instructional leadership at the secondary school level, have outlined a four-stage process that describes how the administrator can establish a team with this type of authority. Their guidelines may be adapted for use as initial procedures for setting up the interactive team, as outlined in Figure 7–2. These initial steps are taken to ensure that the current official leader—the administrator of the unit—is involved and supportive, and that all members of the staff understand that specific responsibilities, which are consistent with the organization's overall goals, have been delegated to the interactive team. From that point on, the leadership is vested in the team itself, to be exercised by its designated leader.

Identifying Resources

The initial team leader will want to take steps to identify the human and fiscal resources that are available for the team's use. These steps include analyzing the expertise of potential team members, identifying the available fiscal resources that might be used to support the team's efforts, and organizing information about community resources that are available. These steps are illustrated in Figure 7–3.

As a first step, it will be useful for the team leader to analyze and prepare a brief outline of the professional training and expertise of potential team members, such as that provided in Chapter 4. This analysis will help team members understand the types of knowledge and skills they and others can contribute to the solution of a given student's problems. It will also be useful in helping the team identify the person who should serve as *major service coordinator*—described in Total Quality Management terms as the *quality advisor*—for each student's program planning, implementation, and evaluation.

1. Conduct observations and interviews with administrator and staff to determine:
   - What is the administrator's leadership style?
   - Which individuals are currently performing leadership functions?
   - Which individuals are believed to be capable of leadership?

2. Meet with the administrator to determine:
   - Which leadership functions he or she wishes to perform and which functions may—given the organizational constraints—be delegated to others?

3. Ask administrator in a general meeting of the organization's entire staff to address two issues:
   - Explain how the team's duties are consistent with the overall goals of the organization.
   - Delegate functions to be carried out by the team, under the direction of its leader, with the support of the administrator.

Figure 7–2
Sequence of initial steps in setting up the interactive team

Second, the team leader will need to obtain from the organization's administrator an outline of the *fiscal resources* that have been budgeted for use by the team. This outline will be useful in preventing misunderstandings, such as assuming the budget is unlimited or not knowing that funds are available for particular purposes.

Finally, the team leader will want to obtain a list of community, state, and national resources (advocacy groups, professional organizations, and service agencies) that might contribute their expertise to the cases addressed by the team. It will be useful, during the initial stages of establishing the team's workscope, to compile a reference guide of these resources. This step is the leader's way of showing that people are viewed as major resources, and that the team is concerned with helping people do their jobs effectively.

The types of resources that might be available are shown in Table 7–1.

Wittenmyer (1983) has outlined a systematic procedure for identifying these resources, which are available in any community. She suggests that several resources are available within any community, including the following:

◆ Public interest law firms.
◆ Jaycees/Chamber of Commerce school-business partners.
◆ Big Brother/Big Sister groups.
◆ Foster homes/group homes.

Outline expertise of members

List community resources

Identify budgeted funds

Figure 7–3
Initial steps in identifying resources available to the team

Table 7-1
Possible Community Resources for Special Needs Students

Resources for Prereferral/Service Provision/Evaluation	
General	**Specialized**
Physicians	Clinics: vision, hearing, CP, OT,
Dentists	speech
Mental health clinics	
Social Security offices	
Resources for Instructional Planning	
General	**Specialized**
Day care, nursery	Public schools
YMCA, YWCA	Special day care
Social services	Special groups: ARC, LD, CP, etc.
Welfare services	Special programs: cystic fibrosis,
Community groups: Lions, Elks, Shriners,	sheltered workshops, etc.
Catholic Charities, Jaycees, etc.	Home training
Parent Groups	

Note: From, in part, "Unit Five: Referral, Coordination, and Management of Services by J. Wittenmyer, 1983, in C. M. Del Polito & J.G. Barresi (Eds.), Alliances in Health and Education: Serving Youngsters with Special Needs (pp. 115-133), Washington, DC: American Society of Allied Health Professions.

Establishing Operating Procedures

The team will function more effectively if it has a set of operating procedures that are understood by all members. This involves outlining the legal requirements establishing the mission and conducting effective meetings.

Outlining Legal Requirements.   It is important for the team leader to coordinate the legal requirements for procedures as team members work through the decision points of prereferral, screening, services, instructional planning, and evaluation. The leader will find it particularly useful to provide each team member with a written summary of required legal procedures under which the team needs to operate. Because the legal requirements for the classification and placement of students as "disabled" are the most rigorous, they will be summarized briefly. These requirements include, but are not limited to, information on *informed consent* and *due process* (Howe, 1981). A document explaining these procedures, as required by the jurisdiction in which the organization operates, is always available from the organization's administrator. Gilliam, Kaye, and Soffer (1982) have summarized the legal guidelines required under Public Law 94-142 at each stage of planning and implementing the program for a student who is classified as disabled. Their suggestions for decisions on referral and screening for eligibility, are adapted as Table 7–2.

Specific procedural guidelines are also required during the team meeting for planning the special student's instructional program. Courtnage and Healy (1984) have provided a checklist of these procedures, which may serve as a guide to essential procedures during the program-planning meeting. A brief version of this checklist is shown in Figure 7–4 . These legal procedures must be followed in the event of official referral and screening for placement in special education programs.

Establishing Team Mission.   During its early meetings, the team should establish its mission. The group mission, if stated as a focused and relatively narrow purpose, will help the team direct its actions and set reachable goals. The team leader assists the group in seeing its mission as a clear statement of a problem to be solved. The problem statement guides decisions about what the team wants to accomplish, the information it needs to collect, and the strategies it should select (Scholtes, 1988).

In establishing the mission, the team might use interactive discussions designed to help groups reach consensus. Although many strategies are available, only one is outlined here for illustrative purposes.

The procedures focus first on a *brainstorming* technique, modified from the outline by Dunn and Dunn (1970), which includes a series of questions to help the group

Table 7-2

Legal Requirements and Tasks for Student Referral and Screening for Eligibility Decisions Under Public Law 94-142

Law Requires	
Identification and Referral	**Eligibility**
Identification, location, evaluation, of disabled children (section 121a, 128)	Statement of child's present levels of educational performance
Evaluation to determine disabling condition (121a, 530–532)	
Documented impairment; need for special education and related services	
Tasks Required	
Observe student	Collect data on:
Refer, with data	• Work samples
Advocate for services	• Personal relations
Provide information to parents	• Strengths, weaknesses
Evaluate continually during referral process	
	Attend meeting to:
	• Validate findings
	• Report on effective strategies used

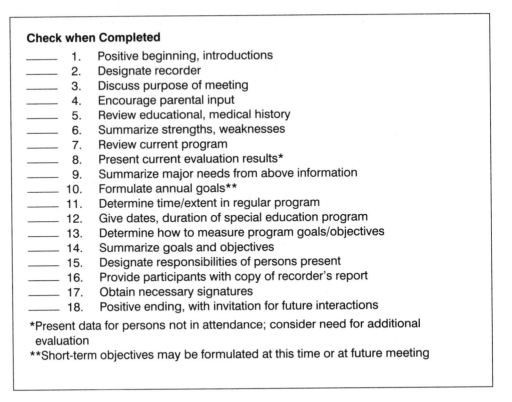

Check when Completed

_____	1.	Positive beginning, introductions
_____	2.	Designate recorder
_____	3.	Discuss purpose of meeting
_____	4.	Encourage parental input
_____	5.	Review educational, medical history
_____	6.	Summarize strengths, weaknesses
_____	7.	Review current program
_____	8.	Present current evaluation results*
_____	9.	Summarize major needs from above information
_____	10.	Formulate annual goals**
_____	11.	Determine time/extent in regular program
_____	12.	Give dates, duration of special education program
_____	13.	Determine how to measure program goals/objectives
_____	14.	Summarize goals and objectives
_____	15.	Designate responsibilities of persons present
_____	16.	Provide participants with copy of recorder's report
_____	17.	Obtain necessary signatures
_____	18.	Positive ending, with invitation for future interactions

*Present data for persons not in attendance; consider need for additional evaluation

**Short-term objectives may be formulated at this time or at future meeting

Figure 7–4
Procedures for use in team meeting to plan student's instructional program

Note: From *A Model in Team Building*, by L. Courtnage and H. Healy, 1984, Cedar Falls: University of Northern Iowa, College of Education. Adapted by permission.

focus. In implementing this technique, the leader poses written questions, which alternate from positive to negative and back again; for example, "What is the ideal mission of our team? What might prevent us from reaching this ideal? In what ways might we begin to solve the problems that confront us? What might prevent us from succeeding? What are our next steps?" The idea behind brainstorming is to allow the members to state, in a series of rapid responses, all possible ideas that might help them define their group mission, before narrowing down their focus to the most realistic set of guidelines.

The second part of the initial procedures for consensus building uses a concept outlined by Powers and Powers (1983) to facilitate participative management by all members of the team. After obtaining information from the group during a brainstorming session, the leader summarizes the statements that were made, giving credit to the individuals who suggested them. The leader then returns this summary to the group for review and feedback on its accuracy. This material thus represents the group's thinking, rewritten in a way to facilitate consensus building. The team leader may find that when a group disagrees or is simply unsure about what course to take, the techniques of brainstorming and consensus building are instrumental in maintaining the focus on mission.

During the initial stages of operation, the leader will also want to guide the group in deciding how it will reach consensus in the event of disagreement (Glatthorn & Newberg, 1984). For example, will they vote and be guided by majority rule? Or will they defer to the opinion of the person with the highest degree of knowledge about the issue? On a team in which professionals have specific types of expertise, intensive training, and strong opinions, it is difficult to establish meaningful interactions. The team's leader, by establishing effective operating procedures, can enable this group to function as a unit.

Conducting Effective Team Meetings.   Scholtes (1988) has listed a detailed set of guidelines to help teams conduct effective meetings. The modified components of selected guidelines that apply most directly to the interactive school-based team are summarized below.

1. *Pre-meeting preparation:* The preparation for a meeting begins when members collect information on the nature of the problem to be discussed. Those who plan to present obtain data and organize it to support their description of the current situation:

- When, how often, under what conditions does the problem occur?

- How does the current situation compare with the goal, ideal situation, or problem solution?

2. *Presentation/discussion:* Each team member who has relevant information prepares a brief presentation, taking care to communicate in jargon-free language. The procedures for effective communication within teams have been presented in previous chapters.

3. *Agenda development:* A meeting agenda should be circulated in advance. Scholtes suggests that it include the topic, time for each item, presenter, and item type (discussion item or announcement). A well-designed agenda can double as a record of the meeting, and be used as a presentation outline for the team to communicate with the organization's administrator, funding agency, and others. Ideally, the final agenda item involves drafting the next meeting's agenda.

4. *Documentation procedures:* When item follow-up is required, it should be documented so each member's responsibilities are clear. A standard form might be developed for recording progress, using the meeting's agenda as an outline. Scholtes suggests that the record include a description of topics, each followed by a summary of main points, decisions/conclusions, and next steps. Most useful of all in documenting procedures is the picture book format, developed by Scholtes and associates (see Figure 7–5). Its designers suggest that the team leader or quality advisor complete the three entries in the left column before the meeting.

5. *Evaluation procedures:* The most effective meetings are those that are evaluated by participants. This procedure helps the team leader make continuous improvements in the meeting process.

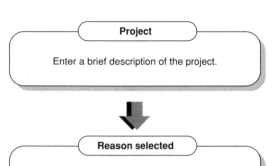

The first three segments of a Picture Book are standard:

Project

Enter a brief description of the project.

Reason selected

Summarize the issues that led to selection of this project, including its importance to customers.

Situation analysis

Summarize any data and include any flowcharts (probably at least a top-down flowchart) or cause-and-effect diagrams that show what the team learned about the status of the process or problem at the beginning of the project. (This box may take up a page or more if you have detailed records.)

Other segments will depend on your project. Some typical items included (not necessarily in this order) are:

Data collection

Show charts or graphs of data the team collects.

Data analysis

Show conclusions from data analysis. Include charts or graphs as appropriate.

Goal

State the goal of the next phase of the project.

Actions

Summarize the actions taken during a certain phase of the project. With a slight twist, a similar box could state actions the team recommends to follow up on its project.

Evaluation

Present summary data and conclusions from the project. Include evaluation of the project, especially what actions or decision were most and least effective, and things the team could improve on next time.

Description: The picture book format displays the milestones in a project through a series of flowchart-like entries. The project team leader and/or quality advisor should fill in the first two or three entries prior to the team's first meeting.

Figure 7–5

Picture book format for documenting team procedures

Note: From *The Team Handbook* (pp. 4–14) by P. Scholtes, 1988, Madison, WI: Joiner Associates. Copyright 1988 by Joiner Associates Inc. Reprinted with permission of the author.

SERVICE COORDINATION PROCEDURES FOR QUALITY ADVISORS

The functions of the team leader, who organizes and facilitates the team's operations, differ from those of another member of the team who also fills a leadership role. We will call this second individual the *quality advisor,* a term borrowed from the literature on Total Quality Management. While the team leader is the same person throughout the team's existence, the quality advisor changes according to the case being handled by the team. The quality advisor—who might be the special educator, school counselor, a parent, or someone else—is the member with the greatest expertise in this particular case, and therefore is its major advisor in coordination of services.

The quality advisor fills a leadership role traditionally called *care manager* (Young, 1987) or *case manager.* Case management is defined as "a set of logical steps and a process of interaction within a service network which assure that a client receives needed services in a supportive, effective, and cost effective manner" (Weil, Karls, & Associates, 1985, p. 2).

The *quality advisor* who manages a specific case, has four major responsibilities:

1. Coordinating the services needed by the student/client and family.

2. Delegating responsibility for providing those services to the individuals best able to provide them.

3. Providing follow-up to ensure that goals are being met.

4. Guiding the contributions of paraprofessionals and volunteers who assist on the case.

Each of these responsibilities will be discussed briefly.

Coordinating Needed Services

Each quality advisor needs to coordinate the special student's program by interacting with other team members and agencies. Because the team will be working with individuals and groups from agencies outside its own organization, it is important for the quality advisor to follow established guidelines for *interagency collaboration*. If the initial tasks of the team leader have been completed, each quality advisor will find that the team has access to a resource file showing the agencies with which the team may need to interact to obtain necessary services.

The quality advisor will need to make certain the file includes all necessary information about the agency's services and its procedures for referral. This file might take the form of a set of index cards, on which the following information is recorded:

◆ The name, address, and phone number of the contact person.

◆ Days and times information about new referrals is taken.

◆ Type of information required (birth certificate, test data, etc.).

◆ Type of release form the agency requires, and its confidentiality.

◆ Type of service responsibilities the agency has.

◆ The agency's available funding options and constraints.

The Regional Resource Center Task Force on Interagency Collaboration (1979) has suggested that this information be organized at the state level into a common format so that the services of each agency can be readily compared with those of other potential providers. A modified version of their format is shown as Table 7–3.

Table 7–3

Common Format for Comparison of Agency Programs

Agency Name _____

Service Description _____

Operates Under Which State/Federal Laws? _____

Client Eligibility (age, income, disability, other) _____

Early and Multidisciplinary Assessment

Early Identification? _____

Types of Assessments Checklist

_____ Medical	_____ Academic performance
_____ Vision	_____ Adaptive behavior
_____ Hearing	_____ Motor abilities
_____ Speech and language	_____ Prevocational
_____ Social history	_____ Vocational
_____ Psychological	_____ Other
_____ General intelligence	

Where Services Are Delivered Checklist

_____ Regular program	_____ Home-based
_____ Part-time special program	_____ Group home facilities
_____ Full-time special program	_____ Work-training center
_____ Long-term residential facility	_____ Job placement
_____ Short-term medical facility	_____ Job coaching
_____ Clinics	_____ Other

Types of Services Checklist

_____ Case management	_____ Recreation
_____ Academic instruction	_____ Client counseling
_____ Independent living skills	_____ Parent training
_____ Speech and language development	_____ Family, genetic counseling
_____ Social/sexual training	_____ Nutrition services
_____ Prevocation/career training	_____ Respite care
_____ Vocational training	_____ Income maintenance
_____ On-the-job training	_____ Transportation
_____ Psychological services	_____ Protective services
_____ Physical or occupational therapy	_____ Crisis intervention
_____ Medical and dental services	_____ Other

Note: Adapted from *Interagency collaboration on full services for handicapped children and youth,* by Regional Resource Task Force on Interagency Collaboration, 1979, Washington, DC: U.S. Department of Health, Education, and Welfare, Bureau of Education for the Handicapped.

In addition to coordinating the student's program through interagency collaboration, the quality advisor should maintain records of the decisions the team has made, their dates, and the people responsible for their implementation. These records will enable the quality advisor to track the progress of the case and request additional assistance from one or several members of the team as necessary.

Delegating Responsibility

Since no quality advisor has either the time or the expertise to implement personally all aspects of the student's program, he or she needs to be able to delegate responsibilities to others. The process of *delegating* is most productive when it is guided by the leader's knowledge of each team member's task strengths and preferences (SRI, 1980). The quality advisor who is most effective in delegating understands the importance of providing resources, encouragement, and supportive feedback (Gersten, Carnine, & Green, 1982).

Delegating refers to the assignment of part of the duties to another person who will assist with this task. The following guidelines for effective delegating are derived from the work of Developmental Dimensions (1981) for school teams and of Milch (1984) for teams of health-related professionals; they have been modified to fit the role of the quality advisor as service coordinator. In delegating responsibility, the quality advisor should:

1. *State the task clearly and objectively to the person who will do it.*
2. *Tell this person why the task is important.*
3. *Give "permission".* Others in the work environment need to know who has been delegated authority to accomplish the task so they will give full cooperation rather than resistance.
4. *Clarify the results that are expected.* It is important to tell the designee what to accomplish, but not how to do the job.
5. *Allow for interaction.* Make certain the task and its results are clear by asking the designee to restate what is to be done.
6. *Agree on follow-up.* Be sure to set a time and place to meet after the task is completed to monitor the results. It is not adequate to say, "Let's get together *sometime* and talk about it *some more.*"

Throughout these steps, the effective quality advisor — as team leader — is communicating clearly, showing high expectations for results, and expressing confidence in both the importance of the task and the ability of the person to whom it is delegated. In the vignette that introduced this chapter, the team leader made major errors in delegating responsibility. He neither stated expectations clearly nor clarified the results that were required. Not granting "permission" to the special education teacher to conduct observations in the regular classroom was another major error, which resulted in the classroom teacher's feeling that the special educator was interfering.

Moreover, he did not establish guidelines for follow-up, so team members did not know they were expected to do more than just talk about the problem.

In explaining the importance of stating the task clearly, Milch (1984) indicates that an unclear task statement may cause the team member to spend a large amount of time and effort, only to be told that "this is not what was expected." It is easy to see how such misunderstanding can foster frustration and even resentment among the team members. Milch also elaborates on the importance of clarifying the results that are expected, as opposed to specifying the exact procedures to be used. When the leader clarifies results, the person to whom the task is delegated feels free to apply professional knowledge and skill in determining how to achieve these results. Conversely, when the leader prescribes the details by which the task is to be accomplished, there is no respect shown for the person to whom the task is delegated. This type of delegating is a "put down," likely to be met with the (usually unspoken) response, "Well, if you know so much about my job, why don't you do it yourself?" Most people have experienced this type of delegating, which is illustrated in Figure 7–6.

Figure 7–6
Ineffective delegating and follow-up

Providing Follow-Up

It has been emphasized throughout the chapter that the quality advisor who assumes the leadership position is not an authoritarian: The quality advisor develops the goals and objectives the team wishes the student to meet in collaboration with other team members. It is the quality advisor, however, who delegates specific responsibilities and then follows up by monitoring the progress of these assignments. The quality advisor gives both positive and corrective feedback during follow-up to the people to whom responsibility has been delegated. The cartoon in Figure 7–6 illustrated not only ineffective delegating, but also highly insensitive follow-up on the part of the special educator.

While providing follow-up, the quality advisor needs to use the key principles that have been shown to motivate staff to improve their performance: enhancing self-esteem, expressing empathy, and asking for help (Developmental Dimensions, 1981). The quality advisor continually seeks information about the progress and problems of those to whom specific responsibility is delegated. Using a calendar with timelines for follow-up, the quality advisor initiates contact with other members of the team. It is important for this leader to provide *supportive feedback* to all members of the group (Gersten et al., 1982). Supportive feedback is based on guidelines that enhance future interactions, and it includes the expression of willingness to help the team member who encounters difficulty in completing delegated tasks. The guidelines that seem most appropriate for the quality advisor's provision of feedback are adapted from the work of Developmental Dimensions (1981) and incorporate some of the strategies suggested by Blanchard and Johnson (1982). They include the following:

1. *Describe the problem clearly.* This is done by the member of the team who has experienced the problem. The team member who has made a direct observation that includes data-based input should use the data base to describe the problem.

2. *Ask for the person's help in solving the problem.*

3. *Talk about causes of the problem.* The quality advisor should initiate this part of the discussion as an expression of empathy for the team member. The quality advisor should take care, however, not to let the discussion of causes become a dead-end explanation of why nothing can be done to solve the problem. The discussion should be kept short, then shifted to solutions.

4. *Brainstorm possible solutions.* The quality advisor requests possible solutions, saying, "Let's list some solutions we might try." The quality advisor writes them down, using phrases to describe each idea. When three or four potential solutions have been written, the quality advisor and team member look at them again and pick the one that has the best chance of initial success.

5. *Agree on the action and a follow-up discussion time.* Decide what role each person will play in the implementation of this solution. For example, the quality advisor might say, "OK, then, you're going to . . . and I'm going to help you by. . . . Let's meet again Friday at 2 o'clock to talk about how well this solution is working."

Positive Feedback.   When providing feedback to the person to whom a task has been delegated, the quality advisor hopes to be able to acknowledge the job's having been done well, thank the person, and praise the person's efforts. Praise is easier to provide than corrective feedback, although adults sometimes find it difficult to praise other adults in a sincere, helpful manner. It is easier to provide praise when the team has an established pattern in which the person to whom the advisor has delegated a task expects feedback on performance (Milch, 1984). *Positive feedback* is most effective when it is delivered immediately, or as soon after task completion as feasible. It should be brief and highly specific, specifying the results that were accomplished (Blanchard & Johnson, 1982; Milch, 1984). The quality advisor should also thank the person for helping and encourage the continuation of efforts on behalf of the team (Developmental Dimensions, 1981). An illustration of effective praise between professionals is as follows:

The school psychologist, as quality advisor, has delegated to the classroom teacher the task of implementing a behavior modification program for a boy named Tracy, who has been engaging in disruptive, off-task conversations during academic instruction. The psychologist, coming in to observe the effects of the program, notices great improvement in the boy's behavior because of the teacher's implementation of the plan. The psychologist says, "You really kept Tracy on task during math class today! When he started talking about his favorite TV show, you just ignored him and called on Barbara. Preventing him from going off on a tangent increased the accuracy of the whole group on their math facts. Thanks for sticking with me on this. I know it's hard to ignore off-task behavior, but it pays off!"

This kind of specific feedback relates the teacher's contribution to the team's results, thus showing the effect of the new program. It heightens the feeling that the person being praised has accomplished something of importance and lessens the possibility that the praise will sound phony or exaggerated, as it would if the quality advisor simply had said, "You're doing just great!"

Corrective Feedback.   It is less pleasant for the quality advisor to give *corrective feedback* to a person whose work has not supported the team's efforts. But without corrective feedback, tasks lack clarity, and positive feedback eventually loses its meaning. Corrective feedback should be specific, including descriptions of both the behavior and its negative effect on the situation (Blanchard & Johnson, 1982; Developmental Dimensions, 1981; Milch, 1984). Beyond this, the quality advisor should show a desire to be helpful, rather than appear punitive or vengeful. The quality advisor can demonstrate helpfulness by asking for reasons for the lack of effective contributions and by listening to the reasons with empathy, but without accepting them as excuses for continued ineffectiveness. The quality advisor can focus on problem solving by saying, "What can we do to prevent this problem from recurring?" The quality advisor and team member engage in some collaborative problem solving; then they agree on a follow-up to determine whether the proposed solution is working. Finally, and most important of all, the quality advisor expresses confidence in the person's ability to contribute increasingly to the team's efforts.

The emphasis in corrective feedback is on task completion that enables the team to reach its goal, rather than on the personal performance of the team member. The quality advisor's role is to work collaboratively with the person in need of assistance to design the solution to a shared problem. Although the leader is a collaborator, he or she is also the person in charge, the one who will follow up on the strategy and retain ultimate responsibility for its effectiveness. It is important in this role to maintain a careful balance between being too directive and too "friendly." The overly directive quality advisor allows the team member to avoid assuming ownership or responsibility for the problem; the overly friendly leader appears too weak to provide the follow-up necessary for task completion.

Guiding Paraprofessionals and Volunteers

The team member who functions as quality advisor may also have the task of coordinating the work of *paraprofessionals, preservice trainees,* and *volunteers* who assist the team members in their roles as service providers or collaborators. In a number of school districts and clinical programs, paraprofessionals, who have some training but less than full certification in their field, are employed as assistants for the professionals in special programs. In many other programs, people with expertise in their own fields volunteer their time to help school or health-related personnel. The team member's role in recruiting, training, and coordinating the work of these people is becoming increasingly important.

Paraprofessionals.   The role of the paraprofessional is to supplement the instructional or other support services provided to the special needs student, under the supervision of the teacher or other professional responsible for those services. For the purpose of this discussion, the preservice trainee, who may be a student teacher or health professions-related intern, is considered a paraprofessional, because this person is not yet certified to conduct the duties of a professional. According to O'Shea and Hendrickson (1987), the paraprofessional in the classroom most often engages in activities such as the following:

◆ Provides follow-up tutoring.
◆ Circulates throughout the room to check students' progress.
◆ Provides students with drills and reviews.
◆ Prepares instructional materials and games.
◆ Reads stories to students.
◆ Conducts small group noninstructional activities.
◆ Corrects homework and workbook assignments.
◆ Arranges learning centers, demonstrations, bulletin boards.

In a classroom for students with physical disabilities, the paraprofessional also assists students with functional skills such as dressing and eating, with the use of braces and other prosthetic devices, and with lifting and transferring, as from a wheelchair to a toilet. The paraprofessional may also help other members of the team, such as the computer specialist and the physical or occupational therapist.

O'Shea and Hendrickson (1987) suggest that the professional can guide the paraprofessional most effectively by using certain interpersonal and management strategies, modified in Figure 7–7. O'Shea and Hendrickson stress the importance of working with paraprofessionals in a team relationship, in which the professional is the leader. The teacher, related professional, or quality advisor assumes the role of helping the paraprofessional develop additional skills. Through observation, supervision, and specific feedback, the professional with good communication skills can promote positive growth in the paraprofessional, ensuring that this individual will be a more effective member of the interactive team.

Volunteers. Volunteers have assisted in schools on an organized basis since the National School Volunteer Program began in 1950. In 1981, leaders in business and industry joined the efforts to provide assistance to school programs through the creation of the Advisory Council on Private Sector Initiatives (National Association of Partners in Education, 1988). NAPE has combined the two groups of volunteers, the

1. **Praise** the paraprofessional for specific tasks that are well done.
2. **Provide corrective feedback privately,** not in the presence of students or clients.
3. **Teach** the paraprofessional to use the disciplinary system designed by the professional, with rules that are consistent, as agreed upon by all.
4. **Encourage** the paraprofessional to handle discipline problems, but provide support when needed.
5. **Remind** the paraprofessional to set a good example, to show respect and courtesy to others.
6. **Discuss** the importance of fairness to all.
7. **Stress** the importance of using the school day for worthwhile tasks, not busy-work.
8. **Stress** the necessity of not being overly friendly with students.
9. **Demonstrate** how to select students who get along well together when organizing committees and work groups.
10. **Encourage** the paraprofessional to keep a sense of humor!

Figure 7–7
Effective guidance of paraprofessionals

Note: From *Training Module: Using Teacher Aides Effectively* by D. O'Shea and J. Hendrickson, 1987, Gainesville: University of Florida, Multidisciplinary Diagnostic and Training Program. Adapted by permission.

school volunteers and the school-business partnerships. Volunteer support for schools by business and industry now involves at least 17% of the nation's schools and 9 million of our children (Greer, 1989).

School volunteers may be specialists in their own fields—writers, researchers, vice presidents, designers, marketing personnel, physicians, attorneys, photographers—some of whom are actively involved in their professions, and some of whom are retired. Several schools have used volunteers to assist with programs in literacy, dropout prevention, and drug abuse prevention. These volunteer partners represent a rich resource of knowledge and support for the interactive team. Volunteers may engage in activities such as the following:

◆ Tutoring students with special needs.

◆ Serving as mentors for students who lack adult role models.

◆ Sponsoring training, demonstrations, and tours for students.

◆ Assisting with projects or judging contests.

◆ Providing work internships for students.

◆ Donating equipment and materials.

It is important for team members to work within the overall system of their organization to identify and coordinate the efforts of volunteers, and to assist in the design of a training program that will enable volunteers to work effectively with students who have special needs. These volunteers will appreciate guidance about the rules of the organization and the instructional and management techniques that are effective with the type of special students to whom they are assigned. They will also appreciate both positive and constructive feedback when it is delivered sensitively, although the team leader is not in the position of serving as a "supervisor" of their efforts.

McCauley (1989), who has suggested that the nurturing of *school-community partnerships* is like growing a garden, has developed guidelines for the successful use of volunteers and business partners. These guidelines are adapted in Figure 7–8. Both paraprofessionals and volunteers should be provided with guidance that recognizes their contributions and allows them to become respected members of the interactive team. The quality advisor is the team member in the best position to ensure that this occurs.

APPLICATION

The following application illustrates the correct way for the team leader or quality advisor to delegate a task to a paraprofessional and to provide effective feedback while monitoring the completion of the task. The task is presented as a series of examples, with comments on their appropriateness.

The quality advisor is a classroom teacher.

The task: conducting a follow-up review for a special needs student on a lesson the teacher has taught in reading.

Step one	PREPARE:	identify planners
		define partnership
		determine roles, responsibilities
Step two	GATHER TOOLS:	identify resources
		design contract
		hold training session
Step three	SOW SEEDS:	find partners to make school "bloom"
Step four	WATER AND FEED OFTEN:	match programs with partners
		provide positive feedback,
		recognition of efforts in public
Step five	Enjoy the bountiful harvest of your "garden"

Figure 7–8

Building and managing educational partnerships with volunteers

Note: From a chart presented by B. McCauley at conference sponsored by the Florida Department of Education and the Florida Chamber of Commerce, March 1989.

Step 1: State the Task Clearly

Clear	Unclear
I'd like you to help Jimmy master these five words he missed in reading today.	I'd like you to help Jimmy in reading for about 20 minutes.

In the unclear example, the task is unclear and unfocused; in addition, the element of time is specified objectively, but the task is not.

Step 2: Tell Why the Task Is Important

Nobody likes the feeling of being delegated a task because it is unimportant or unworthy of the attention of the "boss."

Clear	Unclear
It's really important for him to have extra practice because it takes a lot of time and repetition for him to learn.	It's really important for him to learn to read.

The unclear example states something so obvious that it sounds as if the teacher is talking down to the paraprofessional. In the first example, the paraprofessional is addressed in a way that shows respect for his or her skill. The teacher is sharing knowledge about the nature of the student's difficulty and relating it to the task delegated, which heightens the importance of the task.

Step 3: Give Permission

Others in the work environment need to know that the "boss" has delegated task authority to someone else so that they will give full cooperation rather than resistance. In our example, the child with whom the paraprofessional will work needs to know that this person is the "acting teacher." Assurance of permission would be given to the paraprofessional in the child's presence.

Clear	Unclear
I've told Jimmy that you're going to be his reading teacher for the next 20 minutes and that I expect him to work just as well for you as he does for me.	You have my permission to use this reading book to work with Jimmy.

The word *permission* is used here to mean that the delegator confers an "acting in my place" title upon the person to whom responsibility is being delegated. It is important that knowledge of this permission be shared with the individual over whom the paraprofessional has been delegated responsibility.

Step 4: Clarify Results

It is important for the delegator to tell the designee what is to be accomplished, but not how to do the job. In the cartoon shown as Figure 7–6, the special educator delegated the details on how to do the task of making flashcards. The effect was predictable: The paraprofessional gave the job back to him.

Clear	**Unclear**
Mastery of each word means he can read it correctly within five seconds and that he gets it right three times in a row.	Use these flashcards instead of letting him practice writing the words or playing a game.

The unclear example suggests that the quality advisor—the teacher—does not trust the paraprofessional to make decisions about how the task is accomplished. The quality advisor also gives no guidance on what is expected as a result of the efforts—the behavior expected or product to be completed.

Step 5: Allow for Interaction

The quality advisor should make certain the task and its results are clear by asking the paraprofessional to restate what is to be done.

Clear	**Unclear**
Let's be sure we're both clear on what is to happen. Can you summarize what I'd like you to do?	Do you have any questions about what you are to do?

In the unclear example, the quality advisor will not know whether the task is understood, because it is unlikely that the paraprofessional will ask any questions.

Step 6: Agree on Follow-Up

The quality advisor should set a time and place to meet after the task is completed to monitor the results. This will allow her to thank the paraprofessional for assistance and to include the paraprofessional in deciding whether the task should be modified to increase its effectiveness with the student.

Clear	Unclear
Could we meet at 3 o'clock today in my office to analyze the progress Jimmy has made?	If Jimmy has trouble, let's get together and talk about it some more.

In the unclear example, the plan for monitoring effectiveness is so open that nothing further will happen.

All the way through these steps, the effective leader is communicating clearly, showing high expectations for results, and expressing confidence in both the importance of the task and the ability of the person to whom it is delegated. By using these procedures, it is more likely that the paraprofessional will become a valued and valuable member of the interactive team.

Step 7: Conduct Follow-Up

The effective leader gives both positive and corrective feedback during follow-up of delegated activities. The specific substeps for conducting follow-up to encourage improved performance have been outlined earlier in the chapter. In this application, only the most important of the substeps—describing the problem, discussing possible causes, listing alternative solutions, and agreeing on next steps—will be illustrated.

The paraprofessional (PP) who has worked with Jimmy describes a problem during the scheduled follow-up conference with the quality advisor, the teacher/leader (TL):

PP: Jimmy mastered three of the five words I taught him, but he is still having trouble reading the other two words.

TL: What do you think caused this problem?

PP: I'm not sure. It could be that the two words were so much alike that they were confusing to him. The words were *horse* and *house*.

TL: Yes, those words do look a lot alike. That's a good observation. Do you have any other ideas?

PP: It was close to the end of the 20 minutes when I presented those words. He might have been more tired then. He seemed to be looking around at the other kids instead of concentrating.

TL: That's certainly consistent with what we know about Jimmy's behavior and attention span. Let's list a few ideas about how we might modify the task next time you work with him to make it more effective.

The paraprofessional and the teacher/leader list four possible alternatives for task modification:

1. Reduce practice time from 20 minutes to 10 minutes at a time; repeat practice twice a day.

2. Remove Jimmy from his desk during work on reading; place him in a quiet corner away from distractions.

3. Use practice alternatives that are more motivating, such as word games or computer-assisted instruction on the troublesome words.

4. Highlight the differences between the words *horse* and *house,* either by printing the contrasting letter in red; or pairing each word with a picture illustrating its meaning, to help Jimmy develop his own device for learning the differences between the two words.

TL: Which of these alternative ways of changing the task do you think would be most effective the next time you work with Jimmy?

PP: I'd like to try the last one—helping him develop some kind of trick for learning the differences in the two words.

TL: That sounds as if it might help him—not just for the next practice time, but over the long term—to develop a strategy for telling the difference between words that look alike. Why don't you design a set of materials that highlight the differences in these words and their meanings. Then try it with him tomorrow and see whether he masters all five words, including *horse* and *house.* Let's get together again after school at this time tomorrow to see how well our new plan worked.

In this example of follow-up, the teacher serving as quality advisor provided an opportunity for the paraprofessional to function as an important part of the interactive team. The emphasis in follow-up was on the task, rather than on the performance of the paraprofessional. It was possible for the two team members to function well together because they focused on solution of the problem—designing a task that was more effective in helping their shared student learn the target words. Moreover, although the professional was clearly "in charge" of the conference, the paraprofessional's observations, ideas, and contributions were important. This is how the team leader can obtain maximum efforts from all members of the interactive team.

SUMMARY

There are two types of team leaders. The person who calls and conducts meetings, collects and distributes information on resources, and maintains records, is the official, designated, ongoing team leader. The temporary leader, called the quality advisor, changes with each case; this leadership role is given to the person with the greatest knowledge about the specific case being considered by the team. Both types of team leaders need special skills in the leadership of professionals:

◆ Skills that are similar to the skills, attributes, and behaviors of effective leaders in other organizations, including business and industry.

◆ Skills that focus on the management of tasks, rather than on individuals.

The ongoing, designated team leader has three tasks that set the stage for the effective functioning of the team in the future:

◆ Set up the team within the context of the organization.

◆ Identify resources for use by the team.

◆ Establish operating procedures.

Each designated leader, called a quality advisor, is responsible for overall coordination of a case that involves a specific special needs student. The quality advisor is responsible for:

◆ Coordinating the services provided to the student or client.

◆ Delegating responsibility to other team members.

◆ Providing follow-up on the effectiveness of delegated tasks.

◆ Guiding the activities of paraprofessionals and volunteers who assist the team.

In this chapter, the work of the team leader has been outlined. The emphasis of the chapter has been on the use of the leader as a collaborator who can encourage the full participation of each team member to reach the team's goal: the best possible program for a given student.

In the next chapter, the dimension of leadership as a facilitating factor will be explored further. The discussion will focus on ways that professional development can be used to empower team members in their efforts to bring about long-term systematic change, which enhances the effectiveness of programs for special needs students.

ACTIVITIES

1. Using the six steps presented in the chapter, write or act out the conversation you would use to delegate a teaching task to a practicum student in your classroom or clinical program. (Use any task of your choice.)

2. Explain the difference between listening with empathy to the reasons for a paraprofessional's problem in completing a task and accepting those reasons as excuses for failure to complete the task.

3. Using the guidelines presented in the chapter, write or act out the conversation you would use in giving your paraprofessional corrective feedback during follow-up on a task you had delegated. (Use any situation of your choice.)

4. Using the guidelines presented in this chapter, delegate a task to a paraprofessional or practicum student in your program, observe that person completing the task, and provide feedback on the task performance during a follow-up conference.

5. Use directories, interviews, and other sources of information to develop a card file of community resources that might be used by an interactive team in your area. The following sample, shown as Figure 7–9, provides a useful format for this activity.

Using directories, knowledgeable people, the phone book, and other resources you can muster, prepare a resource card file.

Card Entry Format
1. Upper right—name of agency or service
2. Left margin, line two—address and phone number
3. Left margin, line three—service description
4. Back of card, line one—hours of operation
5. Back of card, line two—area served
6. Back of card, line three—fee charged and financial notes
7. Back of card, line four—name of contacts

Example:

1. County office of Child Services	4. M–Sa, 8 a.m.–6 p.m. and 24 hours emergency
2. 429 Elm Street 307-4569	5. Whole County
3. Assigns case worker to home of child who has been abused. Makes referrals or gives shelter when necessary.	6. No Charge
	7. George Bundy
Front	Back

Figure 7–9
Community resources card file

REFERENCES

Audette, B., & Algozzine, G. (1992). Free and appropriate education for all students: Total quality and the transformation of American public education. *Remedial and Special Education, 13*(6), 8–18.

Bennis, W. (1989). *Why leaders can't lead: The unconscious conspiracy continues.* San Francisco: Jossey-Bass.

Blanchard, K., & Johnson, S. (1982). *The one minute manager.* New York: Wm. Morrow.

Bonstingl, J. (1992). The quality revolution in education. *Educational Leadership, 50*(3), 4–9.

Courtnage, L., & Healy, H. (1984). *A model in team building.* Cedar Falls: University of Northern Iowa, College of Education.

Covey, S. (1990). *The 7 habits of highly effective people.* New York: Simon & Schuster Fireside.

DeBevoise, W. (1984). Synthesis of research on the principal as instructional leader. *Educational Leadership, 41*(5) 14–20.

Deming, W. E. (1986). *Out of the crisis.* Boston: MIT Center for Advanced Engineering Studies.

Developmental Dimensions. (1981). *Interaction management system.* Pittsburgh: Author.

Drucker, P. (1969). *The age of discontinuity: Guidelines for our changing society.* New York: Harper & Row.

Dunn, R., & Dunn, K. (1970). *Practical approaches to individualizing instruction.* West Nyack, NY: Parker.

Gersten, R., Carnine, D., & Green, S. (1982, March). *Administrative supervisory support functions for the implementation of effective educational programs for low income students.* Paper presented at the annual meeting of the American Educational Research Association, New York.

Gilliam, J., Kaye, N., & Soffer, R. (1982). Collaborative planning and multidisciplinary team development. In L. Burrello & N. Kaye (Eds.), *Developing the roles of the teacher and the team* (pp. 1–55). Falls Church, VA: Counterpoint Books.

Glatthorn, A., & Newberg, N. (1984). A team approach to instructional leadership. *Educational Leadership 39*(3), 60–63.

Greer, J. (1989). Partnerships: What is our contribution? *Exceptional Children, 55,* 391–393.

Hall, G., Rutherford, W., Hord, S., & Huling, L. (1984). Effects of three principal styles on school improvement. *Educational Leadership, 41*(5), 22–31.

Halpin, A. (1959). *The leadership behavior of school superintendents.* Chicago: University of Chicago, Midwest Administration Center.

Halpin, A., & Winer, B. J. (1957). A factorial study of the leader behavior descriptors. In R. Stogdill & A. Coons (Eds.), *Leader behavior: Its description and measurement.* Columbus, OH: Ohio State University.

Hempfill, J., (1958). Administration as problem solving. In A. Halpin (Ed.), *Administrative theory in education.* Chicago: University of Chicago, Midwest Administration Center.

Hempfill, J., & Coons, A. (1957). Development of the leader behavior description questionnaire. In R. Stogdill & A. Coons (Eds.), *Leader behavior: Its description and measurement.* Columbus, OH: Ohio State University.

Hersey, P., & Blanchard, K. (1974). So you want to know your leadership style? *Training and Development Journal, 28*(2), 22–36.

Howe, C. (1981). *Administration of special education.* Denver, CO: Love.

Juran, J. (1992, July 29). Managing for world class quality. Keynote address at the Third Annual Symposium: Quality in Action in Academe. Lehigh University, PA.

Kaplan, G. (1985). Shining lights in high places: Education's top four leaders and their heirs. *Phi Delta Kappan, 67*(1), 7–16.

Kouzes, J., & Posner, B. (1990). *The leadership challenge: How to get extraordinary things done in organizations.* San Francisco: Jossey-Bass.

Lazarsfeld, P. (1963). The social sciences and administration: A rationale. In L. Downey & F. Enns (Eds.), *The social sciences and educational administration.* Edmonton, Alberta, Canada: University of Alberta.

Lipham, J. (1964). Leadership and administration. In D. Griffiths (Ed.), *Behavioral science and educational administration.* 63rd Yearbook of the NSSE. Chicago: University of Chicago Press.

McCauley, B. (1989, March). *Creating and managing an educational partnership program.* Presentation to Partners in the Business of Education, a Joint Conference by the Florida Department of Education and the Florida Chamber of Commerce, Ft. Lauderdale, FL.

McClelland, D. (1975). *Power: The inner experience.* New York: Irvington.

McGregor, D. (1960). *The human side of enterprise.* New York: McGraw-Hill.

Milch, E. (1984). *Delegating and monitoring staff performance.* Gainesville, FL: Alachua General Hospital.

National Association of Partners in Education. (1988). *1988 Annual report.* Alexandria, VA: Author.

O'Shea, D., & Hendrickson, J. (1987). *Training module: Using teacher aides effectively.* Gainesville: University of Florida, Multidisciplinary Diagnostic and Training Program.

Peters, T., & Austin, N. (1985). *A passion for excellence: The leadership difference.* New York: Warner Books.

Powers, D., & Powers, M. (1983). *Making participatory management work.* San Francisco: Jossey-Bass.

Regional Resource Center Task Force on Interagency Collaboration. (1979). *Interagency collaboration on full services for handicapped children and youth.* Washington, DC: U.S. Department of Health, Education, and Welfare, Bureau of Education for the Handicapped.

Scholtes, P. (1988). *The team handbook.* Madison, WI: Joiner Associates.

Senge, P. (1990). *The fifth discipline: The art and practice of the learning organization.* New York: Harper and Row.

Sergiovanni, T. (1992). *Moral leadership.* San Francisco: Jossey-Bass.

SRI. (1980). *Administrator perceiver technical manual.* Lincoln, NE: Selection Research.

Tribus, M. (1992, July 30). Quality management in education. Third Annual Symposium: Quality in Academe. Lehigh University, PA.

Weil, M., Karls, J., & Associates. (1985). *Case management in human service practice.* San Francisco: Jossey-Bass.

Wilson, M. (1993). The search for teacher leaders. *Educational leadership, 50*(6), 24–27.

Wittenmyer, J. (1983). Unit five: Referral, coordination, and management of services. In C. M. Del Polito & J. G. Barresi (Eds.), *Alliances in health and education: Serving youngsters with special needs* (pp. 115–133) Washington, DC: American Society of Allied Health Professions.

Young, T. (1987). Therapeutic case advocacy: A summary. *Focal Point, 1*(3), 1–5.

CHAPTER 8

Empowering Team Members Through Professional Development

Power, Empowerment, and Change
> Responsible and Effective Use of Power
> Bringing About Change
> Empowering Others

Summary of Best Practices

Strategies for Professional Development
> Sharing Knowledge
> Developing Skills
> Developing the Team

Application

Summary

TOPICS IN THIS CHAPTER INCLUDE

◆ Discussion of the terms *power* and *empowerment* as they relate to professional development and the process of change.

◆ Description of the best practices for professional development, summarized from the research.

◆ Description of three types of professional development for teams: sharing knowledge, building skills, and developing the team as a unit.

◆ Guidelines and examples for implementing knowledge sharing and skill development.

◆ An application, showing how the level of a team's development might be viewed from the perspective of the leader's style.

The team that had met to evaluate and place students with special needs in exceptional children's programs at the elementary school was having difficulty implementing its programs. The students they had identified and placed were functioning well, but teacher referrals had increased by 25%. The school psychologist found that teachers were asking for her help in placing problem students in pull-out programs, but that her services as a consultant to others in the building were not welcomed. Three classroom teachers who had been involved in the team were cooperative, but most of their colleagues seemed to resist efforts to provide prereferral programs for students who were having learning or behavior problems in the classroom.

The special education teacher was already overloaded with students who had been placed in the resource room part-time, yet he was reluctant to refuse services to additional students in need because it seemed that "they couldn't get help any other way." He was most frustrated by being unable to arrange a logical plan for scheduling students into the resource room. The classroom teachers indicated the times that referred students could receive resource room services—times that did not conflict with the regular classroom schedule.

At the same time, the school counselor, speech-language therapist, and physical therapist, all of whom served more than one building and were available only at specific times, further restricted the scheduling options by telling the special educator when his students could receive their services.

Together, the special education teacher, the school psychologist, and two of the classroom teachers approached the school principal, who was new in the district and eager to establish her school as a model program for serving students with a variety of special needs. The team agreed to support the principal's efforts in professional development by presenting inservice training on the potential contributions and limitations of their roles. They also agreed to serve, along with selected classroom teachers, as "mentors" who would conduct follow-up observations and assist in program planning and the coaching of teachers who wished to implement alternative learning strategies for the special needs students in their classrooms.

The team members, under the direction of the school principal, conducted a needs assessment to determine the types of problems school personnel were having with their special needs students and the areas in which they felt least effective in assisting these students. They learned that teachers were most concerned about managing the behavior of special needs students during large group instruction and providing students with academic instruction that would enable them to master the basic skills. With this information in hand, the team members began to design a plan for professional development to assist all members of the school staff in working more effectively with students with special needs.

A group representing the leadership in the school's teachers' union and the PTA was asked by the principal to design a formal evaluation of the professional development program's effectiveness and to conduct this evaluation one year after its implementation. The evaluation plan was to focus on the decrease in student referrals to special programs, while also considering the effects of professional development on the whole school's sense of "mission" and teachers' and parents' satisfaction with the program. Evaluation during the second year of implementation was to include an analysis of the effect of the program on the average student's academic achievement, as well as individual learning and behavior changes in special needs students.

This case illustrates the problems encountered by team members who attempt to implement programs for special needs students without the support of the entire school staff. Team members often wish they had the power to implement whole-school change by demanding that every teacher learn how to work effectively with special needs students. However, experienced change agents understand that school improvement occurs best when it is based on empowerment, rather than on rule enforcement. In this chapter, the guidelines for use of professional development as a facilitating factor are outlined. Power is defined, and the distinction is drawn between power and empowerment. The best practices for empowering team members through professional development are outlined, and the relevant research on team development in business and industry is summarized. Three levels of professional development—sharing knowledge, developing skill, and changing behavior—are described. Applications of each level are given as the use of professional development as a facilitating factor in interactive teaming is explained.

POWER, EMPOWERMENT, AND CHANGE

Team members who recognize the need for a change in the behavior of others or in the culture of the organization in which they work often wish they had the power to implement this change. Professional development is one of the most effective ways to bring about change. Such development has the greatest effect when it is implemented by people who understand how it relates to the change process by empowering people rather than by imposing power upon them.

Bennis (1989) also pointed out that effective leaders manage conflict creatively, encouraging both innovation and challenges presented as divergent points of view. Covey (1990) added that the leader's power is based on the group's respect for his or her credibility and genuineness, as opposed to the leader's ability to act out superficial behaviors that give the appearance of power.

Responsible and Effective Use of Power

The term *power* is used here in the positive sense as the ability to accomplish the goals of the team in providing the best possible program for each student with special needs. The use of power is discussed along two dimensions: (a) understanding the positive aspects of power and (b) recognizing and using established power. Each of these dimensions will be discussed briefly.

Understanding the Positive Aspects of Power.   It should be emphasized that power is equated with strength or effectiveness, but is not used as a synonym for autocratic leadership. As shown in Chapter 7, power is essential in the exercise of leadership that facilitates change.

Several types of power are available to the team member who wishes to be a change agent. The types of power have been discussed by French and Raven (1959) as including coercive, reward, legitimate, expert, and charismatic power. *Coercive power,* which involves the use of threat or punishment, is used least often by leaders who wish to obtain cooperation; likewise, *reward power* is of only temporary value in facilitating behavioral or organizational change. *Legitimate power,* which is based on the group's acceptance of a common purpose, requires that the leader conform to this purpose and fit the group's concept of how their leader should behave. The use of legitimate power is the most desirable within the interactive team, although this is not the only type of power available to the team leader.

The leader who is perceived to have *expert power* is felt to have knowledge, insight, and vision. For the interactive team, expert power can also be appropriately used to initiate the changes necessary to implement a student's program. The expert is viewed as the one who can solve the problem or make something happen. The person who demonstrates expert power in a group is the one who comes prepared with facts and information. The data collected may take the form of charts and graphs, showing the student's responses to various types of programs; historical information, including test scores and work samples; or a summary of the research on a particular program that has been found effective. The team member with data is the individual most likely to be perceived by others as having the necessary expert power to bring about desired change.

Recognizing and Using Established Power.   The team member who wishes to bring about positive change does not always have the power—either legitimate or expert—to do so. In this case, it is important for the person who wishes to facilitate change to recognize and use *established power* within the organization. Tucker (1972) has developed a key to planning change based on an understanding of power. This key is presented as a flow chart, which follows a series of questions. In Question 1, team members who wish to be *change agents* are asked to determine whether they have power. If they answer "yes," they have no obstacle and can go all the way through the flow chart, even skipping steps to accomplish their change. (There may be later consequences to skipping steps, because they may not have "institutionalized" the changes.)

If the change agents have no power, they must decide whether to behave as revolutionaries or to "communicate the importance of that change to persons in power" (p. 2). In most instances, team members do not have power and must propose their change through a third party who is known and respected by the power structure in the organization. Tucker pointed out that this sharing of power involves both risk and compromise, but he suggested that it is the most effective strategy for the powerless beginner. Tucker's key for planning change has been adapted for use by the interactive team member and is presented as Figure 8–1. The "change" presented in the flow chart is the new program, which the interactive team wishes to implement to improve the services offered to special needs students. The team members responsible for implementing this program are "change agents" who work within the *power structure* of the organization to be sure the changes required by this program will be accepted by members of the organization.

In the flow chart, the team member asks a series of questions, in which the key issues are the following:

◆   Does the member have the power to bring about the desired change? If not, shall power be seized, or should the team member "give" the change idea to another person who may be more successful?

◆   Is the member willing to discuss the change with others, knowing that the proposal will be modified in the process of discussion?

◆   Is the team member known and respected by the power structure? If not, should the team member try to gain respect or, alternatively, "give" the change to a known and respected person for implementation?

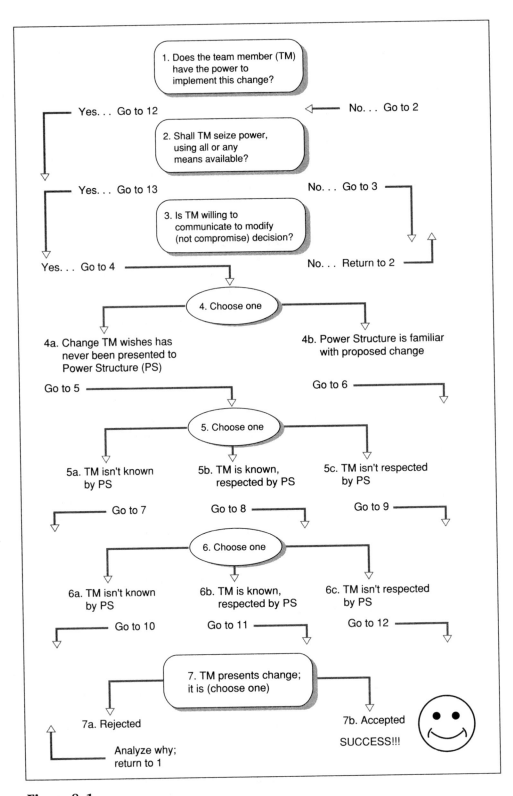

Figure 8–1

A flow chart for planning change

Note: From *A Plan to Achieve Change* by J. Tucker, 1972, Austin: University of Texas, Department of Special Education. Adapted by permission.

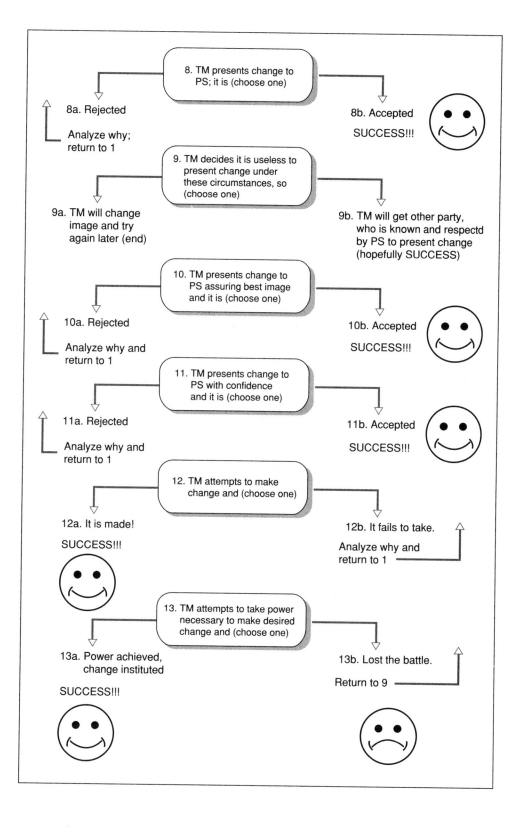

8. TM presents change to PS; it is (choose one)

8a. Rejected

Analyze why; return to 1

8b. Accepted

SUCCESS!!!

9. TM decides it is useless to present change under these circumstances, so (choose one)

9a. TM will change image and try again later (end)

9b. TM will get other party, who is known and respectd by PS to present change (hopefully SUCCESS)

10. TM presents change to PS assuring best image and it is (choose one)

10a. Rejected

Analyze why and return to 1

10b. Accepted

SUCCESS!!!

11. TM presents change to PS with confidence and it is (choose one)

11a. Rejected

Analyze why and return to 1

11b. Accepted

SUCCESS!!!

12. TM attempts to make change and (choose one)

12a. It is made!

SUCCESS!!!

12b. It fails to take.

Analyze why and return to 1

13. TM attempts to take power necessary to make desired change and (choose one)

13a. Power achieved, change instituted

SUCCESS!!!

13b. Lost the battle.

Return to 9

As shown in Figure 8–1, the team member who is established within or respected by the power structure of the organization will be able to get necessary program changes accepted more readily than a person who is rejected by the power structure or is new to the organization. In the latter instance, the team member will find that the most effective way to implement changes is by *giving ideas away to an established person who is respected and accepted by the power structure*. This concept is key to the understanding of how to use power by sharing it; this is called *empowerment*. Empowerment is essential in the process of change.

Bringing About Change

One might assume that when there is a compelling need for change, it would be easy to implement this change. Those who study the change process caution that this is not so (Bennis, 1989; Cuban, 1988; Gartner & Lipsky, 1987; Skrtic, 1987). The difficulties in implementing change are related to the structure of schools, the societal value system, and the current status of fragmented services for special needs students.

Guidelines for Implementation.   From both successful and unsuccessful attempts at change, one can abstract the importance of a supportive climate created by an internal team, rather than imposed by outside experts. The prospective *change agent* or developer needs to understand that successful change can occur only when people or groups directly responsible for problems are involved in the design and implementation of the *change strategy*.

Two theories of change have been selected as most relevant to the design of an educational change strategy. The first is a theory based on the analysis of the forces for and against change; the second is a theory based on the study of change as a process, which takes place at the personal level.

The work of Lewin (1975) on force field analysis in change has often been considered by those who study change within organizations. Lewin has classified forces as *driving* and *restraining* in regard to change and stated that an imbalance between these forces precipitates change. Sage and Burrello (1986) have analyzed the driving and restraining forces for change in special education. As driving forces they included the social climate, the courts and legislation. As restraining forces, they cited isolated and conflicting professions, bureaucratic regulations, money, and tradition. Sage and Burrello noted the irony that some of the same forces that initially facilitate change later become restraining factors. For instance, P.L. 94-142 included new categorical definitions for various disabling conditions. School districts received additional funds on the basis of the number of students who could be classified by these definitions. The definitions became part of the bureaucracy, forcing districts to label students to receive funds to assist them. The new generation of innovators, who wished to fund special programs according to functional disabilities rather than categorical labels, were forced into an adversarial position with those professionals who had been instrumental in initially facilitating change.

Extensive studies have been conducted of change in educational organizations (Hall, George, & Rutherford, 1977; Hall, Loucks, & Newlove, 1976). They believe change is a process rather than a single event, and that change takes place slowly, at the personal rather than the system level. They have designed two frameworks for analyzing change. The first is based on the individual's stages of concern for the change (Hall, George, et al., 1977). These levels range from awareness to refocus, and they indicate the individual's readiness for acceptance of change. Individual teachers faced with change progress through the levels of basic awareness to concern about how the innovation will affect them, how they are going to manage the change, and then concern for the effect of the innovation on the entire class.

Ultimately people incorporating change progress to a concern for collaboration with others and then to refocusing—thinking about how the innovation might be used to modify the whole system. This conceptual framework also includes a set of strategies through which the change agent or developer can affect individuals who are at different levels of concern. According to this theory, the effectiveness of interventions will be determined by the change agent's understanding of the stage of the "client's" concern about the change.

Hall, Loucks, et al. (1976) have also looked at the effect of change as measured by the levels of use by individuals within the system. Studying several innovations over a 15-year period, they have determined that 40% of the teachers remain at the routine level of innovation, even three or four years after the innovation has been implemented. McLaughlin and Marsh (1978) have summarized the effect of federally funded school innovations and have concluded that innovative programs remain as a permanent part of the school structure only when teachers believe the change has made a difference in the lives of the most difficult children. Hall, Rutherford, Hord, and Huling (1984) also found that the principal's style determines whether an innovation remains. They classified school principals as responders (those who do what central office asks), managers (those who take an innovation and adapt it to their own school), or initiators (those who start with analysis of their own district and teachers, then design their response to change around the analysis of what needs to occur within their context). These researchers concluded that changes are of a higher quality and quantity in schools where the leader is classified as an initiator.

A. Tucker (1984) has analyzed change in higher education and suggested guidelines for selecting strategies to implement change. These guidelines are adapted here to focus on change in special programs provided by interactive teams. Guidelines include selecting the focus for change, determining who to involve, and deciding how to intervene.

The first guideline for the developer is to determine the *focus for change*. Exactly what needs to be modified or developed? A. Tucker (1984) lists six factors to consider in selecting the change focus:

1. Change will occur more easily when it is *timely* and appropriate.
2. The developer should determine whether the innovation has a *reasonable chance* of success.
3. The developer should select the *least drastic* solution as the answer to the problem.

4. Plans for change are more effective when they are designed with built-in *responses to the personal needs* of those affected by the change.

5. In addition to communicating with those affected by the change, the developer must also remember to *communicate with those within the system who must approve the change*.

6. The developer should remain *sensitive to the values* of those for whom the change is implemented.

Bennis (1989) has added suggestions for some ways to avoid disastrous conflicts and counter-productive efforts to bring about needed changes. For the purpose of the interactive school team, we have selected only a few of these, then modified and adapted them for the team's consideration, as follows:

◆ Discuss the proposed change honestly, rather than overselling its potential benefits.

◆ Avoid involving those with fanatical positions on a team that plans change strategy.

◆ Focus on action, rather than depending on rhetoric.

◆ Be cautious about proposals that would "turn off" the key people in the organization.

Fullan (1993) discussed the need for effective teachers to combine ability as change agents with a strong sense of moral purpose (i.e, desire to make a difference in the lives of children). To do this, he believes, teachers need to develop (a) a personal vision of why they became teachers; (b) habit of inquiry—continuous questioning, renewal, vitality in lifelong learning; (c) mastery of a high level of skill and knowledge; and (d) the ability to collaborate with others. Collaboration is emphasized as a way to increase individual strength, by joining with others in continuous growth.

Next, it is useful to *determine who to involve* in the design of the change strategy. These individuals may be labeled *change agents*. Every group has influential people who must be involved if change is to occur. Even if the developer does not conduct a systematic study of the "real power" people, the developer can identify some people who need to be involved as change agents in any change strategy (A. Tucker, 1984). Certainly the developer must include the individuals with administrative titles, who have responsibility for the program to be changed. Those who make decisions about the spending of funds will need to be consulted when money is involved. Elected or appointed representatives of particular constituencies must also be included. Individuals in the system with knowledge about the particular topic need to be involved (e.g., the school nurse when the education of children with AIDS is the issue; the building director when the change involves designing classrooms that are free of architectural barriers). It is important to remember that anyone who will be affected by the change should be involved in some way in its design.

In trying to select specific individuals to involve as change agents in a planning group, the developer should consider the characteristics of the people themselves.

How will they react to the proposal? Will they be able to function with others in the group? The group should include people who may oppose the change, so a sense of ownership can be developed among diverse constituencies. This concept of extending ownership was implemented quite effectively by Pelfry (1988), who selected a planning committee for a change that involved the extensive acquisition of computers. He included on this committee a board member who had previously opposed all changes that required substantial expenditures, thus converting a potential opponent into a strong ally.

After deciding on a focus and the people who will be involved, the developer decides *how to intervene* to facilitate the change. A. Tucker (1984) has suggested seven generic *change strategies*:

1. Call attention to a contradiction.
2. Use research.
3. Lower the situational conflict (involve persons in social interactions).
4. Adopt two or more options.
5. Identify the alternative solutions, citing the probable consequences.
6. Apply a historical approach.
7. Appeal to values and traditions.

Those who are involved in or affected by the proposed change need to have a sense of ownership of the new plan. Their sense of ownership is established by joint participation in planning for, developing, implementing, and evaluating the plan.

Application of Change Strategy.   In designing a change strategy, the developer first considers the generic intervention plans and determines the individuals who need to be involved as change agents. Then the developer plans the sequence of steps to be taken in facilitating the change. The following guidelines for designing these steps have been synthesized from the work of J. Tucker (1972), A. Tucker (1984), Grosenick and Reynolds (1978), and Losen and Losen (1985).

1. *Identify real and potential supporters.* These may be friends or colleagues who share the belief in a need for change. Or they might be people who, with additional information, could become supporters. Losen and Losen (1985) suggest that special educators may be able to engage the school board attorney as an ally by providing this individual with the latest information on school law as it relates to disabled students. The attorney, who is obligated to remain current in a range of topics related to school law, may appreciate this highly specialized information. The special educator, who can obtain this information from current journals and professional societies, is able to develop a dimension of expert power by providing this technical knowledge.

2. *Test the waters.* The developer might visit someone else's classroom or office and say, "I have an idea that I think might improve the program. I don't even know

whether it's feasible, but this is what it is. . . . What do you think about it? What are the chances we might be able to do that? Who else might be interested in this idea? Who would be against it? What problems might we face if we really wanted to do it?" In this manner, the developer talks informally with as many people as possible, modifying the plan as others make important suggestions. The individual who skips this step and presents the entire, new idea to the group will frequently find that the idea is rejected (A. Tucker, 1984). Individual contacts enable the developer to count the votes and incorporate the ideas of many persons who subsequently develop ownership in the plan.

3. *Translate the change into language that others can understand.* For advocates, the language of change is based on values, such as "equal opportunity" and "student rights." For policy makers, the language of change is directly related to dollars and cents. Successful change agents may convince even a conservative administration that special education makes sense in terms of cost effectiveness, because it is cheaper to provide preventive programs to children in school than to institutionalize them for a lifetime, during which they would drain, rather than contribute to, the tax base.

4. *Identify additional sources of support* that may be used to supplement the regular budget. Both governmental agencies and charitable foundations often fund special projects through grants. Service clubs, which exist in every community, are always looking for worthy projects. Lions Clubs give glasses to needy children; Shriners help build hospitals. Locate some other sources of funding that may help to get the project "off the ground."

5. *Ask for technical assistance.* If the proposal for change is technical or complex, ask for help from experts. On a public health issue, help may be available from the public health department or the public information office of the local hospital. When proposing a change that involves computer use, involve business and industry personnel who are prominent in computer technology. Be sure that these people and their organizations are recognized for their contributions—through media exposure and letters of appreciation to their superiors—so they will share ownership of the new idea. Failing to ask for help may be a serious error, because those who could be your strongest allies may become opponents if they think they are being bypassed or that the change agent is setting up a program that is competitive with theirs.

6. *Share information on success.* When students in a new reading program improve their achievement scores or work-study students receive excellent reports from their employers, let the media know. Pictures of successful students and human interest stories can enhance the public relations of the organization. Again, the "power people" (school principal or program director) should share in the good press so they can develop an even stronger sense of commitment to continue the innovative program.

Team members who attempt to bring about change will encounter false starts, resistance, and the need to go "back to the drawing board" many times before real progress can be made. The task requires patience and perseverance, as well as an understanding of the theories and strategies for facilitating change. The individual who follows these guidelines, however, may be able to minimize the discouragement and negative personal consequences of repeated failure.

Empowering Others

The discussion of empowerment in this chapter is focused on providing team members with both *legitimate power* through decision sharing and *expert power* through information sharing. Both types of empowerment are based on professional development, and their purpose is to enable team members to accomplish changes that benefit special needs students.

Empowerment as Power Sharing.   Empowerment is illustrated in the way the team leader—a person with power—shares this power with others who can help to implement the necessary change. Powers and Powers (1983) have shown how *participatory management* can be used successfully by leaders who are perceived as powerful. Participatory management includes the use of consultation (in a process that emphasizes information exchange), coalition building, task orientation, conflict resolution, and flexibility. Many of these techniques have been presented earlier in the discussions on consultation and communication skills. Powers and Powers show also that, although the participatory structure operates more slowly, it is no less decisive, and that the leader who is effective within this framework sets clear goals that have a greater chance for successful implementation because they are based on group consensus. Those who wish to establish their leadership on behalf of educational teams will be interested in developing the shared power more descriptive of participatory rather than of autocratic management.

Leaders in business and industry have long been concerned with this type of empowerment. The development of individual skills and group cohesiveness among members of their organization's staff, which culminates in the building of an organizational team, has been summarized by Ends and Page (1984) and by Scholtes (1988). It is worthwhile to note that these procedures have much in common with those suggested as the best practices for professional development in educational organizations.

In the business and industry model for team building, summarized by Ends and Page (1984), the organization's manager is the team builder, who initially has power. The word *power* is defined as "the ability to influence the behavior of others" (p. 53). These authors describe the process of team building as a sequence in which the leader learns to influence the behavior of individuals, then develops small- and large-group leadership skills, and finally demonstrates the ability to allow members of the group to influence group decisions in an interactive manner. Their point is clear and consistent with the entire body of literature on change: People do not become involved in activities over which they have no influence. They point out that this interaction is important both in allowing team members to have influence in the group, and in seeing that the group leader has used their ideas to influence those above this group in the organization's power structure. Once the team is functioning as a unit, there is a sense of pride among group members in their belonging to a winning team. In effective schools, this same sharing of common goals and pride in teamwork is present (Audette & Algozzine, 1992; Levine, 1985).

Empowerment also takes on a dimension of personal development within the context of group growth. Covey (1990) emphasizes the importance of each individual's attention to his or her own personal energy needs, and suggests replenishment, inspiration, and stress reduction as forms of personal empowerment. Some of this inspiration and stress reduction that facilitate personal empowerment can result from the provision of a supportive work environment, respect and recognition for each member's contributions to the team effort (Jackman, 1991). Jackman, who has assisted in the analysis of successful teams in business and industry, emphasizes the importance of shared respect and support among members of the winning team. Jackman indicates that the "key player" is one who values consensus based on shared goals and that a "star team" is one in which all members are nurturing and enthusiastic about each other's contributions to the group effort. The team is more effective, then, when each member is empowered, and when the team itself has developed as a mature, supportive unit.

Empowerment as Knowledge Sharing.   Empowerment also involves the development of expert power or knowledge among members of the staff. In the interactive team, knowledge acquisition begins with information sharing among team members. Individuals engage in a type of professional development based on the sharing of the specialized knowledge about their roles with other members of the team (Lyon & Lyon, 1980). Such information sharing has been illustrated in the Chapter 4 Application showing an informational interview between a special educator and a speech-language therapist.

Ends and Page (1984) emphasized that the process of organizational team building begins with the development of skills in individual team members. They indicated that the process must be nonthreatening and that the change needs to be consistent with the individual's self-image. If these conditions are met, the team member goes through a four-stage process of change in learning the new behavior: recognizing the need to change, knowing what to change, desiring to learn, and practicing until the new behavior is acquired. These authors indicated clearly that the strongest teams are those in which individual members possess knowledge and skill.

In the educational literature, the acquisition of knowledge and skill that results in empowerment is referred to as *professional development*. The educational organizations that are most effective in implementing needed changes are those in which a large number of individuals have been involved and have developed a sense of ownership for the new program (Glatthorn & Newberg, 1984; Lieberman, 1988; Sickler, 1988). These organizations are characterized by a sense of shared understanding about the changes that are necessary. Gersten, Carnine, and Green (1982) have added that accurate group implementation and clear, specific supervisory instructions are the common elements in effective innovative programs for difficult students. Finally, Stedman (1987), summarizing the school effectiveness research, has shown that the best schools for disadvantaged students are those in which the entire staff and the community share a sense of ownership for and a belief in the ability of low-functioning students. This sense of shared purpose originates in the development of knowledge and skills through professional development.

SUMMARY OF BEST PRACTICES

The process of professional development in educational organizations was originally summarized by the National Inservice Network (NIN), a governmental agency active in the 1970s (Hutson, 1979). More current summaries of effective practices and their relationship to school improvement have been completed by Showers, Joyce, and Bennett (1987), by Joyce, Showers and Rolheiser-Bennett (1987), and by Schmoker and Wilson (1993).

The content presented in a professional development program is focused directly on the behavior of teachers and indirectly on the behavior of students. The best kind of professional development will affect student behavior because it results in the enhancement of teacher competency. Joyce et al. (1987) have shown evidence that professional development programs for several models of teaching result in higher student achievement. These include strategies often used with special needs students—cooperative learning approaches, information-processing models that include the use of advanced organizers and mnemonics, and DISTAR as a model of direct instruction. The developer should know that these models have proved their effectiveness with students and would therefore be appropriate for use in whole-school professional development programs.

The decision about content for professional development should also take into consideration the need of participants to obtain a basic level of knowledge about a program before they are able to "buy into" it (Showers et al., 1987). Moreover, the selection of content should include four components that have been found useful in enabling teachers to take new information back to their classrooms: (a) presentation of theory, (b) demonstration of the new strategy, (c) initial practice with supervision, and (d) feedback on their performance (Showers et al., 1987). By incorporating these features, training conducted as part of professional development can also serve as a model of effective instruction. The presenter models direct instruction with active learner participation. This type of content consists of activities that are appropriate for adult learners, as described previously, and includes activities through which the participants can reflect on new ideas, discuss issues, and apply new learning to their own classrooms or clinical programs.

The NIN literature also contains suggestions for the selection of an underlying philosophy for implementing professional development programs. The most important philosophical guideline is that programs should be based on a developmental model, not a deficit model. That is, the developers view members of the staff as effective teachers and team members who want to improve, not as ineffective participants in need of remediation. The logic behind this concept is that education and related services personnel cannot learn everything they need to know during preservice training; nor can professionals learn all they need to know at a fixed point in time, because new knowledge continues to make existing practice obsolete.

There are three other special considerations for professional developers who wish to implement best practices. First, activities that are effective with one group may not be appropriate for others. That is, it may be important to design programs that are responsive to differences in the language and culture of various groups, such as providing evening sessions with supper and child care (Boone, 1990) or assisting participants in environments closer to their homes (Padilla, 1989), rather than requiring them to attend meetings at school. Second, developers should conceptualize the total plan for professional development, rather than view it as a single event in which all participants assemble to be lectured for an hour and then go back to their classrooms where nothing will change. The positive effects of continued support after the initial presentation of the idea, through coaching by an expert or peer, have been especially strong (Glatthorn, 1987; Showers et al., 1987). These will be discussed in greater detail later in the chapter. Finally, developers should be aware that certain individual traits or characteristics may influence the effectiveness of professional development programs. These include the probability of more positive responses by those who exhibit flexibility in thinking, and the effect of what the teacher believes about teaching and the way he or she teaches (Showers et al., 1987). Developers who wish to bring about change through empowerment of team members will be aware of these and other findings identified earlier as "best practices."

STRATEGIES FOR PROFESSIONAL DEVELOPMENT

Three of the most widely used types of professional development for teams are (a) knowledge sharing, (b) skill development through coaching/reflection, and (c) team development. One way to empower team members is to provide them with new knowledge or skills in formal, scheduled learning activities. This is usually done through traditional professional development activities, in which team members share knowledge that enhances their colleagues' understanding. Skill development can be accomplished through a combination of peer coaching and individual reflection, in which team members observe each other and incorporate new learning into their existing structure of knowledge and skills. Finally, professional development can become an ongoing activity, through which the team itself matures as a unit capable of functioning effectively. In the following discussion, strategies for professional development through formal knowledge sharing and coaching with reflection will be presented. The chapter's application will provide an activity for identifying the team's maturity level and need for professional development as a unit.

Sharing Knowledge

Two aspects of knowledge sharing will be discussed: (a) the importance of determining the knowledge or content to be shared, through a needs assessment; (b) the guidelines for presentation. This discussion is directed at the formal sharing of knowledge, through professional development activities. Informal knowledge sharing, which occurs more frequently, has been described in the informational interview, Chapter 4, and in the Chapter 5 discussions of communication skills.

Needs Assessment.   NIN researchers summarizing best practices suggest that content should be based on a needs assessment. That is, the content is selected on the basis of a survey of the staff members who will receive the new information. In the survey, they have been asked what they need to know, have stated their major problems, and have suggested needs for further training. Through this needs assessment, those who share their knowledge determine the information that should be presented. An example of a needs assessment instrument, developed by members of a team of special educators who serve children with mild learning disabilities, is presented as Figure 8–2. This needs assessment was used to plan the content for a professional development program in which these team members participated. A modified version of the instrument was used as a post-test, to determine the effect of the knowledge sharing program on its participants.

Guidelines for Presentation.   The effective presenter of the professional development program establishes expert power by demonstrating knowledge and speaking with confidence. This person uses visual aids to help focus information on the topic, establishes eye contact with other members of the group, and sits or stands in a position that is higher than others while presenting information. When the presenter is a newcomer or is younger than others in the group, it is particularly important for him or her to acquire the knowledge necessary for establishing the impression of expert power and to use effective presentation skills to enhance this image. A person who is highly respected by the group might help establish the newcomer's credibility by indicating that this person is an expert in the field and by showing some relationship between the experience of the presenter and that of the participants.

Information presenters should communicate clearly, through correct use of media and an understanding of the most effective ways of presenting information. Effective use of media involves both its selection and its use. The first tendency of planners may be to overuse media, thinking that more is always better, as was shown tongue-in-cheek in the comic strip, *Beetle Bailey*. In the strip, General Halftrack was once shown conducting an inservice for his troops. He began by giving a progress report: "Enlistments are down," said the general as he pushed a button and a big foot clamped down on the floor, "while discharges are up." The general shot off a rocket. "The picture looks cloudy," he said as smoke poured out of the chart. "Original estimates have been shot full of holes." You can picture his demonstration of a shower of bullets. "There is nothing to do but pick up the pieces and start over," he said as little bits of paper were tossed into the room by a small catapult. The result was that people left the meeting whispering, "I could do without some of the visual aids." The point, of course, is for the presenter to consider whether visual aids will enhance or distract the audience from the message.

Visual aids are important because they help the presenter to focus the attention of the audience, enhancing the presenter's image as one with expert power. Transparencies, charts, and slides are the most frequently used types of visual aids. To be effective, the visual aid should focus on key words, while the presenter elaborates on each point. If the presenter wishes to provide the audience with details on the information being presented, handouts would be more effective than a transparency or chart. An attempt to provide these factual details without handouts would result in an

For each item, please circle the number that shows the degree to which you feel you can demonstrate the skill (1 = **low**, 5 = **high ability** to perform).

1. Establish positive motivational strategies that can be used with students with varying learning styles and ages.

    1   2   3   4   5

2. Analyze materials according to appropriateness for students.

    1   2   3   4   5

3. Develop lesson plans that assist my students in learning the skills I want to teach.

    1   2   3   4   5

4. Develop a schedule that allows me to work effectively with the variety of students in my classroom.

    1   2   3   4   5

5. Respond appropriately to the learning needs of students from different cultures.

    1   2   3   4   5

6. Resolve behavioral difficulties between emotionally handicapped students and other exceptionalities.

    1   2   3   4   5

7. Develop a plan of intervention for deviant behaviors.

    1   2   3   4   5

8. Identify specific teaching materials to meet needs of a given exceptionality.

    1   2   3   4   5

9. Create positive public relations within the community regarding my classroom.

    1   2   3   4   5

10. What is your major problem in your classroom at this time? Describe it briefly.

11. What change would you most like to make in your classroom, if you had the authority to make this change? Describe what you would change.

Figure 8–2
Pretest/assessment of skills for teachers

overload of verbal information, increasing the chances for misunderstanding. The type of media selection, then, should fit the purpose of sharing knowledge as outlined in the presenter's objectives.

Knowledge sharing is also enhanced when the presenter uses *summative,* rather than redundant or interfering *media combinations* (Deterline, 1968). A summative combination combines auditory and visual input in a complementary way. Suppose the presenter is teaching an audience about hearing impairments and is describing "how we hear." The speaker using summative media combinations would use a visual presentation that enhances, summarizes, and clarifies the auditory description of the concept. Thus, the speaker might present a model of the route that sound waves travel while saying, "We hear when sound waves are transmitted through the ear to the brain." The summative media combination is illustrated in Figure 8-3.

In a *redundant* media combination the leader would say, "We hear when sound waves are transmitted through the ear to the brain," while showing a transparency with just those words. The redundant use of media is boring, because the audio and visual components repeat rather than enhance each other. Such redundancy may even encourage the audience to tune out either the auditory or the visual component of the message.

The *interfering media combination* presents a visual that goes beyond the image of the auditory and distracts the audience from the major message. Thus, presenting the auditory description of how we hear with a visual showing a child with a hearing aid (Figure 8–4) is an interfering use of media combinations. Rather than helping the audience to visualize the route or even repeating the verbal message, this visual causes the audience to focus on an external aid to hearing and the boy's raised hand, thus making processing the verbal message more difficult.

Figure 8–3
Summative media combination: How we hear

Figure 8–4
Interfering media combination: How we hear

The use of summative media combinations that clarify information being pre-sented is one way to enhance the professional development program. Effective pre-senters also employ other ways to enhance knowledge sharing in professional devel-opment programs. The following presentation guidelines have been modified from the work of LeRoux (1984)[1]:

1. Establish credibility through demonstration of knowledge.
2. Use cue cards for notes, rather than read from a script.
3. Face the audience directly, keeping your weight distributed equally on both feet and standing without hands in pockets.
4. Use gestures to enhance the presentation.
5. To use eye contact effectively, focus for about three seconds on each person.
6. Practice the art of asking questions.
7. Answer questions appropriately.
8. Build rapport with the audience by giving equal recognition to all participants.

LeRoux (1984) elaborates on the correct ways to ask and answer questions, as these are among the most difficult parts of any presentation. He suggests that the pre-senter begin by giving the audience permission to interrupt with questions and by mentioning that there will be a question-and-answer time at the end of the presenta-

[1]*Note:* From *Selling to a Group* by P. LeRoux, 1984, New York: Harper & Row. Adapted by permission of Harper & Row Publishers, Inc.

tion. When finished, the presenter should say, "Now it's time for questions." The speaker can "warm up" the audience by saying, "First I want to ask you a question." The presenter should ask a simple question that participants can answer by raising hands. The presenter might also prime the audience for questions by saying, "The question most frequently asked is. . . . Now, what are your questions?"

Finally, the correct way to field a question is to use this three-step process:

1. Indicate whose question you are answering: Point to the person.
2. Give eye contact to the person asking the question.
3. When the person has finished, repeat the question so the entire group can hear it.

LeRoux also suggests that the presenter try to neutralize negative questions so they do not build up resistance from the audience. For instance, after a presentation on mainstreaming, a classroom teacher in the audience might ask, "How am I going to have time to work with students with disabilities in my classroom when I have 35 other children?" The presenter could rephrase the question in a neutral way, as "You're wondering whether you can deal with the increasing demands on your time in the classroom. Let me answer that by giving you some examples of how other teachers who are concerned about all of their students have dealt with this issue. . . ." The presenter is then in a position to give some useful suggestions, rather than being forced into a defensive posture. The answer should be brief, and the presenter should move on quickly to the next question.

Application of Knowledge Sharing.   Suppose the presenter has identified the inability to work effectively with hearing-impaired students as a major need among members of the staff. She designs a one-hour presentation aimed at attitude change and knowledge sharing for the whole staff. After a brief introduction and overview that establish her credibility and relate the presentation to the needs identified by the group, she presents:

1. An opening simulation, during which she plays a record of conversations as heard by people with different types of hearing impairments.
2. A group discussion of the feelings and insights experienced by participants as they listened to the record, followed by the development of a group-generated list of the types of difficulties that might be experienced by hearing-impaired students in the classroom.
3. A brief overview of information on hearing impairment, which includes the use of summative transparencies such as those shown in Figure 8–3 to illustrate how we hear and to present information about the three major types of hearing impairments.
4. An illustration of one method teachers can use to help hearing-impaired students in the classroom. This part of the presentation incorporates transparencies made from Figure 8–3 and Figure 8–4, which illustrate the value of using summative visual aids to clarify auditory information presented.

5. A small-group activity, during which participants work together to develop a set of lesson materials for use with hearing-impaired students in their classes (these materials would be equally appropriate for use with all of their students). Participants work with others at their grade level to design a set of summative visual aids with an accompanying auditory script for a lesson they might teach in math, science, or social studies. The presenter circulates to give assistance while the participants work and collects the materials at the end of the session.

6. The presenter hands out a list of other suggestions that teachers might use to increase their effectiveness with students who are hearing impaired. She indicates that the lesson materials developed by each group will be typed and that the visual aids will be redrawn as transparencies by students in the school's art class; these materials will then be distributed to all members of the group for use in their classes.

7. The presenter obtains the participants' opinions about the effectiveness of the professional development program, including (a) how much they had enjoyed the presentation, (b) the degree to which they had learned how to work more effectively with hearing-impaired students in their classroom, and (c) whether they planned to use any of the knowledge they had acquired during the session.

This example of a professional development program aimed at knowledge sharing has shown how the presenter can transmit relevant information to a diverse group of individuals. It has also shown how to use professional development activities not only to increase the knowledge of participants, but also to establish a sense of teaming among members of the staff. The provision of follow-up materials, designed by participants, will further enhance the opportunities for continued interaction and cooperation among those who collaborated in their design.

Developing Skills

Team members can empower each other by engaging in activities that enhance their skills. The most effective means are based on knowledge about adults as learners. These include (a) skill development through peer observation and coaching, and (b) opportunities for the learner to reflect upon what is learned, and to incorporate new learning into ones' own existing knowledge structure.

Developing Skills Through Coaching.   Team members can empower each other by developing skills through mutual assistance known as coaching. In coaching, team members engage in frequent, ongoing observations of each other's performance, followed by conferences that focus on constructive feedback (O'Shea, 1987). Coaching provides team members with an increased amount and quality of supervised practice, as well as assistance in the transfer of newly developed skills (Ackland, 1991; Joyce & Showers, 1988; Neubert, 1988). Coaching has been used effectively at both the preservice and inservice levels. In one interesting program, special education seniors were coached by teams of mentors, who included special educators, general educators, and university faculty members (Duarte, 1992–93).

In preservice education, coaching has been shown to improve the learner's ability to transfer new learning (Peterson & Hudson, 1989; Wynn, 1987; 1988).

Coaching also increases desirable teaching behaviors and decreases undesirable ones (Peterson & Hudson, 1989). Coached teachers also seem to retain information longer and to have a greater effect on the learning improvement of pupils in their classrooms (Showers, 1984). Most significant for team members, it has been found that coaching improves collegiality, because it reduces teachers' isolation and provides them with peer support (Wynn, 1987; 1988).[2]

During coaching, team members are asked to practice the skill in a professional development session while their performance is being observed. After demonstrating mastery during the training session, participants are asked to practice the skill in their own classroom or program while their performance is being observed. The observer—who may be the presenter, a supervisor, or a peer—engages in coaching to help the performer in skill development. Coaching has been effective in numerous professional development programs in enabling teachers to demonstrate skill mastery (Glatthorn, 1987; McREL, 1984/1985).

Coaching seems to be most effective when implemented by teacher groups who observe and assist each other as peers. Rogers (1987) has described one of these programs in detail, showing how teachers within the school worked together in teams of two or three to observe and videotape each other's teaching. Members of these teams asked their partners to help them identify a goal for improvement and then engage in observation of teaching performance. This nonjudgmental, supportive observation provided constructive feedback and thus facilitated the goal of self-improvement. Leggett and Hoyle (1987) have developed a program in which preservice students learn to work together as teams, using observation and feedback in a spirit of collegiality for instructional improvement.

Ends and Page (1984) have developed a checklist for coaching, used in the development of skills by members of an organizational team. It has been modified for use by the interactive team and is presented as Figure 8–5. Ends and Page suggest that the checklist be used in the joint goal-setting and planning process, which should precede coaching for skill development.

In the coaching conferences that follow observations, team members should remember to:

◆ Establish a positive climate for collaboration.

◆ Use persuasive data.

◆ Deal with feelings and attitudes.

◆ Avoid giving direct advice.

◆ Pursue alternative strategies.

◆ Plan for next steps.

◆ Encourage input from the person you are coaching.

---

[2]The assistance of Tracy Hines on this literature review is gratefully acknowledged.

---

1. Does the team member agree the skill needs to be developed?

2. Does the team member understand exactly what is to be done?

3. Does the team member want to develop the skill?

4. Will the team member have responsibility for the outcome of the skill application (or is the outcome determined by something over which the member has no control)?

5. Is the goal realistic, but challenging (neither too simple nor too advanced for the member's current level)?

6. Can the coach provide immediate, concrete feedback so the team member will know how well he or she is doing?

Figure 8-5

A coaching checklist

Note: From *Organizational Team Building* (p. 186) by E. Ends and C. Page, 1984, Lanham, MD: University Press of America. Adapted by permission.

Developing Skills Through Reflection.   During the process of coaching, the team member is confronted with new information in the form of peer feedback, new research, and data on the performance of students. To increase the effectiveness of existing practices and to make new decisions, the team member needs to be able to synthesize this new information, reflect on its meaning, and incorporate it into his or her current cognitive framework. Because interactive teaming, like teaching, is an involved task which requires problem solving within circumstances lacking certainty, effective team members need to become deliberate and reflective decision makers (Patricia & Lamb, 1990). There is a considerable body of knowledge that supports the value of critical reflection in teacher education (Ross & Krogh, 1988; Roth, 1989). During field-based experiences, the intern analyzes relevant research and theory, while documenting the process and outcomes of teaching through a format such as a journal. This opportunity allows the intern to formulate possible solutions to classroom problems, while linking theory with practice and establishing the relationship between action and reflection (Krutilla & Safford, 1990; Valli, 1989; Zeichner & Liston, 1987).

Professionals who recommend preparing students as active decision-makers through the process of reflection on self and data may do so in response to studies which disclose that student teachers become less creative, more rigid, more authoritarian, and less responsive to the needs of pupils when they complete their field-based experiences than when they began (Thies-Sprinthall, 1984). Findings from the work of Johnson (1986) and Goodlad (1990) suggest that student teachers may learn less during the latter part of their field experiences, either believing they have already mastered all they need to know, or that the theory taught earlier has little relevance to classroom practice. Blase (1985) further suggests that over time teachers narrow and routinize their methods, materials and content to conform with the expectations of the bureaucracy. All this evidence suggests the need for development of decision-making and problem-solving skills, through teacher's critical reflection on personal performance and research data.[3]

It is suggested, then, that the team member can develop and retain new professional skills most effectively when encouraged to reflect on the observations made by a peer during coaching. The use of a data base in problem-solving has long been advocated in special education programs. It is consistent also with the basic principles of Total Quality Management (Deming, 1986), and the guidelines for development of effective teams (Scholtes, 1988). Professional development is facilitated both through coaching and by opportunities to develop decision-making skills through reflection on personal performance and student achievement data (Peterson & Hudson, 1989; Showers, 1984).

Developing the Team

The final type of professional development to be discussed is the development of the team itself, as a mature, supportive, effective functional unit. The team's development is the focus of this entire book, and its importance is highlighted in the basic principles of Total Quality Management (Deming, 1986), particularly those of "constancy of purpose," responsiveness to the "customer," and continuous improvement. Although it is not our intention to review these guidelines at this point, we have selected a summative activity, through which the reader may consider data and reflect upon information about the hypothetical team's need for professional development, and the leadership style most effective for teams at varying developmental or maturity levels.

APPLICATION

This activity is based on the early work of Hersey and Blanchard (1974), related to the leadership styles needed for effective management of groups. As indicated in Chapter 7, these authors have described the leader's behavior as either task-oriented or relationship-oriented. They have further indicated that the maturity of the group determines the degrees of directiveness and personal relationship that are appropriate for leadership of the group. It is important to specify that *maturity*, as used here, refers to the group's maturity as a team, a functional unit (not to the age level or the personality variables that may be synonyms for maturity in other contexts). Classifying leadership into four quadrants, Hersey and Blanchard indicate that the immature group needs the highest level of task direction and the lowest level of personal relationship. Conversely, the most mature group requires neither task direction nor relationship development. The four categories are as follows:

---

[3]This summary of the literature on reflective teaching was completed by Linda Lenk, University of Florida.

1. Below-average maturity group—high task/low relationship.
2. Average maturity group—high task/high relationship.
3. Average maturity group—low task/high relationship.
4. Above-average maturity group—low task/low relationship.

In the application that follows (Figure 8–6), read each of the 10 situations describing the team's behavior, and make a decision about the team's maturity level as a functional group based on this information. Then select one of the four alternative actions, each of which indicates a particular level of the leader's style in task and relationship response.

When you finish, compare your selected actions with those of the designers, using the Style Range answer chart (Figure 8–7). The answers A.B.C.D. are listed in rows reading across from the situation number. All answers that indicate the response for a particular "style" are found in the columns, reading down. That is:

1. Responses (high task/low relationship) for below-average maturity group
2. Responses (high task/high relationship) OR
3. Responses (high relationship/low task) for average maturity group
4. Responses (low task/low relationship) for above-average maturity group

Absolute "right" and "wrong" responses are not given, both because we have taken some liberty with the original authors' ideas, and because we think your reflection upon these decisions will lead to a lively discussion. From this activity, you should be able to make decisions about the types of behaviors that characterize mature and immature teams, and to formulate some suggestions about the types of professional development activities that might be appropriate for groups that exhibit these behaviors.

SUMMARY

Members of the interactive team are interested in obtaining *power,* which is defined as the ability to facilitate change that improves programs for special needs students. Power is obtained through empowerment—the provision of knowledge, skill, and change strategies to persons within the organization who serve these students or clients. The empowerment of individuals is accomplished through professional development, designed in accordance with information about the best practices for its use.

Three types of professional development programs, increasing in complexity and effectiveness, are available to members of the interactive team:

◆ Sharing knowledge.
◆ Developing skills.
◆ Developing the team.

"You are the group leader. . ."

SITUATION

1. Your team members are not responding lately to your friendly conversation and low-key directions. They haven't followed through on I.E.P. assignments.

ALTERNATIVE ACTIONS

A. Insist on uniform procedures and task accomplishment.
B. Make yourself available for discussion but don't push.
C. Talk with team members, then set goals.
D. Do not intervene.

SITUATION

2. The effectiveness of your team is increasing. You have been making sure that all members were aware of their roles and performance expectations.

ALTERNATIVE ACTIONS

A. Be friendly, but continue to make sure that all members are aware of their roles and tasks.
B. Take no definite action.
C. Do what you can to make the members feel important and involved.
D. Emphasize the importance of timeliness and tasks.

SITUATION

3. Members of your team are unable to solve a problem. You have previously left them alone. Group performance and interpersonal relations have been good.

ALTERNATIVE ACTIONS

A. Get involved with the group and work with the members in problem-solving.
B. Let the group work it out.
C. Intervene quickly to correct and redirect.
D. Encourage group work on problem and be available for discussion.

SITUATION

4. You are considering a major change in referral procedures. Your subordinates have a fine record of accomplishment. They respect the need for change.

ALTERNATIVE ACTIONS

A. Allow group involvement in developing the change, but don't push.
B. Announce changes and then implement with close supervision.
C. Let group formulate its own direction.
D. Incorporate group recommendations, but design change yourself.

SITUATION

5. The achievement of your group has dropped during the last few months. Members have been unconcerned with meeting objectives, and have continually needed reminding to have their tasks done on time. Redefining roles has helped in the past.

ALTERNATIVE ACTIONS

A. Allow group to determine its own direction.
B. Incorporate group recommendations, but see that objectives are met.
C. Redefine goals and supervise carefully.
D. Allow group involvement in setting goals, but don't push.

Figure 8–6

What is your leadership style?

Note: Reprinted from the Training & Development Journal. Copyright (February 1974), the American Society for Training and Development. Reprinted with permission. All rights reserved.

SITUATION	ALTERNATIVE ACTIONS
6. You are considering major changes in your team's structure. Members of the group have made suggestions about needed changes. The group has demonstrated flexibility in its day-to-day operations.	A. Define the change and supervise carefully. B. Acquire group's approval on the change and allow members to decide on implementation. C. Be willing to make changes as recommended, but maintain control of implementation. D. Avoid confrontations; leave things alone.
SITUATION	ALTERNATIVE ACTIONS
7. Group performance and interactions are good. You feel somewhat unsure about your lack of direction of the group.	A. Leave the group alone. B. Discuss the situation with the group and then initiate necessary changes. C. Take steps to direct team members toward working in a well-defined manner. D. Be careful of hurting leader-subordinate relations by being too directive.
SITUATION	ALTERNATIVE ACTIONS
8. Your superior has appointed you to head a task force that is far overdue in making requested recommendations for change. The group is not clear on its goals. Attendance at sessions has been poor. Their meetings have turned into social gatherings. The group has the necessary talent.	A. Let the group work it out. B. Incorporate group recommendations, but see that objectives are met. C. Redefine goals and supervise carefully. D. Allow group involvement in setting goals, and don't push.
SITUATION	ALTERNATIVE ACTIONS
9. Your team members, usually able to take responsibility, are not responding to your recent redefining of standards.	A. Allow group involvement in redefining standards, but don't push. B. Redefine standards and supervise carefully. C. Avoid confrontation by not applying pressure. D. Incorporate group recommendations, but see that new standards are met.
SITUATION	ALTERNATIVE ACTIONS
10. Recent information indicates some internal difficulties among team members. The group has a remarkable record of accomplishment. Members have effectively maintained long range goals. They have worked in harmony for the past year. All are well qualified for the task.	A. Try out your solution with subordinates and examine the need for new practices. B. Allow group members to work it out themselves. C. Act quickly and firmly to correct and redirect. D. Make yourself available for discussion, but be careful of hurting leader-member relationships.

Figure 8–6, *continued*

Figure 8–7

Style range

	(1)	(2)	(3)	(4)
1	A	C	B	D
2	D	A	C	B
3	C	A	D	B
4	B	D	A	C
5	C	B	D	A
6	A	C	B	D
7	C	B	D	A
8	C	B	D	A
9	B	D	A	C
10	C	A	D	B
	(1)	(2)	(3)	(4)
	HT/LR	HT/HR	HR/LT	LT/LR

Professional development requires an understanding of the process of change and an ability by the developer to design a change strategy that will affect the entire organization in which special needs students are served. Effective professional development increases the power of the team by empowering its members with knowledge and skills that assist them in implementing needed changes. The empowerment of family members, which enables them to function as full members of the interactive team, is described in the following chapter.

ACTIVITIES

1. Compare and contrast the following pairs of terms:
    - power structure; change agent
    - inservice training; professional development
    - power; empowerment
    - legitimate power; expert power

2. Through observation and discussion, identify one or two professionals in your program who demonstrate excellent skills that might be used by others. Plan a professional development program that includes modeling, demonstration, and follow-up coaching by these exemplary professionals.

3. Conduct or design a needs assessment that might be used in planning a professional development program for your organization.

4. Observe a meeting of a team that is planning a program for a special needs student. List your observations of the personal and professional characteristics of those with the most power and least power. Compare your observations with those made earlier, following the guidelines for observation of the team at the end of Chapter 1. List the procedures the high-power person used to facilitate the team efforts. Describe any attempts by the high-power person to empower others in the decision-making process.

5. Design a knowledge-sharing professional development program that meets the following criteria for oral presentation. Present it to members of your group and obtain their evaluation of its effectiveness.

    a. Brief overview/theoretical base presented.

    b. Interesting opener/closing.

    c. Appropriate media and handouts used.
        - Designed to match purpose.
        - Audio-visual combinations are summative.
        - Momentum maintained during handout distribution.

    d. Effective activities.
        - Designed to match objective(s).
        - Designed to involve audience.

    e. Effective presentation.
        - Demonstrated professionalism.
        - Demonstrated knowledge.
        - Used notes appropriately.
        - Used nonverbals effectively (eyes, stance, gestures).
        - Used verbals effectively (volume, inflections).
        - Used questions appropriately (eliciting, responding, answering).
        - Managed audience (developing rapport, managing disruptions).
        - Used humor and/or examples.
        - Avoided information overload.

REFERENCES

Ackland, R. (1991). A review of the peer coaching literature. *Journal of Staff Development, 12,* 22–27.

Audette, B., & Algozzine, B. (1992). Free and appropriate education for all students: Total quality and the transformation of American public education. *Remedial and Special Education, 13*(6), 8–18.

Bennis, W. (1989). *Why leaders can't lead: The unconscious conspiracy continues.* San Francisco: Jossey-Bass.

Blase, J. (1985). The socialization of teachers. *Urban Education, 20,* 235–256.

Boone, R. (1990). The development, implementation, and evaluation of a preconference training strategy for enhancing parental participation in and satisfaction with the individual transition conference. (Doctoral dissertation, University of Florida, 1989). *Dissertation Abstracts International, 51*(3), 816A.

Covey, S. (1990). *The 7 habits of highly effective people.* New York: Simon & Schuster.

Cuban, L. (1988). A fundamental puzzle of school reform. *Phi Delta Kappan, 69,* 341–344.

Deming, W. E. (1986). *Out of the crisis.* Boston: MIT Center for Advanced Engineering Studies.

Deterline, W. (1968). *Instructional technology workshop.* San Rafael, CA: General Programmed Teaching.

Duarte, P. (1992–93). A mentorship program for special education seniors. *National Forum of Applied Educational Research Journal, 6*(1), 54–67.

Ends, E., & Page, C. (1984). *Organizational team building.* Lanham, MD: University Press of America.

French, J., & Raven, B. (1959). The bases of social power. In D. Cartwright (Ed.), *Studies in social power.* Ann Arbor, MI: University of Michigan, Institute for Social Research.

Gartner, A., & Lipsky, D. (1987). Beyond special education: Toward a quality system for all students. *Harvard Educational Review, 57,* 367–395.

Gersten, R., Carnine, D., & Green, S. (1982, March). *Administrative supervisory support functions for the implementation of effective educational programs for low income students.* Paper presented at the annual meeting, American Educational Research Association, New York.

Glatthorn, A. (1987). Cooperative professional development: Peer-centered options for teacher growth. *Educational Leadership, 45,* 31–35.

Glatthorn, A., & Newberg, J. (1984). A team approach to instructional leadership. *Educational Leadership, 39*(3), 60–63.

Goodlad, J. (1990). *Teachers for our nation's schools.* San Francisco: Jossey-Bass.

Grosenick, J., & Reynolds, M. (1978). *Teacher education: Renegotiating roles for mainstreaming.* Reston, VA: The Council for Exceptional Children.

Hall, G., George, A., & Rutherford, W. (1977). *Measuring stages of concern about the innovation: A manual for use of the SOC Questionnaire.* Austin, TX: University of Texas, R & D Center for Teacher Education.

Hall, G., Loucks, S., & Newlove, B. (1976). *Measuring levels of use of the innovation: A manual for trainers, interviewers and raters.* Austin, TX: University of Texas, R & D Center for Teacher Education.

Hall, G., Rutherford, W., Hord, S., & Huling, L. (1984). Effects of three principal styles on school improvement. *Educational Leadership, 41*(5), 22–31.

Hersey, P., & Blanchard, K. (1974). So you want to know your leadership style? *Training and Development Journal, 28*(2), 22–36.

Hutson, H. (1979). *Inservice best practices: The learnings of general education.* Bloomington, IN: National Inservice Network.

Jackman, M. (1991). The queen of team. *Executive Female,* July–August, 37–40.

Johnson, L. (1986). Factors that influence skill acquisition of practicum students during a field-based experience. *Teacher Education and Special Education, 9*(3), 89–103.

Joyce, B., & Showers, B. (1988). *Student achievement through staff development.* New York: Longman Publishers.

Joyce, B., Showers, B., & Rolheiser-Bennett, C. (1987). Staff development and student learning: A synthesis of research on models of teaching *Educational Leadership, 45,* 11–23.

Krutilla, J., & Safford, P. (1990). Portrait of the shared student teaching experience: Owning reflection and action. *Teacher Education and Special Education, 13*(3–4), 217–220.

Leggett, D., & Hoyle, S. (1987). Preparing teachers for collaboration. *Educational Leadership, 44,* 58–63.

LeRoux, P. (1984). *Selling to a group.* New York: Harper & Row.

Levine, M. (1985). Excellent companies and exemplary schools: Common goals and characteristics. *NASSP Bulletin, 69*(7), 56–59.

Lewin, K. (1975). Field theory in social science. In D. Cartwright (Ed.), *Field theory in social science.* Westport, CT: Greenwood.

Lieberman, A. (1988). Expanding the leadership team. *Educational Leadership, 45,* 4–9.

Losen, S., & Losen, J. (1985). *The special education team.* Boston: Allyn & Bacon.

Lyon, S., & Lyon, G. (1980). Team functioning and staff development: A role release approach to providing integrated services for severely handicapped students. *Journal of the Association for the Severely Handicapped, 5*(3), 250–263.

McClelland, D. (1975). *Power: The inner experience.* New York: Irvington.

McLaughlin, M., & Marsh, D. (1978). Staff development and school change. *Teacher's College Record, 80,* 70–95.

McREL (Mid-continental Regional Educational Laboratory). (1984/1985, Winter). Coaching: A powerful strategy for improving staff development and inservice education. *Noteworthy,* 40–46.

Neubert, G. (1988). *Improving teaching through coaching.* (Fastback 277). Bloomington, IN: Phi Delta Kappa.

O'Shea, L. (1987). The supervision throughput model: Interpersonal communication skills and problem-solving procedures for effective intern supervision. *Teacher Education and Special Education, 10,* 71–80.

Padilla, S. (1989). *The effect of teacher's home visits on special student's school performance.* Unpublished manuscript, University of Florida, Department of Special Education, Gainesville.

Patricia, L., & Lamb, M. (1990). Preparing secondary special education teachers to be collaborative decision makers and reflective practitioners: A promising practicum model. *Teacher Education and Special Education, 13*(3–4), 228–232.

Pelfry, R. (1988, February). How to sell a school board by really trying. *Electronic Learning,* 16.

Peterson, S., & Hudson, P. (1989). Coaching: A strategy to enhance preservice teacher behaviors. *Teacher Education and Special Education, 12,* 56–60.

Powers, D., & Powers, M. (1983). *Making participatory management work.* San Francisco: Jossey-Bass.

Rogers, S. (1987). If I can see myself, I can change. *Educational Leadership, 45,* 64–67.

Ross, D., & Krogh, S. (1988). From paper to program: A story from elementary PROTEACH. *Peabody Journal of Education, 65*(2), 19–34.

Roth, R. (1989). Preparing the reflective practitioner: Transforming the apprentice through the dialectic. *Journal of Teacher Education, 40*(2), 31–35.

Sage, D., & Burrello, L. (1986). *Policy and management in special education.* Englewood Cliffs, NJ: Prentice-Hall.

Schmoker, M., & Wilson, R. (1993). Transforming schools through total quality education. *Phi Delta Kappan, 74,* 389–395.

Scholtes, P. (1988). *The team handbook.* Madison, WI: Joiner Associates.

Showers, B. (1984). *Peer coaching: A strategy for facilitating transfer of training.* Report to the U.S. Department of Education. Eugene, OR: University of Oregon, Center for Educational Policy and Management. (ERIC Document ED 271 849).

Showers, B., Joyce, B., & Bennett, B. (1987). Synthesis of research on staff development: A framework for future study and a state-of-the-art analysis. *Educational Leadership, 45,* 77–87.

Sickler, J. (1988). Teachers in charge: Empowering the professionals. *Phi Delta Kappan, 69,* 354–356.

Skrtic, T. (1987). *An organizational analysis of special education reform.* Washington, DC: The National Inquiry into the Future of Education for Students with Special Needs.

Stedman, L. (1987). It's time we changed the effective schools formula. *Phi Delta Kappan, 69,* 215–224.

Thies-Sprinthall, L. (1984). Promoting the developmental growth of supervising teachers: Theory, research programs, and implications. *Journal of Teacher Education, 35*(3), 53–60.

Tucker, A. (1984). *Chairing the academic department: Leadership among peers* (2nd ed.). New York: American Council on Education–Macmillan.

Tucker, J. (1972). *A plan to achieve change*. Austin, TX: University of Texas, Department of Special Education.

Valli, L. (1989). Collaboration for transfer of learning: Preparing preservice teachers. *Teacher Education Quarterly, 16*(1), 85–95.

Wynn, M. (1987). Student teacher transfer of training to the classroom: Effects of an experimental model. (Doctoral dissertation, University of Florida, 1986). *Dissertation Abstracts International, 47*, 3008A.

Wynn, M. (1988, April). Transfer of training to the classroom by student teachers: Effects of an experimental model. Paper presented at the annual meeting of the American Educational Research Association, New Orleans, LA. (ERIC Document ED 239 830).

Zeichner, K., & Liston, D. (1987). Teaching student teachers to reflect. *Harvard Educational Review, 57*, 23–48.

CHAPTER 9

Enabling and Supporting Families

Factors that Have Influenced Changes in Attitudes

Legislative Factors
Theoretical Factors
Research Factors

Role of the Professional

Providing Basic Information
Reporting Evaluation Results
Understanding and Gathering Family Information
Providing Instruction to Families
Understanding Culturally Diverse Families
Interpreting Information
Communicating Effectively

Role of the Family

Providing Information
Reinforcing School Program at Home
Advocating for Quality Services
Understanding the Professional's Perspective

Strategies for Supporting Families

Application

Summary

TOPICS IN THIS CHAPTER INCLUDE

◆ The changing view of families of children with disabilities.

◆ The various roles of professionals supporting families.

◆ The unique roles of family members collaborating with professionals.

◆ Strategies for collaborating effectively with families.

◆ An application for involving families in special education.

Linda is the single mother of a 6-year-old child with disabilities, Miriam, and a 4-year-old child, Carlos. Linda lives in Miami with her mother, a native Cuban, who speaks very little English. Linda has fought many battles in the past six years. Physicians told her that Miriam would not live to see her first birthday, ophthalmologists reported that the girl was totally blind, and physical therapists said she would never walk.

In spite of the gloomy prognosis, Linda was committed to making Miriam's life the best that it could be. Linda searched for early intervention services when Miriam was 18 months old. They attended early intervention clinics; Linda spoke with other parents of infants with disabilities. Linda placed Miriam in public school programs for toddlers with disabilities. She and Miriam attended summer camps for children with visual impairments and their families. Linda learned physical therapy techniques needed to help Miriam with motor control and eating.

If there is a typical story of a parent of a child with disabilities, this may be one. But Linda brings a new twist to the story. Linda is currently running her own advocacy consultation business. She collaborates with professionals and parents in school districts around Florida in an effort to meet the needs of children with visual and multiple disabilities. She serves as an advocate in due process hearings, and makes presentations at legislative hearings and many special education national conferences. Linda continues her battles for appropriate services for her daughter, and fights for better services for other children with disabilities. She is a distinct kind of parent, well versed in legal and educational issues, articulate in presenting her opinion, and an equal partner on the special education team.

During the last 20 years, much has been written about families of students with disabilities. With the passage of Public Law 94-142 in 1975, and subsequent legislation of the Individuals with Disabilities Education Act in 1990 (P.L. 101-476), the role of the family as an integral part of the special education process was recognized. Special education personnel became aware of the need to develop skills in supporting and involving families. Although families were encouraged to participate in the development of their child's IEP program, there were indefinite attempts for such involvement.

Parental involvement usually was limited to attending IEP conferences and approving program and placement decisions made by special education personnel (Meyers & Blacher, 1987). Parents were often intimidated by the process, rarely contributed to the development of the IEP, and typically were viewed by professional staff members as submissive or passive participants in the IEP process. Furthermore, school administrators discouraged the involvement of parents in school functions (Fuqua, Hegland, & Karas, 1985) for fear that agitated and unsatisfied parents would instigate due process hearings and lawsuits. If school personnel did encourage *family-centered involvement,* it usually was regarded as more of a kindhearted or paternalistic gesture.

With the passage of Public Law 99-457 (U.S. Code, 1986), the early intervention amendment to the Education of All Handicapped Children's Act, professionals' knowledge and perceptions of families of children with disabilities have been significantly influenced. Families are respected as experts on their children and are valued for their equal partnership in the educational process. The purpose of this chapter is to present the factors that have influenced the changing attitudes of professionals about families of children with disabilities.

A contemporary view of the role of the professional and parent in a collaborative partnership also will be described. Understanding families from culturally and linguistically diverse backgrounds will be highlighted and strategies for involving families will be discussed.

FACTORS THAT HAVE INFLUENCED CHANGES IN ATTITUDES

American families have changed dramatically during the last few decades. These changes have implications for professionals working with families today (Hanson & Lynch, 1992). Reports on the diverse structures of today's families indicate the following:

◆ 59% of children born in 1983 lived with only one parent (Williams, 1992).

◆ Cohabitation has become a common family form, replacing the old stepfamily structure (Levin, 1993).

◆ In Florida, 1 out of every 5 children resides with another relative or outside the family structure (Florida Kids Count, 1993).

◆ In 1990, one of ten Florida babies was born to an unmarried teen mother (Florida Kids Count, 1993).

◆ In 1990, the majority of the nation's preschoolers (57%) had parents in the work force; by the year 2000 that proportion will grow to 7 in 10 (Florida Kids Count, 1993).

◆ An estimated 100,000 children are homeless (Children's Defense Fund, 1991; Hanson/Lynch, 1992).

◆ Most homeless women are "mothers, are under 35 years, are members of a minority group, have not completed high school, and have experienced more than one episode of homelessness in their lifetimes" (Milburn & D'Ercole, 1991, p. 1161).

◆ More than 46% of children under the age of 5 receive care outside the home from a nonfamily caregiver (Hayes, Palmer, & Zaslow, 1990).

◆ More same-sex partners are now raising children (Lynch & Hanson, 1992).

◆ More grandparents are becoming custodial parents of young children (Lynch & Hanson, 1992).

◆ By the year 2000, one fourth to one third of the U.S. population will be African-American, Asian, and Hispanic (Williams, 1992).

◆ 60% of all immigrants were from either Mexico, Central America, or South America; and the second largest number of immigrants came from Asia (Moore, 1993).

In recent years, the idea that families of children with disabilities function normally and that the child exerts positive influences on family members has been stated definitively (Dunst, Trivette, & Deal, 1988; Powell & Gallagher, 1993; Turnbull & Turnbull, 1990). The role of the family and their involvement with special education personnel have improved significantly. Factors that may have influenced these changes are in the areas of legislation, theory development, and improved research on family adjustment.

Legislative Factors

The passage of P.L. 99-457 considerably influenced the roles and responsibilities of the parent and the professional in meeting the educational needs of children with disabilities. For families receiving services under early intervention programs, the Individualized Family Support Plan (IFSP) is required under this legislation. The intent of the service plan is similar to that of an IEP for a child. However, the IFSP is designed to focus on generating individualized goals and services for meeting the needs of the families and young children with disabilities being served in early intervention programs. Those needs may include parent support, counseling services, or parent education. Although P.L.99-457 mandates services for families of young children with disabilities, the implications of the IFSP will ultimately be to older children with disabilities and their families.

Theoretical Factors

Various theoretical points of view related to families of children with disabilities have been presented in recent literature. One of the most applicable is the *family systems theory* (Carter & McGoldrick, 1980; Minuchin, 1974; Turnbull & Turnbull, 1990). Theorists maintain that the underlying structure of the family can be conceptualized into four *family subsystems: marital, sibling, parental,* and *extrafamilial.*

The ability of the family to function effectively depends on how clearly the boundaries and rules of the family are defined and how cohesive and flexible the family is during life cycle changes. The underlying premise is that life events, such as the birth of a child with disabilities, will affect not only the parents but also the siblings, grandparents, and friends. The implications of this theoretical framework are that interventionists are a part of the extrafamilial subsystem and therefore affect each member of the family, even though they may be involved directly with only one member, usually the mother. The traditional view of parent involvement and training with only mothers of children with disabilities must be broadened to include fathers, siblings, grandparents, and others who share in the care of these children.

Literature on theoretical approaches for understanding families provides professionals with a wealth of information. The social support perspective (Dunst, Cooper, Weeldreyer, Snyder, & Chase, 1988; Dunst, Trivette, & Cross, 1986), cognitive coping approach (Turnbull et al., 1993), stress and adaptation theory (McCubbin & Patterson, 1983), feminist family theory (Osmond & Thorne, 1993), and ethnocultural application of family theories (Dilworth-Anderson, Burton, & Johnson, 1993) provide a range of perspectives for understanding diverse families and families of children with disabilities. Various approaches to understanding families give professionals many more tools to assess family functioning and adaptation to children with disabilities.

Research Factors

The idea that families have a difficult time adjusting to the presence of a child with disabilities has been a major concern of professionals working in special education. In past years researchers have found that many families of children with disabilities were dysfunctional and in need of counseling (c.f. Farber & Ryckman, 1965). For example, some studies have reported a higher incidence of divorce (Murphy, 1982), drug and alcohol abuse (Shapiro, 1982), and child abuse (Frodi, 1981) in families of children with disabilities.

Dunst (1985) stated that the traditional view of families of children with disabilities was based on a deficit model in which much attention was placed on the pathology in families. In the traditional view, the goal of the professional was to remediate the deficits by helping families come to grips with the problems of having a child with disabilities. Families were viewed as overly emotional; family members were rejecting or struggling with the acceptance of the child with disabilities. These families were viewed as dysfunctional in contributing to their child's general welfare and educational program. Traditionally, the image of the family with a child with disabilities was one of chronic sorrow, severe depression, and emotional turmoil.

No longer is the family viewed as pathological and unhealthy. Instead, the family is portrayed positively. During the past few years, researchers have reported on studies supporting the notion that families are not necessarily adversely affected by the presence of a child with disabilities (Dunst et al., 1988; Dunst, 1985; Turnbull et al., 1993; Turnbull & Turnbull, 1990; Powell & Gallagher, 1993; Zeitlin, Williamson, & Rosenblatt, 1987). In fact, some researchers found that families of children with disabilities are as well adjusted as families with nondisabled children (Dunlap, Ondelacyt, & Sells, 1979; Gallagher, Cross, & Scharfman, 1981; Salisbury, 1987). The availability of *multifaceted family assessment* procedures—including tests, survey instruments, rating forms, natural observation, and interviews—have yielded more sensitive data on families of children with disabilities (Bailey & Simeonsson, 1988).

Some studies, however, report increased amounts of *family stress* when family members are coping with children with disabilities (Crnic, Friedrich, & Greenberg, 1983; Gallagher, Beckman, & Cross, 1983). How families cope with this stress influences their interaction with professionals in special education and other related fields. For example, Shuster, Guskin, Hawkins, and Okolo (1986) reported that mothers were reluctant to share information about their infants with disabilities with medical and early intervention personnel if the mothers were stressed, felt devalued, or lacked respect for the service provider. Thus, the goal of family intervention is to help families expand internal and external resources to meet the challenges and take advantage of the opportunities of family life (Zeitlin & Williamson, 1988). Providing families with support networks that help them cope with the stress of caring for a child with disabilities should be one aim of special education professionals.

Some research on diverse families of children with disabilities is appearing in the literature (Behar, Correa, & Beverly, 1993; Hanline & Daley, 1992), but more is needed. Additionally, research methods using ethnographic and qualitative approaches have proved valuable in expanding the knowledge-base on families of children with disabilities (Able-Boone, Sandall, Loughry, & Frederick, 1990; Teachman & Neustadtl, 1993).

Golan (1980) stated that families should be viewed as "normal people with normal troubles engaged in developmental processes of change and adaptation" (p. 266). Moreover, through parent training, support networking, and advocacy efforts, parents are educated to be equal partners with special educators. Many families have become sophisticated in working with school personnel by taking on a more active role in the educational process. Clearly, the relationship of the family and the professional has changed from coexistence to collaboration. In the next section, the roles and responsibilities of professionals and parents within the collaborative partnership will be delineated.

ROLE OF THE PROFESSIONAL

School personnel are responsible for initiating and maintaining a positive, interactive, and facilitative relationship with families of children with disabilities. In this regard, the role of the professional is multifaceted. Many school personnel feel comfortable with the more traditional responsibilities of providing information on students' progress, results of diagnostic evaluations, inclusive educational placement strategies, and schedules of upcoming school events.

But the role of the professional has expanded to include parent education and advocacy, medical report interpretation, active listening, and working with culturally diverse students and their families. The family's needs can range from information about due process hearings to help obtaining transportation, welfare payments, and food stamps. School personnel may take on the shared roles of social worker, attorney, physician, therapist, psychologist, clergy, and friend. The professional should not assume all these jobs without assistance or training, however.

Collaboration, role sharing, and role release are required for special educators and other team members to be successful in their expanded job responsibilities. Although many professionals may be willing to expand their roles in encouraging family involvement, few are trained to assume the added responsibilities. The various roles and responsibilities of the special education team members as collaborators are discussed below.

Providing Basic Information

The traditional role of the professional working with families has been as information provider. Teachers of students with mild disabilities, for example, usually provide the family with information on academic and emotional/social progress. The teachers and therapists of students with severe disabilities provide information on developmental progress, self-care skills, communication, and progress on related therapies such as occupational, physical, and speech. As educators and families move toward more inclusive settings for students with disabilities, the educator will need to provide information on students' integration into general education classrooms. Both general and special educators will need to be involved in information dissemination.

Information has been provided to families in many ways. Formal staffing and IFSP or IEP meetings are the most common arenas for professionals and families to interact. In some cases, special educators contact family members by phone, share daily logs with parents, or send notes home informing the family of the child's program.

Generally, it is helpful for professionals to provide parents with a checklist to help them prepare for the IEP conference. Figure 9–1 is an example of such a checklist. For more detailed information on preparing families for the IEP meeting, see Turnbull, Strickland, and Brantley (1982). For more detailed information on the IFSP meeting, see McGonigel, Kaufmann, and Johnson (1992) and Bennett, Lingerfelt, and Nelson (1990). Informal meetings provide professionals with time to share information with parents related to early developmental intervention, academic changes, behavioral problems, and therapy prescriptions.

How to Get Ready

_____ 1. Make a list of questions and concerns.
_____ 2. Ask your child if he/she has questions for the teacher.
_____ 3. Arrange for a babysitter for small children.

Questions You May Want to Ask

_____ 1. In which subjects does my child do well? Is my child having any trouble?
_____ 2. Does my child get along with other children?
_____ 3. Does my child obey the teacher?
_____ 4. How can I help at home?

Questions the Teacher May Ask You

_____ 1. What does your child like the best about school?
_____ 2. What does your child do after school? (Where are his/her interests?)
_____ 3. Does your child have time and space set aside for homework?
_____ 4. How is your child's health?
_____ 5. Are there any problems that may affect your child's learning?
_____ 6. What type of discipline works well at home?

At the Conference

_____ 1. Please arrive on time.
_____ 2. Discuss your questions and concerns.
_____ 3. Share information that will help the teacher know your child better.
_____ 4. Take notes if you wish.

After the Conference

_____ 1. If you have more questions or you ran out of time, make another appointment.
_____ 2. Tell your child about the conference.
_____ 3. Plan to keep in touch with the teacher.
_____ 4. If you were satisfied with the conference, write a note to the teacher.

Figure 9–1

Parent checklist for IEP meetings

Note: From _Communicating with Parents of Exceptional Children: Improving Parent-Teacher Relationships_ (p. 186) by R. L. Kroth, 1985, Denver: Love Publishing Company. Reprinted by permission.

Reporting Evaluation Results

The role of the special education team has been to interpret results of diagnostic evaluations to families. Providing diagnostic feedback is frequently the responsibility of a school psychologist or special education teacher. Informing parents about their child's educational or physical disabilities can be extremely sensitive and requires skills typically associated with problem solving, collaborating, and counseling. The following case illustrates the sensitive situation of a family hearing evaluation results.

Christopher, a 4-year-old child with multiple disabilities, was tested by a four-member evaluation team. During the diagnostic feedback session, all members were present with the parents. The psychologist reported to the parents first. He did an excellent job in providing the family with an overview of the evaluation results. However, at the end of his report the psychologist stated that Christopher was mentally retarded with adaptive behavior deficits in communication and self-care skills. The boy's mother became enraged and stood up screaming and crying that her son was not retarded. She was upset by the term *retardation,* and said she would leave the room if that word was used again. The family counselor intervened and calmed the mother down, agreeing that the word would not be used again in the session.

For these parents, the term *retardation* was offensive. The mother accepted the fact that her child had developmental delays, but she was unwilling to accept the diagnosis of retardation. The psychologist's role as information provider was to report test results according to the child's global intelligence scores. The professional who reports evaluation results in a sensitive way may still have families who are discouraged and, at times, shocked by the results of the evaluation (Turnbull & Turnbull, 1990). Guidelines for providing families with test results have been stated in various sources (Hirsh, 1981; Rockowitz & Davidson, 1979). Additionally, Fish (1990) and Margolis and Branningan (1990) provide special educators with strategies for interacting with angry parents, including active listening, empathizing, establishing trust, and systematic problem-solving techniques. Special education team members should adhere to the following when providing diagnostic feedback:

◆ Provide feedback in a private, safe, comfortable environment.

◆ Keep the number of professionals to a minimum.

◆ Begin by asking parents their feelings about the child's strengths as well as weaknesses.

◆ Provide the evaluation results in a *jargon-free* manner, using examples of test items and behavioral observations throughout.

◆ Provide parents results from a variety of assessment activities, including standardized tests, criterion-referenced tests, direct behavioral observations, play-based or community-based assessment, and judgment-based approaches.

◆ Be sensitive to viewing the child as an individual and a "whole" child when reporting various evaluation results.

◆ Allow the parent time to digest the results before educational planning begins.

◆ Be sensitive to linguistically different families and the use of interpreters.

◆ Prepare for the session with other team members, clarifying any possible conflicts before the meeting.

◆ Use conflict resolution strategies to clarify any possible conflicts with families.

Understanding and Gathering Family Information

The role of the professional working with students with disabilities has expanded significantly in the area of assessment instruments and analysis. No longer are team members asked to assess only the student's needs, but they now are being asked to assess the family's needs as well. Special education teams must understand the complex family system and know how to match intervention with the service needs of individual families. The linear view of the child with disabilities and the parent (most typically the mother) has been replaced with a systemic view of *family subsystems* (parental, marital, sibling, and extrafamilial) (Turnbull & Turnbull, 1990). Bailey and Simeonsson (1988) stated that conducting family assessments:

◆ Helps the professional understand the child as part of a family system.

◆ Identifies the family's service needs.

◆ Specifies the family's strengths and adaptations.

◆ Expands the efficacy of services and intervention.

Table 9–1 provides a list of the most commonly used instruments and checklists for assessing family functioning and needs. Although these instruments have been recommended by experts in the field, several cautions should be taken when using the instruments. Many assessment tools involve personal questions, which some families might consider overly intrusive. The responsibility for administering such instruments may fall on a psychologist or social worker, neither of whom usually has the time to conduct such assessments. Special education teachers may find the instruments too detailed for use in the school setting. Furthermore, professionals have not received training in administering many of the assessment tools and interpreting their results into concrete family plans (Bailey & Simeonsson, 1988).

Research by Garshelis and McConnell (1993) found that individual professionals on interdisciplinary teams did not do well in matching the family's needs with the mothers' perceptions of family needs. The collaborative teaming process helped professionals come to consensus and more closely match the parents' perceived needs.

Table 9–1

Sample of Assessment Instruments Useful for Gathering Family Information

---

Instrument Name: Variables Assessed

Caldwell Home Observation for Measurement of Environment (Caldwell & Bradley, 1979): Home variables

Carolina Family Responsibilities Scale (Gallagher, Scharfman, & Bristol, 1984): Perceptions of support from spouse

Child Improvement Locus of Control Scale (DeVillis et al., 1985): Locus of control

Client Patient Satisfaction Scale (Larsen, Attkisson, Hargreaves, & Nguyen, 1979): Parental satisfaction with services

Dyadic Adjustment (Spanier, 1976): Spouse relations

Family Crisis Oriented Personal Evaluation Scales (F-COPES) (Olson et al., 1985): Coping and adaptation to stress

Family Functioning Style Scale (Deal, Trivette, & Dunst, 1988): Family strengths

Family Needs Survey (Bailey & Simeonsson, 1990): Family needs

Locke-Wallace Marital Adjustment Scale (Locke & Wallace, 1959): Home quality and impact measures based on interview protocol

Parent Needs' Survey (Seligman & Darling, 1989): Parent needs

Parenting Stress Index (Abidin, 1986): Stress

The researchers concluded that professionals should allow parents to provide the team with perceived family needs, and should use those needs to guide the interventions developed with the family. Professionally directed assessments of family needs may not be accurate.

Professionals must be cautious in using family surveys with families of children with disabilities. Some of the instruments lack validity and reliability and have small norming populations (L'Abate & Bagarozzi, 1993; McGrew, Gilman, & Johnson, 1992). Furthermore, professionals should be overly cautious when using the surveys with families from culturally and linguistically diverse backgrounds (Behar, Correa, & Beverly, 1993). Few family instruments have been normed on minority families, and the families' cultural values and beliefs might not be taken into consideration when interpreting the results. Professionals should keep in mind that each family of a child with a disability has unique characteristics and should be evaluated on an individual basis.

Providing Instruction to Families

Professionals in special programs frequently are involved in educating parents to implement educational programs at home. The educational objectives can vary from teaching parents specific strategies such as learning strategies for increasing word recognition to teaching parents time-out procedures for decreasing tantrum behavior.

An abundance of research is available that supports the efficacy of educating parents in skills related to teaching students with disabilities (Johnson & Katz, 1973; Turnbull & Turnbull, 1990).

However, more recent trends in family literature indicate that the concept of parents as teachers and of professionals as parent trainers is questionable. Professionals must understand that although parents are effective in teaching and reinforcing behavior in their children, their role as teachers can be an added burden and source of stress for the family. Turnbull and Turnbull pointed out that families often do not have the time outside of their work and household responsibilities to "teach" their children. In many families the stress of daily intervention with their children can have detrimental effects on family members' interaction. Dunst, Leet, and Trivette (1988) found that adequacy of family resources and personal well-being affected the families' ability to adhere to prescribed interventions for the child. They concluded that some families did not follow through on prescribed interventions because they had to invest time and energy in meeting other family needs. Families with inadequate resources and social support did not carry out child treatments. To presume these families are resistant, uncooperative, or noncompliant is a grave error in professional judgment. The following vignette illustrates these issues:

Mrs. Green has a 4-year-old daughter, Kinesha, with severe visual and motor disabilities and mental retardation requiring extensive supports. At a recent IEP meeting, the special education professionals recommended that Mrs. Green continue the physical therapy interventions at home. The techniques prescribed involve 30 to 40 minutes a day of range-of-motion exercises and movement facilitation techniques to enhance posture and movement. Kinesha cries during much of the therapy sessions conducted at school and may vomit when she gets extremely upset. In addition, the special education teacher has asked Mrs. Green to provide Kinesha with 10 to 15 minutes of language stimulation a day to enhance her understanding of simple labels for familiar objects. The teacher provides the mother with a simple data collection sheet for the object labeling program. She also recommends that Mrs. Green spend extra time during meals to encourage Kinesha to feed herself. Lastly, the school psychologist is concerned about Kinesha's tantrums and vomiting and would like the mother to implement a time-out procedure for the next few months and report Kinesha's progress at the end of each week. Mrs. Green leaves the meeting with four training programs to be conducted each day at home. On a follow-up visit to the school, Mrs. Green is asked to report on the progress of all the programs. She is embarrassed and says she has been unable to conduct the programs at home.

The professionals involved with Mrs. Green have good intentions for Kinesha's educational program, but they have not made a thorough assessment of the family's needs. Before recommending family intervention programs, professionals should have asked about other family members, working responsibilities of both parents, and daily routines and schedules of the family. The family systems approach acknowledges the right of Mrs. Green and other family members to identify their own priorities for Kinesha. Professionals must consider individualizing their approach to providing families with information about intervention strategies, resources, and advocacy (Dunst, Leet, & Trivette, 1988; Turnbull & Turnbull, 1990). Specific suggestions for providing parents with information will be discussed in the last part of this chapter on involvement strategies. Providing information is especially difficult when families are culturally and linguistically different from mainstream school professionals.

Understanding Culturally Diverse Families

Statisticians indicate that by the turn of the century the minority cultures will be in the majority in many urban centers (Lynch & Stein, 1987; Moore, 1993; Williams, 1992). In the 1990 Census Report (1992) it was stated that nearly 32 million U.S. respondents claimed to speak a language other than English at home. This was an increase of 38% over the numbers reported in 1980. In 1984, more than 4.6 million school-age students spoke a language other than English at home (Plisko, 1984). Those numbers have continued to increase; for example, in Florida in 1991, public schools identified 98,229 *limited English proficient* (LEP) students, a 59% increase over the past two years (MIS Report, 1991–1992). The majority of the LEP and *non-English language background* (NELB) students in the United States are Hispanic. About 78% of the total LEP population is Hispanic (Waggoner, 1984). As a result of sustained immigration and high birth rates among some Hispanic subgroups, Hispanics are projected to become the largest minority in the nation shortly after the turn of the century (Bouvier & Davis, 1982; Moore, 1993; Reich, 1986).

Because of the increased incidence of minority populations in many school districts, special educators are required to work with students and families from diverse cultural groups. Unfortunately, most studies of families of children with disabilities have been directed toward Anglo-American families in the mainstream culture (Behar, Correa, & Beverly, 1993; Hanline & Daley, 1992; Lynch & Hanson, 1992; Harry, 1992; Lynch & Stein, 1987). The culturally diverse family—that is, the family from a cultural background other than Anglo-American—may not understand the special education needs of their child. They may not understand the nature of the child's disability, the educational services available for the child, or the expectations of professionals working with the child and family (Heron & Harris, 1987; Lynch & Hanson, 1992; Harry, 1992). Nevertheless, the professional must view the culturally diverse family not as inferior, but as having different values and beliefs that are positive (Behar, Correa, & Beverly, 1993; Correa, 1989). The belief system held by the family may actually be a strength for coping with and caring for the child with a disability.

The role of the professional working with the culturally diverse family is multifaceted. Professionals must first assess their own biases toward different ethnic groups. Second, they must make an effort to understand the family. At the same time, the minority family must be helped to understand and participate in the traditional Anglo mainstream culture. Acculturation into school life is a two-way process in which professionals and families collaborate.

Wayman, Lynch, and Hanson (1990) have provided guidelines for professionals making home visits to families from diverse backgrounds. Additionally, Correa (1989) described strategies for professionals working with culturally diverse families. Effective strategies include the following:

◆ Empowering families with skills for adapting and coping with a school system that may be very different from what they are accustomed to.

◆ Enabling families to reinforce educational programs at home in natural and functional ways.

◆ Assisting families through the transition from their native culture to the mainstream school culture.

◆ Serving as *culture brokers* by providing a link between the majority and minority cultures.

◆ Serving as mediators and advocates for the minority group.

◆ Removing barriers such as cultural differences, and linguistic and communication differences to enhance interaction between professionals and families.

◆ Assessing the family in terms of their experiences in their native country; the role of extended family members and siblings; the amount of community support available; religious, spiritual and/or cultural beliefs; and parenting practices (e.g., discipline, independence).

◆ Providing information, written and oral, in ways that enable families to comprehend.

Interpreting Information

For many families of children with disabilities, the information given to them on their child's disability can be overwhelming. In particular, medical information can be difficult to understand and interpret. Professionals in special programs are typically the only people parents can turn to when deciphering medical, psychological, and insurance reports. Interpreting information in terminology that a parent understands is an appropriate role for the professional. Special educators and other school-based professionals may be more available than physicians to families seeking information. Special educators, particularly school counselors and teachers of students with severe disabilities, can be greatly helped when team members, such as school nurses and public health officials, provide relevant medical information. Additionally, teachers of students with severe disabilities should have access to reference guides (e.g., *Merck Manual; Physicians' Desk Reference;* medical dictionaries; ophthalmology, ontology, anatomy, and physiology textbooks) that may help in the interpretation of medical reports.

The following vignette illustrates the role of the special education professional in translating information and the difficulty that may arise from that role.

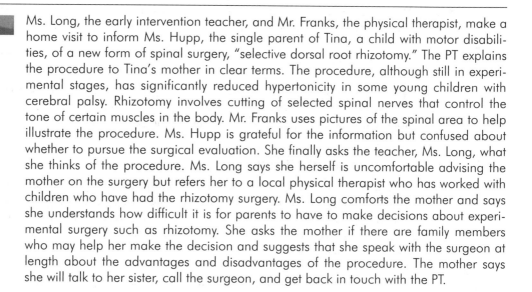

Ms. Long, the early intervention teacher, and Mr. Franks, the physical therapist, make a home visit to inform Ms. Hupp, the single parent of Tina, a child with motor disabilities, of a new form of spinal surgery, "selective dorsal root rhizotomy." The PT explains the procedure to Tina's mother in clear terms. The procedure, although still in experimental stages, has significantly reduced hypertonicity in some young children with cerebral palsy. Rhizotomy involves cutting of selected spinal nerves that control the tone of certain muscles in the body. Mr. Franks uses pictures of the spinal area to help illustrate the procedure. Ms. Hupp is grateful for the information but confused about whether to pursue the surgical evaluation. She finally asks the teacher, Ms. Long, what she thinks of the procedure. Ms. Long says she herself is uncomfortable advising the mother on the surgery but refers her to a local physical therapist who has worked with children who have had the rhizotomy surgery. Ms. Long comforts the mother and says she understands how difficult it is for parents to have to make decisions about experimental surgery such as rhizotomy. She asks the mother if there are family members who may help her make the decision and suggests that she speak with the surgeon at length about the advantages and disadvantages of the procedure. The mother says she will talk to her sister, call the surgeon, and get back in touch with the PT.

Parents often ask teachers to help them make decisions regarding medical, financial, or personal family matters. Parents who are young, inexperienced, less educated, or from minority cultures often are the ones who turn to school personnel for such help. Although this situation indicates that the parent trusts the professional, professionals may be uncomfortable with advising the parent on decisions involving an issue that is outside of their expertise. Professionals should provide as much information as possible and allow the parents to share their feelings. However, professionals make it clear that the final decision lies with the family.

Furthermore, professionals are frequently put in the role of interpreting special education information for families who do not speak English or who cannot read. Using interpreters for non-English speaking families can be a major help. Unfortunately, many interpreters used in the schools are not knowledgeable about special education terminology. The following illustrates the dilemma.

Mr. Agard, the father of a 9-year-old child with learning disabilities speaks only Haitian Creole. For lack of other resources, the special education teacher, Mr. Weaver, has asked the Haitian custodian to sit in on the IEP meeting and assist in interpreting the information. During the psychological report the term *visual perceptual dysfunction* was used. Not knowing exactly how to translate the diagnosis, the custodian told the father that his son was visually impaired. Mr. Agard became confused and asked if he should take his son to the eye doctor. With continued struggling, both Mr. Weaver and the custodian tried to clear up the confusion. However, Mr. Weaver was never totally confident that the father had understood the diagnosis. To minimize the confusion, Mr.

Weaver should have contacted local churches and outreach agencies within the Haitian community to recruit a trained volunteer translator for the IEP meeting.

Providing parents with information and support may appear basic to school professionals. The task becomes a challenge when families lack basic information on special education, legal, medical, financial, and psychological information.

Communicating Effectively

As illustrated in the previous section, the importance of being sensitive to the language and culture of parents is a prerequisite to effective communication with families of children with disabilities. There are other prerequisites to developing positive communication between families and professionals. Turnbull and Turnbull (1990) outlined three major skills needed:

1. Professionals must understand themselves and appreciate the personalities and behaviors of others.
2. Professionals and families must have mutual respect for and trust in each other.
3. Both families and professionals must view their relationship as a partnership and work collaboratively.

In their effort to communicate openly with parents, professionals must use good interpersonal communication skills. A comprehensive discussion of interpersonal communication including both verbal and nonverbal skills has been outlined in Chapter 5. Rogers (1961) said when working with parents, the professional's most important communication attributes are empathy, genuineness, and unconditional positive regard.

As professionals expand their roles and responsibility in family involvement, they will most likely come across difficult parents, who for various reasons may be angry, resistant, pushy, adversarial, or noncaring. Sonnenschein (1984) warns that professionals may label parents inaccurately based on the parents' behaviors. Parents may be accurate in their feelings and perceptions of certain situations and factors that affect their children. Roos (1985) further warns that professionals often yield to the temptation to blame, compete with, or undermine parents of children with disabilities. Those who react to "difficult" parents by becoming defensive and fighting back will soon find that the foundation for developing a partnership will be weak. As mentioned earlier, Fish (1990) and Margolis and Branningan (1990) provide strategies for interacting with angry parents and resolving conflicts.

Communicating with families from diverse cultural and linguistic backgrounds can also be challenging to professionals. Several guidelines have been provided specifically to interpersonal communication with diverse families (Wittmer, 1992; Lynch & Hanson, 1992). In particular, professionals should be sensitive to issues of nonverbal communication (e.g. eye contact, facial expressions, gestures, proximity, touching) among diverse cultural groups.

Professionals must understand that most parents are not dysfunctional (Behar, Correa, & Beverly, 1993; Dunst, Trivette, & Deal, 1988; Turnbull & Turnbull, 1990; Webster, 1977) and, in fact, that many parents are emotionally stronger as a result of having a child with disabilities in the family (Turnbull et al., 1993; Wikler, Wasow, & Hatfield, 1983). It is critical for professionals to refrain from viewing parents of children with disabilities as abnormal and to respect their involvement on the educational team. The roles and responsibilities of professionals in creating a positive partnership with families are extensive. Nonetheless, it is not a one-sided association. The next section relates to the family's role in the establishment of the special education team.

ROLE OF THE FAMILY

As the term implies, a partnership involves parents becoming equal and active in the association with special educators. For most families, the role of a collaborative partner is foreign and uncomfortable. Therefore, the responsibility for initiating the partnership may fall on the professional. However, for the relationship to be maintained, the parent must commit to helping professionals meet the unique needs of their children by providing information, reinforcing school programs at home, asserting and advocating for quality services, and understanding the professionals' role.

Providing Information

For professionals in special programs to understand their students' educational, medical, and emotional needs, comprehensive information is often required. The family is usually in the best position to provide teachers and other professionals with such information. First, parents should feel comfortable in releasing consent to the schools for medical information on their children, especially in the areas of vision, hearing, and neurological status. If such information takes some time to be received by the professionals, the parent should try to keep the teacher and related service staff informed of any medical information that may indirectly or directly affect the child's physical and educational needs. The following illustrates how one parent designed a practical way of informing teachers and other school personnel about the medical and educational history of her child with emotional disabilities.

In September, Mr. and Mrs. Bell, the parents of Michael, a 7-year-old boy with autism, came to school to visit with the special education teacher. Mrs. Bell brought a three-ring notebook with comprehensive information on Michael's disability. She had divided the notebook into five sections: medical, psychiatric, educational, financial, and resources. In addition, the Bells had included yearly pictures of Michael and samples of his drawings and preacademic work. During the conference, the Bells shared information on Michael's last school placement and on current psychiatric reports. The teacher appreciated the information, because she was still waiting for Michael's school folders to be transferred. She was unaware that Michael had been diagnosed with infantile autism at the age of 3 and was currently taking Ritalin. Mr. and Mrs. Bell signed consent for release of information forms for the teacher and left the teacher with copies of the most relevant reports.

In this case, Michael's parents were able to provide professionals with a comprehensive compilation of information on his medical and educational history. To help organize the numerous documents gathered over the years, the Bells assembled a notebook. For parents of children with medical needs and severe disabilities, keeping track of medical and educational information is critical. However, professionals must respect the fact that family history or social work reports may be too sensitive to release. If parents do not provide the teacher with important information, the teacher may become frustrated with getting the information from physicians, therapists, and other professionals.

Other information parents can provide to teachers involves family activities that may affect the child's behavior or assist in supplementing educational programs. For example, families can tell teachers about vacations; relatives or friends the child cares about; and favorite restaurants, TV shows, or games the family enjoys. Teachers can relate the child's home experiences to educational activities at school. In particular, parents should keep professionals informed of any changes in the health of the child or family situations that may affect emotional behavior.

Reinforcing School Program at Home

Many families are under added pressures with both parents regularly working outside of the home or single parents needing to work full-time. Professionals must understand that parents often have to take care of family priorities before they can attend to school responsibilities. All children need unstructured time with their parents for fun, play, and sharing. It is easy for school personnel to so burden families with "ought to's" that parents feel guilty about taking time to simply play with their children. The parent must be viewed as a parent, not as another teacher.

Professionals can provide parents with intervention programs that can be easily integrated into normal family routines without making the parents feel guilty for not being able to spend more time "teaching" their child. If math is an area that teachers think should be reinforced at home, they can ask parents to have their children add items at the grocery store or check the bill at a fast-food restaurant. For children with more severe disabilities, parents and siblings can usually help in activities such as teaching table setting, recognizing photographs of familiar objects, and even stimulating vision or hearing. Only if the family is willing should teachers provide families with sophisticated educational lessons requiring data collection or lengthy practice. Home programs often will not be effective if they are time consuming or complex.

If possible, parents should try to attend school events involving their child's program. It may be helpful for them to meet and talk with other families. The school can often provide helpful information on various topics. Parents do not attend school meetings for many reasons. Meetings are often scheduled at a time that interrupts work (e.g., 3 p.m.) or mealtimes. Meetings take place in school buildings that may be far from home, in unfamiliar surroundings. For parents from diverse backgrounds, schools may be threatening places. School desks are uncomfortable, no drinks are offered, nor are babysitting services provided. Topics may be of no interest, or they may be subjects that some families consider inappropriate. Speakers may use jargon or present complicated concepts. Professionals and middle-class Anglo parents may dominate discussions. Culturally diverse parents who do not attend meetings may actually use their time more effectively at home with their children. Effective programs can be developed by asking a sample of parents from different groups within the school population what topics they want information about, when to schedule meetings, and where to have the meetings. Interpreters may be needed in some locations.

Advocating for Quality Services

As mentioned in Chapter 5, the professional who is competent in collaborating with others on the educational team must develop skills in assertive communication. This holds true for parents as well. The traditional role of parents involved in their child's educational program has been either passive, submissive behavior or aggressive, hostile behavior. These behaviors are exhibited in reactions to what parents perceive as intimidation and seizure of control by school professionals. In turn, submissive or aggressive parental behaviors fail to earn respect from school professionals. Parents as well as professionals need to learn how to communicate effectively, showing respect for others while stating facts and opinions based on evidence in such a way that listeners do not become defensive. Training in advocacy and assertiveness is important for parents and other family members. The responsibility for this training can fall on either the school or national parent organizations such as Parent to Parent. The following narrative illustrates why it is important for parents to communicate their expectations and goals assertively to professionals working with their children.

Mrs. Avila, a native Puerto Rican mother of an 18-year-old daughter with mild disabilities, attended an IEP meeting at which her daughter's transition program was discussed. Mrs. Avila was asked if she would consent to her daughter's attending the local sheltered workshop for vocational training in assembling packages of Christmas bows. Mrs. Avila's first reaction was to ask the professionals if those were realistic expectations for her daughter's future. The special education teacher said it was an excellent opportunity for the daughter and presented retainment and productivity statistics on the workshop. Mrs. Avila was intimidated by the professionals and consented to the transition program without further discussion. During the following six months, her daughter developed aggressive behaviors, appeared to lose motivation in school, and regressed in her social and communication skills. Mrs. Avila became depressed and angry about the school's decision to place her daughter in the sheltered workshop. She had higher expectations for her daughter and wanted her to work in the community. Mrs. Avila did not know how to work with the professionals on changing the transition program. She felt a loss of power and control over her daughter's training.

Mrs. Avila clearly exemplifies what many families experience when working with professionals. The fact that Mrs. Avila came from a Hispanic culture that does not encourage women to be assertive may add to the problem. Turnbull and Turnbull (1990) explained that parents' diminished sense of status and power in decision making is common. Parents are usually outnumbered by professionals and made to feel unimportant in the educational process.

Parents should not settle for second best. They should understand the limitations of the school system, but still push for quality programming. Families with skills in assertive communication and knowledge of the IEP process are able to represent their child's interest in securing the best possible educational services (Turnbull & Turnbull, 1990). While their child is receiving services, parents should remain involved and assertive. They should provide professionals in special programs with regular feedback on the educational program. Telling teachers what their goals, priorities, and expectations are for their child is important. If a problem arises, the parent should respect the chain of command and begin by speaking directly with the professional responsible for the child. If the problem cannot be resolved at that level, the parent should contact the teacher's supervisor, principal, and finally the superintendent for action. Most problems, however, can be resolved when an open, honest relationship exists between parents and professionals at the school level.

Understanding the Professional's Perspective

If a collaborative partnership is to be maintained, parents must understand the professionals' perspective and the limitations the system places on their ability to act. With some insight into school policies such as teachers' contracts and teachers unions, parents can begin to understand the conditions under which the teacher functions. Employers, on one hand, expect the teacher to advocate on behalf of the school district. Parents, on the other hand, need the teacher to advocate for better services for their children. If there is a conflict in providing the services, the teacher is often caught in between. To illustrate this dilemma, the following vignette is offered.

Ms. Leslie, the special education teacher, was asked to speak with the principal of the school in which she has been employed for one year. Mr. Jones, the principal, was angry with Ms. Leslie for telling a parent that she had the right to get a second opinion on a psychological assessment of a 4-year-old student with physical disabilities. The initial assessment was conducted by a psychologist employed by the school board who had not made any effort to adapt the administrative procedures and reported a developmental age score that was significantly different from that reported by Ms. Leslie and the mother. Mr. Jones asked Ms. Leslie what she thought she was doing by giving parents ammunition to fight the school district. The mother of the child had requested a second evaluation and had threatened the school with due process proceedings because her daughter's IEP was not designed to meet her intellectual capabilities. Mr. Jones presented an ultimatum to Ms. Leslie. If she continued to undermine school personnel such as the psychologist, she would have to find herself a new job.

Schools today are under extreme pressure from state education departments, and many face lawsuits from parents regarding appropriate services for students with disabilities. Mr. Jones may not be the "bad guy" in this scenario, considering that his superintendent and state department are trying to stop expensive lawsuits. Moreover, state and local communities are under pressure to provide better services with diminishing funds and personnel. Parents must understand the complexities of school systems and put themselves in the shoes of the professional. Many authors provide useful information for both professionals and parents who want to advocate for quality services for children in the areas of due process (Brock & Shangberg, 1990; Sussan, 1990), conflict resolution (Margolis & Brannigan, 1990; Fish, 1990), advocacy (Friesen & Huff, 1990), and parent involvement (Katsiyannis & Ward, 1992).

Parents need to see professionals as people who may become extremely emotionally attached to a child, typically acting as if they were the child's prime expert. Parents must remember that professionals can become protective of students and sometimes may not behave objectively. Professionals with special programs have a vested interest in their students' programs and are committed to getting the best possible services for their students. It is sometimes difficult for special education team members to remain completely objective about students. Both parents and professionals need to balance caring and objectivity.

A professional may wear a cloak of objectivity to hide feelings. But objectivity without caring is not desirable. It is not an error or a weakness to *care* or show authentic feelings. It is an error to allow feelings to overcome objectivity. Team members can help each other maintain this delicate balance, rather than scorning the member who errs in either direction. Together parents and professionals can come to an excellent association, if they remember that the goal of the partnership is to improve services to children with disabilities.

STRATEGIES FOR SUPPORTING FAMILIES

The major roles and responsibilities of professionals and parents have now been outlined. How professionals establish collaborative relationships with families is a concern that special education professionals will have for years to come. There are no simple guidelines for involving parents in the educational program of their children with disabilities. However, for families of infants and toddlers with disabilities, individualizing family support plans (IFSP) will require school personnel to concentrate on assessing the needs of each family individually, and to work together on designing programs that meet the family's needs directly.

Establishing effective interactions between families and professionals takes a commitment of time, energy, financial resources, and sensitivity from school administrators, direct service providers and related service personnel. In Figure 9–2, practical strategies to meet the needs of families in special education programs are presented.

1. *Establish an advisory committee with parents and professionals* to outline and monitor the "parent-professional" goals of the school. Have the committee follow a systematic plan for implementing parent training, advocacy, and information exchange (Heward & Dardig, 1978).

2. *Gather extensive information on the families' strengths and needs.* Use a variety of instruments listed in Figure 9–1. For special education teachers, formal psychosocial instruments may be too detailed. The Family Assessment Interview Guide (Turnbull & Turnbull, 1990) serves as a school-based interview that can provide teachers with practical information on family resources, family interaction, family functions, and family life cycle.

3. *Identify family needs and preferences for school involvement.* The Family Information Preference Inventory (Turnbull & Turnbull, 1990) can be adapted to provide school personnel with information on the needs of parents in the areas of teaching the child at home, advocacy and working with professionals planning for the future, coping with family stress, and using resources.

4. *Develop school manuals on school policies and procedures, curriculum, and transition.* Manuals for parents are available from many parent organizations such as PACER centers (PACER Center, 1984). However, individualizing manuals for each school district is advantageous because policies and procedures may be different across states, and curriculum, transition, and resource information may be specific to a school district.

5. *Provide parents with videotapes, films, and slide-tape presentations that provide instruction and support to families.* A resource center for such materials has been established by the Young Adult Institute, 4602 34th Street, New York, NY 10001. Materials on various aspects of educating children with disabilities are available for use with parents. In addition, establish a materials lending library for families and a toy lending library for parents of young children.

Figure 9–2
Strategies for involving families

APPLICATION

The following is an example of sections of an Individualized Family Support Plan (IFSP) developed for the family of Rachel, a 2-year-old with disabilities. Rachel was premature and evidenced retinopathy of prematurity (retinal damage that left her with only light perception), motor impairment, and cognitive delays. The development of this plan involved all the skills described in interactive teaming. The parent, Janet Howe, a single mother with two children, was asked to provide the team with goals and needs relevant to her own family. The parent, early intervention teacher, psychologist, school counselor, and physical therapist attended the initial planning meeting. The meeting took place at the local community day-care center, where the early intervention program is located. Ms. Howe began the meeting by stating her perceptions of Rachel's educational needs as well as the family's needs. Table 9–2 is an example of the goals developed based on Ms. Howe's family needs.

6. *Involve parents in individual classroom projects* such as publishing family recipe calendars in which each family has a favorite recipe printed. Also, publish a classroom newsletter in which current activities and news on each student or family can be distributed among the families. Design home-school diaries for the purpose of sharing individual information with families daily or weekly. Include photographs and charts that illustrate examples of the children's progress. Provide a system for distributing feedback on the child's behavior and progress using "happy-grams," phone calls, or videotape.

7. *Develop a survival vocabulary list in the* native language(s) of your families for use with parents and school personnel. Include basic special education terminology, greetings, body parts, action words, calendar words, etc. Silberman and Correa (1989) have published a Spanish survival vocabulary list for use with children with physical disabilities and their families.

8. *Provide parents with a current listing of respite care and babysitting services for children with disabilities.* Keep a list of other resources on a bulletin board near the entrance of the classroom, such as announcements on family group meetings, weekend workshops, state or national conferences, television programs pertaining to special education, and handouts on preparation for IFSP or IEP meetings.

9. *Include parents* in transition planning, discussing the expectations of the next environment, issues of inclusion, materials or equipment necessary for the next environment. Have parents visit potential receiving classrooms. Provide team meetings with both exiting and receiving classroom personnel and families.

Ms. Howe and all the team members will meet every six months to discuss progress on the Individualized Family Support Plan. In meeting the needs of the Green family, described earlier in this chapter, the early interventionists will arrange a meeting for all related service personnel such as the family therapist, speech therapist, and physicians to discuss the Green's family program and learn more from each other as team members. This meeting will be arranged as a luncheon, with the food donated by a local Lions Club.

SUMMARY

This chapter has presented the issues related to establishing a partnership among professionals and families of children with disabilities. Developing a collaborative relationship is not simple.

Table 9–2

Sample of an Individualized Family Support Plan

Area of Need	Suggested Goals
1. Ms. Howe needs babysitting once a week to attend the infant program's parent support group.	1. The local high school has developed a respite care program for parents in the community who need babysitting or homecare. The group will be contacted to provide Ms. Howe with volunteer babysitting services every week. The early interventionist will consult with the high school volunteer, orienting her to Rachel's special physical and cognitive needs.
2. Ms. Howe wants help in interpreting and understanding the ophthalmologist's reports.	2. The local itinerant vision teacher will be contacted to help Ms. Howe understand the effects of visual impairment on Rachel's overall development. Additionally, the vision teacher will sit down with Ms. Howe and review tape-recorded sessions of Ms. Howe's visits to the ophthalmologist. The ophthalmologist has agreed to be available to school personnel for added explanation of Rachel's condition on a consultative basis.
3. Ms. Howe is concerned about Rachel's language development. In particular, Rachel is using echolalia when engaged in communication.	3. The early interventionist and physical therapist will consult with the local university speech clinic/laboratory in an effort to improve their skills in early language development. The speech-and-language therapist will conduct a staff development workshop for all the personnel at the early intervention program on how to stimulate language in young children. If necessary a formal referral will be made to the speech clinic.
4. Ms. Howe reports that her other child, Ricky, age 10, is exhibiting resentment toward Rachel by not helping around the house and refusing to watch Rachel while mother is cooking dinner. Ms. Howe would like some suggestions as to what to do.	4. The school counselor has arranged a sibling support group for brothers and sisters of children with disabilities attending the early intervention program. A family therapist, Mr. Dodd, himself a sibling of an adult with disabilities, conducts the groups once a month at the day-care center.

Professionals and parents must understand their roles and responsibilities in the partnership. The association involves a two-way commitment.

Many families are unable to find the time or energy to get actively involved with the school program.

Parents may feel powerless and insignificant in the education of their child. They may be timid and nonassertive about their feelings, especially if they come from a diverse cultural background.

Professionals must not mistake a family's lack of involvement or shyness as not caring. Instead, they should find creative ways to keep parents informed and make families feel as though the "door is always open" to involvement.

The professional must view the family as a normal family dealing with an abnormal task, caring for a child with disabilities. Special education professionals clearly serve a role in empathizing with families who are coping with and adjusting to having a child with a disability. However, to perceive the family as being dysfunctional because of those feelings would be a grave error.

Providing families with the tools (support services) to cope with the care of a child with disabilities becomes the major role of professionals. Support can come from many parts of the family subsystem, but for professionals it includes providing them information and resources on services for their children.

The professional must view the family as being the child's best expert. Families frequently report that professionals make them feel as if they do not understand their own child's problems. Families know and understand their children better than any professional can. Likewise, professionals working with children with disabilities have expertise in specialized areas that parents may not realize. The mutual knowledge and expertise of both parents and professionals can be shared, and the result is quality services for children with disabilities. Professionals must view the parents as equal and valued team members.

Clearly, professionals today see the value of involving families in the educational process. However, professionals may lack the skills needed to establish the parent-professional relationship. This chapter has attempted to provide special education personnel with insight into the skills that are needed for the partnership. As stated by Will (1988), "professionals must be flexible, and be willing to 'go the extra mile,' in spite of limited resources, to provide family members with the tools necessary to live and work cohesively as a unit. This is not an easy task, but it is one which will yield tremendous results" (p. 2).

ACTIVITIES

1. Generate a list of informational interview questions to ask parents of children with disabilities. Make sure the questions are stated in a manner that shows respect for the families. Practice asking the questions in a simulated role-play situation.

2. Make a home visit with someone at the local school (e.g., special education teacher, psychologist, social worker, counselor). Observe how the home visit is

conducted. Be prepared to ask some general information questions about the child. For example, ask family members (e.g., parent, sibling, extended family member) to describe things the child likes to do at home.

3. Attend a local community parent support group. Observe the group interactions. Write a brief reaction to the meeting, listing the activities that were most effective and least effective during the meeting.

4. Analyze published videotapes on the reaction of parents to having a child with disabilities. Discuss how the videotapes depict the strengths and the needs of the families of children with disabilities.

5. Review selected articles from the journal *Exceptional Parent*. Abstract the articles selected for their portrayal of the family experiences associated with caring for a child with disabilities.

REFERENCES

Abidin, R. R. (1986). *Parenting stress index* (2nd ed.). Charlottesville, VA: Pediatric Psychology Press.

Able-Boone, H., Sandall, S., Loughry, A., & Frederick, L. (1990). An informed, family-centered approach to Public Law 99-457: Parental views. *Topics of Early Childhood Special Education*, *10*, 100–111.

Bailey, D. B., Jr., & Simeonsson, R. J. (1988). Assessing the needs of families with handicapped infants. *Journal of Special Education, 22,* 117–127.

Bailey, D. B., & Simeonsson, R. J. (1990). *Family needs survey*. Chapel Hill: University of North Carolina, Frank Porter Graham Child Development Center, F.A.M.I.L.I.E.S. Project.

Behar, L., Correa, V. I., & Beverly, C. (1993). *Family functioning analysis of Hispanic families of young children with disabilities: Implications for P.L. 99-457 and personnel preparation*. Manuscript submitted for publication.

Bennett, T., Lingerfelt, B., & Nelson, D. (Eds.). (1990). *Developing individual family support plans*. Cambridge, MA: Brookline Books.

Bouvier, L. F., & Davis, C. B. (1982). *The future racial composition of the United States*. Washington, DC: Population.

Brock, K. A. (1990). Avoiding unnecessary due process hearings. *Journal of Reading, Writing, and Learning Disabilities International, 6,* 33–39.

Caldwell, B., & Bradley, R. (1979). *Home observation for measurement of the environment manual*.

Little Rock: University of Arkansas, The Center for Child Development and Education.

Carter, E. A., & McGoldrick, M. (Eds.). (1980). *The family life cycle: A framework for family therapy*. New York: Gardner Press.

Children's Defense Fund. (1991). *The state of America's children 1991*. Washington, DC: Author.

Correa, V. C. (1989). Involving culturally diverse families in the education of their limited English proficient handicapped and at risk children. In S. Fradd & M. J. Weismantel (Eds.), *Bilingual and bilingual special education: An administrator's handbook* (pp. 130–144). San Diego: College-Hill Press.

Crnic, K. A., Friedrich, W. N., & Greenberg, M. T. (1983). Adaptation of families with mentally retarded children: A model of stress, coping, and family ecology. *American Journal of Mental Deficiency, 88*(2), 125–138.

Deal, A. G., Trivette, C. M., & Dunst, C. J. (1988). Family functioning style scale. In C. J. Dunst, C. M. Trivette, & A. G. Deal (Eds.), *Enabling and empowering families: Principles and guidelines for practice* (pp. 179–184). Cambridge, MA: Brookline Books.

DeVillis, R. F., DeVillis, B. E., Revicki, D. A., Lurie, S. J., Runyan, D. K., & Bristol, M. (1985). Development and validations of the child improvement locus of control scales. *Journal of Social and Clinical Psychology, 3,* 308–325.

Dilworth-Anderson, P., Burton, L., & Johnson, B. (1993). Reframing theories for understanding race, ethnicity, and families. In P. G. Boss, W. J. Doherty, R. LaRoss, W. R. Schumm, & S. K. Steinmetz (Eds.), *Sourcebook of family theories and methods: A contextual approach* (pp. 627–649). New York: Plenum.

Dunlap, W. R., Ondelacyt, J., & Sells, E. (1979). Videotape involves parents. *Journal of American Indian Education, 19*(1), 1–7.

Dunst, C. J. (1985). Rethinking early intervention. *Analysis and Intervention in Developmental Disabilities, 5,* 165–201.

Dunst, C. J., Cooper, C. S., Weeldreyer, J. C., Snyder, K. D., & Chase, J. H. (1988). Family needs scales. In C. J. Dunst, C. M. Trivette, & A. G. Deal (Eds.), *Enabling and empowering families: Principles and guidelines for practice*. Cambridge, MA: Brookline Books.

Dunst, C. J., Leet, H. E., & Trivette, C. M. (1988). Family resources, personal well-being, and early intervention. *The Journal of Special Education,* 22, 108–116.

Dunst, C. J., Trivette, C. M., & Cross, A. H. (1986). Mediating influences of social support: Personal, family and child outcomes. *American Journal of Mental Deficiency, 90*(4), 403–417.

Dunst, C. J., Trivette, C. M., & Deal, A. G. (1988). *Enabling and empowering families: Principles and guidelines for practice*. Cambridge, MA: Brookline Books.

Farber, B., & Ryckman, D. B. (1965). Effects of severely mentally retarded children on family relationships. *Mental Retardation Abstracts, 2,* 1–17.

Fish, M. C. (1990). Family-school conflict: Implications for the family. *Journal of Reading, Writing, and Learning Disabilities International, 6,* 71–79

Florida Kids Count (1993). *Key facts about the children: A report on the status of Florida's children.* Tallahassee, FL: Florida Center for Children and Youth [or Washington, DC: The Center for the Study of Social Policy].

Friesen, B. J. (1990). Parents and professionals as advocacy partners. *Preventing School Failure, 34,* 31–35.

Frodi, A. M. (1981). Contribution of infant characteristics to child abuse. *American Journal of Mental Deficiency, 85,* 341–349.

Fuqua, R. W., Hegland, S. M., & Karas, S. C. (1985). Processes influencing linkages between preschool handicapped classrooms and homes. *Exceptional Children, 51,* 307–314.

Gallagher, J. J., Beckman, P., & Cross, A. H. (1983). Families of handicapped children: Sources of stress and its amelioration. *Exceptional Children, 50*(1), 10–19.

Gallagher, J. J., Cross, A., & Scharfman, W. (1981). The father's role. *Journal of the Division for Early Childhood, 3,* 3–14.

Gallagher, J. J., Scharfman, W., & Bristol, M. (1984). The division of responsibilities in families with preschool handicapped and nonhandicapped children. *Journal of the Division for Early Childhood, 8,* 3–11.

Garshelis, J. A., & McConnell, S. R. (1993). Comparison of family needs assessed by mothers, individual professionals, and interdisciplinary teams. *Journal of Early Intervention, 17,* 36–49.

Golan, N. (1980, May). Intervention at times of transition: Sources and forms of help. *Social Casework,* 259–266.

Hanline, M. F., & Daley, S. E. (1992). Family coping strategies and strengths in Hispanic, African-American, and Caucasian families of young children. *Topics in Early Childhood Special Education, 12,* 351–366.

Hanson, M. J., & Lynch, E. W. (1992). Family diversity: Implications for policy and practice. *Topics in Early Childhood Special Education, 12,* 283–306.

Harry, B. (1992b). *Cultural diversity, families, and the special education system: Communication and empowerment*. New York: Teachers College Press.

Hayes, C. D., Palmer, J. L., & Zaslow, M. J. (1990). *Who cares for America's children? Child care policy for the 1990s*. Washington, DC: National Academy Press.

Heron, T. E., & Harris, K. C. (1987). *The educational consultant: Helping professionals, parents, and mainstreamed students*. Austin, TX: Pro-Ed.

Heward, W. L., & Dardig, J. C. (1978). Inservice for parents of special needs children. *Viewpoints in Teaching and Learning, 54,* 127–137.

Hirsh, G. P. (1981). *Training developmental disability specialists in parent conference skills.* (Doctoral dissertation, University of Kansas, Lawrence, 1981). Dissertation Abstracts International, 42, 3425.

Johnson, C. A., & Katz, R. C. (1973). Using parents as change agents for their children: A review.

Journal of Clinical Psychology and Psychiatry, 4, 181–200.

Katsiyannis, A., & Ward, T. J. (1992). Parent participation in special education: Compliance issues as reported by parent surveys and state compliance reports. *Remedial and Special Education, 13,* 50–55.

Kroth, R. L. (1985). *Communicating with parents of exceptional children: Improving parent-teacher relationships.* Denver, CO: Love Publishing Company.

L'Abate, L., & Bagarozzi, D. A. (1993). *Sourcebook of marriage and family evaluation.* New York: Brunner/Mazel.

Larsen, D., Attkisson, C., Hargreaves, W., & Nguyen, T. (1979). Assessment of client patient satisfaction: Development of a general scale. *Evaluation and Program Planning, 2,* 197–207.

Levin, I. (1993) Family as mapped realities. *Journal of Family Issues, 14,* 82–91.

Locke, H. J., & Wallace, K. M. (1959). Short marital-adjustment and prediction tests: Their reliability and validity. *Journal of Marriage and Family Living, 21,* 251–255.

Lynch, E. W., & Hanson, M. J. (1992). *Developing cross-cultural competence: A guide for working with young children and their families.* Baltimore: Paul Brookes.

Lynch, E. W., & Stein, R. C. (1987). Parent participation by ethnicity: A comparison of Hispanic, black, and Anglo families. *Exceptional Children, 54*(2), 105–111.

Margolis, H., & Brannigan, G. (1990). Calming the storm. *Learning, 18,* 40–42.

McCubbin, H. I., & Patterson, J. M. (1983). Family stress and adaptation to crises: A Double ABCX Model of family behavior. In D. Olson & B. Miler (Eds.), *Family studies review yearbook* (pp. 87–106). Beverly Hills, CA: Sage Publications.

McGonigel, M. J., Kaufmann, R. K., & Johnson, B. H. (1991). *Guidelines and recommended practices for the Individualized Family Service Plan* (2nd ed.). Bethesda, MD: Association for the Care of Children's Health.

McGrew, K. S., Gilman, C. J., & Johnson, S. (1992). A review of scales to assess family needs. *Journal of Psychoeducational Assessment, 10,* 4–25.

Meyers, C. E., & Blacher, J. (1987). Parents' perceptions of schooling for severely handicapped

children: Home and family variables. *Exceptional Children, 53,* 441–449.

Milburn, N., & D'Ercole, A. (1991). Homeless women. *American Psychologist, 46,* 1161–1169.

Minuchin, S. (1974). *Families and family therapy.* Cambridge, MA: Harvard University Press.

MIS Report (1991–1992). Tallahassee: Florida Department of Education.

Moore, L. (1993). Re-defining, re-inventing, and re-establishing community. *Equity & Choice, 9*(2), 5–9.

Murphy, A. T. (1982). The family with a handicapped child: A review of the literature. *Developmental and Behavioral Pediatrics, 3*(2), 73-82.

1990 Census Report. (1992, September). Education & Social Stratification Division.

Olson, D. H., McCubbin, H. I., Barnes, H., Larsen, A., Muxen, M., & Wilson, M. (1985). *Family inventories.* St. Paul: University of Minnesota.

Osmond, M. W., & Thorne, B. (1993). Feminist theories. In P. G. Boss, W. J. Doherty, R. LaRoss, W. R. Schumm, & S. K. Steinmetz (Eds.), *Sourcebook of family theories and methods: A contextual approach* (pp. 591–625). New York: Plenum.

PACER Center. (1984). *Parents Helping Parents* (Evaluation Report). Minneapolis, MN: Author.

Plisko, V. W. (Ed.). (1984). *The condition of education.* Washington, DC: U.S. Department of Education, National Center for Education Statistics.

Powell, T., & Gallagher, P. A. (1993). *Brothers and sisters: A special part of exceptional families (2nd Ed).* Baltimore: Paul Brookes.

Reich, K. (1986, September 26). Hispanic population likely to double by 2020. *Austin American-Statesman,* A4.

Rockowitz, R. J., & Davidson, P. W. (1979). Discussing diagnostic findings with parents. *Journal of Learning Disabilities, 12*(1), 11–16.

Rogers, C. R. (1961). *On becoming a person: A therapist's view of psychotherapy.* Boston: Houghton-Mifflin.

Roos, P. (1985). Parents of mentally retarded children—misunderstood and mistreated. In H. R. Turnbull & A. P. Turnbull (Eds.), *Parents speak out: Then and now* (pp. 245–260). New York: Merrill/Macmillan.

Salisbury, C. L. (1987). Stressors of parents with young handicapped and nonhandicapped children. *Journal of the Division for Early Childhood, 11,* 154–160.

Seligman, M., & Darling, R. B. (1989). Parent needs survey. In M. Seligman, & R. Benjamin Darling (Eds.) *Ordinary families, special children: A systems approach to childhood disability*. New York: Guilford Press.

Seligman, M., & Darling, R. B. (1989). *Ordinary families, special children: A systems approach to childhood disability*. New York: Guilford Press.

Shapiro, R. (1982). Alcohol and family violence. In L. R. Burnhill (Ed.), *Clinical approaches to family violence* (pp. 69–86). In J. C. Hansen (Ed.), *Family therapy collections*. Aspen: Aspen Publications.

Shuster, S., Guskin, S., Hawkins, B., & Okolo, C. (1986). Views of health and development: Six mothers and their infants. *Journal of the Division for Early Childhood, 11,* 18–27.

Silberman, R., & Correa, V. I. (1989). Spanish survival words and phrases for professionals who work with students who are bilingual and severely/multiply handicapped and their families. *Journal of the Division of Physically Handicapped, 10,* 57–88.

Sonnenschein, P. (1984). Parents and professionals: An uneasy relationship. In M. L. Henniger & E. M. Nesselroad (Eds.), *Working with parents of handicapped children: A book of readings for school personnel* (pp. 129–139). Lanham, MD: University Press of America.

Spanier, G. B. (1976). Measuring dyadic adjustment: New scales for assessing the quality of marriage and similar dyads. *Journal of Marriage and the Family, 38,* 15–28.

Sussan, T. A. (1990). How to handle due process litigation effectively under the education for all handicapped children act of 1975. *Journal of Reading, Writing, and Learning Disabilities International, 6,* 63–70.

Teachman, J. D., & Neustadtl, A. (1993). Emerging methods. In P. G. Boss, W. J. Doherty, R. LaRossa, W. R. Schumm, & S. K. Steinmetz, *Sourcebook of family theories and methods: A contextual approach* (pp. 715–727). Plenum Press: New York.

Turnbull, A. P., Patterson, J. M., Behr, S. K., Murphy, D. L., Marquis, J. G., & Blue-Banning, M. J. (1993). *Cognitive coping, families, and disabilities*. Baltimore: Paul Brookes.

Turnbull, A. P., Strickland, B., & Brantley, J. C. (1982). *Developing and Implementing Individualized Education Programs* (2nd ed.). Columbus, OH: Merrill.

Turnbull, A. P., & Turnbull, H. R. (1990). *Families, professionals, and exceptionality: A special partnership* (2nd ed.). New York: Merrill/Macmillan.

U.S. Code, 99th Congress, 2nd Session. Education of the Handicapped Act Amendments of 1986.

Waggoner, D. (1984). *Minority children at risk in America: Concepts, definitions and estimates*. Washington, DC: National Council of La Raza. (ERIC Document Reproduction Service No. ED 254 633).

Wayman, K., Lynch, E., & Hanson, M. (1990). Home based early childhood services: Cultural sensitivity in a family systems approach. *Topics in Early Childhood Special Education, 10,* 56–75.

Webster, E. J. (1977). *Counseling with parents of handicapped children: Guidelines for improving communication*. New York: Grune & Stratton.

Wikler, L., Wasow, M., & Hatfield, E. (1983). Seeking strengths in families of developmentally disabled children. In L. Wikler and M. P. Keenan (Eds.), *Developmental disabilities: No longer a private tragedy* (pp. 111–114). Silver Spring, MD: National Association of Social Workers.

Will, M. (1988, Spring). Family support: Perspectives on the provision of family support services. *Focal Point, 2,* 1–2.

Williams, B. F. (1992). Changing demographics: Challenges for educators. *Intervention in School and Clinic, 3,* 157–163.

Wittmer, J. (1992). *Valuing diversity and similarity: Bridging the gap through interpersonal skills*. Minneapolis, MN: Educational Media Corporation.

Zeitlin, S., & Williamson, G. (1988). Developing family resources for adaptive coping. *Journal of the Division for Early Childhood, 12,* 137–146.

Zeitlin, S., Williamson, G. G., & Rosenblatt, W. P. (1987). The coping with stress model: A counseling approach for families with a handicapped child. *Journal of Counseling and Development, 65,* 443–446.

PART III

Implementation of
Interactive Teaming

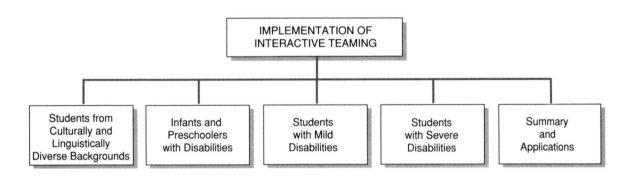

IMPLEMENTATION OF
INTERACTIVE TEAMING

Students from
Culturally and
Linguistically
Diverse Backgrounds

Infants and
Preschoolers
with Disabilities

Students
with Mild
Disabilities

Students
with Severe
Disabilities

Summary
and
Applications

OVERVIEW

In Part II, the facilitating factors that contribute to the effective implementation of interactive teaming were examined. All the factors described affect in various ways the implementation of services for students who are at-risk or disabled.

Regardless of the category or label of students, all interactive teams operate within a common framework of problem identification, intervention design and implementation, and evaluation of effectiveness. Other similarities include the necessity of collaboration among all members, role release in the sharing and use of the professional expertise of others, and the need for constant and clear communication among team members so that comprehensive and coordinated services can be provided to children and adolescents with special needs.

Some differences among the categories also exist. The roles of team members will vary in scope, levels of involvement, and the amounts and forms of direct (i.e., teaching) and indirect (i.e., consultation) services provided. In addition, there may be differences in the educational focus, such as academics vs. self-care skills, and in the types of interventions that team members design and implement.

Implementation with culturally diverse students is examined in Chapter 10. How interactive teaming can be implemented, considerations and roles of service providers working with infants and preschoolers with disabilities are delineated in Chapter 11. The implementation of interactive teaming with students with mild disabilities and students with severe disabilities is described in chapters 12 and 13 respectively. Student characteristics, considerations for meeting educational needs, and a description of professional roles are presented in each chapter. The concluding chapter comprises a summary and extended case study illustrating the implementation of the interactive teaming model. Current trends and promising practices for the future also are included.

CHAPTER 10

Implementation with Students from Culturally and Linguistically Diverse Backgrounds

Characteristics of Culturally and Linguistically Diverse Students

Language Characteristics
Cultural Characteristics
Socioeconomic Characteristics

Meeting Educational Needs

Service Delivery Options
Assessment and Curricular Design
Instructional Strategies

Roles of Professionals Involved with Culturally Diverse Students

Application

Summary

TOPICS IN THIS CHAPTER INCLUDE

- ◆ The characteristics associated with students from culturally and linguistically diverse backgrounds.
- ◆ The various educational needs of students from diverse backgrounds.
- ◆ Teaching strategies for working with students from diverse backgrounds.
- ◆ The unique roles of professionals working with students from diverse backgrounds.
- ◆ An application for team involvement in educational planning for students from diverse backgrounds.

Chan, a 5-year-old Vietnamese child, has become a problem for his teacher, Ms. Reid. He is failing to pay attention during a language enrichment group, a 15-minute session where students are read a story by the teacher and then asked comprehension questions. Chan speaks some English, but he is more fluent in Vietnamese, according to his parents. During this group session, Chan does not look at the book being read and gets up to leave the group at least five times during the session. Ms. Reid has tried many strategies for keeping Chan on task, but most have failed.

Frustrated with the situation, Ms. Reid has decided to let Chan play alone in the free-play area of the classroom during the language group sessions. Chan's peers have complained how unfair it is that Chan gets to play while they work. Ms. Reid has explained to the students that Chan needs some time to adjust to the classroom routines because he has just arrived from Vietnam, he is just starting to learn English, and he does not yet understand the way things are done in schools in the United States. She, however, does not seek any help from other professionals and Chan remains in her classroom falling further behind each day.

The education of students and families from linguistically and culturally different backgrounds in today's public schools is a critical and specialized area within general education and special education because of the dramatically changing demographics of the United States. Large numbers of immigrant and U.S.-born children from culturally diverse populations are entering public schools. Although this chapter focuses on students from ethnically or linguistically diverse backgrounds, it is important to note that today a broader definition of diversity must be understood. Many students live in situations that may place them at risk for school discrimination or school failure. These at-risk situations include the following:

◆ Students who are gay or lesbian.

◆ Students who come from migrant families.

◆ Students who live in poor inner city or rural areas.

◆ Students who are homeless.

◆ Students who have HIV or AIDS.

◆ Students who are victims of child abuse or live in violent environments.

◆ Students who live with relatives, guardians, or foster parents.

◆ Students who are latchkey and unsupervised at home (Salend, 1994).

The interactive team of professionals working with this special population must have a strong knowledge base in understanding differences (e.g., cultural, linguistic, religious, environmental, lifestyle) and in preparing these students for successful experiences in inclusive general education. As discussed in Chapter 6, cultural sensitivity by professionals to these students and their families is essential.

The vignette about Chan is an example of what might happen if professionals are not sensitive to the special needs of students from diverse cultures and if collaboration with other professionals is not sought. Ms. Reid should have contacted other professionals for consultation on Chan's attention problems. With the help of other professionals knowledgeable about Vietnamese students, an appropriate assessment of the situation and plan of action could have been implemented.

The purpose of this chapter is to introduce the specific needs of students from culturally and linguistically diverse backgrounds and to delineate the various roles of the professionals working with these students. First, a brief overview of cultural and linguistic differences will illustrate characteristics of students from culturally and linguistically diverse backgrounds. Some of these students are limited English proficient students, which may put them at risk for special education services. Second, a short discussion of the educational needs of students from culturally and linguistically diverse backgrounds is presented to suggest various service delivery options available for these students. Within the description of the educational needs of these students, assessment techniques and modified teaching strategies used for students from diverse backgrounds will be delineated. Third, the role of the professionals involved in the education and treatment of students from culturally and linguistically diverse backgrounds is presented. Cultural insensitivities can be found in all aspects of educating students from diverse backgrounds. The key to overcoming these insensitivities is to have a culturally competent interactive team available for instruction and collaboration.

CHARACTERISTICS OF CULTURALLY DIVERSE STUDENTS

Students from culturally diverse populations are at risk for placement into special education due in part to their linguistic differences, their culturally determined behavioral characteristics, and their socioeconomic status. If placed in special education, they are not provided support in their native language which can have an even greater effect on their linguistic and academic development (Briscoe; 1991; Correa & Tulbert, 1991; Figueroa, Fradd, & Correa, 1989; Saville-Troike, 1991). Similarly, students from culturally and linguistically diverse backgrounds are underrepresented in programs for gifted students (Chinn & Hughes, 1987; Rhodes, 1992).

The interactive team is responsible for distinguishing actual learning problems and giftedness from problems associated with learning English as a second language (ESL) or other linguistic differences, being in the process of acculturation to the mainstream Anglo school culture, or lacking educational experiences because of impoverished home environments. The following sections discuss characteristics that may be associated with students from diverse backgrounds. However, it is important to emphasize that the following descriptions of diverse students are not stereotypical of these students' overall personal characteristics. No matter what cultural background students come from, each should be regarded as an individual possessing unique traits that must be considered if adequate educational services are to be provided.

Culture is a dynamic process, full of changes. Minority culture students and their families change as they come into contact with the mainstream culture and their community's culture. Glenn (1989) warns that "we need an approach to education that takes seriously the *lived culture* of children and their families, not the fiestas and folklore that had meaning for their grandparents but are not part of the lives of families coming to terms with the losses and gains of immigration" (p. 779). Therefore, professionals must not assume that culture is an imprint that can be used with all individuals from that culture. To say that a child from Cuba lives the Cuban culture, thinks a certain way, and experiences a family structure particular to Cubans would be wrong. Given these cautions, the following sections outline characteristics that may place the student at risk for receiving appropriate educational services.

Language Characteristics

Many students from culturally diverse backgrounds have linguistic differences that affect their ability to succeed in an English-dominant school system. It is often critical to understand these linguistic differences so that professionals can accurately discriminate an actual language disorder from the natural progression of *second language acquisition* and acculturation. All aspects of language and speech development must be considered. These students often exhibit the usual problems associated with learning a second language, such as poor comprehension, limited vocabulary, grammatical and syntactical mistakes, and articulation difficulties (First, 1991). Ambert (1982) discusses how the identification of a language problem in English could be explained by understanding aspects of the child's native language. Table 10–1 shows some examples.

There is evidence that many language minority students are identified as having a language disorder, usually related to articulation, when in fact they are exhibiting normal characteristics of second language acquisition (Ortiz & Polyzoi, 1988). Therefore, it is critical for professionals working with students who are limited English proficient to know the differences between an actual language disorder and that of second language acquisition. A child who has a language disorder will evidence the problem in the native language as well. For example, a Hispanic child who has a problem with the omission of initial sounds will say "mida" for *comida* (food) or "anjo" for *banjo* (bathroom). Assessing students in their native language becomes a critical component of a multiculturally responsive educational process.

Furthermore, Cummins (1985) states that students learning a second language learn basic interpersonal communication skills (BICS) more easily than cognitive/academic language proficiency (CALPS). Social language usually develops within two years, however cognitive and academic language could take up to seven years to learn, requiring extended instruction in the student's native language.

Table 10-1

Examples of LEP Students' Language Problems

Language Area	Example
Phonology	A Hispanic child may say "choo" for the English word *shoe,* because the *sh* sound is not found in Spanish.
Semantics	When shown a picture of an umbrella and asked to tell the teacher what you use it for, a Haitian child might state that it is used for the sun. In Haiti, the meaning or use of an umbrella is for protection from both the intense tropical sun and the rain.
Morphology	Chinese children indicate plural by placing a number in front of the noun. Therefore, a child who is asked to tell the teacher how many arms and legs he has, may respond by saying "two arm" and "two leg."
Syntax	In Spanish, an adjective follows a noun it is describing. Therefore, a child who comments on the teacher's dress as being pretty may say "the dress pretty."

Note: From "The Identification of LEP Children with Special Needs" by A. N. Ambert, 1982, *Bilingual Journal, 7*(1).

Additionally, students who speak with a *nonstandard dialect,* but are competent in English frequently are discriminated against by professionals and peers (Cecil, 1988; Salend, 1994; Taylor, 1987; Toohey, 1986). For example, it is estimated that between 80% and 90% of African-Americans in the United States use some form of Black English (Smitherman, 1985). Often, Chicano, Puerto Rican, and African-American students with nonstandard English dialects will be considered inferior by classmates and teachers. Teachers may have negative attitudes toward students and lowered expectations of these students' linguistic abilities (Harry, 1992). This comes at a time when the use of nonstandard English dialect among the youth culture is becoming more popular (Salend, 1994). Many may be referred to special education merely because the professionals believe that nonstandard English dialects convey an inability to function in a mainstream classroom. Professionals should respect these students and encourage bidialectal use of language, teaching students when to use standard English and when to use other dialects (Salend, 1994).

Cultural Characteristics

Various learning and behavioral characteristics associated with students from culturally diverse populations are provided in this section. In general, professionals should avoid negative stereotypes when considering this information. There is, however, sufficient literature to support the differences in children's learning and behavioral styles, depending on their socioeconomic backgrounds and the individual child's cultural dominance.

Learning Styles.   Many authors have written about the diverse learning styles of students from multicultural backgrounds. According to Salend (1994), dimensions of learning styles instruction include the following:

◆ Environmental considerations such as background noise levels, lighting, temperature, and seating arrangements.

◆ Emotional considerations such as individual levels of motivation, persistence, conformity, responsibility, and need for structure.

◆ Grouping considerations such as learning alone or in groups, and with or without adults present.

◆ Physical considerations such as learning modality preferences, time of day, and need for food, drink, and mobility while learning.

◆ Psychological considerations such as approaching a task globally or analytically (Salend, 1994, p. 313).

Salend (1994) described high-context cultures as those in which cooperation is encouraged, time schedules are flexible, and less authoritarian approaches are emphasized. In a low-context culture, competition, individualization, and strict adherence to time are the norm. An example of a low-context classroom environment is described as follows:

Arnaldo, a Dominican ninth-grade migrant student, has been asked to go to the office by his science teacher, Mr. Brown, because of his lack of attention. Mr. Brown teaches science by lecturing students from the front of the class and asking them to follow his lecture in their science book. On this day, Mr. Brown lectured for 40 minutes on the phenomenon of the lunar eclipse. The students were to follow along in their books. After the lecture, they were to write the answers to the questions in the back of the chapter on eclipses. Mr. Brown did not allow students to interact with each other during his lectures or the writing period. All students were seated in rows facing the front of the class, and all written work had to be turned in with a specific format for the student's name, date, science unit, and chapter pages. Arnaldo asked a classmate if he had understood the directions, and Mr. Brown sent him to the office.

For students from high-context cultures, school activities such as the teacher lecturing at the front of a class of 20 to 40 children seated in rows of desks cause much difficulty. For Arnaldo, a student who evidenced high-context needs, the science class was frustrating. In fact, if Arnaldo could not adjust to the low-context nature of Mr. Brown's science class, he was in danger of failing ninth-grade science.

The current Anglo middle-class culture of schools must be flexible enough to accommodate the diverse learning styles of multicultural students. Alternative learning environments have been recommended for culturally diverse students (Cuban, 1989; Fradd & Weismantel, 1989; Gilbert & Gay, 1985; Salend, 1994; Westby & Rouse, 1985). Classroom environments should include activities that are group negotiated, controlled, noncompetitive, and relatively unrestricted in terms of time. Activities that actively involve students in the learning process—such as field trips, art projects, experience stories, and pretend play—would provide a better match for the needs of high-context learners.

Gilbert and Gay (1988) described the need for teachers to modify their instructional methods to better accommodate poor urban African-American students' cultural styles. These children may function better in school environments that are more cooperative, informal, and loosely structured. Students possess both strengths and weaknesses in their learning styles. According to Gilbert and Gay, African-American students lack written test-taking abilities, but are adept in verbal expression with dramatization. The way to provide culturally and linguistically diverse students with an appropriate education is to teach them academic and social skills while reinforcing their cultural heritage. Educators should expect high achievement from culturally diverse students. However, teaching methods should be modified to better match the students' learning styles.

The learning styles of culturally diverse students also have been described as being more related to *field-sensitive* or *field-dependent behavior,* vs. the *field-independent behavior* often associated with Anglo middle-class students (Castañeda & Gray, 1974; Gollnick & Chinn, 1994). Field-sensitive learners are concerned with social environment. They react to support or doubt from others, prefer more personal relationships with teachers, and work cooperatively with others. Field-independent learners are task-oriented, more independent of external judgment, prefer formal relationships with teachers, and work independently and for individual recognition. For students who evidence field-dependent behaviors, teaching should more closely relate to a personalized and humanized curriculum that emphasizes the interests and experiences of the students. Teachers should display physical and verbal expressions of approval and warmth together with providing lessons that encourage cooperation, informal class discussions, and the development of group feelings. A balance between both field-independent and field-dependent curricula should be maintained by professionals when working with students from diverse cultural and linguistic backgrounds. However, educators must realize that no two students are alike and, therefore, each educational program must be based on individual student needs rather than on stereotyped learning styles (Salend, 1994).

Behavioral Styles.   Culturally and linguistically different students are often referred to special education because of certain behavioral characteristics that appear abnormal in United States classrooms (Hoover & Collier, 1985; 1991). However, the behaviors exhibited by students from different cultures may be culturally appropriate in their native culture or may be normal reactions in the process of adjusting to culture shock or acquiring a second language.

Tao, a newly arrived Cambodian student, has been referred to the school psychologist for counseling. His teacher describes Tao as severely withdrawn, not making eye contact or speaking to her when she talks to him. She is concerned that Tao is emotionally disabled and unable to survive in the mainstream classroom. The school psychologist contacts the social worker for the state Department of Human Resources. Tao was recently placed in foster care. Before his arrival in the United States, he had been living in a refugee camp with other Cambodian orphan children. Although Tao's records did not clearly state his history, it was suspected that Tao had been traumatized by the war and was experiencing post-traumatic stress disorder. He arrived severely malnourished and with no educational experience. His enrollment into the sixth grade was his first experience with a school culture.

An interactive team will need to collaborate with people in the local Cambodian community to obtain information that might provide them some insight into Tao's withdrawn behavior. Providing Tao with a school buddy and contacting a local Cambodian college student to volunteer to work with Tao a few hours a week might reduce Tao's anxiety and resistance to the school environment. Careful follow-up of Tao's behavior in the classroom should be carried out by all team members. If his behavior does not change, a referral would be warranted.

Professionals working with culturally diverse students must obtain information about the conditions in which these students have lived. Many abnormal behaviors, including withdrawal, defensiveness, disorganization, and aggression, may be attributed to various sociocultural influences (Hoover & Collier, 1985). Students adjusting to being refugees of war-torn countries, and entering a new culture will most probably experience some degree of social trauma and emotional problems (DeBlassie & Franco, 1983), often described as post-traumatic stress disorders (Carlin & Sokoloff, 1985). However, interactive teams can carefully observe students over time to separate the more subtle behaviors of second language acquisition and cultural adjustment from behaviors related to emotional problems (Fradd, Barona, & Santos de Barona, 1989).

Socioeconomic Characteristics

Some culturally and linguistically diverse students who have had extensive training in both public and private schools are from middle-class or upper-class families. A large percentage of culturally and linguistically diverse students come from poor homes and have had little preparation for school (Fradd & Weismantel, 1989). For example, whereas about 42 percent of the African-American and 35 percent of the Latino youths age 6 to 17 live in poverty, the poverty rate among their white counterparts is estimated at 14 percent (Children's Defense Fund, 1990). It is estimated that by the year 2000, 25 percent of America's children, many of these culturally and linguistically diverse, will be living in poverty (Children's Defense Fund, 1989). Furthermore, it is estimated that more than 1 million children are homeless (O'Connor, 1989; Linehan, 1992) and about 28 percent of the homeless students are not attending school (Pear, 1991). These students suffer from poor health, have no transportation to school, and do not retain important records and forms for school files. Many poor and culturally different students have been placed in special education or have dropped out of school (Ortiz & Garcia, 1988; Salend, 1994).

Some professionals view the lack of achievement by poor students as a problem inherent in the student, and they often assume that the families have failed to prepare their children for school and do not teach them the value of education (Cuban, 1989). Teachers may fail to recognize that economic differences affect cognitive and learning styles of students, causing them to respond differently to instruction (Ortiz & Garcia, 1988). Further, studies have shown that teachers pay more attention to students who are attractive, well dressed, and well behaved, whereas they may ignore or discriminate against students who may have unwashed and worn clothing or who are not so well groomed (Harry, 1992). The attitudes of educators must change if students from poor environments are to survive in school.

Cuban (1989) provides an alternative way to frame the problem of poor and at-risk students in schools today. He states that the reason students fail in school is that the school culture ignores and devalues the students' own cultural backgrounds and seldom adapts to students' individual differences. Cuban further states that "instead, schools seek uniformity, and departures from the norm in achievement and behavior are defined as problems. Social, racial, and ethnic discrimination are embedded in the routine practices of schools and districts" (p. 781).

The need for restructuring schools to accommodate the special needs of students from poor and culturally diverse populations is urgent. Around the nation many school leaders are recognizing the need for more parental input, teacher-run schools, alternative schools, dropout prevention programs, and other innovative ways to adapt to the changing school population. Mobiles (motorized classrooms delivering instruction in the community) have been used for tutoring homeless students (Pear, 1991). Milwaukee public schools have implemented two experimental programs based on the African-American immersion schools model. The model encompasses concepts, content, themes, perspective, and pedagogy reflective of the African and African-American ontology (Holt, 1991; Leake & Leake, 1992; Leake, 1992; Scherer, 1991; Tatum, 1992).

Professionals serving migrant students can access a nationwide computerized communication system, the Migrant Students Record Transfer System (MSRTS) to monitor student records and progress. In addition, professionals can use the Portable Assisted Study Sequence (PASS) curriculum and correspondence materials to encourage students to earn school credits toward graduation (Reynolds & Salend, 1990). Innovative programs are crucial to the success of culturally and linguistically diverse students in today's schools.

MEETING EDUCATIONAL NEEDS

A major function of the team serving students from culturally and linguistically diverse backgrounds is to prepare these students for acculturation to the mainstream American culture without unwarranted stripping away of their linguistic and cultural characteristics. Each member of the team must work cooperatively to assess and develop intervention programs that prepare students for their roles in their native community and in the larger Anglo-American communities. The educational needs of students from culturally and linguistically diverse backgrounds are complex in the areas of service delivery options, assessment, program design, and teacher competencies. The following section will address these needs.

Service Delivery Options

Various service delivery models are being used with students from culturally and linguistically diverse backgrounds. Most schools are providing students who are significantly limited English proficient (LEP) with alternative programs such as bilingual education or *English to Speakers of Other Languages* (ESOL). Some programs offer instruction in the native language; all provide specialized instruction in English. The programs last one to three years, with transition into the general education classroom occurring to some degree throughout this period. However, if the LEP student evidences learning problems warranting special education, a combination of language and special education services must be provided. In a recent study on Hispanic students, language therapy was the most frequently recommended service, and articulation therapy was next (Ortiz & Yates, 1988). Preferably ESOL and special education services should be provided using a consultant teacher assistance model within an inclusive general education classroom. Methods for successful inclusion have been described by Salend (1994). Figure 10–1 illustrates the cascade of service delivery options available to students who are limited-English proficient and receiving special education services.

Assessment and Curricular Design

The most startling effect of cultural and linguistic differences on children occurs when professionals assume that students from culturally and linguistically diverse backgrounds appear to be developmentally delayed, learning disabled, emotionally disabled, or mentally disabled (Fradd & Tikunoff, 1987; Salend, 1994). Students from diverse backgrounds taking standardized tests are hindered by "their limited proficiency in English, their lack of familiarity with the tests' content and with test-taking strategies, and the failure of test administrators to understand the social and cultural factors associated with the assessment process" (Salend, 1994, p. 481). The school psychologist is in a particularly sensitive position when it comes to the use of standardized assessment instruments to place students from culturally and linguistically

Figure 10–1

Special education placement alternatives

Note: From The Bilingual Special Education Interface (p. 193) by L. Baca and H. Cervantes, 1986, Columbus, OH: Merrill. Adapted from "A Framework for Considering Some Issues in Special Education" by M. Reynolds, 1962, *Exceptional Children, 28,* pp. 367–370. Adaptation reprinted by permission.

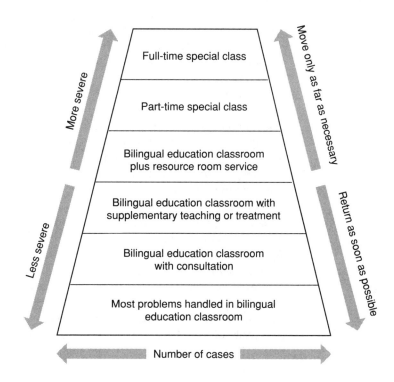

diverse backgrounds in special programs. This professional, more than any other member of the team, needs to take special care in assessing students using procedures for measuring first and second language proficiency, examining achievement and intelligence testing in students' primary languages, and documenting students' language use in natural environments (Rueda, 1989).

By not understanding the cultural values of students and their families, professionals may erroneously assess students' abilities, refer them to special education, and implement special programs ineffectively. Conversely, a professional who believes a student's learning difficulties are related only to the child's adjustment to the dominant culture may underestimate a true learning problem. Teachers in general, special, and bilingual education, together with speech and language professionals, and school psychologists must understand the cultural and linguistic context of the student's behavior and language when they observe the child to determine whether a true learning problem exists. Good observations of the child's behavior and native language in school and at home will help the professionals make these difficult decisions. Teamwork is critical in this process. Collaboration with families, communities, and related service professionals will be necessary for making an appropriate special education placement decision. Table 10–2 provides a list of the test instruments most frequently used with limited English proficient students.

Many of the tests are available in Spanish, but few are available in other languages, such as Haitian Creole, Vietnamese, Korean, Chinese, or Japanese. These languages are prevalent in schools with a high enrollment of culturally diverse students. Although the list in Table 10–2 is not exhaustive, it can guide professionals in providing a comprehensive battery of tests when assessing limited English proficient students. Readers are referred to recent publications (Baca & Cervantes, 1989; Fradd & Weismantel, 1989; Ortiz & Ramirez, 1988) for further guidance in selecting assessment and curriculum instruments.

Additionally, other forms of evaluation are necessary with this population. Informal assessment procedures—including sampling language, direct observation, anecdotal records, videotapes, and writing samples—have been extremely effective in providing the interactive team with information on the culturally diverse students' abilities (Fradd, Barona, & Santos de Barona, 1989). Procedures for collecting oral *language samples* usually involve tape-recording a sample of the student's conversations for 15 to 30 minutes on three occasions. A language sample provides the education professional with data on aspects of the student's language such as subject-verb agreement, past and future tenses, and vocabulary. It also samples the child's knowledge of various experiences within his or her own cultural and linguistic framework. Written language samples provide information about students' level of achievement in writing ability. Samples should be taken in both the students' own language and English. Analysis of the samples provides a basis both for assessment of students' skills and for planning instructional programs. Table 10–3 outlines several alternatives to traditional assessment that have been proposed for students from culturally and linguistically diverse backgrounds (Duran, 1989; Guerin & Maier, 1983; McLoughlin & Lewis, 1990).

Table 10-2
Tests Frequently Used with Limited English Proficient Students

TEST AREA: LANGUAGE	
Test Name	**Reference**
Boehm Test of Basic Concepts—Revised	Boehm (1986)
Dos Amigos Verbal Language Scales	Critchlow (1973)
Language Assessment Scales	DeAvila & Duncan (1981)
Pictorial Test of Bilingualism and Language Dominance	Nelson, Fellner, & Norrell (1975)
Test of Auditory Comprehension of Language —Revised (English/Spanish)	Carrow-Woolfolk (1985)
Test of Language Development—Primary (TOLD—P)	Newcomer & Hammil (1982)
Woodcock Language Proficiency Battery— Spanish Form	Woodcock (1981)
TEST AREA: ACADEMICS	
Wide-Range Achievement Test—Revised	Jastak & Wilerson (1984)
Bateria Woodcock Psycho-Educativa en Español	Woodcock (1982)
Peabody Individual Achievement Test	Dunn & Markwardt (1970)
Brigance Assessment of Basic Skills—Spanish Edition	Brigance (1984)
TEST AREA: INTELLIGENCE	
Wechsler Intelligence Scale for Children—Revised	Wechsler (1974)
Escala de Inteligencia Wechsler Para Niños	Wechsler (1951)
Kaufman Assessment Battery for Children	Kaufman & Kaufman (1983)
System of Multicultural Pluralistic Assessment	Mercer & Lewis (1978)
Leiter International Performance Scale	Leiter (1948)
Raven's Progressive Matrices	Court & Raven (1986)

Instructional Strategies

A number of instructional strategies have been reported to be effective with students from culturally and linguistically diverse backgrounds (Adams & Hamm, 1991; Correa & Tulbert, 1991; Fradd & Weismantel, 1989; Ortiz & Ramirez, 1988; Salend, 1994; Voltz & Damiano-Lantz, 1993; Wigg, Freedman, & Secord, 1992). The basic components for teaching culturally diverse students are that instruction should (a) match the learning style of the student, (b) provide opportunity for the student to use native and English language skills, (c) include the student's native heritage and culture as a context for

Table 10–3

Tests Frequently Used With Limited English Proficient Students

Alternative Assessment Strategies	Description
Culture-Free-/-Fair Tests	Measure aspects of growth presumed to be unrelated to culture. However, no test is completely culture-free.
Culture-Specific Tests	Measure knowledge and competence within a non-dominant culture. Tests are limited in measuring school learning.
Test Translations	English-language tests translated into the student's dominant language. Translations do not remove the bias in the test items.
Pluralistic Assessment	Measures student's medical status, social performance, and learning potential normed on diverse students.
Adaptive Behavior Assessment	Measure student's ability to cope with social and cultural demands. Does not measure academic abilities.
Dynamic Assessment	Employs test-train-test procedures providing information on what instruction is needed for a student to acquire skills.

designing curricula, (d) promote confidence and elevate self-esteem in the student, (e) encourage student-to-student interactions, and (f) prepare the student for inclusion into the dominant school culture.

Research indicates that many bilingual students will benefit in terms of academic progress and acquisition of English skills from *bilingual education* (Cummins, 1989). Various types of bilingual education (Salend, 1994) are described below.

◆ *Transitional bilingualism:* Focuses on transitioning from native language to English, with an emphasis on using English.

◆ *Monoliterate bilingualism:* Focuses on developing oral language in both languages with reading instruction conducted only in native language.

◆ *Partial bilingualism:* Focuses on developing both fluency and literacy in the primary and second languages with some degree of preserving cultural identity.

◆ *Full bilingualism:* Focuses on developing skills in both languages and in all content areas with concentration on developing pride in their cultural and linguistic identity.

Overall, teachers need to employ reciprocal interaction teaching models that foster empowerment and learning through verbal and written exchanges between students and teachers, and among students (Cummins, 1984). Fradd and Bermudez (1991) suggest that teachers use the POWER model, which includes process-oriented instruction, whole language, cooperative learning, cognitive mapping, and reading and writing across the curriculum.

The *whole-language approach* has influenced language instruction for limited English proficient students (Fradd, Barona, & Santos de Barona, 1989; Freeman & Freeman, 1993). The whole-language approach provides the student with language arts activities that focus on the students' language and experiences in and out of school to increase their reading and writing abilities (Weaver, 1991). This approach also gives non-English speaking students reading and language arts instruction while they are developing the background to understand and apply formal language rules (Fradd, Barona, & Santos de Barona, 1989). Students are encouraged to use all sensory modes to learn and appreciate language, including music and movement. Whole-language materials are being adapted for use with limited English proficient students.

Additionally, strategies for teaching students with mild disabilities have potential application for students from culturally and linguistically diverse backgrounds. Numerous strategies have been used with students with mild disabilities, including direct instruction (Gernsten & Keating, 1987; Morsink, Thomas, & Smith-Davis, 1987; Ornstein, 1987), peer tutoring (Maheady, Sacca, & Harper, 1988), and precision teaching (White & Haring, 1976). Some of these strategies will be discussed in Chapter 12, as they relate to working with students with mild disabilities. Because it is beyond the scope of this chapter to describe instructional strategy in detail, readers are referred to the referenced publications for further guidance in implementing the strategies. However, two strategies especially merit discussion in view of their applicability to working with culturally diverse students. They are *cooperative learning* (Hudson, 1989; Johnson & Johnson, 1984; 1986; Slavin, 1990), and *learning strategies* (Deshler & Schumaker, 1986).

Cooperative Learning.   Cooperative learning involves students helping one another in small-group instruction and provides an opportunity for students to develop academic as well as social skills. The major elements of cooperative learning include positive interdependence, individual accountability, collaborative skills, and face-to-face interactions (Johnson & Johnson, 1986). To implement cooperative learning structures, teachers should arrange classrooms to facilitate cooperation, assign two to six students to a group, and plan an instructional activity. Students are responsible for working cooperatively in groups to acquire the skills of the activity assigned. Students can be evaluated on both an individual and group basis for successful completion of assignments. For example, if an educator wants limited English proficient students to learn how to use English vocabulary words needed for ordering at a fast-food restaurant, the following procedures could be implemented:

1.   Assign a set of words for each member of the group to define and learn to pronounce.

2.   Get the small groups together to share and discuss the words.

3. Allow the students to take a group quiz, where they can interact and review the words.

4. Provide an individual quiz for students to reinforce individual accountability.

5. Take the students to a fast-food restaurant to practice their new vocabulary words.

Cooperative learning improves the students' motivation and raises self-esteem, while freeing the teacher from direct instruction, drill, and classroom management. Additionally, for limited English proficient students, interaction with English speaking group peers enhances language development and socialization. Cooperative learning is also a successful tool for promoting social relations between culturally different students (Adams & Hamm, 1991). Readers should refer to Slavin (1990) and Whittaker (1991) for more detailed guidelines on implementing cooperative learning activities.

Learning Strategies.   Learning strategies enable students to meet immediate academic requirements successfully and to generalize those skills to novel situations and settings. Examples of learning strategies developed at the University of Kansas (Deshler & Schumaker, 1986) include paraphrasing, sentence writing, error monitoring, self-questioning, and paragraph and theme writing. For example, the use of a learning strategy for spelling words, reported by Graham and Freeman (1986), can be adapted for working with limited English proficient students who are learning to spell English words associated with a basic anatomy lesson. The words the students would need to spell are associated with body organs, such as *stomach, heart, lungs, brain,* and *kidney.*
The following procedures would be implemented:

1. Teach the student to say the word.

2. Write and say the word.

3. Check the word.

4. Trace and say the word.

5. Write the word from memory.

Pictures or mnemonics can be used to facilitate the students' learning the body organ words. Learning strategies have been shown to improve low-achieving students' academic achievement in mathematics, reading, writing, and spelling (Deshler & Schumaker, 1986). The strategies appear to be excellent learning tools for students from culturally and linguistically diverse backgrounds, as well.
In general, the instructional strategies discussed have been limited to application with students with mild disabilities. However, many of the strategies have been adapted for use with students from culturally and linguistically diverse backgrounds. Some effective instructional practices generated for these students are outlined in Figure 10–2.

1. Allow students to develop ownership in learning by involving them in classroom management (Voltz & Daminano-Lantz, 1993).

2. Use cultural referents and student experiences during instruction (Salend, 1994).

3. Facilitate understanding of new words and phrases through use of rephrasing, pictorials, and pantomimes, and by writing key words (Salend, 1994).

4. Use storytelling to encourage use of oral language skills (Maldonado-Colon, 1990).

5. Develop a reward system, using group or companion contingencies (Echevarria-Ratleff & Graff, 1988).

6. Present daily rehearsal of student expectations (Fradd & Tikunoff, 1987).

7. Offer a buddy or peer tutorial system (Salend, 1994).

8. Use an assortment of culturally appropriate teaching materials (Banks, 1994).

9. Arrange a variety of high-context teaching activities (e.g., field trips, cooking activities, plays) (Westby & Rouse, 1985).

10. Involve families in educational programs by using family and home cultural information to promote engagement in instructional tasks (Correa & Tulbert, 1992).

11. Use active learning techniques by which students can collaboratively share alliances (Adams & Hamm, 1991; Fradd & Bermudez, 1991).

12. Develop student's language competence through use of art forms, drama, simulations, role plays, music, and games (Salend, 1994).

Figure 10–2
Classroom interventions successful with LEP students in the mainstream

Instructional strategies are effective tools for the educator involved with students from culturally and linguistically diverse backgrounds. Additionally, today's educator must incorporate the concept of multicultural education into all aspects of the classroom curriculum. Banks (1994a; 1994b) provided excellent texts for implementing a multicultural curriculum that encourages understanding and respect of *all* students.

Selecting the appropriate curricula to meet the diverse needs of all students in today's classrooms remains a critical aspect of the educator's responsibility. Unfortunately, a paucity of curriculum materials is available for students from culturally and linguistically diverse backgrounds (Fradd & Morsink, 1984; Salend, 1994). By collaborating with other team members, the job of designing effective instruction for students from diverse backgrounds becomes less arduous.

ROLES OF PROFESSIONALS INVOLVED WITH CULTURALLY DIVERSE STUDENTS

Professionals involved with educating students from culturally diverse backgrounds must understand the complex aspects of cultural influences on the student and the family. Often interactive teaming revolves around the general education teacher and the bilingual education teacher. However, for students with limited English proficiency the roles of the school psychologist and the speech and language therapist become critical, and if the student evidences any potential learning or behavioral problems, the special education professional must be involved.

The general roles of professionals have been outlined in Chapter 4. Some specialized contributions of team members who work with students from culturally and linguistically diverse backgrounds are presented in Table 10–4.

APPLICATION

In the vignette at the beginning of the chapter, Ms. Reid, Chan's teacher, had decided that the best way to cope with a limited English proficient student was to provide an alternative activity (free play) that was not as demanding as the one his peers were involved in (story time). Unfortunately, for Chan to succeed in an inclusive education, he will eventually need to attend to large group instruction and stay on task. Providing him with free play during this time will not prepare him for the next environment, first grade. The following solution to this problem exemplifies the interactive team approach.

Interactive Team Plan for Improving Chan's Attention to Task

The general education teacher, Ms. Reid, arranges a series of cooperative planning meetings. She asks each specialist to outline the concerns and needs for Chan's success in an inclusive classroom. Ms. Reid takes on the role of services coordinator by taking charge of coordinating all the information shared by the interactive team. The English to Speakers of Other Languages teachers and bilingual teachers are invited to visit Ms. Reid's classroom and make an anecdotal record of Chan's conduct. Both share their concern that Chan is having difficulty adjusting to the school environment and is behaving much like a child who does not understand the language and is suffering from post-traumatic stress disorder. They recommend that Chan be referred to the school psychologist, speech and language therapist, social worker, and the special education teacher for further follow-up. Both the

ESOL and bilingual teachers agree that Chan should be pulled out for some ESOL instruction, but they want further diagnostic evaluation carried out before recommending a self-contained bilingual program. In addition, the ESOL and bilingual teachers invite Ms. Reid to come to their classrooms, to observe other limited English proficient students, and to get ideas for classroom adaptations.

Ms. Reid contacts the school psychologist, the social worker, the special education teacher, and the speech and language therapist. They also visit Chan's classroom and collect behavioral analysis data on Chan's off-task, withdrawn behavior. Each professional graphs those data and presents them at the prereferral meeting arranged by Ms. Reid. The speech and language therapist informally assesses Chan's ability to understand English. She also contacts a volunteer Vietnamese college student to help assess Chan's language proficiency in Vietnamese.

During the prereferral meeting, all team members are present. Additionally, Chan's foster parents and an interpreter attend. The special education teacher provides the team with a behavior management program that uses social praise as a reinforcer. All team members agree to participate in Chan's behavior management program to the degree appropriate. Everyone agrees that Chan would benefit from a buddy-system program with another student. Each team member speaks empathetically with the foster parents about Chan. Both foster parents are made to feel comfortable and are asked throughout the meeting if they have any questions or suggestions. They help the team understand the experiences they had when they immigrated to the United States from Vietnam. They suspect that Chan had experienced violence, malnourishment, and hardships before arriving in the United States. Chan's foster father says the boy likes to listen to music and that the music seems to bring him out of his depression. The father will bring a few of Chan's favorite cassettes to school, so they can be shared with the other students and be available to Chan when he wants some time away from the stresses of the classroom.

The speech and language therapist, bilingual teacher, and ESOL teacher all agree to give Ms. Reid some strategies that can be integrated into the inclusive classroom. They will visit Chan in the classroom twice a week and facilitate the instructional strategies. The school psychologist is interested in Chan's adjustment to post-traumatic stress and offers to spend 15 minutes once a week with Chan, observing his adjustment to school. The parents also agree to participate in the plan and are given simple and functional ideas for home intervention. The special education teacher will serve as a consultant to the team. If Chan is officially placed in special education, the teacher will take a more active role in intervention. Objectives are developed during the meeting, and various team members share responsibility for conducting the interventions outlined. The chart in Table 10–5 on page 305 is used to delineate the objectives and each team member's responsibility. Team members agree to reconvene within six weeks to discuss Chan's progress. If progress is not seen within the six weeks, a formal referral to special education will be made.

Table 10–4

Roles of Professionals and Others Involved With Culturally and Linguistically Diverse Students

Personnel	Direct Service Provider	Team Member
Bilingual Educator	• Assess language development in student's native language. • Provide academic instruction using native and English language, and native heritage/cultural context. • Communicate with family in native language or with interpreters.	• Serve as culture broker. • Conduct staff development on bilingualism/biculturalism. • Collaborate on bilingual techniques with other team members. • Integrate regular and special education curriculum into bilingual program.
Teacher of English to Speakers of Other Languages (ESOL)	• Instruct in English as a second language, usually with a pull-out approach. • Communicate with family in native language or with interpreters.	• Serve as culture broker. • Conduct staff development on factors affecting second language acquisition and language development. • Consult with team members on effective techniques for teaching student English.
General Educator	• Conduct curriculum-based assessment to develop appropriate academic program. • Provide peer tutoring or a buddy system for adjustment into classroom. • Provide intervention that includes the student's cultural experiences. • Collect data and make referrals to bilingual education or special education when necessary.	• Integrate bilingual and/or special education techniques into general academic program. • Report on progress with inclusion in all areas including social/emotional adjustment. • Use native languages aides, volunteers, parents to assist in classroom program. • Integrate a multicultural education program into the daily curriculum that promotes an understanding and respect for diversity.
Special Educator	• Conduct nondiscriminatory assessment in the areas of achievement and language. • Communicate cross-culturally with student and family. • Adapt teaching materials according to the needs of student. • Develop IEP in cooperation with general and bilingual educators. • Role release to general and bilingual educators effective teaching strategies including direct instruction, cooperative learning, learning strategies, and behavior management techniques.	• Serve as culture broker. • Accept shared responsibilities with bilingual/ESOL/general educators. • Interpret assessment results. • Conduct staff development on special education and remediation techniques

Personnel	Direct Service Provider	Team Member
Chapter 1 Teacher	• Instruct young children who qualify for Chapter 1 federal funds (low SES, LEP).	• Share instruction techniques with special educator. • Prepare team for student's entry into general education. • Serve as culture broker.
Migrant Teacher	• Provide instruction that prepares the child for inclusion in the general education curriculum. • Visit migrant camps or communities and communicate with family.	• Provide team with information on migrant conditions of the family. • Maintain records with the Migrant Students Record Transfer System (MSRTS) • Encourage alternative methods of earning credits toward graduation. • Provide on-site tutoring programs. • Serve as culture broker.
School Psychologist	• Conduct nondiscriminatory assessment in the areas of intelligence/achievement. • Maintain current cumulative records on students.	• Interpret test results. • Conduct staff development on working with culturally diverse families. • Explain all school procedures, policies, legal mandates. • Participate in prereferral process.
Speech-Language Therapist	• Conduct assessment in both English and native language in the areas of language and speech development. • Conduct individual, group, or integrated therapy with students.	• Role release therapy techniques that can be integrated into all educational programs. • Interpret test results.
Guidance Counselor/ Social Worker	• Assess student in the areas of adaptive behavior and vocational planning. • Provide individual or group therapy sessions to work on self-concept and self-esteem. • Communicate with families. • Establish families' concerns, needs, and priorities.	• Interpret results of testing and progress in counseling sessions. • Make home visits and report findings of family status. • Serve as liaison with other nonschool agencies.

Table 10–4, *continued*

Personnel	Direct Service Provider	Team Member
Administrator	• Manage all aspects of school programs. • Assure that all programs are meeting the unique needs of LEP students. • Evaluate staff performance.	• Provide team with guidance on legal and districtwide policies and procedures. • Serve as meeting manager. • Support team in acquiring materials and resources necessary to deliver quality services. • Be available to meet with families and parent groups. • Encourage a multicultural approach to all aspects of school life.
Parents/ Family Members	• Support school programs and assist in enhancing the child's development of English. • Support bicultural instruction.	• Provide team with information on language and cultural background. • Support parent organizations and parent education efforts by the school or community.

SUMMARY

The data on the prevalence of students from linguistically and culturally diverse backgrounds who are at risk for school failure indicate that school personnel must acquire the skills necessary to understand and work with this population. Interactive teaming is the most efficient way to meet the special needs of these students.

By consulting and collaborating with others on the team, school personnel can design educational programs that are sensitive to the students' cultural backgrounds and specific learning styles. This chapter has provided an overview of what research shows are the best practices in working with students from diverse backgrounds. The major points discussed are as follows:

◆ Students from diverse backgrounds are a heterogeneous population, and negative stereotypes should be avoided when learning about cultural characteristics associated with their native cultures.

◆ Certain learning, behavioral, and socioeconomic characteristics related to students from diverse backgrounds place these students at risk for success in schools.

◆ A variety of service delivery options is available for students from diverse backgrounds. The goal, however, is to provide services that assure inclusion into the mainstream school program and protect the student from long-term placement in segregated programs.

Table 10–5

Interactive Team Plan for Chan

1. Chan will sit at story time for 3 minutes and receive social praise from a class-room volunteer if he stays on task.
2. Chan will stay on task during one-to-one instruction, 5-minute drill on English survival words.
3. Chan will stay on task while drawing a picture of his new Vietnamese foster family.
4. Chan will stay on task for 5 to 10 minutes while he listens to and articulates sounds in English associated with functional objects in his environment.

◆ Comprehensive and nondiscriminatory assessment practices, involving both formal and informal procedures, will assist in deciding whether a student evidences a significant learning problem or evidences characteristics associated with second language acquisition and cultural assimilation.

◆ A variety of instructional strategies can be used in working with students from diverse backgrounds, including strategies developed for students with mild disabilities. Cooperative learning and learning strategies are two strategies that can be adapted to working with students from diverse backgrounds.

◆ The various roles of school personnel involved with students from diverse backgrounds are focused on enhancing students' use of English, providing a learning environment that promotes inclusion into the mainstream, developing confidence and self-esteem in students, and providing family involvement in a manner that is sensitive to the native culture.

ACTIVITIES

1. Conduct an informational interview with a professional who is involved in the educational programs of students from diverse cultural backgrounds. Use the guidelines provided in Chapter 4.

2. Tour a school program serving limited English proficient students. Observe the students' activities and schedules. Note if any special adaptations or curricula are being used. Observe any bilingual instruction occurring, and note the personnel who are proficient in two or more languages.

3. Volunteer in an after-school program for bilingual students, at-risk students, or immigrant adults. Note the characteristics of the students as related to their cultural backgrounds. Tutor non-English speaking students in English. Find topics related to their culture to use as conversation warm-ups.

4. Obtain a language sample from a limited English proficient student. Consult with a speech and language therapist or a bilingual teacher regarding the grammatical language structures used by the student. Evaluate the child's proficiency in English.

5. Compile a resource file of materials for your classroom that promote multicultural education. Order catalogs that have multicultural educational materials such as books, dolls, crayons, and construction paper.

REFERENCES

Adams, D., & Hamm, M. (1991). Diversity gives schools infinite learning possibilities. *School Administrator, 48*(4), p. 20–22.

Ambert, A. (1982). The identification of LEP children with special needs. *Bilingual Journal, 7,* 17–22.

Baca, L., & Cervantes, H. (1989). *The bilingual special education interface* (2nd Edition). New York: Merrill/Macmillan.

Banks, J. A. (1994a). *An introduction to multicultural education.* Boston: Allyn & Bacon.

Banks, J. A. (1994b). *Multiethnic education: Theory and practice* (3rd ed.). Boston: Allyn & Bacon.

Boehm, A. E. (1986). *Boehm test of basic concepts— revised.* San Antonio: Psychological Corporation.

Brigance, A. H. (1984). *Brigance diagnostic assessment of basic skills, Spanish edition.* North Billerica, MA: Curriculum Associates.

Briscoe, D. B. (1991). Designing for diversity in school success: Capitalizing on culture. *Preventing School Failure, 36*(1), 13–18.

Carlin, J., & Sokoloff, B. (1985). Mental health treatment issues for Southeast Asian refugee children. In T. Owan (Ed.), *Southeast Asian mental health: Treatment, prevention, services, training, and research* (pp. 91–112). Washington, DC: U.S. Department of Health and Human Services.

Carrow-Woolfolk, E. (1985). *Test for auditory comprehension of language: Revised.* Allen, TX: DLM Teaching Resources.

Castañeda, A., & Gray, T. (1974). Bicognitive processes in multicultural education. *Educational Leadership, 32,*(3), 203–207.

Cecil, N. L. (1988). Black dialect and academic success: A study of teacher expectations. *Reading Improvement, 25*(1), 34–37.

Children's Defense Fund. (1989). *A vision for America's future.* Washington, DC: Author.

Children's Defense Fund. (1990). *Latino youths at a crossroads.* Washington, DC: Author.

Chinn, P., & Hughes, S. (1987). Representation of minority students in special classes. *Remedial and Special Education, 8*(4), 41–46.

Correa, V., & Tulbert, B. (1991). Teaching culturally diverse students. *Preventing School Failure, 35*(3), 20–25.

Court, J. H., & Raven, J. (1986). *Manual for Raven's progressive matrices and vocabulary scales (section 2): Colored progressive matrices* (1986 ed. with U.S. norms). London: Lewis.

Critchlow, D. C. (1973). *Dos amigos verbal language scale.* Novato, CA: Academic Therapy.

Cuban, L. (1989). The at-risk label and the problem of urban school reform. *Phi Delta Kappan, 10*(70), 780–784, 799–801.

Cummins, J. (1985). *Bilingualism and special education: Issues in assessment and pedagogy.* San Diego: College-Hill.

DeAvila, E., & Duncan, S. E. (1981). *Language assessment scales.* San Rafael, CA: Linguametrics Group.

DeBlassie, R. R., & Franco, J. N. (1983). Psychological and educational assessment of bilingual children. In D. R. Omark & J. G. Erickson (Eds.), *The bilingual exceptional child* (pp. 55–68) . Boston: College-Hill.

Deshler, D. D., & Schumaker, J. B. (1986). Learning strategies: An instructional alternative for low-achieving adolescents. *Exceptional Children, 52,* 583–590.

Dunn, L. M., & Markwardt, F. C. (1970). *Peabody individual achievement test.* Circle Pines, MN: American Guidance Service.

Duran, R. P. (1989). Assessment and instruction of at-risk Hispanic students. *Exceptional Children, 56*(2), 154–159.

Echevarria-Ratleff, J., & Graff, V. L. (1988). California bilingual special education model sites (1984-1986): Programs and research. In A. Ortiz & B. A. Ramirez (Eds.), *Schools and the culturally diverse exceptional student: Promising practices and future directions* (pp. 104–111). Reston, VA: Council for Exceptional Children.

Figueroa, R. A., Fradd, S. H., & Correa, V. I. (1989). Bilingual special education and this special issue. *Exceptional Children, 56*, 174–178.

First, J. (1991). *The common school: Making the vision work for all children.* Boston: National Coalition of Advocates for Students.

Fradd, S., & Morsink, C. (1984). Curriculum development in bilingual special education. In L. Baca (Ed.), *The second annual symposium on evaluation and interdisciplinary research in bilingual education* (pp. 69–86). Denver, CO: BUENO Center for Multicultural Education.

Fradd, S., & Tikunoff, W. (1987). *Bilingual education and bilingual special education: A guide for administrators.* Boston: College-Hill.

Fradd, S., & Weismantel, M. J. (1989). *Meeting the needs of culturally and linguistically different students: A handbook for educators.* Boston: College-Hill.

Fradd, S., Barona, A., & Santos de Barona, M. (1989). Implementing change and monitoring progress. In S. Fradd & M. J. Weismantel (Ed.), *Meeting the needs of culturally and linguistically different students: A handbook for educators* (pp. 63–105). Boston: College-Hill.

Fradd, S. H., & Bermudez, A. B. (1991). POWER: A process for meeting the instructional needs of handicapped language-minority students. *Teacher Education and Special Education, 14*(1), 19–24.

Freeman, D. E., & Freeman, Y. S. (1993). Strategies for promoting the primary languages of all students. *Reading Teacher, 46,* 552–558.

Gernsten, R., & Keating, T. (1987). Long-term benefits from direct instruction. *Educational Leadership, 44*(6), 28–31.

Gilbert, S. E., & Gay, G. (1985). Improving the success in school of poor black children. *Phi Delta Kappan, 67,* 133–137.

Glenn, C. L. (1989). Just schools for minority children. *Phi Delta Kappan, 10*(70), 777–779.

Gollnick, D. M., & Chinn, P. C. (1994). *Multicultural education in a pluralistic society* (4th ed.). New York: Merrill/Macmillan.

Graham, S., & Freeman, S. (1986). Strategy training and teacher-vs.-student controlled study conditions: Effects on LD students' spelling performance. *Learning Disability Quarterly, 9,* 15–21.

Guerin, G. R., & Maier, A. S. (1983). *Informal assessment in education.* Palo Alto, CA: Mayfield.

Harry, B. (1992). *Cultural diversity, families, and the special education system: Communication and empowerment.* New York: Teachers College Press.

Holt, K. C., (1991). A rationale for creating African-American immersion schools. *Educational Leadership, 49*(4), 18.

Hoover, J. J., & Collier, C. (1985). Referring culturally different children: Sociocultural considerations. *Academic Therapy, 20,* 503–509.

Hoover, J. J., & Collier, C., (1991). Meeting the needs of culturally and linguistically diverse exceptional learners: Prereferral to mainstreaming. *Teacher Education and Special Education, 14*(1), 30–34.

Hudson, P. J. (1989). Instructional collaboration: Creating the learning environment. In S. Fradd & M. J. Weismantel (Eds.), *Meeting the needs of culturally and linguistically different students: A handbook for educators* (pp. 63–105). Boston: College-Hill.

Jastak, J. F., & Wilerson, G. S. (1984). *The wide range achievement test: Revised.* Wilmington, DE: Jastak Associates.

Johnson, D. W., & Johnson, R. T. (1984). *Cooperation in the classroom.* Minneapolis, MN: Interaction Book Company.

Johnson, D. W., & Johnson, R. T. (1986). Mainstreaming and cooperative learning strategies. *Exceptional Children, 52,* 553–561.

Kaufman, A. S., & Kaufman, N. L. (1983). *Kaufman assessment battery for children.* Circle Pines, MN: American Guidance Service.

Leake, D. O. (1992). Milwaukee's African American immersion middle school: Meeting special needs. *Schools in the Middle,* Summer, 27–30.

Leake, D. O., & Leake, B. (1992). Islands of hope: Milwaukee's African American immersion schools. *Journal of Negro Education, 61*(1), 24–29.

Leiter, R. G. (1948). *Leiter international performance scale*. Chicago: Stoelting.

Linehan, M. F. (September, 1992). Children who are homeless: Educational strategies for school personnel. *Phi Delta Kappan, 74*(1), 61–66.

Maheady, L., Sacca, M. K., & Harper, G. (1988). Classwide peer tutoring with mildly handicapped high school students. *Exceptional Children, 55,* 52–59.

Maldonado-Colon, E. (1990). Development of second language learners' linguistic and cognitive abilities. *The Journal of Educational Issues of Language Minority Students, 9,* 37–48.

McLoughlin, J. A., & Lewis, R. B. (1990). *Assessing special students* (2nd ed.). New York: Merrill/Macmillan.

Mercer, J. R., & Lewis, J. F. (1978). *System of multipluralistic assessment*. Cleveland: Psychological Corporation.

Morsink, C. V., Thomas, C., & Smith-Davis, J. (1987). Noncategorical special education programs: Process and outcomes. In M. Wang, M. Reynolds, & H. Walberg (Eds.), *Handbook of special education: Research and practice, Volume 1* (pp. 287–312). Oxford, England: Pergamon.

Nelson, D., Fellner, M. J., & Norrell, C. L. (1975). *Pictorial test of bilingualism and language dominance*. Corpus Christi, TX: South Texas Testing Service.

Newcomer, P. L., & Hammil, D. (1982). *Test of language development—primary*. Austin, TX: Pro-Ed.

O'Connor, K. (1989). *Homeless children*. San Diego, CA: Lucent.

Ornstein, A. C. (1987). Emphasis on student outcomes focuses attention on quality of instruction. *NASSP Bulletin, 71*(495), 88–95.

Ortiz, A., & Garcia, S. (1988). A prereferral process for preventing inappropriate referrals of Hispanic students to special education. In A. Ortiz & B. A. Ramirez (Eds.), *Schools and the culturally diverse exceptional student: Promising practices and future directions* (pp. 6–18). Reston, VA: Council for Exceptional Children.

Ortiz, A., & Polyzoi, E. (1988). Language assessment of Hispanic learning disabled and speech and language handicapped students: Research in progress. In A. Ortiz & B. A. Ramirez (Eds.), *Schools and the culturally diverse student: Promising practice and future directions* (pp. 32–44). Reston, VA: Council for Exceptional Children.

Ortiz, A., & Ramirez, B. A. (Eds.). (1988). *Schools and the culturally diverse exceptional student: Promising practices and future directions*. Reston, VA: Council for Exceptional Children.

Ortiz, A., & Yates, J. (1988). Characteristics of learning disabled, mentally retarded, and speech-language handicapped Hispanic students at initial evaluation and reevaluation. In A. Ortiz & B. A. Ramirez (Eds.), *Schools and the culturally diverse exceptional student: Promising practices and future directions* (pp. 51–62). Reston, VA: Council for Exceptional Children.

Pear, R. (1991, Sept. 9). Homeless children challenge schools. *The New York Times*. p. A10.

Reynolds, C. J., & Salend, S. J. (1990) Issues and programs in the delivery of special education services to migrant students with disabilities. *The Journal of Educational Issues of Language Minority Students, 7,* 69–83.

Reynolds, M. (1962). A framework for considering some issues in special education. *Exceptional Children, 28,* 367–370.

Rhodes, L. (1992). Focusing attention on the individual in identification of gifted black students. *Roeper Review, 14*(3), 108–110.

Rueda, R. (1989). Defining mild disabilities with language-minority students. *Exceptional Children, 56,* 121–129.

Salend, S. J., (1994). *Effective mainstreaming: Creating inclusive classroom* (2nd ed.). New York: Merrill/Macmillan.

Saville-Troike, M. (1991). *Teaching and testing for academic achievement: The role of language development*. Washington, DC: National Clearinghouse for Bilingual Education.

Scherer, M. (1991). School snapshot: Focus on African-American culture. *Educational Leadership, 49*(4), 17,19.

Slavin, R.E. (1990). *Cooperative learning: Theory, research, and practice*. Englewood Cliffs, NJ: Prentice-Hall.

Smitherman, G. (1985). What go round come round: King in perspective. In C. K. Brooks (Ed.), *Tapping potential: English and language arts for the black learner* (pp. 41–62). Urbana, IL: National Council for Teachers of English.

Tatum, B. D. (1992). African-American identity development, academic achievement, and missing history. *Social Education, 56*(6), p. 331–334.

Taylor, J. (1987). Teaching children who speak a non-standard dialect to read. *Reading Improvement, 24*(3), 160–162.

Toohey, K. (1986). Minority educational failure: Is dialect a factor? *Curriculum Inquiry, 16*(2), 127–145.

Voltz, D. L., & Damiano-Lantz, M. (1993). Developing ownership in learning. *Teaching Exceptional Children, 25*(4), 18–22.

Weaver, C. (1991). Whole language and its potential for developing readers. *Topics in Language Disorders, 11,* 28–44.

Wechsler, D. (1951). *Escala de inteligencia Wechsler para niños.* Cleveland: Psychological Corporation.

Wechsler, D. (1974). *Wechsler intelligence scale for children: Revised.* Cleveland: Psychological Corporation.

Westby, C. E., & Rouse, G. R. (1985). Culture in education and the instruction of language learning-disabled students. *Topics in Language Disorders, 5*(4), 15–28.

White, O., & Haring, N. (1976). *Exceptional teaching: A multimedia training package.* Columbus, OH: Merrill.

Whittaker, C. R. (1991). *The cooperative learning planner.* Ann Arbor, MI: Exceptional Innovations.

Wigg, E. H., Freedman, E., & Secord, W. A. (1992). Developing words and concepts in the classroom: A holistic-thematic approach. *Intervention in School and Clinic, 27*(5), 278–285.

Woodcock, R. W. (1981). *Woodcock language proficiency battery: Spanish form.* Allen, TX: DLM Teaching Resources.

Woodcock, R. W. (1982). *Bateria Woodcock psico-educativea en Español.* Allen, TX: DLM Teaching Resources.

CHAPTER 11

Implementation with Infants and Preschoolers with Disabilities

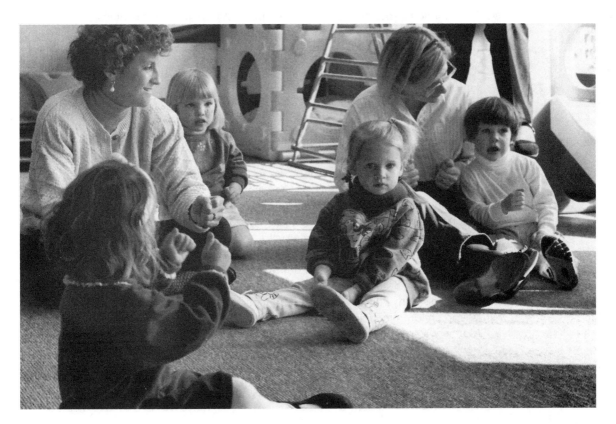

Characteristics of Young Children with Disabilities and Their Families

Intervention Needs of Young Children with Disabilities

Family-Centered Approaches
Service Delivery Options
Assessment Techniques
Intervention Strategies

The Role of the Professionals

Application

Hospital Transition
Neonatal Follow-Up Transition
Home-Based and Clinic-Based Early Intervention Transition
School District Transition
Observations

Summary

Activities

TOPICS IN THIS CHAPTER INCLUDE

◆ The characteristics associated with young children and their families.

◆ The various developmental and service delivery needs of young children and their families.

◆ The unique roles of professionals working with young children and their families.

Matthew, a 3-year-old with Down syndrome, attends a Montessori preschool in his local community. The public school program provides him with services from an itinerant early childhood special education teacher twice a week. The Montessori teacher and the early interventionist work closely on (a) adapting the preschool environment for his language needs, including sign language and picture cards for expressive communication; (b) facilitating social interaction with same-age peers; (c) integrating his special language, cognitive, and physical therapy goals into a developmentally appropriate program; and (d) designing a data-collection system for monitoring his developmental progress. Both teachers graduated from the local university's unified early childhood and early childhood special education program and were prepared to work with young children in inclusive settings using an interactive teaming approach.

Matthew's speech and physical therapists and his service coordinator at the local children's medical center meet monthly with his parents and the early intervention teachers to discuss his progress, the family's needs, and preparations for Matthew's transition to the kindergarten program in the local public school.

Interactive teaming may never be more important than when working with children like Matthew and his parents. With the passage of P.L. 99-457 and the mandated services for free and appropriate education for all children with disabilities starting at age 3, early childhood personnel are realizing that skills in coordination of services, consultation with related personnel, and collaboration with families are critical. Transdisciplinary teaming approaches are necessary in serving young children because of the large numbers of professionals involved in early intervention (Landerholm, 1990). Full-service programs for young children with disabilities and their families involve professionals from health, education, and human services.

Part H of P.L. 99-457 also mandates the expansion of interagency collaboration. States and local agencies serving infants and toddlers (birth to age 3) with disabilities developed interagency collaboration councils (ICC) as mechanisms for coordination of services. Never has interagency collaboration been taken more seriously by professionals in special education (Stegelin & Jones, 1991; Brown, Thurman, & Pearl, 1993). Successful interagency collaboration requires all the interactive teaming skills outlined in Part II of this book.

This chapter will focus on the specific components of early intervention that incorporate interactive teaming skills. First, a brief overview of the various conditions that make children eligible for early intervention services will be provided to acquaint the reader with the increasing numbers of young children who are at risk. Second, a discussion of the intervention needs of young children with disabilities suggests various service delivery options available for these children and their families. Within the description of the intervention needs of these children, assessment techniques and intervention strategies used for young children will be delineated. Third, the role of the professionals involved in intervention with young children and their families is presented. The key to providing a successful early intervention program requires that an interactive team be available for intervention, consultation, and collaboration.

CHARACTERISTICS OF YOUNG CHILDREN WITH DISABILITIES AND THEIR FAMILIES

Regulations under Part H of P.L. 99-457 provide eligibility criteria for three subgroups receiving early intervention: *established conditions*, *developmental delays*, and *at risk*. Some states serve all three subgroups of children while other states with large numbers of at-risk children have elected to use the criteria for established conditions and developmental delays. *Established conditions* refers to young children who have a genetic disorder, congenital malformation, or a neurologic disorder that has a high probability of resulting in a developmental delay. *Developmental delays* refers to young children who evidence a certain percentage of difference between their performance level and chronological age or a certain number of standard deviations below their chronological age based on quantitative and/or qualitative assessment. For a child to be eligible for services under the *at-risk* group, "children may currently demonstrate no abnormality, but have biological or environmental factors associated with their medical history or home context that increase the risk of delay in the future" (Brown, Thurman, & Pearl, 1991, p. 30).

The numbers of young children who could be eligible for early intervention services is dramatically increasing (Anastasiow & Harel, 1993). For example, the increased numbers of infants suffering from fetal alcohol syndrome and fetal alcohol effects challenge early interventionists. These children may have lifelong disabilities caused by prenatal neurological damage resulting in cognitive and language delays as well as the presence of challenging behaviors (Burgess & Streissguth, 1992). Similarly, children exposed to cocaine and other drugs pose a challenge to early intervention programs. Although the initial sensationalized problems of these children are not substantiated by current research, some research indicates that about one-third of cocaine/polydrug-exposed children evidence some delays in language, problems in attention, and self-regulation (Griffith, 1992). The practice of categorizing these children as a new breed of disability or designing special programs for cocaine/polydrug-exposed children is not supported by professionals in the field (Griffith, 1992; Schutter & Brinker, 1992). However, intervention does require (a) a collaborative effort with medical, educational, and therapeutic programs, (b) treatment of the mothers' addiction and (c) parental involvement, empowerment, and education.

Other groups of young children who are entering the early intervention arena include students exposed to lead poisoning. Needleman (1992) reported that 16% of all American children have blood lead levels in the neurotoxic range, placing them at risk for impaired neurobehavioral functioning. Most of those children are inner-city African-Americans living in poverty. Delays in development have been noted in these children including inattentiveness and mild learning disabilities.

Furthermore, a growing number of children are homeless or living in violent environments. Homeless young children may be at risk for developmental delays due to their transitory state and lack of access to basic resources such as food and medical care (Linehan, 1992). The effects of violence on young children also place the child at risk for normal development. Children who are abused can suffer significant emotional delays. However, current research indicates that children who witness violence and live in unsafe and stressful environments are also affected adversely, sometimes evidencing post-traumatic stress disorder symptoms such as emotional withdrawal, aggression, and inattentiveness (Craig, 1992).

Finally, the number of children affected by medical conditions such as prematurity, cancer, medically fragile status (Bartel & Thurman, 1992), or human immunodeficiency virus (HIV) (Seidel, 1992) have needs that challenge early interventionists. Collaboration with medical personnel as well as social service personnel will be necessary. Personnel will need knowledge and understanding of the issues related to terminal illness, death, and dying. Collaboration with families whose young children are dying may be extremely difficult for early interventionists not prepared in these areas. Consulting with social workers, family therapists, and other mental health professionals may be an important first step for the interventionists.

The discussion of the increasing numbers of children at-risk illustrates the changing causes of developmental delays today. By adding these at-risk children to the existing numbers of children with established conditions, one can better understand the enormous challenges that face early interventionists. Further complicating the challenges is the fact that families no longer comprise a working husband, a wife who stays at home, and siblings. Instead, today's family can include custodial grandparents, foster parents, same-sex partners, co-habitating couples, teen parents, parents with disabilities, and single parents. Meeting the intervention needs of young children and their families finds today's early intervention team engaged in an extremely complex enterprise.

INTERVENTION NEEDS OF YOUNG CHILDREN WITH DISABILITIES

The needs of young children with disabilities are different from the needs of elementary- or secondary-age children. Early intervention programs serving children from birth to age 5 *should not* involve teaching a lower extension of the elementary education curriculum. Early intervention programs should be **family-centered**; include **coordinated service delivery options** that promote inclusion; use **transdisciplinary play-based assessment** approaches; and provide the child with **individually and developmentally appropriate** intervention.

Family-Centered Approaches

Family-centered early intervention has been defined as an approach to intervention that recognizes and respects the pivotal role the family plays in the lives of young children with disabilities (Association for the Care of Children's Health, 1989). The major goal of this approach is to support families in their natural caregiving roles by building on unique individual and family strengths, and to enable and empower families to meet their own needs in ways that create self-competence (Bailey, Palsha, & Simeonsson, 1991; Bailey, McWilliam, & Winton, 1992; Caro & Derevensky, 1991). The following nine essential elements characterize family-centered care:

1. Recognizing the family as a constant in the child's life and intervention settings as temporary.

2. Facilitating parent/professional collaboration in the care of the child; in the child's program; and in intervention policy.

3. Sharing information about the child in an unbiased, supportive manner.

4. Implementing comprehensive intervention programs that include emotional and financial services for families, as well as child-directed services.

5. Recognizing the individuality of families, including their strengths and patterns of coping and adjusting.

6. Incorporating the unique developmental needs of young children into the service-delivery system.

7. Encouraging parent to parent support systems.

8. Designing intervention systems that are flexible, accessible, and responsive to the unique needs of different families.

9. Recognizing and respecting cultural and linguistic difference (Association for the Care of Children's Health, 1989).

Service Delivery Options

Meeting the complex needs of today's young children and families requires the involvement of multiple agencies and programs. Most children who have significant disabilities due to established conditions or developmental delays receive services from the state's lead agency for Part H of P.L. 99-457. These services can involve various agencies. Espe-Sherwindt (1991) estimated that the average number of agencies involved with families receiving Part H services was 4.7. The agencies included primary physician/health clinics, the Special Supplemental Food Program for Women, Infants, and Children, educational and therapeutic services for the child, protective services, mental health services, and case management services. Young children who are at risk are served by other agencies such as Head Start, Medicaid, Maternal and Child Health Block Grants, Chapter 1 Handicapped Programs, Social Services Block Grants, or state appropriations programs. The high number of agencies and programs available for young children with disabilities or at-risk children necessitates interactive teaming efforts by all personnel and the family.

Perhaps one of the most impressive models of interactive teaming can be found in the establishment of local interagency collaborative councils (ICC) (Stegelin & Jones, 1991; Morgan, Guetzloe, & Swan, 1991; Peterson, 1991; Swan & Morgan, 1993). ICCs were first mandated by P.L. 99-457 and are now operating in all communities serving young children with disabilities or at-risk populations. The following vignette helps illustrate the function of an ICC.

The case of Ryan, a 2½-year-old diagnosed with lead poisoning is discussed at the February meeting of the Jones County ICC. At the ICC meeting are Ryan's mother and his health-care provider, the service coordinator for Part H, the Part H early interventionists, the director from First Start, the school district's prekindergarten special education supervisor, the school psychologists, the Head Start director, the supervisor for the elementary education program, the director of the regional resources center, and the social services worker. The service coordinator introduces the mother to the team and provides some background on Ryan's case. The boy receives services from the Part H early interventionists, but has been tested by the school psychologist and found to be ineligible for special education services when he turns 3 years old. The service coordinator would like to make sure Ryan remains in an early intervention program until he is 4, when he can attend Head Start.

The mother and health-care provider provide the team with information on how Ryan is progressing. His major IFSP goals are in increasing his attention and engagement with toys and adult-child interactions. He has been improving since he started receiving early intervention services at home. The mother wants to earn her GED and get off welfare by working part time. But she fears the home visit program will be discontinued. The First Start director believes Ryan would qualify for First Start services until he turns 4. She asks the mother if she would be interested in placing Ryan in a home-care provider program on the days she is working. The mother says she would like to visit the program first but is interested in the option. The First Start parent liaison would provide support to the home-care provider and make home visits in the evenings when the mother comes home from work.

The First Start director would like to work closely with the Part H early interventionist to transition the IFSP to First Start. Head Start is now alerted to Ryan's referral when he turns 4, and the school district will monitor his progress as he nears kindergarten. The service coordinator suggests scheduling an IFSP transition meeting for all interested. The resource materials director offers office space for the meeting and reminds the First Start director that she may check out any early childhood materials Ryan might need in the home-care program. The school's prekindergarten special education consultant offers to help the home-care provider on a short-term basis. The social services worker mentions that his agency can provide transportation for Ryan to the home-care program if necessary. They will continue to provide Ryan and his mother transportation to his health-care provider.

Interagency coordinating councils integrate services for young children and their families. Cooperation, collaboration, and a genuine desire to share information are requirements for successful councils. The ICC has the potential of providing seamless services to young children and their families. Swan and Morgan (1993) provide an excellent guide for creating effective local interagency coordinating councils. They outline the following eight basic premises of ICC collaboration:

1. One agency alone cannot provide all the services needed for a young child with disabilities or at high risk and his or her family.

2. With limited resources and categorical focus, agency programs must coordinate efforts to avoid waste, unnecessary duplication, and service gaps.

3. There is nothing to be gained by competition. The agency that provides the service is not as important as the fact that the child and family are appropriately served.

4. The differences across agency programs represent a strength, not a weakness or problem to be eliminated.

5. The service delivery system must consist of a variety of options from which families may choose.

6. Agency programs are "equal" in importance.

7. Agencies must provide mutual support and assistance to one another. Favorable trade-offs exist.

8. A structured system of interagency collaboration must exist (Swan & Morgan, 1993, p.15).

Once an ICC is created, service delivery options can be expanded. For example, if the ICC had not been working cooperatively, Ryan may have gone without services for a year and his mother might have felt pressured to stay at home, opting to remain on welfare and not earn her GED. The absence of early intervention between ages 3 and 4 may have placed Ryan at risk for further developmental delay and placement into special education.

Service delivery options vary depending on the age and special needs of the young child. For newborns and infants with significant disabilities service delivery begins in a *hospital-based program*. Neonatal intensive care units (NICU) are graded by level of care provided with the Level 1 NICU providing the most significant treatment for infants with severe illness. The Level II and III NICUs provide care for newborns with a moderate degree of illness or newborns with illnesses that are complex or difficult to diagnose (Brown et al., 1993). NICU programs have expanded to encompass a range of professionals, including pediatricians; neonatologists; NICU nurses; social workers; physical, occupational, speech-language, and respiratory therapists; audiologists; and infant developmental specialists (i.e. early childhood special educators). Most NICU programs focus on family support, including programs that encourage social interactions and environments of the infants and their caregivers. A family-centered approach is most critical in the NICU where the emotional and psychological needs of families are emphasized (Long, Artis, & Dobbins, 1993). Another goal of NICU-based programs is preparing families for the transition from hospital to home.

Infants being discharged from NICU are often linked to *developmental follow-up programs*. The purposes of this service delivery option include: 1. providing ongoing support for families, 2. to smooth the transition for the infant and families, 3. to direct the family toward appropriate community resources, and 4. to provide ongoing secondary care of infants (Brown et al., 1993, p. 224). Professionals involved with developmental follow-up programs must be closely linked with community services and the local ICC. Follow-up programs are important for infants with established conditions as well as infants who are at-risk for developmental delays. Example of specific follow-up program models are described in Brown et al. (1993).

Home-based programs are most appropriate for infants and toddlers with disabilities who are younger than 36 months. Home-based programs require that professionals be competent in working with families within their home environment. This model of service delivery reinforces family-centered vs. child-centered intervention; however, intervention is provided less frequently. Related service personnel must be careful to coordinate services with the quality advisor or home visitor to assure that families are not overwhelmed by home visits and intrusion into their private lives. Transdisciplinary models of teaming are critical in home-based programs, where the home visitor has knowledge of all aspects of the infant's intervention program. Other team members serve as consultants to the home visitor.

For some toddlers and preschoolers ages 18 months to 5 years, *center-based programs* can be beneficial. For younger toddlers, half-day center-based programs may be more appropriate. Although contact with families may be less frequent, professionals must continue providing a family-centered approach to center-based services. Evening or weekend parent support programs can be established to meet the needs of some families. Additionally, early interventionists should collaborate with community day care center providers to ensure that inclusive environments are made available to preschoolers with disabilities and their families (Hanline & Hanson, 1989). Consulting and collaborating with general early childhood educators becomes one of the most important roles of early childhood special educators as inclusive educational settings become an available option for service delivery.

Assessment Techniques

An important component of early intervention programs involves assessment of young children and their families. The IFSP should address both child and family needs and outcomes requiring professionals to understand comprehensive ecological assessment techniques.

Arena assessments have become one of the most promising approaches to child assessment. These assessments require interactive teaming skills from each professional. Working together with the family, early intervention professionals provide a natural play environment in which to observe the infant interacting with toys, objects, adults, and peers. Linder (1993) describes a transdisciplinary play-based assessment technique that involves multiple professionals observing the abilities of young children through play. The play facilitator interacts with the child, providing opportunities for other team members to observe developmental skills in the language, cognition, motor, and social/emotional domains. Planning the play activities is an important initial step for the transdisciplinary assessment team. A parent facilitator is selected to work with the family member present during the play session and gather information on the family's needs and concerns. After the assessment, team members review the videotaped assessment and work together to interpret the results and plan the intervention. The arena model of assessment encourages collaboration and consultation from all team members.

Intervention Strategies

Effective early intervention programs provide individualized (Fewell & Oelwein, 1991) and developmentally appropriate practices to young children with disabilities (Bredekamp, 1986; 1991; Bailey & Wolery, 1992). For some children, specialized instructional strategies may be required. Bailey and Wolery (1992) describe the following strategies for intervention:

1. Structure the physical space to promote play, engagement, and learning.
2. Structure the social environment by using models, proximity, and responsive adults to promote engagement and learning.

3. Use children's preferences to promote learning.

4. Structuring routines using violation of expectancy, naturalistic time delay, and transition-based teaching.

5. Use structured play activities.

6. Use differential reinforcement, response shaping, and correspondence training.

7. Use peer-mediated strategies to promote communication and social skills.

8. Use naturalistic or milieu teaching strategies to promote communication and social skills.

9. Use response prompting procedures.

10. Use stimulus modification.

Many of these instructional strategies will have to be understood by parents, paraprofessionals, and general early childhood educators serving young children with disabilities in their general education classrooms. Special education personnel will help educators integrate these strategies into an early childhood program that supports developmentally appropriate practices (DAP). The following guidelines characterize DAP:

1. Activities should be integrated across developmental domains.

2. Children's interests and progress should be identified through teacher observation.

3. Teachers should prepare the environment to facilitate children's active exploration and interaction.

4. Learning activities and materials should be concrete, real, and relevant to the lives of young children.

5. A wide range of interesting activities should be provided.

6. The complexity and challenge of activities should increase as children understand the skills involved (Bredekamp, 1987 as cited in Bailey & Wolery, 1992, p. 540).

No single philosophical approach to early intervention meets the needs of the diverse population. A combination of individualized and adapted instructional strategies with a DAP approach is the ideal model for early intervention. Teachers, parents, and related personnel must collaborate to provide quality services to young children.

Essential features of effective early intervention services include family-centered approaches, coordinated service delivery options, transdisciplinary assessments, and individualized and developmentally appropriate practices of instruction. Professionals from many disciplines are involved in providing effective services to young children and their families. Their roles and responsibilities are critical to the success of early intervention programs. The next section will address the various roles of early intervention professionals.

THE ROLE OF THE PROFESSIONALS

"Multidisciplinary coordination between personnel was mandated for early intervention services because no single agency, group, or discipline could meet all of the needs of eligible children and their families" (Brown & Rule, 1992, p. 246). Part H of P.L. 99-457 specified 11 disciplines to be actively involved in early intervention services in every state. The general roles of professionals have been outlined in Chapter 4. Specialized contributions of team members who work with infants, toddlers, and preschoolers with disabilities are outlined in this chapter.

Delineating the roles of each of the team members within the educational and community setting is a first step in clarifying each group's function on the team. Table 11–1 outlines the various roles and responsibilities in both direct service and team involvement.

Although family members are not delineated as one of the 11 disciplines in the Part H legislation, they play one of the most important roles on the interactive team. Families can do the following (a) reinforce developmental and therapeutic programs in the home and community setting, (b) inform team members of the results of health-related appointments and treatment recommendations, and (c) provide team members with information on medical, behavioral, and family issues. Also, families should be respected if they choose not to be actively involved because of external or family stresses (e.g. work schedules, family crisis) (LeLaurin, 1992).

Other team members that may participate in interactive teams are agency or school administrators and paraprofessionals. Administrators may (a) support inclusive early education programs by providing resources and materials for those programs, (b) provide professional development to team members, and (c) advocate for the program. Paraprofessionals can (a) assure that the environment is ready and safe for young children, (b) provide follow-up to instructional programs throughout the day, and (c) assist in all early intervention activities by valuing child-directed and child-initiated responses. Paraprofessionals are often from the children's community culture and can serve as cultural mediators to the team.

The role of the *quality advisor* or *service coordinator* can vary with individual children and families. A paradigm of service coordination has emerged under P.L. 99-457 that emphasizes family-driven vs. agency-driven practices (Dunst & Trivette, 1989; Swan & Morgan, 1993). Two levels of service coordination have been defined in the literature (Swan & Morgan, 1993). One level is coordination of community services and the other level is coordination of child and family services. The interagency coordinating councils are the primary vehicles for the community level of service coordination. The service coordinator's role is to organize comprehensive services and mobilize resources when necessary. At the family level, the service coordinator assists specific families in the ongoing process of coordinating and monitoring services across the various providers. The individual service coordinator helps the family identify short-term and long-term outcomes and support services needed and helps the family gain access to these services (Swan & Morgan, 1993). If services do not exist, the service coordinator mobilizes resources and services required.

Table 11–1

Roles of Professionals and Others Involved with Infants, Toddlers, and Preschoolers with Disabilities and Their Families

Personnel	Direct Service Provider	Team Member
Audiologists	• Determine auditory function and characteristic of hearing losses • Assess and monitor middle ear infections • Determine relationship of auditory function and communication development • Recommend appropriate amplification or assistive devices	• Interpret all auditory function reports to family and professionals • Provide team members with instruction on hearing loss and use of amplification or assistive devices
Early Childhood Special Educators	• Conduct screening and child-find programs • Assess children's developmental competence • Develop an individualized IFSP or IEP for each child and family • Assess family needs and strengths • Implement family support services or parent education • Evaluate program effectiveness • Advocate for children and families	• Coordinate interdisciplinary services • Integrate and implement interdisciplinary team recommendations • Coordinate services from multiple agencies • Provide consultation to other professionals, families, and other caregivers • Support inclusive early intervention by serving as itinerant/consultant to the early childhood educators
Early Childhood General Educators	• Develop learning environments and activities that promote DAP philosophy. • Develop learning environments and activities that promote social interactions of children with and without disabilities. • Integrate multicultural education into all aspects of program • Provide families with information and support related to enhancing the development of the child. • Evaluate program effectiveness • Advocate for children and families	• Integrate interdisciplinary team recommendations • Collaborate with ECSE on instructional strategies and social integration for children with disabilities • Provide consultation to other professionals, families, and other caregivers
Nutritionists	• Develop nutrition care plans through assessments of nutritional status, food intake, eating behavior, and feeding skills.	• Coordinate nutrition services • Provide consultation and technical assistance to parents and team members • Provide preventive nutrition information, services, guidance • Make referrals to community resources

Note: Adapted from Bailey (1989).

Personnel	Direct Service Provider	Team Member
Nurses	• Assess physiological, psychological, and developmental characteristics of the child and family • Plan and implement interventions to improve the child's health and developmental status • Develop medical plans to treat underlying causes of medical or developmental problems • Administer medications, treatments, and regimens prescribed by a licensed physician • Monitor complex medical procedures (tracheotomy suctioning, catheterization procedures, G–tube feeding, mechanical ventilation, etc.)	• Collaborate with caregivers and team members to meet basic health and daily-care needs of the child • Assist in interpreting all medical information and reports • Make referrals to community resources
Occupational Therapists	• Assess children's developmental levels, functional performance, sensory processing, and adaptive responses • Assess family-infant interactions • Recommend, select, design, and fabricate assistive seating and orthotic devices • Prevent secondary impairments	• Provide consultation to other professionals, families on the child's functioning and integrate therapy recommendations • Consult with caregivers and team members on adaptive or assistive devices
Physicians	• Provide services to the child, including assessment, provision of a "medical home", comprehensive medical care, diagnosis, treatment, and referral	• Provide consultation and instruction to parents and team members • Consult with community settings service the child on diagnosis and treatment
Psychologists	• Administer psychological and developmental tests and other assessment procedures • Plan a program of psychological services, including family counseling, parent training, and child development	• Integrate and interpret assessment information to parents and team members • Coordinate psychological services • Collaborate with team members on family needs and strengths

Table 11–1, *continued*

Personnel	Direct Service Provider	Team Member
Physical Therapists	• Assess for motor skills, neuromotor, neuromusculoskeletal, cardiopulmonary, oral motor, and feeding • Implement environmental modifications and recommend adaptive equipment and mobility devices	• Provide consultation to teach handling, positioning, and movement techniques to facilitate motor functioning and posture • Collaborate on methods for integrating therapy into the child's program
Social workers	• Make home visits to evaluate a child's living conditions and patterns of parent-child interaction • Assess psychosocial development of the child within the family context • Provide individual or group counseling for family members	• Build partnerships with the family • Consult with team members on family needs and strengths • Coordinate community services • Consult with team members on the impact of culture on the family, and how to provide culturally competent intervention
Speech-Language Pathologists	• Assess communication and oral-motor abilities • Plan and implement appropriate therapeutic programs • Design augmentative communication systems including manual sign language, computerized communication devices, or picture/symbol systems	• Provide consultation to caregivers and team members regarding communication and oral-motor therapy programs • Refer children to medical or other professional services necessary
Vision Specialist	• Conduct assessment of functional vision • Determine the relationship of development and visual loss • Provide early orientation and mobility programs • Recommend assistive or low-vision devices	• Interpret visual functioning to caregivers and team members • Consult and refer children to medical or other professional services necessary • Collaborate on designing environments that accommodate the child's visual loss • Teach caregivers and team members sighted-guide techniques • Assist caregivers and team members with pre-Braille or low-vision instruction

The role of each team member is critical to the success of providing coordinated and appropriate services to young children and their families. The efforts being done in early childhood special education toward this end are commendable. General educators and special educators of school-age children might benefit from adopting or adapting the unique features of early intervention collaboration outlined in this chapter.

APPLICATION

Anthony's parents have worked with personnel from the local hospital, follow-up clinic, early intervention program, day care center, and school district during the past five years as they have been transitioned from one service agency to another. They say the transitions have been smooth and the personnel supportive and collaborative. The following describes the various steps and strategies that were used during each of the six transitions. The *assess-plan-implement-evaluate* framework for transition planning was used by each sending and receiving program or agency (Rosenkoetter, Hains, & Fowler, 1994).

Hospital Transition

Anthony was born three months premature and weighed less than 4 pounds. He stayed in a Level I NICU for three months while physicians monitored bleeding in his head, respiratory problems, and severe jaundice. During that time, Anthony's parents connected with the NICU family support program. The program team consisted of a social worker specialized in NICU families, a developmental psychologist, Anthony's primary physicians, a nurse, and a service coordinator from the hospital's Neonatal Follow-Up program. Team members met regularly to discuss Anthony's progress with the family, and extended family members were encouraged to participate in these sessions. The social worker invited the parents to attend a NICU parent support group, which met in the evenings once a week. Anthony showed much improvement during his stay in the NICU and was moved to a Level II NICU after three months.

The team began to prepare the family for the first transition: taking Anthony home. The nurse provided the family with instructions for Anthony's heart monitor, medication regimen, and dates for home visits. The service coordinator provided the family with information on the follow-up clinic and scheduled their first appointment. The developmental psychologist reported her findings from neurobehavioral and developmental assessments. Anthony appeared to have some moderate developmental delays. Early stimulation and intervention strategies were discussed with the family. The social worker invited the parents to attend the one-year reunion for families that had been part of the support group. A discharge conference was scheduled with the family and the team. All the information on the transition activities, programs, and agencies, phone numbers, and scheduled appointments were given to the parents in the transition notebook.

Neonatal Follow-Up Transition

Anthony was home at five months and was being followed up by the nurse and service coordinator. The primary concerns and intervention program was focused on Anthony's medical stability and early development. After three months, the family and service coordinator met with the home-based teacher from the local early intervention center (EIC). A new transition team was formed consisting of the home-based teacher, family therapists, and center psychologist. They met for a few evenings to discuss the transition from follow-up clinic to the home visitation program. Anthony had improved medically and was to be monitored by the follow-up clinic annually. The team discussed Anthony's continued delay in gross motor and cognitive skill development and an IFSP was created. The family concerns and outcomes were focused on providing an early stimulation program and finding a support group for the mother, who was feeling isolated from other parents.

Home-Based and Clinic-Based Early Intervention Transition

The home-based teacher visited the family every week, providing them with activities for developmental stimulation. The EIC began providing monthly physical therapy and speech therapy services. The teacher and parents, however, were shown the therapeutic programs to integrate into Anthony's daily routines. His mother began attending a support group at the EIC.

When Anthony turned 15 months, the home-based teacher initiated the transition plan for him to enter the center-based program. The parents and home-based teacher observed the classroom and evaluated what would be necessary for him to attend. The parents attended the IFSP transition meeting and three new members joined the team: the classroom teacher, the nutritionists, and the occupational therapist. A plan was developed that included scheduling transportation, ordering positioning equipment and feeding utensils, and scheduling a phase-in period. Three months later Anthony began to attend the EIC. The program was inclusive and provided day care for children without disabilities. Anthony's parents linked up with the center-based family support group. The parents and team met every six months to review the IFSP.

When Anthony turned 28 months old, another transition meeting was scheduled. This time the center teacher and parents went to the local school district prekindergarten program. They evaluated the environment, and talked with the principal, teacher, and school psychologist. The school's early childhood teacher also visited Anthony in his EIC classroom. He was referred to the special education program and a psychological assessment was completed. The EIC team (sending agency) and the school district team (receiving agency) met to plan for the transition to the prekindergarten program at the elementary school. The plan included (a) a sending and receiving agency communication plan; (b) a plan to expand the IFSP outcomes to IEP goals; and (c) a plan to evaluate Anthony's transition.

School District Transition

The receiving agency implemented the specified objectives in the transition plan and prepared the environment to meet his needs. When Anthony turned 3, the parents and team met once again and evaluated if the school district was ready to receive Anthony. All documents were transferred to the early childhood teacher, including data collection and anecdotal progress notes. The parents were linked with the school's parent support group and were introduced to all school staff. The first day of school, the EIC teacher stayed with Anthony in the classroom. The transition was smooth, and Anthony adapted well to his new program.

Observations

In less than three years, Anthony's family dealt with more than 13 professionals. Each transition brought the parents stress and anxiety. However, the team members were sensitive to the needs of the family adjusting to an infant with disabilities. The family-centered approach was evident throughout the process. Parents were included in all meetings when they were able to attend. No decisions were made without them. They were empowered to assess-plan-implement-evaluate each of the programs before the transitions. Each team member was treated with equal respect and openness. Documentation was provided for the family at each step of the way. For programs serving young children with disabilities to be seamless in the delivery of services, professionals and parents must communicate, collaborate, and consult.

SUMMARY

Collaboration and teaming are integral components to serving young children with disabilities and their families. Legislative backing for cooperation and integration of a system that has typically been fragmented has created a great opportunity to improve services to these individuals. The diverse characteristics of the young children receiving services in early intervention programs further justifies the need for interactive teaming. More and more children live in environments or suffer from physiological conditions that put them at risk for developmental delays. Additionally, personnel must understand that the advantages of family-centered approaches far outweigh the agency-driven or child-centered approaches of yesterday's programs.

A continuum of service delivery options is necessary to meet the needs of infants, toddlers, and preschoolers with disabilities and their families. However, those options and array of services must be closely coordinated and monitored. Intervention strategies must be individualized and developmentally appropriate for all children, and transdisciplinary arena assessments should be supported by the team. The family should be empowered to take an active role in deciding what they need and how they want those needs met. The roles of professionals on the early intervention team should be formed around the family, enabling the family to make informed decisions. As equal partners, each team member can offer valuable information and skills development to the team. Collaboration and consultation among early interventionists can result in high quality services for young children and their families.

ACTIVITIES

1. Conduct an informational interview with a professional who is involved in early intervention programs for young children with disabilities or at risk. Use the guidelines provided in Chapter 4.

2. Attend a local interagency coordinating council meeting. Observe the teaming and collaboration skills among the professionals.

3. Volunteer at a local day care center, an early childhood prekindergarten program, a Head Start classroom, or NICU "cuddle program". Use child-directed approaches to play and social interactions.

4. Ask family members of young children with disabilities to speak to the class about family-centered intervention.

5. Attend tours of schools and community agencies serving young children with disabilities or at risk. Note the goal and mission of the various agencies as related to the quality of services provided to the children and their families.

REFERENCES

Anastasiow, N. J., & Harel, S. (1993). *At-risk infants: Interventions, families, and research.* Baltimore: Paul H. Brookes.

Association for the Care of Children's Health. (1989, Spring). *Family Support Bulletin.* Bethesda, MD: Author.

Bailey, D. B. (1989). Case management in early intervention. *Journal of Early Intervention, 13,* 120–134.

Bailey, D. B., McWilliam, R. A., & Winton, P. S. (1992). Building family-centered practices in early intervention: A team-based model for change. *Infants and Young Children, 5*(1), 78–82.

Bailey, D. B., Palsha, S. A., & Simeonsson, R. J. (1991). Professional skills, concerns, and perceived importance of work with families in early intervention. *Exceptional Children, 58*(2), 156–165.

Bailey, D., & Wolery, M. (1992). *Teaching infants and preschoolers with disabilities* (2nd ed.). New York: Merrill/Macmillan.

Bartel, N. R., & Thurman, S. K. (1992). Medical treatment and educational problems in children. *Phi Delta Kappan, 74*(1), 57–61.

Bredekamp, S. (1986). *Developmentally appropriate practice.* Washington, DC: National Association for the Education of Young Children.

Bredekamp, S. (1987). *Developmentally appropriate practice in early childhood programs serving children from birth through age 8.* Washington, DC: National Association for the Education of Young Children.

Bredekamp, S. (1991). *Guidelines for appropriate curriculum content and assessment in programs serving children ages three through eight.* Washington, DC: National Association for the Education of Young Children.

Brown, W., & Rule, S. (1993). Personnel and disciplines in early intervention. In W. Brown, S. Thurman, & L. E. Pearl (Eds.), *Family-centered early intervention with infants and toddlers: Innovative cross-disciplinary approaches* (pp. 245–268). Baltimore: Paul H. Brookes.

Brown, W., Thurman, S. K., & Pearl, L. E. (1993). *Family-centered early intervention with infants and toddlers: Innovative cross-disciplinary approaches.* Baltimore: Paul H. Brookes.

Burgess, D. M., & Streissguth, A. P. (1992). Fetal alcohol syndrome and fetal alcohol effects: Principles for educators. *Phi Delta Kappan, 74*(1), 24–30.

Caro, P., & Derevensky, J. L. (1991). Family focused intervention model: Implementation and research findings. *Topics in Early Childhood Special Education, 11*(3), 66–80.

Craig, S. E. (1992). The educational needs of children living with violence. *Phi Delta Kappan, 74,* 67–68, 70–71.

Dunst, C. J., & Trivette, C. M., (1989). An enablement and empowerment perspective of case management. *Topics in Early Childhood Special Education, 8*(4), 87–102.

Espe-Sherwindt, M. (1991). The IFSP and parents with special needs/mental retardation. *Topics in Early Childhood Special Education, 11*(3), 107–120.

Fewell, R. R., & Oelwein, P. L. (1991). Effective early intervention: Results from the model preschool program for children with Down syndrome and other developmental delays. *Topics in Early Childhood Special Education, 11*(1), 56–68.

Griffith, D. R. (1992). Prenatal exposure to cocaine and other drugs: Developmental and educational prognoses. *Phi Delta Kappan, 74*(1), 30–34.

Hanline, M. F., & Hanson, M. J. (1989). Integration considerations for infants and toddlers with multiple disabilities. *Journal of the Association for Per-*

sons with Severe Handicaps (JASH), 14(3), 178–183.

Landerholm, E. (1990). The transdisciplinary team approach in infant intervention programs. *Teaching Exceptional Children, 22*(2), 66–70.

LeLaurin, K. (1992). Infant and toddler models of service delivery: Are they detrimental for some children and families? *Topics in Early Childhood Special Education, 12,* 82–104.

Linder, T. W. (1993). *Transdisciplinary play-based assessment: A functional approach to working with young children.* Baltimore: Paul H. Brookes.

Linehan, M. F. (1992). Children who are homeless: Educational strategies for school personnel. *Phi Delta Kappan, 74*(1), 61–66.

Long, C. E., Artis, N. E., & Dobbins, N. J. (1993). The hospital: An important site for family-centered early intervention. *Topics in Early Childhood Special Education, 13*(1), 106–119.

Morgan, J. L., Guetzloe, E. C., & Swan, W. (1991). Leadership for local interagency coordinating councils. *Journal of Early Intervention, 15,* 255–267.

Needleman, H. L. (1992). Childhood exposure to lead: A common cause of school failure. *Phi Delta Kappan, 74*(1), 35–37.

Peterson, N. L. (1991). Interagency collaboration under part H: The key to comprehensive, multidisciplinary, coordinated infant/toddler intervention services. *Journal of Early Intervention, 15,* 89–105.

Rosenkoetter, S. E., Hains, A. H., & Fowler, S. (1994). *Bridging early services for children with special needs and their family.* Baltimore: Paul H. Brookes.

Schutter, L. S., & Brinker, R. P. (1992). Conjuring a new category of disability from prenatal cocaine exposure: Are the infants unique biological or caretaking casualties? *Topics for Early Childhood Special Education, 11,* 84–111.

Seidel, J. F. (1992). Children with HIV related developmental difficulties. *Phi Delta Kappan, 74*(1), 38–40, 56.

Stegelin, D. A., & Jones, S. D. (1991). Components of early childhood interagency collaboration: Results of a statewide study. *Early Education and Development, 2*(1), 54–67.

Swan, W. W., & Morgan, J. L. (1993). *Collaborating for comprehensive services for young children and their families: The local interagency coordinating council.* Baltimore: Paul H. Brookes.

CHAPTER **12**

Implementation for Students with Mild Disabilities

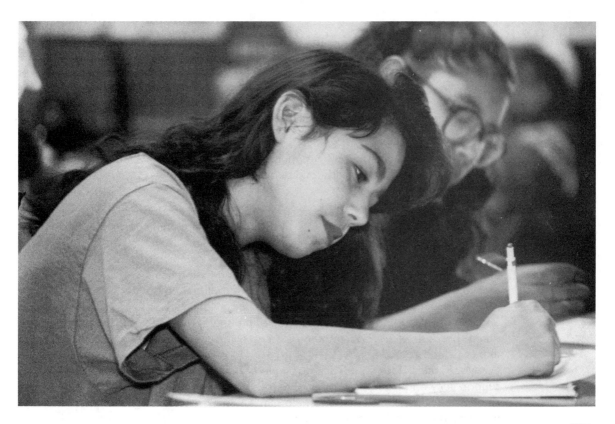

Characteristics of Students with Mild Disabilities
Learning Disabilities
Mental Retardation
Emotional Disturbances/Behavior Disorders
Visual Impairments
Hearing Impairments
Physical Impairments
Communication Disorders
Considerations

Meeting Educational Needs
Problem Identification and Designing Interventions
Service Delivery Options
Teacher Competencies

Selected Teaching Strategies
Considerations

Roles of Professionals Involved with Students with Mild Disabilities

Application

Summary

TOPICS IN THIS CHAPTER INCLUDE

◆ Characteristics of students with mild disabilities.

◆ Educational needs of students with mild disabilities.

◆ Service delivery options.

◆ Teacher competencies and selected teaching strategies.

◆ Description of roles of interactive team members.

◆ An application illustrating team members working together to meet the needs of a student with mild disabilities.

 Joey, a personable 9-year-old, has become increasingly difficult to manage in Ms. Alley's third-grade class. Although Joey repeated first grade, he is still behind in reading compared with his classmates. He seems to be aware of his slow progress, and lately he has been acting out as a way of avoiding assignments. Rather than begin his seatwork when Ms. Alley gives an assignment, he will get up out of his seat to sharpen his just broken pencil, or he will turn to another child to talk. If he does get started on an assignment and has to erase a mistake, he angrily wads up the paper and begins again. Because of his poor reading skills and the avoidance behaviors, he is falling further behind each day.

Ms. Rhodes, Joey's mother, is a single parent holding down two part-time jobs to support Joey and his older brother, Gregory. She is aware of his problems and is concerned, but when she has time to help him with his homework, he often demonstrates the same behaviors he does at school.

Joey was referred for testing in the middle of second grade, and by the end of the year, he was placed in a resource room for students with learning disabilities. In her summary of the psychological assessment, Dr. Eaddy noted Joey's low tolerance for frustration and his reluctance to attempt tasks because he did not want to fail.

Ms. Jackson, the resource teacher, has begun to work with Joey on his reading skills for 45 minutes each day. He seems to look forward to coming to the resource room because there are only six other students in the class, and he receives more individual attention. Even in this small setting, though, he glances around to see if other students are listening before he begins to read aloud.

Ms. Jackson and Ms. Alley have asked the speech-language therapist for assistance in developing Joey's vocabulary and other types of language activities in which he can be successful. Mr. Morrow, the therapist, provided a number of activities that Joey seemed to enjoy initially, but he now appears to be growing wary of doing them because none of the other children is doing similar assignments.

Joey's strongest suit is his skill in sports. Lately he has become increasingly competitive because this is the only outlet in which he thinks he can do better than his peers. The emphasis on winning has alienated two of his friends, who have chosen to play with others because Joey seems so intent on winning rather than having fun or participating as a team player. The adapted physical education teacher, Ms. DiCicco, has suggested that during recess the teachers involve all the students in cooperative games so the interactions among the students will be more positive.

This vignette illustrates the complex array of problems that many students with mild disabilities or those considered "at risk" often face in school settings. This complexity presents real challenges to interactive team members in their roles as collaborators with other professionals and as direct service providers. In cases like Joey's, the interactive teaming model requires cooperation, commitment, and coordination of efforts among all the personnel involved to ensure continuity and comprehensive academic, social, and behavioral programming.

This chapter includes a discussion of the characteristics and needs of students with mild disabilities. Service delivery options, teacher competencies, and selected strategies also are presented. The last section of the chapter contains information on the roles of the professionals who may be involved in programming for children and adolescents with mild disabilities.

CHARACTERISTICS OF STUDENTS WITH MILD DISABILITIES

As discussed in the first chapter, this country is experiencing a dramatic increase in the number of students considered at risk for school difficulties or failure. Many of these students will eventually be labeled "mildly disabled" at some point in their school years; that is, they will be identified as learning disabled, mentally retarded, or mildly emotionally disturbed/behaviorally disordered. Currently, these students make up almost 90% of the school-age population identified as disabled, and they often have similar characteristics and needs (Mercer & Mercer, 1993; Morsink, Thomas, & Smith-Davis, 1987).

The term "mild disabilities" can also include students with sensory disabilities (i.e., vision and hearing), physical or health impairments, (e.g., cerebral palsy or epilepsy), and communication disorders (e.g., speech and language problems). These students can be considered mildly disabled if the severity of their disability and the extent of their educational needs are such that they are appropriately served in a regular classroom for at least part of the day. In addition, these students would be provided other types of services, such as speech-language therapy or remediation from a special educator, as needed.

Brief descriptions are provided to highlight characteristics of students in each area. Although this information will be familiar to special educators, school psychologists, and other personnel who received training on learners with exceptional needs as part of their programs, it is included here as reference material for interactive team members who may not have this knowledge or who need to update their information. The references cited in each area will be of further assistance to those who need more information. Additional material on pupils whose sensory, physical, or intellectual disabilities are more severe is provided in the next chapter.

Learning Disabilities

Mercer (1992) noted that the "common denominator" among learning disabled students is a discrepancy between the child's estimated ability and his actual performance on academic tasks. Specific academic difficulty areas typically include oral language, reading skills and comprehension, written expression, and mathematics calculation and reasoning. Other characteristics that may be present are visual and auditory perceptual disorders; lack of metacognitive strategies; social-emotional problems, including lack of motivation and hyperactivity; and memory difficulties.

Certain central nervous system dysfunctions often related to learning disabilities include attention deficit disorder (ADD) and attention deficit hyperactivity disorder (ADHD). The exact relationship between learning disabilities and ADD or ADHD remains unclear and is often the subject of debate among educators and medical professionals and parents. A distinction between the terms was described by Silver (1990) who stated that a learning disability affects the brain's ability to learn, and the presence of attention deficit disorders interferes with one's availability for learning.

Mental Retardation

The definition of mental retardation has evolved from one focusing primarily on significantly subaverage intelligence and associated adaptive behavior impairments, to one that stresses interaction among the major dimensions of the capabilities of an individual, the environments in which the person functions, and the need for varying levels of support (Beirne-Smith, Patton, & Ittenbach, 1994).

The definition adopted by the American Association on Mental Retardation (AAMR) in 1992 follows:

Mental retardation refers to substantial limitations in present functioning. It is characterized by significantly subaverage intellectual functioning, existing concurrently with related limitations in two or more of the following applicable adaptive skill areas: communication, self-care, home living, social skills, community use, self-direction, health and safety, functional academics, leisure and work. Mental retardation manifests before age 18.

The needed levels of support are based on four dimensions: (a) intellectual functioning and adaptive skills, (b) psychological/emotional considerations, (c) physical health/etiology considerations, and (d) environmental considerations. The four levels of needed support identified by the American Association on Mental Retardation (1992) are intermittent, limited, extensive and pervasive.

Emotional Disturbances/Behavior Disorders

Kauffman (1993a) commented that the definition of children in this category is subjective, and that identifying children as emotionally disturbed or behaviorally disordered is compounded by the variations in conceptual models and problems in assessment. Another issue is the subjectivity of standards for determining a behavior disorder, because expectations may vary by sex, age, subculture, community, and economic conditions (Cullinan & Epstein, 1994).

Identification procedures vary from state to state, but the most frequently cited characteristics are school learning problems (not due to mental retardation), difficulty in establishing and maintaining satisfactory interpersonal relationships, inappropriate feelings and manifestations of behaviors, unhappiness or depression, and in some cases the existence of physical problems influenced by personal or school situations. Emotionally disturbed children frequently are impulsive, distractible, and hyperactive.

Visual Impairments

Finkelstein (1989) noted that students with visual impairments may have sight that is useful for some purposes, while others are blind or have such profound visual impairments that their vision is not useable as an educational medium. These students may have difficulty with concept development and social problems due to the limitations of their vision and the ways they are treated by others. They often need assistance with orientation and mobility (i.e., moving around in their environment) daily living skills, and language development, in addition to other academic needs (Shea & Bauer, 1994).

Hearing Impairments

Hearing impairments range from mildly hard of hearing to profoundly deaf (Wray, Flexer, & Ireland, 1988). In the hearing-impaired population, two groups typically are described: (a) *deaf* people, whose loss is so great that their hearing is not functional for everyday life; and (b) *hard-of-hearing* people, who have some degree of functional hearing with or without a hearing aid. The two predominant types of hearing impairments are *conductive,* which occurs in the outer or middle ear, and *sensorineural,* which occurs in the inner ear.

Students with hearing losses may experience difficulties in academics, because so much is learned through listening, or personality and emotional problems due to a feeling of isolation and a reduced ability to communicate. In addition to academics and social adjustment, hearing-impaired students may need help with listening skills and other forms of communication such as speech-reading, cued speech, and sign language.

Physical Impairments

Physical impairments were defined in P.L. 94-142 and restated in P.L. 101-476 (Individuals with Disabilities Education Act, or IDEA) in two broad categories: orthopedic impairments and health impairments. The former category includes impairments such as clubfoot, poliomyelitis, and cerebral palsy. Heath impairments include asthma, sickle cell anemia, and diabetes.

Physical impairments may range from mild to severe, and they may or *may not* be accompanied by other disabling conditions such as mental retardation or sensory deficits. Physically impaired students may need education in daily living and social skills, devices to aid them in communication, and modifications for written assignments and tests. They also may require services to help them with physical flexibility and movement, or medication and special diets.

Communication Disorders

Communication disorders often overlap with other types of disabling conditions such as hearing impairments, mental retardation, cerebral palsy, or learning disabilities (Kirk & Gallagher, 1989; Wiig & Semel, 1984). Communication problems may take the form of a speech impairment, language disorder, or both. *Speech impairments* include articulation problems (e.g., substitutions or distortions of sounds), voice disorders (e.g., inappropriate quality or loudness), or fluency disorders (e.g., stuttering). *Language disorders* can be classified as receptive (i.e., problems in understanding language) or expressive (i.e., difficulties in producing language, such as limited vocabulary). In addition to remediation on the specific type of deficit, a student with a speech or language disorder may need help in an academic area, such as reading, or with social interactions with peers.

Considerations

Several considerations regarding students with mild disabilities are worthy of mention at this point. The first is that not all of the students within a category will exhibit all of the characteristics cited at any given time. Second, students may have combinations of conditions, such as behavior and speech disorders, that warrant a variety of services. Third, professionals should try to ensure that the difficulties or disorders being identified are not due to cultural differences discussed in Chapter 10. Finally, labeling should be kept to a minimum because of the possible adverse reactions of parents or students. Instead, interactive team members should focus on students' strengths and specific needs, such as reading comprehension or interacting appropriately with peers, rather than on categorical labels.

MEETING EDUCATIONAL NEEDS

Based on the preceding description of characteristics of students who may be considered mildly disabled, the educational needs that emerge can be put into five major categories: (a) academic remediation, (b) social interactions, (c) self-concept and motivation, (d) behavior management, and (e) special education and support services (e.g., orientation and mobility, counseling, physical therapy, etc.). To consider ways of addressing these needs, four programmatic areas will be discussed: *the process of identifying problems and designing interventions, service delivery options, teacher competencies,* and *selected teaching strategies.*

Although the emphasis in this section is on teachers and teaching strategies, many of the principles can be implemented by team members with other areas of expertise, such as psychology, adapted physical education, and speech-language therapy. These principles should be viewed as supplementary and complementary to existing literature on competencies and effective strategies in each individual field, not as replacements for them. Also, these competencies are in addition to those already discussed as necessary for functioning as a successful team member.

Problem Identification and Designing Interventions

The actual steps used in problem identification and intervention design should be based on the sequence described in Chapter 3. These steps ensure *understanding and clarity of the problem, discussion of previous interventions, identification of data collection procedures and data decision rules, consensus on interventions to be attempted,* and *procedures for evaluating effectiveness and making modifications as necessary.*

These procedures can be beneficial in programming for mildly disabled students at various times or decision points (see Figure 1–3 in Chapter 1). First, for at-risk students, the procedures can be viewed as preventive and prereferral measures. Second, if difficulties persist, team members may decide to proceed with a referral for screening, but they can continue to meet to discuss interventions and provide ideas and support to each other. Third, if the child is placed in a special program or is receiving other types of services, the team members should continue to consult and collaborate to ensure that the child's total program is cohesive. Fourth, if the child is mainstreamed for academic or social skills, the teachers should collaborate on identifying desired student behaviors and appropriate teaching or management strategies. Evaluation should be ongoing during all these situations; that is, team members should be assessing the effectiveness of the interventions, as well as their consultation and collaboration skills, and assisting one another to make whatever modifications are deemed appropriate (Jayanthi & Friend, 1992).

As illustrated in the vignette on Joey, a number of personnel may be involved in the interactive teaming situation and also in follow-up consultation with other team members. Role release will need to occur in all these contexts, along with sensitivity to cultural differences, attention to the perspectives of others, expertise in communication, and effectiveness in leadership strategies.

Service Delivery Options

Students with mild disabilities receive services in several settings, depending on the severity of their problems and where the people involved in placement decisions believe their needs can be best met. If the child evidences severe difficulties in all five of the areas of need previously identified, he/she will likely be placed in a more restrictive setting, such as a full-time special class or in a special class with part of the day spent in a regular classroom. If the difficulties are evidenced primarily in one area such as academic problems, the child may spend the majority of the day in the regular classroom with assistance from a resource teacher or a speech-language therapist. Those whose problems are considered very mild may be in the regular classroom all day, although the teacher will consult as needed with other professionals (e.g., special educator, speech-language therapist, adaptive physical educator). According to the 15th Annual Report to Congress (1993), 69.3% of special education students were in regular classrooms more than 40% of the time during the 1991–92 school year. The continuum of options for service delivery is illustrated in Figure 12–1.

Variations and combinations of the services illustrated on the continuum have been used to meet the needs of students with mild disabilities. Most, if not all, rely on some level of collaboration or teaming among teachers. Bauwens, Hourcade and Friend (1989) described cooperative teaching or co-teaching approaches in which regular and special educators coordinate ways to teach academically and behaviorally heterogeneous groups of students. They described three cooperative teaching options: (a) complementary instruction, in which the regular educator maintains primary responsibility for teaching subject matter and the special educator focuses upon the students' mastery of academic survival skills; (b) team teaching, in which the teachers jointly plan and deliver instruction; and (c) supportive learning activities developed by the special educator to supplement the content delivered by the regular teacher. Simpson and Myles (1990) described a general education collaboration model which incorporated flexible departmentalization and classroom modifications that support mainstreaming. Laycock, Gable, and Korinek (1991) noted that collaborative approaches can provide early intervention for at-risk learners and facilitate access to accommodations in the regular classroom for students with mild disabilities.

Pull-in programs, in which the specialist teaches in the regular classroom were described by Meyers, Gelzheiser, and Yelich (1991). They found that compared with pull-out programs, the teachers in pull-in situations had more collaborative meetings, focused more on specific instructional issues, and learned more instructional techniques. Morsink and Lenk (1992) commented on four promising strategies for inte-

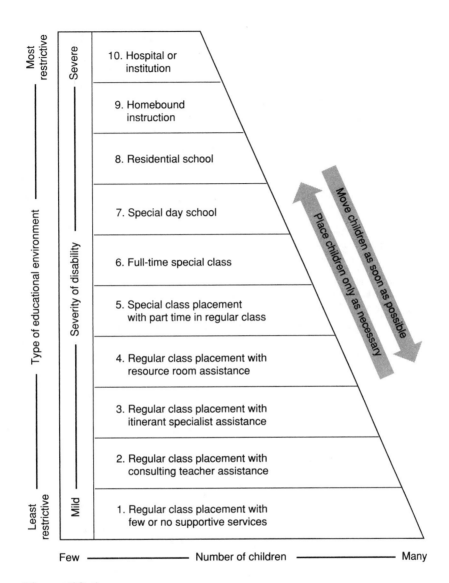

The diagram shows a continuum/pyramid with labels from top (Most restrictive / Severe) to bottom (Least restrictive / Mild):

- 10. Hospital or institution
- 9. Homebound instruction
- 8. Residential school
- 7. Special day school
- 6. Full-time special class
- 5. Special class placement with part time in regular class
- 4. Regular class placement with resource room assistance
- 3. Regular class placement with itinerant specialist assistance
- 2. Regular class placement with consulting teacher assistance
- 1. Regular class placement with few or no supportive services

Left axis labels: Most restrictive — Type of educational environment — Least restrictive; Severe — Severity of disability — Mild

Bottom axis: Few —— Number of children —— Many

Arrows on the right: "Move children as soon as possible" and "Place children only as necessary"

Figure 12–1

Continuum of special education services

Note: From *An Introduction to Special Education,* 2nd ed., by W. H. Berdine and A. E. Blackhurst, 1985, Boston: Little, Brown and Company. Copyright 1985 by William H. Berdine and A. Edward Blackhurst. Reprinted by permission of Scott, Foresman.

grating students with mild disabilities in regular classrooms using collaboration among teachers: adapting learning environments with augmentative technology, learning strategies, peer tutoring, and cooperative learning. They observed that for students at the secondary level, collaborative planning is a major need for transition program delivery. Sileo, Rude, and Luckner (1988) outlined the need for such collaboration among specialists, regular and vocational teachers, and family members to provide transition planning that focuses on relevant life development activities.

A final service delivery option currently receiving much attention and debate among educators who teach students with mild disabilities is full inclusion. Many promote the need for integrating regular and special services to provide high quality education for all students (e.g., Goodlad & Lovitt, 1993), and others have described successful inclusion programs which provide many positive benefits (e.g., Jakupcak, 1993). As the debate continues over the appropriateness of full inclusion for students with mild disabilities, professional organizations reiterate the need for a continuum of services as mandated by the Individuals with Disabilities Education Act (National Joint Committee on Learning Disabilities, 1993), and leaders in the field call for strengthening the conceptual foundations and empirical base (Kauffman, 1993b) and for pragmatic approaches toward redefining relationships with regular education (Fuchs & Fuchs, 1994). Clearly, however, if inclusion is to be a viable service delivery option for students with mild disabilities, collaborative approaches such as interactive teaming will be required.

Teacher Competencies

A sampling of research in the past 15 years in regular and special education on competencies for regular and special education teachers reveals that the skills identified often are quite similar. Researchers such as Brophy (1979), Good (1979), and Stevens and Rosenshine (1981) stressed teacher behaviors that included a teacher-controlled approach, activities with an academic focus, sufficient time for instruction, an emphasis on classroom management, practice opportunities for student responses, material taught in small steps, and frequent testing of student learning with appropriate feedback.

Englert (1984) identified competencies in the areas of classroom organization; teaching and maintaining rules and procedures; allocated and engaged time; and lesson introduction, demonstration, practice, and evaluation. Morsink, Thomas, and Smith-Davis (1987) suggested that four generic sets of competencies were suitable for teachers of mildly disabled students. Those competencies are (a) teacher-directed instruction, (b) provision for students to engage in active academic responding with teacher feedback, (c) contingent reinforcement of appropriate student behaviors, and (d) adaptive instruction, geared to individual needs for differences such as longer learning time, simplified language, or concrete materials. Wolery, Bailey, and Sugai (1988) listed the areas of child development, curriculum content, disabling conditions, principles of learning and behavioral procedures, and instructional monitoring and evaluation procedures as essential knowledge and skills for teachers.

In a research synthesis by the Northwest Regional Education Laboratory (1990), the following recommendations were developed based on effective teacher practices:

◆ Use a preplanned curriculum with learning goals and objectives sequenced to facilitate student learning.

◆ Form instructional groups based on student achievement levels and review and adjust group membership as skill levels change.

◆ Use classroom management strategies that minimize disruptive behaviors.

◆ Hold students accountable for appropriate behavior and achievement and give help immediately when they experience problems.

◆ Provide additional learning time on priority objectives.

Simmons and Kameenui (1991) described the importance of teachers using principles of instructional design, information analysis, and taxonomies of knowledge. Algozzine and Ysseldyke (1992) designed a conceptual model for effective instruction, which included four components: (a) planning instruction (e.g., deciding what and how to teach), (b) managing instruction (e.g., preparation and establishing a positive environment), (c) delivering instruction (e.g., motivation, feedback, and active involvement), and (d) evaluating instruction (e.g., monitoring student understanding and making decisions about performance). Examples of application of their model are provided in a special focus section on effective instruction in *Teaching Exceptional Children* (see Algozzine, Ysseldyke, & Campbell, 1994).

Based on their review and synthesis of the effectiveness research, Mercer and Mercer (1993) identified eight principles of teaching mildly disabled students:

1. *Use effective classroom management*: Effective management enables students to stay on task and promotes continuous learning. Teachers frequently monitor classroom activities, establish classroom routines and procedures, use effective instructional strategies to teach activities such as transitions between lessons and exchanging papers, and provide reinforcement for student accomplishments.

2. *Use direct systematic teaching*: Effective teachers are well-organized, systematic, efficient, and task-oriented. They also use explicit instructional strategies and formats that involve active participation by students. They provide demonstrations, opportunities for practice, and feedback.

3. *Focus on time for learning*: A strong academic focus is maintained to increase the amount of engaged time that students actually spend performing tasks.

4. *Provide success*: Instructional tasks are individualized so that students can achieve a high rate of success.

5. *Establish goals and expectations*: Rationales for goals are explained and instruction is provided to help the students attain the goals.

6. *Monitor progress and provide feedback*: Active monitoring ensures that students understand the task, and that errors can be corrected quickly. Feedback with elaborations and modeling also are related to improved student achievement.

7. *Provide positive and supportive learning environments*: Effective teachers model supportive and enthusiastic behaviors and believe that all students can learn.

8. *Teach students to generalize and to be independent learners*: In effective classrooms students are taught to generalize appropriate academic and social behaviors to other settings and individuals. They also are taught how to be independent learners through the use of learning strategies and metacognitive instruction. (Summarized from Mercer & Mercer, 1993, pp. 13–42.)

Mercer and Mercer (1993) also provided one additional principle that is important for team members: *Enjoy teaching* by appreciating the humor and ideas of students. Enjoying the successes of students as they make progress can be a motivating force for everyone involved.

SELECTED TEACHING STRATEGIES

In terms of teaching techniques, the team members will need to consider the problems presented by the student. Only a selected number of strategies will be cited to illustrate the range of possibilities that might be appropriate for students with mild disabilities. More detailed information on teaching methods for specific academic and behavioral problems is available in a number of textbooks, such as Bos and Vaughn (1994), Henley, Ramsey, and Algozzine (1993), Kerr and Nelson (1989), Lewis and Doorlag (1991), Meese (1994), Mercer and Mercer (1993), Morsink (1984), Salend (1994), Schloss and Sedlack (1986), Wood (1992), and Wolery, Bailey and Sugai (1988).

Most mildly disabled students will need to be taught general strategies for *how* to learn (Deshler & Schumaker, 1986) or explicit strategies, such as decision trees used in problem-solving exercises in computer simulations (Hollingsworth & Woodward, 1993). Others may need to be taught classroom discourse strategies to promote literacy development (Englert, Raphael, & Mariage, 1994); specific strategies for reading comprehension, such as semantic mapping (Sinatra, Berg, & Dunn, 1985) or reciprocal questions (Manzo & Manzo, 1993); or techniques for written expression (Thomas, Englert, & Gregg, 1987; Thomas, in press).

Students who are experiencing difficulties in mathematics need to acquire a cognitive strategy for solving different types of problems (cf. Montague & Bos, 1986), as well as self-monitoring strategies (Frank & Brown, 1992). Sensory-impaired students may need help developing residual hearing and listening skills. Physically disabled and communication-disordered students may need help with alternative communication strategies. (See also Chapter 13.)

Nevin and Thousand (1986) identified a number of promising practices that can be used in regular classroom settings: (a) curricular adaptations, (b) mastery learning, (c) individualized learning, (d) peer tutoring, (e) accelerated learning systems, and (f) applied behavior analysis. Henley, Ramsey, and Algozzine (1993) described several approaches and strategies that have received attention in recent years including integrated teaching, whole language, Adaptive Learning Environment Model, skillstreaming, and direct instruction. Bos and Vaughn (1994) provided an overview of the use of cognitive behavior modification, modeling and demonstration strategies, reflective thinking, information processing and schema techniques, and micro-computers and multimedia systems. Other methods that have been shown to improve academic functioning, as well as social interactions, are cooperative learning strategies, such as the jigsaw technique (cf. Aronson, Blaney, Stephan, Sikes, & Snapp, 1978; Johnson, Johnson, Warring, & Maruyama, 1986; Lloyd, Crowley, Kohler, & Strain, 1988; Putnam, 1993). Learning styles instruction (Carbo, 1990) and teaching school survival skills to adolescents (Schaeffer, Zigmond, Kerr, & Farra, 1990) also can enhance achievement.

Riegel (1983) presented specific modifications that consultants can suggest, along with their difficulty factors (1 = easy, 2.9-4.0 = difficult or time consuming); typical comments from teachers; and consulting recommendations. Other modifications can be found in Lovitt (1984), Mercer and Mercer (1993), Weller and Buchanan (1988), and textbooks previously listed. Sample strategies for academic difficulties are illustrated in Table 12–1.

Considerations

In trying to determine which strategies to recommend or attempt to implement in a particular situation, there are several considerations to bear in mind. Knight (1976) noted that in working with other professionals it is particularly important to inform them that their role is important (whether it be providing service or following up on a skill), to assure them that they will be helped rather than judged, and to clarify which procedures will be used in evaluation.

Additional considerations on making suggestions to regular classroom teachers about behavior problems were identified by Martens, Peterson, Witt, and Cirone (1986). They noted that teachers classify strategies in terms of effectiveness, ease of use, and frequency of use. They cautioned consultants to be aware of the extent to which the interventions they suggest are similar to those a teacher may already be using, and the degree to which a teacher's behavior will have to change in order to implement an intervention.

Guskey (1990) provided a framework for synthesizing diverse instructional strategies: (a) instructional strategies should share common goals; (b) strategies should complement each other; (c) time should be taken to experiment and adapt strategies to individuals and classrooms; and (d) educators should recognize that the combined beneficial effects of several strategies will surpass the effects of any single strategy. A final set of considerations are the procedural principles identified by Idol, Nevin, and Paolucci-Whitcomb (1994) designed to facilitate performance of learners with special needs in inclusive classrooms:

1. Procedural principles designed to facilitate teaching and learning of difficult-to-teach learners must be easy to implement in inclusive classrooms.

2. Teaching and learning procedures should be designed for use with any student who is achieving poorly, rather than for a single learner with special needs.

3. Teaching and learning procedures need to be based on the use of classroom curricula.

Table 12–1

Strategies To Help Low-Level Students Achieve Basic Academic Skills

Strategies That Help	Strategies That Do Not Help
Mostly narrow teacher questions with a "right" answer	Mostly open-ended questions **or** Nonacademic conversation
Calling on nonvolunteers or using patterned turns to select students to answer questions	Selecting only volunteers when calling on students to answer questions
Immediate feedback (as to right or wrong) to students' answers	Not giving clear feedback to students' answers
"Staying with" a student until he or she answers a question	Quickly letting someone else answer; leaving a student with little or no feedback
Short and frequent—rather than long and occasional—paper and pencil activities	Games, art work, many interest centers
Specific praise for good performance	Vague or general praise, or praise when it isn't especially deserved
Covering material thoroughly	Covering a lot of material quickly
Much time spent in teacher questioning, feedback, and supervised practice	Much class time spent in anything else
Time spent in structured learning activities led by the teacher	Time spent in unstructured or free time
Instruction broken down into small steps, short activities sequenced by the teacher	Long, unbroken periods of seatwork or independent work, with students' choice of activities or sequences
Plenty of practice (repetition) with frequent correction and praise	Little practice **or** Independent practice without prompt feedback
A lot of supervision and help, in whole-class or group settings	Individualized, self-paced instruction; independent work
Continuous teacher direction of student behavior and activity	Situations calling for much pupil self-control or self-direction
Materials or questions at a level of difficulty at which students have a high rate of success	Challenging materials or questions, or work in which students are not likely to know most of the answers
Many opportunities and much encouragement to answer teacher questions	Few opportunities or little encouragement to answer questions frequently

4. Teaching and learning procedures must include components that teach learners to generalize.

5. Teaching and learning procedures need to be useful for group instruction.

6. Learners must be directly taught the skill areas they are required to master.

ROLES OF PROFESSIONALS INVOLVED WITH STUDENTS WITH MILD DISABILITIES

As described in Chapter 4, interactive team members involved in the education of mildly disabled students can serve in two types of roles: collaborator/consultant and direct service provider. In both roles, the professionals will apply the knowledge from their own areas of specialization; participate actively in planning, decision making, implementation, and evaluation of interventions; and ensure that programming is provided in a comprehensive and coordinated way (Johnson, Pugach, & Devlin, 1990).

In the role of collaborator/consultant, team members should consider the types and degree of services required and determine which academic or behavioral management strategies are warranted based upon the student's needs. Donaldson and Christiansen (1990) designed a *Collaborative Decision Making Model* that can be used as a guide to select appropriate options for service delivery, instruction, and behavior management (see Figure 12–2). In this model, team members will need to consult/collaborate by identifying the problems presented, deciding upon the appropriate placement in the continuum of services displayed in Figure 12–1, and determining which instructional or behavior management strategies to implement. The final part of the cycle involves evaluating the success of the options or interventions, and deciding what procedures for follow-up or alternative placements are warranted. Additional examples of the types of contributions and activities interactive team members can participate in as direct service providers and collaborators/consultants are provided in Table 12–2.

APPLICATION

The vignette about Joey at the beginning of this chapter contains descriptions of several behaviors that an interactive team could target for change. However, in a team meeting the professionals and Joey's mother agreed that the most problematic behavior in all settings (e.g., regular classroom, resource room, home, playground) was his unwillingness to begin tasks on time. Instead, Joey used a variety of avoidance tactics, including breaking pencils and arguing, to keep from starting his assignments.

The team members decided that a behavior management system using a contingency contract might help modify Joey's behavior. Because Joey enjoys sports, the adapted physical educator, Ms. DiCicco, agreed to allow him to be her "assistant" when she taught a group of preschoolers with disabilities twice a week if he met the conditions of the contract.

Figure 12–2

Collaborative decision-making model

Note: From "Consultation and Collaboration: A Decision-Making Model" by R. Donaldson and J. Christiansen, 1990, *Teaching Exceptional Children, 22*(2), pp. 22–25. Reprinted by permission of the authors and the Council for Exceptional Children.

Table 12–2

Roles of Professionals and Others Involved With Mildly Disabled Students

Personnel	Direct Service Provider	Team Member
Special Educator	Assess educational achievement. Design instructional program. Implement academic/behavioral strategies. Follow up on skills taught by others.	Serve as case manager. Interpret assessments. Observe in other settings. Consult on individualizing instructional techniques.
Regular Educator	Implement academic/behavioral strategies. Assist in social integration.	Consult on curriculum. Consult on group management techniques.
Parent	Reinforce academic and behavioral programs at home.	Provide background information. Consult on possible interventions.
Administrator	Reinforce appropriate behavior.	Provide information on services available in school and community. Assist with scheduling and class size.
Psychologist	Assess psychological functioning.	Interpret test results. Collaborate in designing interventions and data collection strategies.
Speech-Language Therapist	Assess speech-language development. Remediate speech-language disorders in individual or small group sessions.	Interpret test results. Provide follow-up materials for other team members. Consult on strategies to use.
Counselor	Provide counseling on self-concept, getting along with adults and peers, etc.	Collaborate with others about emotional or behavioral situations.
Physical and Occupational Therapist	Assess physical and occupational needs. Provide physical therapy. Provide occupational therapy.	Interpret test results. Collaborate with others on ways to enhance physical development or classroom modifications.
Hearing and Vision Specialists	Assess hearing and vision. Teach strategies such as auditory training, listening skills, orientation and mobility.	Interpret test results. Teach others how to use special equipment or materials.
Adapted Physical Educator	Assess psychomotor skills. Remediate areas of physical fitness.	Collaborate in designing cooperative games and motor development activities.

The regular classroom teacher, Ms. Alley, said she would like to focus on spelling seatwork for purposes of the contract. Ms. Jackson, the resource teacher, identified reading workbook assignments as the area of concern in her classroom. Mr. Morrow, the speech-language therapist, cited oral language practice activities as a goal, and noted that this should be assessed in all settings because Joey received speech therapy only once a week. Joey's mother, Ms. Rhodes, said she wanted him to begin his homework assignments promptly. The objectives and personnel involved in Joey's program are listed in Table 12–3.

The team members discussed the level of performance that should be required for Joey to earn the privilege of being Ms. DiCicco's assistant and decided that a success rate of 60% (i.e., three out of five assignments) for three consecutive days would

Table 12–3

Interactive Team Plan for Joey

Objectives	Personnel				
	Reg Ed	**Sp Ed**	**Parent**	**APE**	**S/LT**
1. Joey will begin his spelling seatwork within two minutes of the assignments being given.	X				
2. Joey will begin his reading workbook assignment within two minutes of the directions being provided.		X			
3. Joey will begin his homework within two minutes of his mother's request to start.			X		
4. Joey will distribute materials for cooperative games within two minutes of the request by the adapted physical educator.				X	
5. Joey will begin his oral language practice activities within two minutes of the request.	X	X	X	X	X

be a good starting point. They based this decision on a desire for Joey to experience success and receive the reinforcement early in the program so that he would be motivated. They agreed to gradually increase the percentage and the number of days as his behavior improved.

Ms. Rhodes said she would like to be the one to explain the program to her son, and everyone else supported this idea. Then the team members discussed a system for collecting and sharing their data with Ms. Alley, who would determine if the criteria had been met and notify Ms. DiCicco that Joey was eligible for the reward. The team members agreed to meet again in two weeks to evaluate the effectiveness of the program, and discuss any needed modifications.

SUMMARY

The characteristics of students with mild disabilities often are similar. Their needs can be categorized into five areas:

1. Academic remediation
2. Social interactions
3. Self-concept and motivation
4. Behavior management
5. Special education and support services

To meet these needs, interactive team members should implement a process for problem identification and designing interventions, use appropriate service delivery options, demonstrate competencies, intervene with effective teaching strategies, and evaluate and adapt programs as necessary.

A number of personnel are involved in the education of students, both as direct service providers and as team members who serve as collaborators/consultants. It is essential that all these people work together in a cohesive and coordinated manner, keeping students' needs as the focus of attention, in order to provide effective programs. Chapter 13 describes how professionals and parents serve as interactive team members for severely disabled students.

ACTIVITIES

1. Conduct informational interviews with a regular educator, resource teacher, and parent about the characteristics of a mildly disabled child. Compare their comments on the child's academic and behavioral needs.
2. Volunteer to tutor or provide a special activity for a mildly disabled child. Describe your observations of the child's behaviors and interests.

3. Observe a child in three different settings, such as regular and special education classrooms and speech-language therapy. What similarities and differences did you notice in the child's behavior and performance?

4. Attend a school-based committee or teacher-assistance team meeting. Based on your observations of the meeting, answer the following questions: Who attended the meeting, and did everyone participate? How was information presented? What characteristics and needs were mentioned? Which academic and behavior management strategies were discussed? How were decisions made?

REFERENCES

Algozzine, B., & Ysseldyke, J. E. (1992). *Strategies and tactics for effective instruction*. Longmont, CO: Sopris West.

Algozzine, B., Ysseldyke, J. E., & Campbell, P. (1994). Strategies and tactics for effective instruction. *Teaching Exceptional Children, 26* 34–36.

American Association on Mental Retardation (1992). *Mental retardation: Definition, classification, and systems of supports* (9th ed). Washington, DC: Author.

Aronson, E., Blaney, N., Stephan, C., Sikes, J., & Snapp, M. (1978). *The jigsaw classroom*. Beverly Hills, CA: Sage Publications.

Bauwens, J., Hourcade, J. J., & Friend, M. (1989). Cooperative teaching: A model for general and special education integration. *Remedial and Special Education, 10*(2), 17–22.

Beirne-Smith, M., Patton, J., & Ittenbach, R. (1994). *Mental retardation* (4th ed.). New York: Macmillan.

Berdine, W. H., & Blackhurst, A. E. (1985). *An introduction to special education* (2nd ed.). Boston: Little, Brown and Company.

Bos, C. S., & Vaughn, S. (1994). *Strategies for teaching students with learning and behavior problems* (3rd ed.). Boston: Allyn & Bacon.

Brophy, J. E. (1979). Teacher behavior and its effects. *Journal of Educational Psychology, 71,* 733–750.

Carbo, M. (1990). Igniting the literacy revolution through reading styles. *Educational Leadership, 48*(2), 89–92.

Cullinan, D., & Epstein, M. H. (1994). Behavior disorders. In N. G. Haring, L. McCormick, & T. G. Haring (Eds.), *Exceptional children and youth* (6th ed.). New York: Macmillan.

Deshler, D. D., & Schumaker, J. B. (1986). Learning strategies: An instructional alternative for low-achieving adolescents. *Exceptional Children, 52,* 583–590.

Donaldson, R., & Christiansen, J. (1990). Consultation and collaboration: A decision-making model. *Teaching Exceptional Children, 22*(2), 22–25.

Englert, C. S. (1984). Measuring teacher effectiveness from the teacher's point of view. *Focus on Exceptional Children, 17*(2), 1–14.

Englert, C. S., Raphael, T. E., & Mariage, T. V. (1994). Developing a school-based discourse for literacy learning: A principled search for understanding. *Learning Disability Quarterly, 17*(1), 2–32.

15th Annual Report to Congress on the Implementation of the Individuals with Disabilities Education Act (1993). Washington, DC: U.S. Department of Education, Office of Special Education Programs.

Finkelstein, D. (1989). *Blindness and disorders of the eyes*. Baltimore: The National Federation for the Blind.

Frank, A. R., & Brown, D. (1992). Self-monitoring strategies in arithmetic. *Teaching Exceptional Children, 24*(2), 52–54.

Fuchs D., & Fuchs, L. S. (1994). Inclusive schools movement and the radicalization of special education reform. *Exceptional Children, 60*(4), 294–309.

Good, T. L. (1979). Teacher effectiveness in the elementary school. *Journal of Teacher Education, 30,* 52–64.

Goodlad, J. I., & Lovitt, T. C. (1993). *Integrating general and special education.* New York: Macmillan.

Guskey, T. R. (1990). Integrating innovations. *Educational Leadership, 47*(5), 11–15.

Henley, M., Ramsey, R. S., & Algozzine, R. (1993). *Characteristics of and strategies for teaching students with mild disabilities.* Boston: Allyn & Bacon.

Hollingsworth, M., & Woodward, J. (1993). Integrated learning: Explicit strategies and their role in problem-solving instruction for students with learning disabilities. *Exceptional Children, 59*(4), 444–455.

Idol, L., Nevin, A., & Paolucci-Whitcomb, P. (1994). *Collaborative consultation* (2nd ed.). Austin, TX: Pro-Ed.

Jakupcak, J. (1993). Innovative classroom programs for full inclusion. In J. W. Putnam, *Cooperative learning and strategies for inclusion: Celebrating diversity in the classroom.* Baltimore: Paul H. Brookes.

Jayanthi, M., & Friend, M. (1992). Interpersonal problem solving: A selective literature review to guide practice. *Journal of Educational and Psychological Consultation, 3*(1), 39–53.

Johnson, D. W., Johnson, R. T., Warring, D., & Maruyama, G. (1986). Different cooperative learning procedures and cross-handicap relationships. *Exceptional Children, 53,* 245–252.

Johnson, L. J., Pugach, M. C., & Devlin, S. (1990). Professional collaboration. *Teaching Exceptional Children, 22*(2), 9–11.

Kauffman, J. M. (1993a). *Characteristics of emotional and behavioral disorders of children and youth* (5th ed.). New York: Merrill/Macmillan.

Kauffman, J. M. (1993b). How we might achieve the radical reform of special education. *Exceptional Children, 60*(1), 6–16.

Kerr, M. M., & Nelson C. M. (1989). *Helping adolescents with learning and behavior problems.* New York: Merrill/Macmillan.

Kirk, S. A., & Gallagher, J. J. (1989). *Educating exceptional children* (6th ed.). Boston: Houghton Mifflin.

Knight, N. (1976). Working relationships that work. *Teaching Exceptional Children, 8,* 113–115.

Laycock, V. K., Gable, R. A., & Korinek, L. (1991). Alternative structures for collaboration in the delivery of special services. *Preventing School Failure, 35*(4), 15–18.

Lewis, R. B., & Doorlag, D. H. (1991). *Teaching special students in the mainstream* (3rd ed.). New York: Macmillan.

Lloyd, J. W., Crowley, E. P., Kohler, F. W., & Strain, P. S. (1988). Redefining the applied research agenda: Cooperative learning, prereferral, teacher consultation, and peer-mediated interventions. *Journal of Learning Disabilities, 21,* 43–52.

Lovitt, T. C. (1984). *Tactics for teaching.* New York: Merrill/Macmillan.

Manzo, A. V., & Manzo, M. C. (1993). *Literacy disorders: Holistic diagnosis and remediation.* Fort Worth, TX: Harcourt Brace Jovanovich.

Martens, B. K., Peterson, R. L., Witt, J. C., & Cirone, S. (1986). Teacher perceptions of school-based interventions. *Exceptional Children, 53,* 213–223.

Meese, R. L. (1994). *Teaching learners with mild disabilities: Integrating research and practice.* Pacific Grove, CA: Brooks/Cole Publishing Co.

Mercer, C. D. (1992). *Students with learning disabilities* (4th ed.). New York: Merrill/Macmillan.

Mercer, C. D., & Mercer, A. R. (1993). *Teaching students with learning problems* (4th ed.). New York: Macmillan.

Meyers, J., Gelzheiser, L. M., & Yelich, G. (1991). Do pull-in programs foster teacher collaboration? *Remedial and Special Education, 12*(2), 7–15.

Montague, M., & Bos, C. S. (1986). The effect of cognitive strategy training on verbal problem solving performance of learning disabled adolescents. *Journal of Learning Disabilities, 19,* 26–33.

Morsink, C. V. (1984). *Teaching special needs students in regular classrooms.* Boston: Little, Brown and Company.

Morsink, C. V., & Lenk, L. L. (1992). The delivery of special education programs and services. *Remedial and Special Education, 15*(6), 33–43.

Morsink, C. V., Thomas, C. C., & Smith-Davis, J. (1987). Noncategorical special education programs: Process and outcomes. In M. C. Wang, M. C. Reynolds, & H. J. Walberg (Eds.), *Handbook of special education: Research and practice* (Vol. 1). New York: Pergamon Press.

National Joint Committee on Learning Disabilities (1993). *A reaction to "full inclusion": A reaffirmation of the right of students with learning disabilities to a continuum of services.* Author.

Nevin, A., & Thousand, J. (1986). What the research says about limiting or avoiding referrals to special education. *Teacher Education and Special Education, 9,* 149–161.

Northwest Regional Educational Laboratory (1990). *Effective schooling practices: A research synthesis 1990 update.* Portland, OR: Author.

Putnam, J. W. (1993). *Cooperative learning and strategies for inclusion: Celebrating diversity in the classroom.* Baltimore: Paul H. Brookes.

Riegel, R. H. (1983). Mainstreaming equals cooperative planning. *Academic Therapy, 18,* 285–298.

Salend, S. J. (1994). *Effective mainstreaming: Creating inclusive classrooms* (2nd ed.). New York: Macmillan.

Schaeffer, A. L., Zigmond, N., Kerr, M., & Farra, H. E. (1990). Helping teenagers develop school survival skills. *Teaching Exceptional Children, 23*(1), 6–9.

Schloss, P. J., & Sedlak, R. A. (1986). *Instructional methods for students with learning and behavior problems.* Boston: Allyn & Bacon.

Shea, T. M., & Bauer, A. M. (1994). *Learners with disabilities: A social systems perspective of special education.* Madison, WI: Brown & Benchmark Publishers.

Sileo, T. W., Rude, H. A., & Luckner, J. L. (1988). Collaborative consultation: A model for transition planning for handicapped youth. *Education and Training in Mental Retardation 23*(2) 333–339.

Silver, L. B. (1990). Attention deficit-hyperactivity disorder: Is it a learning disability or a related disorder? *Journal of Learning Disabilities, 23,* 394–397.

Simmons, D. C., & Kameenui, E. J. (1991). Knowing what you teach: A first step in instructional design. *LD Forum, 17*(1), 23–26.

Simpson, R. L., & Myles, B. S. (1990). The general education collaboration model: A model for successful mainstreaming. *Focus on Exceptional Children, 23*(4), 1–10.

Sinatra, R. C., Berg, D., & Dunn, R. (1985). Semantic mapping improves reading comprehension of learning disabled students. *Teaching Exceptional Children, 17*(4), 310–314.

Stevens, R., & Rosenshine, B. (1981). Advances on research in teaching. *Exceptional Education Quarterly, 2*(1), 1–9.

Thomas, C. C. (in press). Helping students with learning difficulties develop expressive writing skills. *Reading and Writing Quarterly: Overcoming Learning Disabilities.*

Thomas, C. C., Englert, C. S., & Gregg, S. (1987). An analysis of errors and strategies in the expository writing of learning disabled students. *Remedial Education and Special Education, 8,* 21–30, 46.

Weller, C., & Buchanan, M. (1988). *Educators' desk reference for special learning problems.* Boston: Allyn & Bacon.

Wiig, E. H., & Semel, E. (1984) *Language assessment and intervention for the learning disabled* (2nd ed.). Columbus, OH: Merrill.

Wolery, M., Bailey, D. B., & Sugai, G. M. (1988). *Effective teaching: Principles and procedures of applied behavior analysis with exceptional students.* Boston: Allyn & Bacon.

Wood, J. W. (1992). Adapting instruction for mainstreamed and at-risk students (2nd ed.). New York: Macmillan.

Wray, D., Flexer, C., & Ireland, J. (1988). Mainstreaming hearing-impaired children: Typical questions posed by classroom teachers. *Hearsay* (Fall), 76–79.

CHAPTER 13

Implementation for Students with Severe Disabilities

Characteristics of Students with Severe Disabilities

Physical and Sensory Impairments
Challenging Behavior
Medical Conditions

Meeting Educational and Community Needs

Support Service Options

Assessment and Program Design
Specialized Curriculum Components

Selected Teaching Strategies

Roles of Professionals Involved with Students with Severe Disabilities

Application

Summary

TOPICS IN THIS CHAPTER INCLUDE

◆   The characteristics associated with students who have severe disabilities.

◆   The various educational needs of students with severe disabilities.

◆   Selected teaching strategies for working with students who have severe disabilities.

◆   The unique roles of professionals involved with students who have severe disabilities.

◆   An application for team involvement in educational planning for students with severe disabilities.

Mr. and Mrs. Fredricks arrive at their daughter's elementary school for their annual IEP meeting. Sally, 7, has been diagnosed with severe neurological impairment due to spinal meningitis contracted at age 2. Sally is an attractive child who appears to react positively by smiling at and babbling to her family, teachers, and peers. She enjoys participating in group activities involving a touch screen on a computer, and she loves to swim in the local YWCA swimming pool twice a week. However, Sally evidences severe seizure disorders requiring anticonvulsant medication and is currently fed through a gastrointestinal tube (G-tube).

Additionally, Sally has been diagnosed with cortical blindness, although she is able to track a brightly colored beach ball placed in the swimming pool 2 feet from her eyes. Although she has no severe maladaptive behavior at this point, Sally has required behavioral management procedures to decrease eye poking, which frequently occurs during transition periods throughout the day. Sally has one older brother, who attends the same elementary school. She spends most of her day in an inclusive classroom with her first-grade peers.

As her parents enter the principal's conference room, they are greeted by Sally's first-grade teacher, the special education teacher, the school psychologist, the school counselor, and the principal. At first glance it appears to be a typical reunion in a typical school setting. However, within the next 10 minutes the room slowly fills with the following team of professionals: a physical therapist, an occupational therapist, a school nurse, a pediatric neurologist, a speech/hearing clinician, an itinerant vision teacher, an orientation and mobility specialist, a representative from the Commission for the Blind, the behavioral specialist, and the school district's special education director. The Fredricks have also invited a parent advocate and their personal lawyer. Now, with 19 people in the room, the school counselor begins the meeting by asking all the members of the team to introduce themselves. One and a half hours later, the meeting comes to a close with Mr. and Mrs. Fredricks expressing satisfaction with the decisions made on behalf of Sally's educational services.

Although this scenario does not happen frequently, scenes similar to it occur in many United States schools serving students with severe and multiple disabilities. Such service is perhaps idealistic, but it is warranted by the nature of the students for whom individual educational plans must be developed. The education of students with severe and multiple disabilities requires of professionals an extraordinary amount of cooperation, collaboration, and interaction. In fact, a text has been written devoted to the topic of collaboration and teaming for students with severe disabilities (Rainforth, York, & Macdonald, 1992).

In the vignette, Sally has special educational as well as medical needs that must be met by the educational system. In her case interactive teaming is the *core* of her educational program. This chapter will introduce the specific needs of students with severe and multiple disabilities and delineate the various roles of the professionals working with these students. Within the descriptions of the students and of the roles of the professionals working with these students, strategies and techniques used for students with severe or multiple disabilities are presented. More than any group of at-risk students, the group evidencing severe impairments requires a comprehensive interactive team approach. Before discussing the role of the professionals involved in the education and treatment of students with severe disabilities, this chapter will first describe the general characteristics and needs of these students.

CHARACTERISTICS OF STUDENTS WITH SEVERE DISABILITIES

Although students with severe disabilities are a fairly heterogeneous group, they have some common characteristics and educational and medical needs. The abilities of this population are sometimes overlooked when a description of their disabilities is presented. Students with severe disabilities have much to offer society. The types of students considered severely disabled vary from state to state. For purposes of this chapter, students with severe disabilities have the following diagnoses:

◆ Severely impaired intellectual functioning.

◆ Severe physical and multiple impairments due to cerebral palsy, spina bifida, or neurological damage.

◆ Visual impairment associated with other disabilities.

◆ Hearing impairment associated with other disabilities.

◆ Deaf/blindness.

◆ Autism.

Students with severe disabilities have been described as having learning difficulties, including (a) acquiring new skills rapidly, (b) retaining skills they've learned, (c) generalizing skills from one situation to another, and (d) synthesizing skills learned separately into meaningful and functional routines (Rainforth, York, & Macdonald, 1992). The following discussion provides additional descriptions of some of the characteristics found in this population. However, it is important to remember that all students are individuals with unique capabilities. Generalizations of these characteristics to all students with severe disabilities would be inaccurate. The information helps establish the need for medical, social, and educational collaboration when providing services to them.

Physical and Sensory Impairments

Students with severe disabilities frequently evidence orthopedic and sensory disabilities (Sailor, Gee, Goetz, & Graham, 1988). Many students evidence severe motor impairments due to cerebral palsy (Orelove & Sobsey, 1991). About 43% of students with severe disabilities have associated visual impairments, and about 22% of the population have hearing impairments (Jacobson & Janicki, 1985). Additionally, Wolf-Schein (1989) estimated that 747,457 individuals in the United States were deaf-blind and severely developmentally delayed. Students with both physical and sensory impairments have a number of needs. Appropriate intervention requires attention from medical personnel in the areas of physical and occupational therapy, as well as neurology, ophthalmology, and audiology.

Challenging Behavior

Students with severe disabilities often have associated *excessive behaviors* such as self-injury, stereotypy, aggression, or social isolation. Students need treatment in these areas if their behaviors appear to be interfering with school and community functioning. With the most severe behaviors, professionals will usually need to form a committee to assist in monitoring treatment and progress, and to assure that the rights of the individual are respected. A comprehensive and functional analysis of what may be causing the behavior is important (Iwata, Dorsey, Slifer, Bauman, & Richman, 1982; Snell, 1993). Understanding the communicative function of excessive behavior is a promising approach to intervention (Donnellan, Mirenda, Mesaros, & Fassbender,

1984; Durand, 1990). However, in some of the most severe situations medical professionals are likely to be involved in the intervention of the most severe behavior problems if medication is required, such as Tegritol (an *anticonvulsant* used to tranquilize), Haldol, Mellaril, or Prolixin (*antipsychotic/neuroleptic* drugs). Other medication, such as Cogentin, Artane, or Benadryl, is given to counter the side effects of the neuroleptic drugs. Considered anticholinergic and anti-Parkinson medications, these drugs combat the tremors and rigidity often associated with the neuroleptic drugs (A. L. Correa, personal communication, 1988).

Medical Conditions

Students with the most severe disabilities often have associated medical problems such as the need for *tracheostomy suctioning, gastrostomy feeding, oxygen supplementation, seizure monitoring,* or *clean intermittent catheterization* (CIC) (Ault, Graff, & Rues, 1993). The ability to administer routine medical and emergency procedures will be required of all professionals working directly with the student who has complicated medical needs (McCubbin, 1987; Mulligan-Ault, Guess, Struth, & Thompson, 1988; Sailor, Gee, Goetz, & Graham, 1988). Additionally, the increased numbers of students with traumatic brain injuries, fetal alcohol syndrome, and prenatal exposure to polydrug use challenges medical, social, and school personnel.

Certification in procedures such as cardiopulmonary resuscitation (CPR) and the Heimlich maneuver should be required of all professionals working with this population. Additionally, special education personnel should know about communicable diseases such as infectious hepatitis, herpes, cytomegalovirus (CMV), and acquired immune deficiency syndrome (AIDS). Students with severe disabilities may also be taking anticonvulsant medication such as phenobarbital, Dilantin, Mysolin, and Tegritol to control seizure activity. Professionals must understand their side effects (e.g., drowsiness, lethargy, and impaired vision) and their influence on students' performance (Ault, Guy, Guess, & Rues, 1991).

The characteristics associated with students with severe disabilities are numerous, complex, and often not consistent among the population. By assessing and analyzing these students' strengths and weaknesses, team members can develop appropriate instructional programs. The complex nature of these students' disabilities make program development a challenge.

MEETING EDUCATIONAL AND COMMUNITY NEEDS

A major function of the team serving students with severe disabilities is to help them reach their optimal potential for independence and community living with nondisabled people. Summarizing the factors that predict the ultimate success of community living for people with severe disabilities, Haney (1988) has indicated that good personal appearance and social skills are related to success and that the absence of excessive behavior is the best predictor of successful placement. These findings suggest that normalization strategies be used that emphasize students' abilities and develop behaviors that help students become included in families, schools, and communities. Each member of the team must work cooperatively to assess and develop intervention programs that prepare students for their roles in the community.

Today, interactive teams in special education are being challenged by the movement toward inclusive education (National Association of School Boards, 1993), including inclusion of students with the most severe disabilities into general education (Sailor, Gee, & Karasoff, 1993). Early participation in inclusive classrooms can prepare students to function successfully in their home communities. Unique support from family and professional team members involves adapting the curriculum, providing specialized services such as sign language in the inclusive setting, and creating opportunities for increased social interactions (Goetz, 1993). The educational needs of students with severe disabilities are complex in the areas of support services, assessment, program design, and teacher competencies. The following section will address these needs.

SUPPORT SERVICE OPTIONS

The nature of support services provided to students with severe disabilities *does not* typically include academic instruction (Izen & Brown, 1991), but focuses on functional life routines necessary for community life (Snell, 1993). The interactive team that promotes inclusive education comprises parents, members from allied health professionals, general and special education, and vocational and community personnel. However, some programs serving students with severe and multiple impairments have been segregated from regular education programs. In fact, residential programs serving students who are deaf-blind, multidisabled blind, or multidisabled deaf still exist in many regions of the United States. Segregated programs have made it easier for allied health professionals such as physical therapists and occupational therapists to serve a large population of students with disabilities in one central location.

However, a strong campaign has been initiated to move programs serving even students with the most severe disabilities into general education settings (National Association of School Boards, 1993). This campaign has left many professionals in a quandary about how best to provide support services such as physical therapy to students in their home-schools. A transdisciplinary team model is critical and allows the general and special educator the opportunity to integrate therapy techniques throughout the student's daily program.

Ultimately, the optimal inclusive placement for a student would be in a *chronological-age-appropriate* school setting, with the natural proportion of students with disabilities to students without disabilities, and incorporating *community-referenced programming* (Certo, Haring, & York, 1984; Orelove & Sobsey, 1991; Snell, 1993). New and creative placement options have also been proposed for young preschoolers with disabilities under P.L. 99-457 and young adults with disabilities under *transition* programs required by the Individuals with Disabilities Education Act. For infants and preschoolers, service can be provided in a home-based program or a clinical-based center. Placing early intervention programs in regular day-care or Head Start settings is strongly supported by many school districts. Similarly, secondary transition programs are being developed in many middle and high schools. The goals for many of these programs involve integration into the community both through *group-home* or supported-living arrangements, supported employment, and community-based vocational programs. Collaboration with adult services agencies such as vocational rehabilitation and development disability councils are critical for successful transition to post-school life.

Assessment and Program Design

Assessment and program development for students with severe disabilities are not simple. The interactive team must be prepared to provide *multifaceted assessment* of students in the areas of vision, hearing, sensorimotor development, functional/ecological inventories, and family functioning. Rainforth, Macdonald, York, and Dunn (1992) provide an excellent description of the assessment process and procedures recommended for developing an appropriate and functional IEP for students with severe disabilities.

Assessments require a team effort that may include the special education teacher, the parent, the school psychologist, and allied health professionals. Natural observations of the student, arena assessments, interviews with direct service staff, and ecological inventories in the areas of school, domestic, vocational, leisure/recreation, and community living for the student's present and future environments are imperative.

The published curricula for students with severe disabilities is limited. Two of the most widely used curricula for program development are the *Syracuse Community-Referenced Curriculum Guide* (Ford, Schnorr, Meyer, Davern, Black, & Dempsey, 1989) and the *Activities Catalog* (Wilcox & Bellamy, 1987). *Perkins Activity and Resource Guide*, a curriculum for students who are deaf-blind, would also be beneficial for some students who are severely disabled but not sensory impaired (Cushman, Heydt, Edwards, Clark, & Allon, 1992). Additionally, Brown (1987) and Brown, Evans, Weed, and Owen (1987) have described an assessment-curriculum model for designing intervention programs for students. The *Component Model of Functional Life Routines* offers a curriculum model for generating skills that are functional, structured, and comprehensive in the domain areas of personal management, vocational school, leisure, and mobility. Additionally, Brown, Falvey et al. (1980) described the *ecological inventory,* which generates skills by breaking down the domains into environments, subenvironments, activities, and skill sequences. Table 13–1 illustrates the functional analysis conducted in assessing the various ecological domains for a 13-year-old student with severe multiple disabilities.

As outlined in Chapter 11, an abundance of assessment/curriculum models is available for use with young children with disabilities. The most recent and promising materials for use with children birth to age 3 are the *Assessment Evaluation Programming System* (AEPS) and its curriculum guide (Bricker, 1993; Cripe, Slentz, & Bricker, 1993).

Table 13–1
Analysis of Functional Domains for Luis (Age 13)

Domain	Environment	Subenvironment	Activity	Skill Sequence
Vocational	School	Library	Attaching cards to books	1. Open book front cover. 2. Paste back of card folder. 3. Place folder inside front page. 4. Slip library card into folder.
Community	Post office	Mail drop-off slot	Taking school mail to post office	1. Pick up mail at school office. 2. Enter school van. 3. Exit school van and enter post office. 4. Approach drop-off slot. 5. Deposit mail in drop-off slot.
Recreation	School	Pep rally	Participating in weekly pep rally	1. Enter gym. 2. Get pom-pom from usher. 3. Find seat in bleachers. 4. Respond by clapping hands, shaking pom-pom, stomping feet, and cheering appropriately. 5. Exit gym.
Domestic	School	Kitchen	Preparing microwavable frozen meal	1. Remove meal from freezer. 2. Remove from box. 3. Remove foil. 4. Place in microwave. 5. Turn timer to spot marked by tape. 6. Wait during cooking. 7. At sound of bell, remove meal. 8. Prepare to eat. 9. Eat meal. 10. Dispose of container.

Specialized Curriculum Components

A variety of domain areas have been proposed for students with severe disabilities. For younger students a developmental model has been used most frequently. For school-age and older students an ecological or functional model has been proposed. The following represents a few of the components included in an individualized education plan for a student with severe disabilities.

Physical Management Component.   Although a large percentage of students with severe disabilities may have physical impairments, some of these students may not need specialized equipment or physical management. However, for those who have physical disabilities, specialized equipment (e.g., wheelchairs, walkers, positioning equipment, prone standers, and adapted bathroom seating) is often required for use in the classroom and at home.

The student with severe impairments often is unable to maintain proper body alignment and posture. Without a stable body, the student will be unable to perform even minimal tasks such as eating, bathing, brushing his teeth, or going to the bathroom. Teachers and parents need basic skills in relaxing the *hypertonic* (spastic/high muscle tone) student to dress the student or change diapers. Additionally, for students with *hypotonic* muscle tone, the physical therapist (PT) or the occupational therapist (OT) can instruct the special education staff and parents on how to alert the child's neurological and motor system to provide the child with appropriate stimulation.

The physical therapist develops a program of assessment and intervention after the physician has referred the student for these services. Assessment of the disability includes a determination of the strength and range of movement, and the relationship between the movement and the individual's ability to learn or perform learning-related functions. Because it is important to continue the physical therapy program regularly, the PT and OT often work collaboratively with special educators, classroom teachers, and parents, who are responsible for carrying out some of the programs in the therapist's absence. The nature and type of program designed for the student with movement disabilities may include the following:

◆ Neurodevelopmental treatment

◆ Lifting, transferring, carrying, and positioning techniques

◆ Adaptive equipment (e.g., rolls, wedges, standing boards, corner chairs, scooter boards, TumbleForm positioning aids, wheelchairs, and transport chairs) (Campbell, 1993; Campbell & Forsyth, 1993).

Sensory Enhancement Component.   With students who have visual or hearing impairments, *sensory aids* such as glasses, contact lenses, or hearing aids may be necessary. Special *mobility aids* such as the traditional long cane, the Mowat Sensor, Pathsounder or Sonicguide, prescribed by an *orientation and mobility specialist,* may be needed for students with multiple disabilities who are blind (Hill, 1986; Joffee & Rikhye, 1991). In some cases, if the student is deaf-blind, a *communication system* such as the Tandom and/or manual signing systems is essential. Interventions with aids such as the Tellatouch (Silberman, 1986) or vibrotactile devices (Niswander, 1987) have been valuable for deaf-blind students. Lastly, the use of functional vision (Langley, 1980; 1986) and auditory assessment will be a critical part of the initial evaluation of students with multiple disabilities. Additionally, interactive team members must strive to achieve an individualized set of environmental adaptations for each student including therapeutic positioning, lighting and contrast, and audition (Utley, 1993). Table 13–2 provides a check list for team members to complete when working with students who are deaf-blind (Utley, 1993). However, the check list can help teams prepare environmental settings for many students with severe disabilities.

Table 13–2
Environmental Check List

Environmental Check List

Name of Student _____ Date _____

SECTION I - THERAPEUTIC POSITIONING
1. Overall Body Positioning (Sitting)
_____ a. Student is upright, or reclined slightly, with hips, knees, and ankles at 90-degree angles, or other angle(s) recommended by a therapist.
_____ b. Student's head is neutral and upright, with or without external support.
_____ c. Student's arms are supported by the table top or wheelchair tray so the elbows are flexed between 90 and 120 degrees.

2. Overall Body Positioning (Sidelying)
_____ a. Student is supported correctly (i.e., lower shoulder is forward; head is in alignment with the spine; hips, knees and ankles are flexed; pillows are placed between and below bony prominences).
_____ b. Student is lying on the side that results in the better eye (if known) being on the upper lateral half of the body. (**Note:** *Consultation with the team is recommended to determine whether sidelying on a particular lateral half of the body may be contraindicated*).

3. Overall Body Positioning (Supported Supine)
_____ a. Student is supported correctly (i.e., head in alignment; chin slightly flexed; shoulders rounded forward slightly; hips, knees, and ankles flexed).
_____ b. Student's head is stable with or without external support.

4. Position of Peers, Adults, and Materials
_____ a. Depending on the student's head control, materials are placed horizontally, vertically, or somewhere in between those points.
_____ b. Peers or adults position themselves at or near the student's eye level during interaction.

Note: From "Assessing the Instructional Environment to Meet the Needs of Learners With Multiple Disabilities Including Students Who Are Deaf-Blind" by B. L. Utley, 1993, *Deaf-Blind Perspective, 1*(2), pp. 5–8. Reprinted by permission.

Medical Support Component.   The special education team can perform most of the techniques required by students with severe disabilities who are medically fragile. With close supervision from medical staff such as the school nurse, team members are administering complex medical procedures such as tracheostomy suctioning or gastrostomy feeding. However, administration of medication and heart or oxygen monitoring procedures may still be the main responsibility of the school nurse. Clear school district policies and procedures must be outlined to protect students, teachers, and medical personnel from accidents.

In a study by Mulligan-Ault, Guess, Struth, and Thompson (1988), teachers reported that for the most part they are responsible for implementing medical procedures on a daily basis. A list of health-related procedures most often cited by the teachers in this study is provided in Figure 13–1 in the order of the frequency of their occurrences.

SECTION II - LIGHTING

1. Amount and Type of Light (indoors)
_____ a. A combination of light sources (i.e., natural light plus incandescent light, etc.) are available.
_____ b. The entire work surface is illuminated evenly (dependent upon specific task requirements).
_____ c. Supplemental lighting is available (if necessary).

2. Position of Light
_____ a. Student is positioned so that all sources of natural light (e.g., windows) are behind him rather than behind the instructional/social/communicative partners.
_____ b. Supplemental light source originates from over the student's lead so the shade directs the light on only the task materials (if necessary).
OR
_____ c. Supplemental light source originates from behind and over the shoulder of the student (e.g., over the left shoulder for those who use the right hand and vice versa).
OR
_____ d. Supplemental light source originates from behind and over the shoulder of the student on the lateral half of the head where the most functional eye is.

3. Glare
_____ a. Work surface is made of (or covered with) nonreflective material.
_____ b. Materials are made of nonreflective material (if possible).
_____ c. The amount of light emitted in the direction of the eye is limited or eliminated.

4. Contrast
_____ a. For tasks that rely on materials that are black or dark in color, the background surface is lighter to enhance contrast. Light colored materials use a dark background surface.
_____ b. Select or purchase materials that contrast with the work surface (if possible).

Note: The items listed on the check list are to be viewed as *preliminary only.* A more thorough assessment should be made by team members according to the knowledge base of their respective disciplines.

Teachers indicated that it would be beneficial if nurses could work in collaboration with the teachers and share the responsibilities of health-related procedures. Additionally, few teachers reported that their districts had written guidelines or procedures to meet the health-related needs of students with severe disabilities. In most schools, medical and educational services may be fragmented and students are still underserved when it comes to their health-related needs. The new requirements for coordinated planning, particularly for early intervention services (P.L. 99-457), are designed to help professionals work together more effectively in the treatment of students with severe or multiple disabilities. As more students who are medically fragile enter the public school system, services for these students will be more clearly defined (Bartel & Thurman, 1992; Izen & Brown, 1991). Students with communicable diseases such as hepatitis, herpes, HIV, and CM require special disease control procedures in classroom environments (Beverly, in press).

Self-Care Component.   A major component of support services for students with severe disabilities is that of developing self-care skills, such as using the toilet, dressing, eating, and bathing. Often, medical professionals can provide information as to

1. Seizure monitoring
2. Teeth and gum care
3. Medication administration
4. Emergency seizure procedure
5. Prevention of skin breakdown
6. Establishing bowel habits
7. Treatment of skin breakdown
8. Diet monitoring
9. Postural drainage
10. Handling and positioning
11. CPR
12. Shunt care
13. Percussion
14. Gastrostomy feeding
15. Prosthesis care
16. Cast care
17. Monitoring glucose levels
18. Colostomy/ileostomy procedures
19. G-tube feeding
20. Administering enema
21. Catheterization procedures
22. Machine suctioning
23. Nasal cannula
24. Oxygen supplementation
25. Bulb syringe suctioning
26. Oxygen mask
27. Mechanical ventilation
28. Changing tracheostomy tubes
29. Changing tracheostomy ties
30. Delee suctioning

Figure 13–1
Rank order of occurrence of health-related procedures for students with severe disabilities

Note: From "The Implementation of Health-Related Procedures in Classrooms for Students with Severe Multiple Impairments" by M. Mulligan-Ault, D. Guess, L. Struth, and B. Thompson, 1988, *Journal of the Association for Persons with Severe Handicaps, 13,* pp. 100–109.

the readiness of the student for toilet training. Additionally, it is common for feeding programs to be designed for students who are dependent on adult intervention. Often, the OT will design or adapt a self-feeding device to help the student gain independence. Moreover, an OT might develop a program for the classroom staff to implement in the area of stimulating the development of *oral-motor skills* such as swallowing, sucking, and chewing.

School personnel will need to provide appropriate facilities for training students in self-care skills such as using the toilet, bathing and dressing (Campbell, 1993). Usually, family involvement is critical in this area of programming.

Communication Component.   The student with severe or multiple disabilities may be able to communicate using alternative and augmentative communication systems. Students who are unable to use speech as their major communication mode may use gestures, manual signing, communication boards, or electronic devices such as the Zygo, Handivoice, LightTalker, and the Cannon Communicator as an alternative to speech. Augmentative communication systems such as communication boards, electronic speech-output or scanning devices will be designed for individual students by the speech-language therapist and a team of service providers (Miller, 1993). Speech-language therapists, occupational therapists, and special and general educators may all need to understand a simple electronic switch assembly for adapting toys and communication devices (Burkhart, 1980, 1984; Miller, 1993).

For the student with severe or multiple disabilities, the team works on developing language production, concept development, and speech articulation (Langley & Lombardino, 1991). Treating a student who has no formal speech production (verbalizations) and may have a poor prognosis for speech involves developing pragmatic and prelinguistic communication behaviors, such as attending, requesting, rejecting, imitating, turn-taking, and naming (Langley & Lombardino, 1991; Orelove & Sobsey, 1991). Siegel-Causey and Guess (1989) provided guidelines on how to recognize, support, and teach nonsymbolic communicative interactions in the context of daily routines. Although controversial, the use of facilitative communication techniques have been used with students with autism (Bilken & Schubert, 1991).

The team also may be involved in analyzing the communicative function of a student's excessive behavior, such as hand biting or aggression, and developing an intervention program that provides the student with an alternative means of communicating frustration, boredom, or attention by using gestures or signs (Durand, 1990). Whether language takes the form of facial reactions, signing, gesturing, pointing or verbalizations, teaching students with severe disabilities functional language communication within a social context is a major educational goal.

Community-Based Functional Component.   For school-age students with severe disabilities, the sole use of developmental checklists describing the step-by-step sequence of infant and early childhood development for program implementation is no longer appropriate. As described earlier, a more functional approach to developing curriculum has become the major focus of special education programs. This requires administrative support and resources to develop intervention programs that integrate training in the areas of school, domestic, vocational, community, and leisure skill development (Brown, 1987; Brown & Snell, 1993; Snell, 1993). Simulated school environments can no longer suffice for all-school training and intervention. School personnel must access natural community environments, which contain normal prompts and cues. Such environments benefit the student learning how to wash clothes in a laundromat, shop for food at the grocery store, or ride the bus to a supported employment program every day.

Family and Friends Involvement Component.   Involvement of the family in teaming is critical to the success of educational and vocational intervention with students who have severe disabilities. Because of the nature of the student's disability, the family may have added pressures and stressors that will affect their life adjustment (Beckman, 1983; Bronicki & Turnbull, 1987; Salisbury, 1992). Families often have the medical information about their children that is needed for school programs. Conversely, school professionals can help families obtain and interpret medical information that is necessary for the student. The ultimate responsibility for care and future adjustment of the child with severe disability lies with the family members. Their involvement through training and advocacy will be critical once the public school program has ended.

Friends and peers also are an important part of the lives of students with severe disabilities. Team members should focus on enhancing and facilitating social and friendship relationships among students with severe disabilities and nondisabled students. The students with severe disabilities and their friends should be included in many aspects of designing educational programs. An excellent method for doing this is personal futures planning (Mount & Zwernik, 1989). It serves as a tool for fostering new ways of thinking about students with severe disabilities. In futures planning a small group of people (e.g., family, peers, neighbors, community leaders, teachers, administrators) agree to meet for mutual support, brainstorming, and strategizing. The goals for this team are to discuss opportunities for the student "to develop personal relationships, have positive roles in community life, increase their control of their own lives, and develop the skills and abilities to achieve these goals" (p. 1). Futures planning can complement the development of an IEP planning process. A similar approach to planning programs for students with severe disabilities is the McGill Action Planning System (Vandercook, York, & Forest, 1989). MAPS uses support teams in a similar way to brainstorm and develop goals for the student.

SELECTED TEACHING STRATEGIES

Several strategies are described in this chapter for the purpose of illustrating the types of techniques that can be used for students with severe disabilities. More detailed explanations of the best practices for teaching these students are found in several textbooks, such as Rainforth, York, and Macdonald (1992), Orelove and Sobsey (1991), and Snell (1993).

One frequently used teaching strategy involves applied behavior analysis. Within the general application of the approach the teacher selects functional skills for the student and breaks down the skill into small, teachable tasks. Examples of task analyses were outlined in Table 13–1. Once the task sequence has been established, educators must provide a consistent application of prompting and reinforcement procedures. Team members must consider the following components of instructional procedures (Rainforth, York, & Macdonald, 1992):

◆ Setting, grouping, positioning

◆ Equipment/materials

◆ Initial instruction and prompt

◆ Correct response

◆ Time delay and correction

◆ Reinforcement

◆ Frequency to teach

◆ Frequency of data

◆ Type of data

◆ Criterion for change

A number of *time delay or prompting sequences* have been shown to be effective with students with severe disabilities. The sequence of providing *least-to-most prompts* involves allowing wait-time for the student to perform the task step independently before providing help. For example, using the *increasing prompts strategy* for teaching a student to feed himself cereal with a spoon involves first providing the student with the natural cue of the cereal and the spoon. If the student does not respond, a verbal prompt, "pick up your spoon," might be used. If after a designated time period, the student does not begin the task, a gesture or model can be used, such as picking up the spoon and scooping up some cereal. Again, a wait-time occurs, and if the student has not responded, the teacher might provide the most intrusive prompt—taking the student's hand and guiding him through the task of scooping the cereal.

The other prompting strategy is that of *graduated guidance*. In this strategy the teacher begins with total physical assistance by taking the student's hands and moving him through the complete task of scooping up the cereal. After repeated trials, the teacher would begin to decrease her physical assistance when she judged that the student was becoming more independent. The teacher would decrease the prompts until she was merely shadowing the student's hand as the student ate the cereal.

Additionally, reinforcement procedures would be implemented when necessary. The most natural reinforcers, such as social praise, should be tried first, before more artificial reinforcers (e.g., toys, prizes, or edibles) are used.

Instruction of students with severe disabilities should occur in the environment most natural to the task. If a student is being taught to brush her hair, the teacher should provide the training in the natural environment (e.g., bathroom, dressing table). Often, instruction occurs in simulated settings due to a lack of available natural environments. Although they are not as effective for maintenance and generalization of skills to the natural environments, simulated settings may be necessary.

Furthermore, when teaching students with severe disabilities, use of functional and age-appropriate materials is critical. For example, in teaching a 16-year-old student to operate a tape recorder, the use of a child's toy machine would not be recommended. Instead, a regular tape recorder should be used. A variety of materials and experiences should also be used for training generalization across tasks. For example, if a student is learning to use bathroom facilities at school, she should eventually be instructed to use facilities in other settings, such as her home, fast-food restaurants, and the laundromat. In particular, the various settings may require different skills in flushing toilets, dispensing soap, and drying hands.

Instruction of students with severe disabilities requires ongoing data-based programs, using effective behavior analysis procedures (Brown & Snell, 1993). Keeping detailed progress of skill sequences helps the teacher make program changes. Additionally, because students with severe disabilities may not progress as quickly as their nondisabled peers, measuring behavior and recording the progress are critical in instruction.

Students with severe disabilities may be limited by physical or sensory impairments; however, their limitations should not exclude them from participating in age-appropriate routines shared by their nondisabled peers. Instruction should be given in inclusive settings with nondisabled peers and involve adaptations when necessary. The *principle of partial participation* (Brown, Branston, Hamre-Nietupski, Pumpian, Certo, & Gruenewald, 1979) affirms that students with severe disabilities can take part to some degree in age-appropriate activities. For example, excluding students from a school play production because they cannot speak clearly would be contrary to the principle of partial participation. Instead, adapting the school play so that students who could not speak could use a tape recorder or hold props during the play would be appropriate.

A variety of teaching strategies has been discussed. Instruction for students with severe disabilities is challenging and complex. As students become more involved in inclusive settings, team members will need specific guidance in instructional procedures for general education classes. Peck, Odom, and Bricker (1993), Stainback and Stainback (1992), York and Vandercook (1990) provide excellent guides for developing instruction in inclusive settings. Repetition and systematic generalization of training are required. If programs are not carefully designed and implemented, students, parents, and teachers will experience failure and frustration. An interactive team can provide support and contribute creative teaching strategies that are sure to be effective with students. These specific roles and responsibilities will be discussed in the next section.

ROLES OF THE PROFESSIONALS INVOLVED WITH STUDENTS WITH SEVERE DISABILITIES

Given the wide range of characteristics of students with severe disabilities, a number of professionals with varying areas of expertise may be needed to plan the students' programs. The professionals who serve these students need to coordinate their efforts. Coordination is facilitated by effective leadership, good communication skills, and effective professional development procedures, all of which have been outlined in previous chapters. The general roles of professionals are discussed in Chapter 4. Specialized contributions of team members who work with students with severe disabilities are outlined in this chapter.

Delineating the roles of each of the team members within the educational and community setting is a first step in clarifying each group's function on the team. Table 13–3 outlines the various roles and responsibilities in both direct service and team involvement.

APPLICATION

The team members who serve students with severe disabilities are often confronted with the need for *role release* (Lyon & Lyon, 1980), in which more than one person on the team performs the same function, such as implementation of a behavior management program. The professional development function, used for related services training, is also important in transdisciplinary teaming. At times this involves sharing information from one's own discipline with others so they can implement their component of the program effectively; at other times it requires the ability to respect and accept the consultation of parents and other professionals who are specialists in various aspects of the student's care program (Bailey, 1984; Rainforth, York, & Macdonald, 1992). The following vignette illustrates the application of the concept of interactive teaming to areas outside of the traditional role responsibilities of the team members.

Jennifer, a 14-year-old student who is deaf-blind, is receiving services from a physical therapist, an itinerant vision teacher, and a speech-language therapist. Jennifer's teacher, Ms. Johnson, coordinates a conference that all three of the related service professionals and the parents attend for purposes of professional development and role release. In the conference, the physical therapist, Ms. Boles, explains *neurodevelopmental treatment* (NDT) techniques (Bobath & Bobath, 1984) for helping Jennifer to lift her head and stabilize her trunk during lunchtime. Ms. Boles demonstrates these techniques with Jennifer while she is engaged in a voice output computer game with a friend. Ms. Johnson and the parent model the facilitation procedure in front of the physical therapist and ask for feedback on their use of the technique. Simultaneously,

Table 13–3

Roles of Professionals and Others Involved With Students With Severe Disabilities

Personnel	Direct Service Provider	Team Member
Special Educator	• Conduct multifaceted assessment in the areas of vision, hearing, sensorimotor development, functional/ecological inventories, family functioning. • Monitor under supervision any medical and behavioral procedures. • Implement computer and augmentative communication systems. • Provide physical management and proper positioning in equipment. • Conduct functional programming emphasizing independence in school and community integration.	• Serve as case manager. • Accept role released responsibilities from related service personnel. • Interpret multifaceted assessments. • Consult on individualized instructional strategies with general educators serving students in inclusive settings. • Advocate for student and family needs.
Physical Therapist	• Assess posture/motor development. • Conduct direct therapy for specific motor problems within an integrated classroom environment. • Order and prepare adaptive equipment. • Monitor use of braces and orthotic devices.	• Conduct staff development on therapy treatment. • Role release the least complex treatment procedures (e.g., range of motion). • Integrate motor goals into daily life routines. • Consult with other medical personnel (orthopedist, neurologist, nurse, etc.).
Occupational Therapist	• Assess fine motor, oral motor, vocational, and leisure skills areas. • Order and modify special devices. • Design feeding programs. • Conduct eye-hand coordination and fine motor skills programs.	• Conduct staff development on therapy treatments. • Role release the least complex treatments (e.g., feeding procedures). • Integrate fine motor goals into daily life routines. • Consult with other medical personnel.
School Nurse/ Nutritionist	• Dispense medication. • Monitor complex medical procedures (tracheostomy suctioning, catheterization procedures, G–tube feeding, mechanical ventilation, etc.). • Conduct first aid and minor emergency safety procedures. • Prepare appropriate well-balanced meal plans.	• Conduct staff development on health-related procedures. • Role release the least complex procedures (e.g., postural drainage, gastrostomy feeding, prosthesis care). • Consult with other medical personnel. • Implement and orient staff to emergency procedures involving life-threatening situations. • Contact family for ongoing status of medical/nutritional needs. • Consult staff on side effects of medications.

Personnel	Direct Service Provider	Team Member
School Psychologist	• Assess psychological and adaptive behavior functioning. • Conduct behavior management programs for severe maladaptive behavior.	• Conduct assessments jointly with other team members if special adaptations must be made (e.g., severe vision, motor, hearing impairments). • Interpret test results to team and family. • Conduct staff development on behavior management procedures.
Family	• Reinforce functional/behavioral programming. • Reinforce related services programs (e.g., PT, OT). • Attend all health-related appointments.	• Provide information on medical, behavioral, and family issues. • Accept role release responsibilities for intervention programs (e.g., PT, OT). • Consult with staff on medication, personal care, physical management, and adaptive devices.
School Counselor/ Social Worker	• Provide individual family assessment and counseling. • Provide social service resources. • Make home visits.	• Consult with staff on foster care or public assistance programs. • Provide information on family needs and adjustment. • Serve as liaison with related social service agencies.
Speech-Language Therapist	• Assess and intervene on speech-language impairments. • Conduct functional assessments of hearing. • Design augmentative communication systems. • Intervene on prelinguistic communication behaviors.	• Interpret results of traditional and informal observations of student's speech-language functions. • Provide staff development on alternative speech communication programs, augmentative communication devices, and prelinguistic communication techniques. • Provide integrated therapy programs throughout the student's functional curriculum.
Para-professional	• Conduct health-related and per-sonal hygiene procedures under supervision. • Prepare inclusive classroom for daily activities. • Prepare and assist at mealtimes. • Conduct small group intervention programs.	• Provide information on progress of assigned data-based programs. • Share ideas for effective classroom management. • Attend staff development programs (e.g., basic first aid, physical management).

Table 13–3, *continued*

Personnel	Direct Service Provider	Team Member
Para-professional (cont.)	• Assure that equipment and classrooms are safe and sterile. • Organize students' personal hygiene and clothing materials. • Assist in community-based programming. • Collect basic intervention data, under supervision. • Support students in inclusive settings.	
Administrator	• Reinforce behavioral management procedures. • Communicate with families as needed.	• Support staff by providing staff development appropriate to their needs. • Support program by providing adaptive equipment and material. • Provide information on funding resources related to hiring of paraprofessionals and contracting with private agencies for PT or OT services. • Provide financial and transportation support to community-referenced programming. • Coordinate parent advisory councils. • Provide information on due process and legal action issues.

the vision teacher shows Ms. Johnson and the parent how to present Jennifer with computer switches in ways that stimulate visual tracking and searching behaviors. Ms. Johnson and the parent now practice both NDT techniques and vision stimulation activities, and they are given feedback by both professionals. Lastly, the speech-language therapist shows Ms. Johnson and the parent the best ways to help Jennifer indicate her desire for "more" by using a gross gesture of hand to mouth. The speech therapist incorporates the neurodevelopmental treatment (NDT) procedure and the vision activity while modeling and prompting Jennifer to gesture "more computer play." Once again, Ms. Johnson and the parents model all the techniques and ask for feedback. By the end of the session, all four professionals and the parents have shared knowledge of their own disciplines and demonstrated the proper use of the techniques with Jennifer.

The professionals and parents leave the conference with added knowledge and skills for integrating the techniques into Jennifer's home, school, and community program. A monthly follow-up consultation will be arranged by the team for purposes of checking appropriate use of the procedures and discussing Jennifer's progress.

The role of the team leader becomes one of service coordinator of an integrated therapy program. Instead of providing Jennifer with an isolated therapy program in which the related service professional removes her from the inclusive classroom and provides treatment in a private therapy room, the therapist trains the general and special education teacher, the parent, and paraprofessionals to perform therapy techniques in the classroom, home, and community. Additionally, Jennifer's friends learn how to best interact with her and support her during activities in the inclusive classroom. In the interactive team approach, the therapist still provides some direct services to the student on a weekly basis. Those services are often provided within the classroom setting, and when appropriate, they are used for demonstration and training of general and special education staff, parents, and peers.

SUMMARY

The transdisciplinary team serving the needs of students with severe or multiple disabilities comprises a complex group of medical and education professionals.

The team serving students with severe disabilities is at risk for wars over turf. The range of differences in the terminology of the disciplines is enough to cause confusion among the group.

The core members of the team, the parents, are often overwhelmed by the meetings conducted by this transdisciplinary team. Yet, as much as any group of professionals, the parents must work cooperatively for the good of the student.

The nature of the student's condition can be so complex that if collaboration is not established, the student's educational as well as health-related needs will not be met.

Working closely with the families and the student's friends, professionals can orchestrate the delivery of services to students with severe disabilities, whether those services involve physical therapy, occupational therapy, speech therapy, medical interventions, or functional community-based programming.

ACTIVITIES

1. Conduct an informational interview with a professional who is involved in the educational programs of students with severe disabilities. Use the guidelines provided in Chapter 4.

2. Attend a group home or vocational program for people with severe disabilities. Observe for skills that will be needed by younger students to function in these future environments.

3. Volunteer to teach a functional skill to a student in a local school program. Offer to take the student into the community to learn this skill. Use a task analytical approach to breaking down the functional skill, and apply intervention strategies to implement the program.

4. Ask people from the community who have multiple disabilities such as cerebral palsy and blindness to speak to the class about their impairments, how they have adapted, problems they have encountered, and the community services available to them.

5. Attend tours of schools and community agencies serving people with severe disabilities. Note the goal and mission of the various agencies as related to the quality of life of people with severe disabilities.

REFERENCES

Ault, M. M, Graff, J. C., & Rues, J. P. (1993). Special health procedures. In M. Snell (Ed.), *Instruction of students with severe disabilities* (4th ed.) (pp. 215–247). New York: Merrill/Macmillan.

Ault, M. M., Guy, B., Guess, D., & Rues, J. P. (1991). Medication information guidelines. Lawrence, KS: Project ABLE, Department of Special Education, University of Kansas.

Bailey, D. (1984). A triaxial model of the interdisciplinary team and group process. *Exceptional Children, 51,* 17–26.

Bartel, N. R., & Thurman, S. K. (1992). Medical treatment and educational problems in children. *Phi Delta Kappan, 74,* 57–61.

Beckman, P. J. (1983). Influence of selected child characteristics on stress in families of handicapped infants. *American Journal of Mental Deficiency, 88,* 150–156.

Beverly, C. (in press). Providing a safe environment for children who are infected with the human immunodeficiency virus. *Topics in Early Childhood Special Education.*

Bilken, D., & Schubert, A. (1991). New words: The communication of students with autism. *Remedial and Special Education, 12*(6), 46–51.

Bobath, B., & Bobath, K. (1984). The neurodevelopmental treatment. In D. Stratton (Ed.), *Management of motor disorders of children with cerebral palsy.* Philadelphia: J. B. Lippincott.

Bricker, D. (1993). *AEPS measurement for birth to three years (Volume 1).* Baltimore: Paul H. Brookes.

Bronicki, G. J., & Turnbull, A. P. (1987). Family-professional interactions. In M. E. Snell (Ed.), *Instruction of students with severe disabilities* (4th ed.). New York: Merrill/Macmillan.

Brown, F. (1987). Meaningful assessment of people with severe and profound handicaps. In M. E. Snell (Ed.), *Systematic instruction of persons with severe handicaps* (pp. 39–63). Columbus, OH: Merrill.

Brown, F., Evans, I., Weed, K., & Owen, V. (1987). Delineating functional competencies: A component model. *Journal of the association for persons with severe handicaps, 12*(2), 117–124.

Brown, F., & Snell, M. E. (1993). Meaningful assessment. In M. E. Snell (Ed.), *Instruction of students with severe disabilities* (4th ed.). New York: Merrill/Macmillan.

Brown, L., Branston, M. B., Hamre-Nietupski, S., Pumpian, I., Certo, N., & Gruenewald, L. A. (1979). A strategy for developing chronological age appropriate and functional curricular content for severely handicapped adolescents and young adults. *Journal of Special Education, 13,* 81–90.

Brown, L., Falvey, M., Vincent, L., Kaye, N., Johnson, F., Ferrara-Parrish, P., & Gruenewald, L. (1980). Strategies for generating comprehensive, longitudinal and chronological-age-appropriate individualized education programs for adolescent and young-adult severely handicapped persons. *The Journal of the Association for the Severely Handicapped, 8*(3), 71–77.

Burkhart, L. J. (1980). *Homemade battery-powered toys and educational devices for severely handicapped children.* 8503 Rhode Island Ave., College Park, MD 20740.

—. (1984). *More homemade battery devices for severely handicapped children—With suggested activities.* 8503 Rhode Island Ave., College Park, MD 20740.

Campbell, P. (1993). Physical management and handling procedures. In M. Snell (Ed.), *Instruction of students with severe disabilities* (4th ed.) (pp. 248–263). New York: Merrill/Macmillan.

Campbell, P., & Forsyth, S. (1993). Integrated programming and movement disabilities. In M. Snell (Ed.), *Instruction of students with severe disabilities* (4th ed.) (pp. 264–289). New York: Merrill/Macmillan.

Certo, N., Haring, N. G., & York, R. (1984). *Public school integration of severely handicapped students.* Baltimore: Paul H. Brookes.

Cripe, J., Slentz, K., & Bricker, D. (1993). *AEPS curriculum for birth to three years (Volume 2).* Baltimore: Paul H. Brookes.

Cushman, C., Heydt, K., Edwards, S., Clark, M.J., & Allon, M. (1992). *Perkins activity and resource guide: A handbook for teachers and parents of students with visual and multiple disabilities.* Boston: Perkins School for the Blind.

Donnellan, A. M., Mirenda, P. L., Mesaros, R. A., & Fassbender, L. L. (1984). Analyzing the communicative functions of aberrant behavior. *Journal of the Association for Persons with Severe Handicaps, 9,* 201–212.

Durand, V. M. (1990). *Severe behavior problems: A functional communication training approach.* New York: Guilford Press.

Ford, A., Schnorr, R., Meyer, L., Davern, L., Black, J., & Dempsey, P. (Eds.). (1989). *The Syracuse community-referenced curriculum guide for students with moderate and severe disabilities.* Baltimore: Paul H. Brookes.

Goetz, L. (1993). Can inclusive education work for students who are deaf-blind? *Deaf-Blind Perspective, 1*(2), 3–5.

Haney, J. (1988). Toward successful community residential placements for individuals with mental retardation. In L. Heal, J. Haney, & A. Novak Amando (Eds.), *Integration of developmentally disabled individuals into the community* (2nd ed.). Baltimore: Paul H. Brookes.

Hill, E. W. (1986). Orientation and mobility. In G. T. Scholl (Ed.), *Foundations of education for blind and visually handicapped children and youth: Theory and practice* (pp. 315–340). New York: American Foundation for the Blind.

Iwata, B. A., Dorsey, M. F., Slifer, K. J., Bauman, K. E., & Richman, G. S. (1982). Toward a functional analysis of self-injury. *Analysis and Intervention in Developmental Disabilities, 2,* 3–20.

Izen, C. L., & Brown, F. (1991). Education and treatment needs of students with profound, multiply handicapping, and medically fragile conditions: A survey of teachers' perceptions. *Journal of the Association for Persons with Severe Handicaps, 16,* 94–103.

Jacobson, J. W., & Janicki, M. P. (1985). Functional and health status characteristics of persons with severe handicaps in New York State. *Journal of the Association for Persons with Severe Handicaps, 10,* 51–60.

Joffee, E., & Rikhye, C.H. (1991). Orientation and mobility for students with severe visual and motor impairment. *Journal of Visual Impairment and Blindness, 85*(5), 211–261.

Langley, B. (1980). *Functional vision inventory for the multiple and severely handicapped.* Chicago: Stoelting.

Langley, M. B. (1986). Psychoeducational assessment of visually impaired students with additional handicaps. In D. Ellis (Ed.), *Sensory impairments in mentally handicapped people* (pp. 253–296). San Diego: College-Hill Press.

Langley, M. B., & Lombardino, L. J. (1991). *Neurodevelopmental strategies for managing communication disorders in children with severe motor dysfunction.* Austin, TX: Pro-ed.

Lyon, S., & Lyon, G. (1980). Team functioning and staff development: A role release approach to providing integrated educational services for severely handicapped students. *Journal of the Association for the Severely Handicapped, 5,* 250–263.

McCubbin, T. (1987). Routine and emergency medical procedures. In M. E. Snell (Ed.). (1993). *Instruction of students with severe disabilities* (4th ed.). (pp. 152-171). New York: Merrill/Macmillan.

Miller, J. (1993). Augmentative and alternative communication. In M. Snell (ed.), *Instruction of students with severe disabilities* (4th ed.) (pp. 319–346). New York: Merrill/Macmillan.

Mount, B., & Zwernik, K. (1989). *It's never too early, it's never too late: A booklet about personal futures planning.* St. Paul, MN: Metropolitan Council.

Mulligan-Ault, M., Guess, D., Struth, L., & Thompson, B. (1988). The implementation of health-related procedures in classrooms for students with severe multiple impairments. *Journal of the Association for Persons with Severe Handicaps, 13,* 100-109.

National Association of School Boards (NASBE) (1993). Winners all: A call for inclusive schools (Monograph). Alexandria, VA: Author.

Niswander, P. S. (1987). Audiometric assessment and management. In L. Goetz, D. Guess, & K. Stremel-Campbell (Eds.), *Innovative program design for individuals with dual sensory impairments* (pp. 99–126). Baltimore: Paul H. Brookes.

Peck, C., Odom, S., & Bricker, D. (1993). *Integrating young children with disabilities into community programs: Ecological perspectives on research and implementation.* Baltimore: Paul H. Brookes.

Rainforth, B., Macdonald, C., York, J., & Dunn, W. (1992). Collaborative assessment. In B. Rainforth, J. York, & C. Macdonald (Eds), *Collaborative teams for students with severe disabilities.* (pp. 105–155). Baltimore: Paul H. Brookes.

Rainforth, B., York, J., & Macdonald, C. (1992). *Collaborative teams for students with severe disabilities.* Baltimore: Paul H. Brookes.

Sailor, W., Gee, K., Goetz, L., & Graham, N. (1988). Progress in educating students with the most severe disabilities: Is there any? *JASH, 13,* 87–99.

Sailor, W., Gee, K., & Karasoff, P. (1993). Full inclusion and school restructuring. In M. Snell (Ed.), *Instruction of students with severe disabilities* (4th ed.) (pp. 1–30). New York: Merrill/Macmillan.

Salisbury, C. (1992). Parents as team members: Inclusive teams, collaborative outcomes. In B. Rainforth, J. York, & C. Macdonald (Eds.), *Collaborative teams for students with severe disabilities.* (pp. 43–65). Baltimore: Paul H. Brookes.

Seigel-Causey, E., & Guess, D. (Eds.). (1989). *Enhancing nonsymbolic communication interactions among learners with severe handicaps.* Baltimore: Paul H. Brookes.

Silberman, R. K. (1986). Severe multiple handicaps. In G. T. Scholl (Ed.), *Foundations of education for blind and visually handicapped children and youth: Theory and practice* (pp. 145–164). New York: American Foundation for the Blind.

Snell, M. (1993). *Instruction of students with severe disabilities* (4th ed.). New York: Merrill/Macmillan.

Stainback, S., & Stainback, W. (1992). *Curriculum considerations in inclusive classrooms: Facilitating learning for all students.* Baltimore: Paul H. Brookes.

Utley, B.L. (1993). Assessing the instructional environment to meet the needs of learners with multiple disabilities including students who are deaf-blind. *Deaf-Blind Perspective, 1*(2), 5–8.

Vandercook, T., York, J., & Forest, M. (1989). MAPS: A strategy for building vision. *Journal of the Association for Persons with Severe Handicaps, 14*(3), 205–215.

Wilcox, B., & Bellamy, G.T. (1987). *The activities catalog: An alternative curriculum for youth and adults with severe disabilities.* Baltimore: Paul H. Brookes.

Wolf-Schein, E. G. (1989). A review of the size, characteristics, and needs of the deaf-blind population of North America. *The ACEHI Journal, 15,* 85–100.

York, J., & Vandercook, T. (1990). Strategies for achieving an integrated education for middle school students with severe disabilities. *Remedial and Special Education, 11*(5), 6–15.

CHAPTER 14

Summary and Application of the Model in the Future

Features of the Interactive Teaming Model

Extended Case Study

Application of the Model in the Future

Previous Predictions and Realities
Current Trends That Affect Programs for Students with Special Needs

Major Trends in Promising Practices

Success of Total Quality Education
Increased Efforts in Restructuring Teacher Education

Promising Solutions: The Future Model

Conclusion

Application

TOPICS IN THIS CHAPTER INCLUDE

◆ Summary of major features of interactive teaming model

◆ An extended case study, showing how the whole model might be implemented.

◆ Application of the model in the future, with summary of current trends and predictions for future implementation.

Teachers and related professionals, who once functioned in isolated classrooms and clinical programs, are now encouraged to collaborate as members of an interactive service team. The factors that provide the context and rationale for this change include the following:

◆ Professionals in special programs face conflicting demands to produce students with high levels of achievement and to respond to those with special needs that range from learning and behavior problems to cultural and linguistic differences.

◆ Educators and related professionals are being increasingly pressured to collaborate in the solution of growing education-related problems, because in the future most of our students will have complex special needs. Current programs are ineffective in serving the increasing numbers of students with such needs; previously proposed solutions that do not take into account the body of knowledge about the process of change will also be ineffective.

◆ Those who have summarized the research on effective schools suggest that teachers in these schools are committed to a central mission: maximizing the educational opportunities for their students by working as a team to achieve this goal. Conversely, researchers who have studied teachers' sense of efficacy have identified teachers' feelings of isolation as a major barrier to their believing that they are facilitating growth in their students.

◆ Public Law 94-142, amended in 1990 as the Individuals with Disabilities Education Act, P.L. 101-476, requires that special education and *related services* be provided for students with disabilities. This requirement suggests that people from many disciplines are potential members of the team. The more effective programs of the future will require collaboration among professionals and between professionals and parents.

◆ Currently, education, medical, and social services professionals are not being prepared as team members. Newly trained professionals in general education and in social services professions lack the ability to address these complex problems and to function as collaborative members of interactive teams.

FEATURES OF THE INTERACTIVE TEAMING MODEL

The model proposed in this book—interactive teaming—is a response to the nation's increasingly complex problems in special needs programs. It incorporates the features of high expectations, teacher empowerment, and parent-professional collaboration, which together characterize effective schools for disabled and at-risk students.

The interactive team is an educational and health-related group that functions at the highest professional level, using both consultation and collaboration in its efforts on behalf of special needs students. Components of this model are used in programs that provide educational, medical, and social services to severely disabled students, and in school-based management programs that are described in the school improvement literature.

This model for interactive teaming has been described in detail in this text. The three sections focus on context and foundations, facilitating factors, and implementation. The context and foundations section includes the framework and rationale, the historical foundations of consultation and teaming, and the dimensions of the interactive team. The facilitating factors are identified as understanding the roles of team members, enhancing communication skills, considering cultural diversity, developing service coordination skills, empowering team members through professional development, and enabling and supporting families. Four types of implementation contexts are presented, including implementation with culturally and linguistically diverse students, infants and preschoolers with disabilities, students with mild disabilities, and students with severe disabilities.

An extended case study, drawing together multiple facets of the model, follows.

EXTENDED CASE STUDY

 Ethan, a minority-group 8-year-old, is both gifted and learning disabled. His mother, who is divorced, is a physician, and Ethan has already decided that he wants to be a lawyer. Born with cerebral palsy that has left him with motor disabilities but without speech impairment, Ethan has an overall measured IQ of 136, with a verbal score that is 40 points higher than his performance score. On the achievement tests measuring basic skills, Ethan scores at the ninth-grade level in reading and at the first-grade level in basic mathematical skills. He also has great difficulty in manuscript handwriting, and he resists his teacher's efforts to instruct him in cursive writing, although all his classmates are beginning to use it and his teacher requires it.

Sometimes Ethan annoys his teachers—the third-grade classroom teacher; the special education resource room teacher; and the music, art, and physical education teachers—because he likes to have them explain their reasons for everything they ask him to do. He is very logical and rule-oriented, in addition to being quite good at verbal reasoning. Ethan argues with teachers when they ask him to do something he chooses not to do, and he is becoming disruptive in the classroom. Ethan realizes that each of his teachers has different expectations for classroom behavior and consequences when the rules are broken, and he has become quite effective in playing one adult against another.

Ethan is talkative and cheerful; he has many friends in his third-grade classroom who volunteer to push him around the school in his wheelchair. They also volunteer to help him with his math and handwriting assignments, which are difficult for him. And, most recently, several other students in his classroom are beginning to use his strategy of arguing with the teacher when they choose not to follow her instructions.

Ethan's classroom teacher, who has taught third grade in this district for 17 years, believes strongly that rules are rules, and that they apply equally to all students in the classroom. She has become frustrated with his behavior, particularly when he fails to turn in his assignments and when he encourages the other students to defy her authority. Ethan's art and PE teachers allow him to do much as he pleases in their classes; they believe he "is physically disabled and we shouldn't expect much from him in art or physical activities." His music teacher encourages him to express himself verbally whenever he chooses and has made him the master of ceremonies at the school's music programs. His special education teacher, who works with him for one hour a day on math skills, has a strict contingency management program, through which he can earn tokens that accumulate for free time.

Ethan's mother, who is nationally recognized as an authority in her field of medicine, is busy and travels a lot. She adores Ethan and gives him every cultural and material advantage—they go to concerts and lectures together, and she has bought him his own computer with a complete set of games. His mother also makes an effort to work with Ethan on his schoolwork at home, but she thinks the behavior problems he is having at school are the school's responsibility. Ethan's mother is pleasant and cooperative, and she has agreed to support the school's efforts by enforcing a consistent regimen for him at home. She believes, however, that the school personnel should design the school-based program.

The district superintendent is pleased that Ethan's mother does not object to his placement in this school, which contains a large number of low-income students. The superintendent is concerned about the school's attrition rate: It has a largely transient population, and students who enter in the fall rarely remain for the entire school year. He is also concerned about the low level of students' academic achievement and about problems with teacher morale as reported by the president of the professional association. The superintendent is considering making Ethan's school a "magnet," to which residents of the community could choose to send their children because of special programs offered. He is particularly interested in the development of science and computer labs for which he has obtained support from the local Chamber of Commerce in a school-business partnership.

The interactive team that meets to review Ethan's progress in his special program has more than his academic achievement to consider. His case is one in which all the issues of interactive teaming will need to be incorporated.

Step 1

The team meets to review Ethan's progress. Those present are the special educator, classroom teacher, music teacher, school principal, and Ethan's mother.

The team follows the steps in program review, shown earlier in Figure 7–4. The special educator will be the team leader, or quality advisor. It is the group's consensus that Ethan should continue in the part-time special education program for help with math. Ethan's mother agrees to make his home use of computer games contingent upon his conceptual understanding and mastery of the math facts for addition and subtraction for the numbers 0 through 20. Plans are made for additional testing of Ethan's fine motor skills by a physical therapist and for suggestions on the development of appropriate adaptive handwriting devices by an occupational therapist. After this testing is completed, the special educator and classroom teacher agree that they will meet to plan a program related to his development of handwriting skills. Ethan's classroom teacher expresses a concern that his behavior problems are related, in part, to the fact that the adults in his life have conflicting standards for his behavior; his mother agrees. The principal, recognizing this statement as an opener for his agenda—establishing schoolwide goals for students—suggests that he will follow up on this problem with the entire school staff and with the PTA. Each team member leaves with a written record of the decisions made, the people responsible for implementing each, and the projected date for their next contacts.

Step 2

The physical therapist and the occupational therapist conduct an assessment of Ethan's abilities and limitations in fine motor skills, and then meet to discuss their findings. They conclude that it is unrealistic to expect him to develop cursive handwriting skills at this time and agree that he might be encouraged to develop keyboard skills on the computer, provided it could be equipped with an adaptive device. They report this decision to the quality advisor, the special educator. Together, this subgroup laments that the school has no current resources for obtaining these specialized materials, although they have heard the rumor that the school may be receiving a computer lab.

Step 3

The classroom teacher teams with Ethan's mother to provide a program for at-home computer game use, contingent upon mastery of math facts. Deprived of the free use of his computer, Ethan becomes furious and begins to throw tantrums at home and in school. Ethan's mother calls to relate her disappointment with the program. The classroom teacher relates her concern to the special educator, the team leader (or quality advisor), who takes two aspirins and goes to bed.

Step 4

The special educator and the classroom teacher meet the next day. The classroom teacher discusses her concern over Ethan's increased behavior problems, and together the two team members brainstorm possible solutions to their problem, using the problem-solving sequence suggested in Chapter 7. They decide to contact Ethan's mother to request an observation of his home computer setup and to enlist her help with the problem.

Step 5

The special educator, classroom teacher, and Ethan's mother meet briefly in Ethan's home, where he proudly shows his teachers his computer games. Ethan's mother, who has learned about the superintendent's proposed program for school computers, suggests that she might work with the Chamber of Commerce's committee to explore the extension of computers into the school's programs for exceptional students. The special education teacher volunteers to explore the use of adaptive equipment that might enable Ethan to develop computer skills as a substitute for cursive writing. The classroom teacher agrees to take data on Ethan's behavior in the classroom in an attempt to isolate the variables that intensify his outbursts and lack of compliance with class rules.

Step 6

The principal calls a meeting of the representatives of the school's professional organization to present the superintendent's request for development of a magnet school program in their building and to obtain their input on needs for professional development and the additional resources needed to make the school program a model. Ethan's teacher, who is a member of this committee, discusses her previous interactions with Ethan's mother about the possibility of obtaining school-business partnership for the new computer lab.

This news is received with enthusiasm, and several teachers suggest that the school plan a professional development program to provide teachers with additional skills related to the effective use of computers. The music teacher cautions that although new skills in computer use might motivate students and enable teachers to better use technology, the acquisition of computers wouldn't solve the school's basic problem: the increase in students' misbehavior. Ethan's classroom teacher agrees that computers are no panacea and again expresses her concern about the lack of consistency in school rules as a contributing factor to students' misbehavior.

The principal, after listing the teacher's ideas for professional development and school improvement, identifies the need for consistent rules as the group's highest priority. He repeats this process in his meeting with the school's PTA steering committee, and he learns that parents share the teachers' concerns about misbehavior. Then he contacts one of his former professors at a nearby university to help the staff and community develop a uniform set of standards for student behavior.

Step 7

Through a needs assessment, the professor determines that teachers and parents have two major concerns about student behavior:

1. *Poor social behavior:* Students lack the ability to get along together.

2. *Inappropriate academic behavior:* Students fail to raise hands, comply with teacher requests, and complete tasks.

In a schoolwide staff meeting attended by representatives from the PTA, the principal shares the results of this needs assessment as the first step in identifying the school's common goals for student expectations. The professor, who serves as their consultant, organizes the teachers, parents, and other professionals into grade-level clusters. Their first task is to generate a list of positive student behaviors that enable students to get along with others; their second is to generate a list of positive student behaviors that enhance learning. The groups are then asked to rewrite these statements as rules for student behaviors. After grade-level consensus has been reached, the groups meet with those in the grades above and below their own to identify the commonalities in their rule statements. The result is a set of school rules for student behavior for which both teachers and parents have ownership.

Step 8

The building staff adopts the schoolwide rules for students' behavior, and Ethan begins to encounter uniform expectations for his performance in all classes. After initial protests, he begins to comply with the rules. His classroom teacher is pleased with this change in his behavior and reports positively to the special educator and to Ethan's mother.

Step 9

The special educator, classroom teacher, and Ethan's mother meet. They discuss both his progress and their efforts in identifying adapted computer equipment that might be used with Ethan in developing his typing skills. The classroom teacher, who is able to see a positive change in Ethan's overall behavior, is now willing to modify her standards for his handwriting performance, and she agrees that the development of keyboard skills for use on the computer would be an acceptable substitute for his learning of cursive writing. Ethan's mother has obtained support from the Chamber to include adaptive computer equipment in its plan for the whole-school computer lab. The special educator, with assistance from the occupational therapist, has identified the necessary software.

Step 10

The Chamber committee approaches the superintendent with a plan to provide the volunteer services of several computer specialists in implementing the lab. When the photographer from the local paper comes to cover the story, Ethan is shown using the new equipment, with assistance from his classroom teacher. The principal is quoted as saying this represents a schoolwide effort to improve the quality of instruction for all students. The superintendent's comment reveals this small step as part of his master plan to make Ethan's school a magnet. Ethan's mother makes a positive statement about the need for professional parents to continue their support of the district's excellent public school program.

The special educator, the team leader (or quality advisor), is present in the background and smiling. This effective leader has empowered others to implement a program that benefits a specific special needs student, while simultaneously contributing to schoolwide improvement.

APPLICATION OF THE MODEL IN THE FUTURE

Futurists examine current trends as a knowledge base from which to predict the future. In making their predictions, futurists tend to be optimistic. The authors of this book are optimistic in their prediction that a collaborative model such as interactive teaming will be the major pattern for future service delivery to special needs students. This optimistic prediction persists, despite acknowledgement of the history of failed past predictions, the barriers to teaming, and the need for continued research, simply because the need for this model is so compelling.

Previous Predictions and Realities

In 1979, forecasting methods employed in the social sciences were used to predict the future of special education for 1993. The 1979 trends in special education were used as a knowledge base to make these predictions along five dimensions: values, social institutions, the economy, technology, and medicine (Safer, Burnette, & Hobbs, 1979). These authors picked variables from these five fields they could use to predict the future. They saw, in 1979, that the traditional values from the industrial revolution were beginning to change. From the value system of that era, as reflected in the culmination of the civil-rights movement, they suggested that equality and full participation for people with disabilities in education and society might be predicted.

Simultaneously, the 1979 economy was characterized by growth and high inflation, a trend that could open future opportunities for people with disabilities. At that time the nation's social institutions promoted equality and normalization; the family unit was changing from the nuclear model to multiple models with shifting roles and a declining birth rate. Technology was growing rapidly: Compressed speech was possible; and radar, biofeedback, the pacemaker, robotics, and computers seemed to offer limitless opportunities for the disabled. In medicine, there were new diagnostic procedures—the CAT and amniocentesis, which offered early diagnosis and genetic screening—improved neonatal care, and an attempt to remove environmental hazards that laid the groundwork for the early identification and treatment of disabilities. In 1979, these futurists predicted a greater emphasis on the quality of life and self-actualization for people with disabilities, although they acknowledged that an economic slowdown could trigger a return to the older values based on workers' productivity.

Few of these predictions came true. The national priority for equality in education did not materialize; it was replaced by the emphasis in the 1980s on excellence. The information-service economy initially reduced unemployment, though not for people with disabilities; more recently, unemployment has risen again. Social institutions included a greater diversity of family types, although husband and wife roles remained relatively constant; the projected decline in the birth rate did not materialize, and a new teacher and classroom shortage was created when increased national debt reduced public spending for education. Technology has continued to expand at a rapid rate; however, research is underfunded, and the benefits of technology are not generally available to the disabled population. Progress in medicine has been related to a lower incidence of some disabling conditions, particularly cerebral palsy and some genetic problems; however, this information is not being disseminated widely. At the same time, new medical crises such as those threatened by drugs and the AIDS epidemic, have arisen. Overall, the current conditions from which to predict future trends for disabled children are similar to those that existed in 1979.

Current Trends That Affect Programs for Students with Special Needs

There is, however, a major difference between the conditions in 1979 and those of the present: Although support for education programs has declined, the number of students at risk for school failure has risen dramatically, and public awareness of the need to collaborate in the solution of this problem has grown. The following discussion summarizes this trend, first, as it relates to the mega level of society along the dimensions of values, social institutions, the economy, technology, and medicine, and second, as it affects the macro level of school restructuring.

Mega Level: Society.

1. *Trends in Values:* The current value system has shifted from an emphasis on human rights to a focus on excellence, partly in response to this nation's declining economic supremacy (National Commission on Excellence, 1983; SCANS, 1991). Excellence was initially defined in terms of more rigorous standards and a greater concern with college-bound students. More recently, however, there has been a growing concern that these standards are, at best, superficial indicators of quality. The educational reforms of the past decade have been focused on the teaching of basic skills, with state control over education and a curriculum driven by basic achievement tests

(Wise, 1988). There is now a concern that the reforms have overemphasized basic skills while neglecting the teaching of thinking and reasoning (Combs, 1988).

Wise has cautioned that the reforms undertaken during the past decade have not been based on a common vision and that although the newly implemented regulations have attempted to raise the quality of education, they have instead ultimately decreased the sensitivity of schools to their clients and actually reduced the quality of education.

The national value system is also characterized by a growth in emphasis on the safety of "old ways." Evidence of this trend is found, for example, in increased censorship (Mirga, 1987) and in controversy over bilingual education (Gold, 1987). This retreat to the old ways is not entirely negative, however, because it includes a renewed emphasis on the work ethic and on the concept of volunteerism, both of which have positive implications for the future of collaborative programs.

2. *Trends in Social Institutions:* There are at least two major trends in social institutions that affect the climate in which education is delivered. One is the growing mistrust of citizens in their existing bureaucratic institutions. The other is the disintegration of the traditional family structure. These trends, too, may have a positive side, because they could facilitate a reconceptualization of both school bureaucracies and family systems.

Naisbitt (1982) posits as a major "megatrend" in the informational-service society the increase in individuals' self-reliance as a reaction against dependency. Dolce (1981) summarized the post-Vietnam era mood of the country as one in which individuals had lost faith in their institutions, and as a result, had a sense of helplessness. The emergence of a strong "third party" mentality was apparent in the 1992 elections, as new coalitions in both liberal and conservative wings began to grow. Adults had developed the belief that old solutions were no longer valid for current problems. The positive aspect of this trend toward mistrust of institutions was the possibility that it would allow citizens to take the first step in recognizing the need for institutional change.

The statistics on the changes in the family institution have been cited previously. In addition to these data, there are other indications of family disintegration. Child abuse increased 55% between 1981 and 1985, with estimates ranging from 150,000 to 1.5 million cases a year (McClellan, 1987); by 1992, there were 2.9 million cases per year, with an increase of 8% from 1991 to 1992 (Peterson, 1993). Children labeled as "latchkey," who come home after school to an empty house until a parent arrives from work, are estimated as 41% of the school population (Flax, 1987). These changes in families as a social institution indicate a need for public assistance that is too complicated to be delegated solely to the public schools. Recent Congressional action on family leave is an indication that this need is being recognized.

3. *Trends in the Economy:* The amount of money available for special programs has continued to decline, primarily because of the increase in the federal debt (Chiles, 1989). Despite this decline, a new positive has emerged: an emphasis on cost effectiveness in education programs.

The initial reaction against increases in the cost of education for special needs students followed the revelation that the average cost of programs for special students is estimated to be between two and four times that of regular education programs (Kakalik, Furry, Thomas, & Carney, 1981; Gough, 1992). Funding for special education programs, authorized at 20% for 1980, with an increase of up to 40%, was cut in half and never regained its previous level (Howe, 1981). As a result of the loss of funds, however, there was a growing backlog of referrals for the placement of students in special programs. These students were not being served effectively in general education programs, which were struggling with fewer teachers and more students, and attempting to respond to individual differences by dividing students into ability tracks (Oakes, 1986). The effect of actions such as these reached the work force, and business leaders began to recognize that poorly supported education programs increased their costs for training (Iacocca, 1989). In addition, new research summaries showed that money spent on early education programs (Hodgkinson, 1988) and transition training for disabled adolescents (Viadero, 1989) was particularly well-spent in terms of cost effectiveness.

4. *Trends in Technology:* The use of computers is a major trend in technology that affects the educational program. Computers are used extensively in school programs, although there is a need for professional development programs that enable teachers to use computers effectively (LaFrenz & Friedman, 1989; Orlando, 1988). Interactive technology is emerging rapidly, as shown by support for home shopping, multimedia learning, and the paperless office ("Technology," 1993). There is continuing work with computers to develop artificial intelligence; meanwhile, microchips have been used to reactivate neurological responses in people whose limbs have been severed. Though computers promise improvements in education for the future, these innovations are still expensive and not widely available. Recognition of this need has prompted the computer and communications giants to initiate a series of education partnerships that have the potential for school improvement.

5. *Trends in Medicine:* A number of diseases—smallpox, TB, measles, polio—have been controlled by advances in medicine, better health care, and widespread immunizations. New diseases, however, have become more prevalent. The increased numbers of school-age children with AIDS are a growing health problem for schools (Reed, 1988). Increased need for funding has strained the health-care system; new proposals for national insurance may compete with funding of education.

Mental health problems have increased significantly. It is estimated that between 12% and 19% of children today are in need of some sort of mental health treatment, and that 70% to 80% of them are not receiving it (Flax, 1989; Tuma, 1989). The school-related problems of drug abuse have been documented in detail (Newcomb & Bentler, 1989). These conditions exist simultaneously with a dramatic increase in antisocial behavior among youth (Patterson, DeBaryshe, & Ramsey, 1989), and the growth of violence is a major societal concern (APA, 1993).

The encouraging aspect of this trend is that it has precipitated a more general recognition of the problems of at-risk students (Brown, 1985). Horowitz and O'Brien

(1989) provided an analysis of current concerns in their introduction to the 1989 special issue of *American Psychologist*. They pointed out that, in contrast with the last special issue in 1979, this issue pays more attention to adolescent sexuality, teen pregnancy, culture and identity, and the effects of the environment in its discussion of child development. New topics include substance abuse, accidents, learning disabilities, and computers. However, the most striking difference, they said, is that in the current issue topics are related to questions of social policy.

Macro Level: School Restructuring.   Restructuring of the public education system is one of the major trends with positive implications for the future of interactive teaming. In an extensive report on the current status of restructuring, writers at *Education Week* have outlined seven areas in which change must occur if renewal is to succeed:

1. *The balance of power:* This requires a shift in power from administration to groups consisting of the principal, teachers, parents, staff, businesspeople, and students. In this team approach, constituents make decisions about issues as diverse as budget, personnel, and curriculum. Although it is difficult for a council that was chosen to represent diverse points of view to develop a shared vision, it is believed that success can be achieved if more team training is provided and results are not expected too soon (Bradley & Olson, 1993).

2. *Time and space:* This involves modification of the regular hours, straight rows, standard way of teaching. Alternatives include the extended day or year, use of learning centers, and incorporation of work outside of school in community projects or real-world applications of learning. Although there are concerns about cost and need for teacher time, there are also some promising innovations, which involve school/university/community partnerships. Again, the need for collaboration is apparent (Sommerfeld, 1993).

3. *The coherent curriculum:* The emphasis on critical thinking requires that teaching and learning become central to reform, using state frameworks for broad concepts, rather than teaching specific lists of competencies. Although there are parental concerns that children will not acquire specific skills, teachers indicate that student interest and risk-taking increase with teaching that is interdisciplinary, rather than fragmented into academic specialty areas (Viadero, 1993).

4. *Outcomes for student performance:* This involves a change from a time-based or credit hours enrolled format to an emphasis on what students will know and be able to do as a result of their education program. This movement has been controversial in many states and there are questions about the measurement of outcomes, although several states have progressed in developing ways to deliver these programs effectively (Rothman, 1993).

5. *Professional development:* This requires implementation of learning communities to overcome teacher isolation and link classrooms to outside real-world experiences. Although the need for additional team training is noted, existing models incor-

porating professional academies and teacher centers have been successful in helping new teachers adapt to special learning needs of the new student population (Bradley, 1993).

6. *Dollars and sense:* This involves attempts to reduce disparities in school spending across rich and poor districts. Initiated by a series of school finance lawsuits against states, it has resulted in development of creative proposals, including the establishment of baseline or supplementary support from state and federal governments (Harp, 1993).

7. *Signing up the public:* This requires development of public awareness of the serious educational problems, their effect on the economy and on global competitiveness. Both the dissemination of information in ways the public can appreciate and the ability of educators to listen to public concerns are suggested. Recent defeats of tax increases and seeming lack of public commitment to the education system are cited. The involvement of business and industry leaders, parents, and volunteers is suggested and examples of success cited (Walsh, 1993).

The need for education in interactive teaming skills, including collaboration, communication, and cultural sensitivity, is apparent in these proposed macro-level changes. The relationship of the macro level to the special program changes is seen in the support from the special education community in inclusion, when possible and appropriate, of special students, as part of the range of services and improvement of the entire educational system (CASE, 1990; Kovaleski, 1992).

MAJOR TRENDS IN PROMISING PRACTICES

There are two major trends in promising practices, which relate to and predict success for the interactive teaming model in the future: (a) the growing success of total quality education — the application of TQM in schools, and (b) the rapidly increasing number of efforts to restructure teacher education. Each is summarized briefly below.

Success of Total Quality Education

Schmoker and Wilson (1993) indicate that the teamwork concepts inherent in Total Quality Management principles have been applied successfully in a variety of schools, which include the following:

◆ *Central Park East (Harlem, NY):* In this school district, 95% of the mostly black and Hispanic students now go on to college. There is a democratic atmosphere, leadership, a common purpose, and use and analysis of data as a measure of improvement. Teams, consisting of teachers and business and community members examine student portfolios. Students are required to convince faculty they are "ready to graduate."

◆ *Comer Schools (New Haven, CT; Prince Georges County, MD)*: Student achievement scores have increased from 35th to 98th percentile. Teams take a scientific approach, involving members of the community and entire staff in decisions. The emphasis is on professional development, no-fault problem solving, consensus and collaboration, in a process resembling TQM.

◆ *Northview Elementary (Manhattan, KS)*: Reading and math scores improved from a low of 31% to 70% competency to a high of 97% to 100%. The environment is collegial and purposeful; teams analyze data to isolate and solve problems.

◆ *Johnson City Schools (NY)*: After six years, passing scores on the state Regent's achievement test have risen from 45% to 77%. The district uses an outcomes-based model, based on Bloom's concept of mastery learning. The district strives for continuous improvement, measured by internal and external information.

◆ *Levin's Accelerated Schools (Daniel Webster Elementary, San Francisco; Hollibrook, Houston, TX)*: One school progressed from 69th to 23rd in district in three years. The model is based on a six-step inquiry similar to Deming's, which helps teams focus on problems and their solutions. The focus is on accelerating, rather than remediating students with poor achievement. The model emphasizes work with the school as a whole, building on strengths; using data to isolate problems, and emphasizing continuous improvement.

◆ *Mt. Edgecumbe High School (Sitka, AK)*: About 49% of the Native American students now attend post-secondary schools, and dropouts have been reduced from 40% a year to 1%. The group has eliminated grades, but teachers insist on high-quality work. Faculty members begin the school year by helping students see a purpose for learning, then students become their own managers. Teachers may supervise a large number of students (100) to free the time for others to work in teams.

Successful implementation of the TQM concepts in educational settings has positive implications for the need for and predicted success of teaming. This trend is particularly promising if paired with the provision of equal "inputs" (resources) to schools, as well as the expectation of equal outcomes (Miller, 1993).

Increased Efforts in Restructuring Teacher Education[1]

Public concern about the quality and accessibility of education has extended to concern about teacher education. In most of the new reports on the status of education, teachers are characterized as both the problem and the potential solution to the problem (Hawley, Austin, & Goldman, 1988; Kramer, 1991; Sizer, 1992). Many university programs have begun to restructure their efforts in teacher education, through initiatives including organized professional networks (Holmes Group, 1990; Goodlad,

---

[1]The contributions of Robert Sattler and of Pamela Soeder in this review of literature are gratefully acknowledged.

1992), recommendations from groups such as the presidents of the American Association of State Colleges and Universities (AASCU, 1991), and proposals from representatives of the teaching profession and 17 state education agencies (Miller & Darling-Hammond, 1992). These efforts have several common areas of emphasis:

◆ A greater emphasis on academic subject area knowledge and the ability to teach higher order thinking skills in and through the content areas.

◆ Encouragement for development of expertise in accessing information and using new technology.

◆ Recognition of the increasing diversity of the school population, with resultant need for teachers to demonstrate competence in multicultural understanding.

◆ More involvement in collaborative efforts that range from school-based management to continuous professional growth.

A centerpiece of most restructured teacher education programs is some type of university-school district collaboration, such as:

◆ "Professional development schools", in which preservice, beginning, and experienced teachers are involved in ongoing professional development activities (Schlecty, Ingwerson & Brooks, 1988)

◆ "Centers of pedagogy" schools, which are jointly operated by universities and school districts, and where preservice teachers have early and frequent field-based experiences, including a yearlong induction program (Goodlad, 1990)

◆ "Clinical schools", such as those supported partially by external funding sources like the Ford Foundation, and include professional organizations as collaborators (AACTE, 1990; Bey & Holmes, 1990).

Additionally, the restructured programs are providing preservice teachers with more and better opportunities to understand students from differing cultural backgrounds. This essential feature enables teachers to comprehend the effects of race, ethnicity, social class and gender on children's formation of knowledge (Banks, 1993). Moreover, teachers with a high degree of multicultural expertise will be able to interact effectively in diverse cultural situations (Smith, 1992; Bell & Morsink, 1986). While about 90% of all teachers are white and female, the number of students from differing backgrounds is increasing rapidly. Kunjufu (1993) emphasizes that the issue is not the race or gender of teachers, but rather the teachers' expectations for students: Too often, teachers believe that children from low-income, single-parent families have no potential. The disproportionate number of students of color who drop out of school or who are placed in low-ability groups or special education programs underscores the importance of preservice education that enables teachers to understand children's individual differences. Increasingly, restructured programs are providing preservice teachers with supervised, directed experiences that prepare them to become culturally responsive (Ford, 1992; Garibaldi, 1992; Klug, Pena, & Whitfield, 1992; Nel & Sherritt, 1992).

PROMISING SOLUTIONS: THE FUTURE MODEL

These trends support the prediction of a growing awareness of the need for professional collaboration and public support for special needs programs. Educators and related professionals are also offered three federal initiatives that will intensify both their need and their opportunities to collaborate.

P.L. 99-457, the Education of the Handicapped Amendments of 1986, provides special education and related services for disabled infants and preschoolers; this law mandates that services for disabled infants and children be provided in a coordinated way, through an integrated family services plan (Gilkerson, Hilliard, Schrag, & Shonkoff, 1987).

The Family Support Act of 1988, a revision in the federal welfare law, requires education and training for the 11 million Americans on the welfare rolls. It includes provisions for young parents without high school diplomas to return to school if they want to continue receiving benefits. It also recommended that all states establish education and training opportunities for welfare recipients (Walker, 1989).

The Elementary and Secondary Improvement Amendments of 1988, reauthorizing the Chapter 1 programs for children from low-income families, offers early education opportunities to preschool children ages 1-7, and it extends the migrant education programs to 3- and 4-year-olds (Mitchell, 1989).

Those who have summarized these programs say the programs emphatically place demands on the education and human services systems that require collaborative efforts. At the same time that recognition of the need to collaborate has grown, professionals have acquired additional evidence that collaborative efforts result in improved education, both for students at risk and for schools in general. Examples of this evidence include the following:

◆ Heightened awareness of the special needs of children from the diverse subgroups within the African-American, Latino, and American Indian communities, and increased understanding of how collaboration can lessen these children's sense of alienation from school (Kunjufu, 1993; Reeves & McDonald, 1989; Snider, 1990; West, 1990).

◆ Understanding that the current increase in problems such as school dropouts is not simple in origin. These difficulties have multiple causes and manifest medical problems such as teen pregnancy, school problems related to failure, and economic problems such as the need for adolescents to work (Gastright, 1989). Consequently, these problems require intervention by multiple agencies.

◆ Insight into the Carnegie Forum's (1986) recommendations for school improvement through school-based leadership and shared governance. The Carnegie report shows how coalitions among citizens and professionals—focused on university-school collaboration, staff development, and teacher empowerment—can work in the nation's worst inner-city schools, including those in Chicago (Walberg, Bakalis, Bast, & Baer, 1989), Los Angeles (Sickler, 1988), New Haven, CT, (Comer, 1989), Miami (Olson, 1989), and Hammond, IN (Olson & Rodman, 1988;

Schmoker & Wilson, 1993). Moreover, it explains how the participative management structure leads to professional renewal and school improvement in high schools as diverse as those representing inner city and suburban/rural communities (Karant, 1989), and in special services organizations that serve multiple schools in remote rural areas (Piechowski, 1987; Raymond, 1986).

◆ Evidence of the effectiveness of collaboration from the synthesis of the knowledge on school-based management (David, 1989), on total quality education (Schmoker & Wilson, 1993), and on professional development involving collaboration through peer coaching, both in general programs (Chrisco, 1989; Glatthorn, 1987; Raney, & Robbins, 1989) and in special education programs (Ludlow, Faieta, & Wienke, 1989; Peterson & Hudson, 1989; Courtnage & Smith Davis, 1987).

◆ A trend for collaboration between and among community service agencies and a growing body of knowledge to provide assistance to those who establish medical/educational/social services family centers (Burns, 1990; Imel, 1992; California School Boards Association, 1992).

◆ Encouraging new studies about the resilience of children who, because of personal and environmental adversities, succeed in spite of predictions that they will fail; from these studies we can abstract the importance of effective nurturing teachers, as well as regain confidence in the human spirit (Cohen, 1993; Edelman, 1992).

◆ Research on literacy, showing not only the effects of parent-child interactions, but also the importance of school and community interactions in the development of family literacy (Auerbach, 1989).

◆ Accumulating data from special education programs that show an increase in the number of schools requiring prereferral student interventions by teams of teachers (Carter & Sugai, 1989; Chalfant, 1989), an increase in the number of districts employing paraprofessionals and the resultant need for special educators to collaborate with them (Lindeman & Beegle, 1988), and the value of teaching special educators to collaborate as a way to increase their effectiveness (Pugach & Allan-Meares, 1985; West & Idol, 1987) and their sense of efficacy (McDaniel & DiBella-McCarthy, 1989).

◆ Research on learning, particularly in the areas of metacognition and cooperative learning, that has sharpened our insight into the teaching-learning process, showing the similarity between effective programs for special needs students and for all students (Glenn, 1989; Larrivee, 1985; Sommerfield, 1993; Brandt, 1992). New techniques—for using structure and advanced organizers, teaching self-questioning skills, and using mnemonics—can help students learn and retain information (Schumaker & Deshler, 1988). Cooperative learning (Johnson & Johnson, 1975), the subject of a large amount of research, shows promise for enhancing the ability of all students to learn and help each other, and for increasing their social interactions (Villa & Thousand, 1988); it has been particularly effective in teaching high-order skills.

◆ Realization that the solution to better programs for students at risk lies in the understanding that these complex problems involve changes in both students and systems, and that these changes are best implemented by groups of the individuals who work together to "make what is into what ought to be" (Cuban, 1989, p. 800) in their individual organizations.

CONCLUSION

The failure to collaborate on problem solutions has intensified professionals' difficulties in providing universal, free, appropriate education through our public schools. Moreover, school failure has been accompanied by economic consequences to industry, and political consequences to the nation. It has, therefore, attracted the attention of leaders in business and industry who now wish to join in partnerships with educators and to assist in school improvement. An abundance of evidence shows that (a) collaboration is needed, (b) increased collaboration results in improved schools, and (c) the improvement of programs for special needs students supports, rather than conflicts with, overall efforts to improve schools. The interactive teaming model presented in this book has shown how professionals who work in programs for special needs students can collaborate and consult effectively.

APPLICATION

Imagine that the year is 2005. You dropped out of teaching during the last decade of the old century. Because you lived in another country and had no further interest in education in the United States, you did not obtain any information about trends and issues. Now in 2005, you return and seek a job as a special education teacher. *You are told that public school special education no longer exists.*

Debate and discuss this scenario, using evidence gathered from your analysis of current issues and trends. *What might have caused this to happen?*

◆ Could it be that the numbers of children with special needs became so large that all education programs were combined into a common, mediocre system?

◆ Or are there no more public schools at all? Are some children now educated in private schools, while others receive instruction on home computers, or do not receive any education?

◆ Did special education programs collapse in failure under the pressure of a new generation of cocaine babies and children damaged by poverty-induced malnutrition and psychological disorders?

◆ Could it be that special educators, in whose classrooms students were taught only basic low-level skills, were viewed as incompetent teachers in the new century, and that special education, now outdated, was eliminated from the public schools?

◆ Or were special educators so idealistic, so naive about the realities of power and politics that they were unable to work constructively within the system to bring about needed changes?

◆ Did teacher's unions, under pressure from child advocates to place all profoundly disabled students in regular classrooms, lead a parent rebellion that resulted in the repeal of P.L. 94-142 and its antecedents, and disabled students were subsequently expelled from the public school system?

◆ Could it be that the costs of the national deficit, health-care spending, and new prison construction became so great that there were no tax dollars left for special education?

What else might have caused the decline of special education? Choose one of these hypotheses or create your own. Then, outline a series of strategies you could begin to implement for reversing these negative trends.

ACTIVITIES

1. Read the case study on Ethan carefully. What do you think might have happened behind the scenes to enable things to happen at just the right times? Who could have been responsible for these covert activities? If you were a member of this team, would you engage in such activities? Why or why not?

2. Design a change strategy for the educational organization in which you work or plan to work. Incorporate the facilitating factors discussed in this book. Identify the barriers you will probably encounter. Then provide a step-by-step set of activities to implement this change. Discuss the strengths and weaknesses of your proposal with others in your class and make revisions, based on their suggestions for improvement.

3. Debate the prediction for the future: The majority of programs for special needs students will be delivered by teams, using models such as interactive teaming. Provide evidence, pro or con, to support your point of view.

REFERENCES

AACTE. (1990). Clinical schools update. *AACTE Briefs, 11*. Washington, DC: American Association of Colleges for Teacher Education, CS1–4.

AASCU. (1991). *Teach America: A president's agenda for improving teacher education.* Washington, DC: American Association of State Colleges and Universities.

APA. (1993). Violence and youth: Psychology's response, Volume I. Washington, DC: American Psychological Association Commission on Violence and Youth.

Auerbach, E. (1989). Toward a social-contextual approach to family literacy. *Harvard Educational Review, 59,* 165–181.

Banks, J. (1993). Multicultural education: Development, dimensions, and challenges. *Phi Delta Kappan, 74,* 22–28.

Bell, M., & Morsink, C. (1986). Quality and equity in the preparation of black teachers. *Journal of Teacher Education, 37*(2), 16–20.

Bey, T., & Holmes, T. (1990). *Mentoring: Developing successful new teachers.* Reston, VA: Association of Teacher Educators.

Bradley, A. (1993, March 24). Basic training. *Education Week, 12*(26), 13–18.

Bradley, A., & Olson, L. (1993, February 24). The balance of power. *Education Week, 12*(22), 9–14.

Brandt, R. (1992). On building learning communities: A conversation with Hank Levin. *Educational Leadership, 50*(1), 19–22.

Brown, R. (1985). *Reconnecting youth: The next stage of reform.* Denver, CO: Business Advisory Commission, Education Commission of the States.

Burns, J. (1990). New start: One stop service center. Gainesville, FL: University of Florida Department of Special Education. Unpublished manuscript.

California School Boards Association. (1992). *Cutting through the red tape: Meeting the needs of California's children.* West Sacramento, CA: Author.

Carnegie Forum on Education and the Economy. (1986). *A nation prepared: Teachers for the 21st century.* New York: Author.

Carter, J., & Sugai, G. (1989). Survey of prereferral practices: Responses from state departments of education. *Exceptional Children, 55,* 298–302.

CASE. (1990, September 29). Council of Administrators of Special Education. *Position paper on least restrictive environment.* Las Vegas: CASE Board of Directors.

Chalfant, J. (1989). Learning disability policy issues and promising approaches. *American Psychologist, 44*(2), 392–398.

Chiles, L. (1989, February). *America in Debt: The Budget Deficit.* Symposium conducted at the University of Florida Law Center, Gainesville, FL.

Chrisco, I. (1989). Peer assistance works. *Educational Leadership, 46*(6), 31–34.

Cohen, D. (1993, June 9). Schools beginning to glean lessons from children who "defy the odds". *Education Week, 12*(37), 1, 16–18.

Combs, A. (1988). New assumptions for educational reform. *Educational Leadership, 45*(5), 38–41.

Comer, J. (1989) Children can: An address on school improvement. In R. Webb & F. Parkay (Eds.), *Children can: An address on school improvement by Dr. James Comer with responses from Florida's educational community* (pp. 4–17). Gainesville, FL: University of Florida, College of Education

Research & Development Center in collaboration with the Alachua County Mental Health Association.

Courtnage, L., & Smith Davis, J. (1987). Interdisciplinary team training: A national survey of special education teacher training programs. *Exceptional Children, 53,* 451–459.

Cuban, L. (1989). The "at-risk" label and the problem of urban school reform. *Phi Delta Kappan, 70,* 780–784.

David, J. (1989). Synthesis of research on school-based management. *Educational Leadership, 46*(8), 45–53.

Dolce, C. (1981). Conservatism in America: What does it mean for teacher education? *Journal of Teacher Education, 32*(4), 15–22.

Edelman, M. (1992). *The measure of our success: A letter to my children and yours.* Boston: Beacon Press.

Flax, E. (1987, September 9). Teachers cite latchkey situation as cause of learning distress. *Education Week, 7*(1), 17.

___. (1989). Serious gaps cited in services aiding child mental health. *Education Week, 8*(38), 1, 27.

Ford, B. (1992). Multicultural education training for special educators working with African American youth. *Exceptional Children, 59,* 107–114.

Fullan, M. (1993). Why teachers must become change agents. *Educational Leadership, 50*(6), 12–16.

Garibaldi, A. (1992). Preparing teachers for culturally diverse classrooms. In M. Dilworth (Ed.), *Diversity in Teacher Education — New Expectations.* San Francisco: Jossey-Bass.

Gastright, J. (1989, April). Don't base your dropout program on somebody else's problem. *Phi Delta Kappa Research Bulletin,* (No. 8), 1–4.

Gilkerson, L., Hilliard, A., Schrag, E., & Shonkoff, J. (1987, April). Commenting on P.L. 99-457. (United Cerebral Palsy Association) *Word from Washington,* 10–12.

Glatthorn, A. (1987). Cooperative professional development: Peer-centered options for teacher growth. *Educational Leadership, 45,* 31–35.

Glenn, C. (1989). Just schools for minority children. *Phi Delta Kappan, 70,* 777–779.

Gold, D. (1987, November 18). New Jersey relaxes bilingual education rules. *Education Week, 7*(11), 5.

Goodlad, J. (1990). *Teachers for our nation's schools.* San Francisco: Jossey-Bass.

Goodlad, J. (1992). On taking school reform seriously. *Phi Delta Kappan, 74,* 232–238.

Gough, P. (1992). Another bad rap. *Phi Delta Kappan, 74,* 3.

Harp, L. (1993, March 31). Dollars and sense. *Education Week, 12*(27), 9–14.

Hawley, W., Austin, A., & Goldman, E. (1988). *Changing the education of teachers.* Atlanta: Southern Regional Educational Board.

Hodgkinson, H. (1988). The right schools for the right kids. *Educational Leadership, 45,* 10–15.

Holmes Group. (1990). *Tomorrow's schools: Principles for the design of professional development schools.* East Lansing, MI: Michigan State University.

Horowitz, F., & O'Brien, M. (1989). Introduction to special issue. Children and their development: Knowledge base, research agenda, and social policy application [Special issue]. *American Psychologist, 44*(2), 95.

Howe, C. (1981). *Administration of special education.* Denver, CO: Love.

Iacocca, L. (1989, March 22). Remarks to the National Association of Manufacturers, Washington, DC.

Imel, S. (1992). *For the common good: A guide to developing local interagency linkage teams.* Columbus, OH: Center on Education and Training for Employment, Ohio State University.

Johnson, D., & Johnson, R. (1975). *Learning together and alone: Cooperation, competition, and individualization.* Englewood Cliffs, NJ: Prentice-Hall.

Kakalik, J., Furry, W., Thomas, M., & Carney, M. (1981). *The cost of special education* (Report No. N-1792-ED). Santa Monica, CA: Rand Corporation. (Prepared for the U.S. Department of Education, Contract No. 300-79-0733).

Karant, V. (1989). Supervision in the age of teacher empowerment. *Educational Leadership, 46*(8), 27–29.

Klug, B., Pena, S., & Whitfield, P. (1992). From awareness to application: Creating multicultural reform despite political correctness, a case study. In C. Grant (Ed.), *Multicultural Education for the Twenty-First Century.* Proceedings of the Second Annual Meeting of the National Association for Multicultural Education. New Jersey: Paramount Publications.

Kovaleski, J. (1992). Developing Effective Instructional Support Systems in Schools: Functions of the IST.

Harrisburgh, PA: Pennsylvania Department of Education.

Kramer, R. (1991). *Education school follies: The miseducation of America's teachers.* New York: Macmillan.

Kunjufu, J. (1993). Developing a positive self-image in black children. Address to University Community, February 24, 1993. Slippery Rock, PA: Slippery Rock University.

LaFrenz, D., & Friedman, J. (1989). Computers don't change education, teachers do! *Harvard Educational Review, 59,* 222–225.

Larrivee, B. (1985) *Effective teaching for successful mainstreaming.* New York: Longman Publishers.

Lindeman, D., & Beegle, G. (1988). Preservice teacher training and use of the classroom paraprofessional: A national survey. *Teacher Education and Special Education, 11,* 183–185.

Ludlow, B., Faieta, J., & Wienke, W. (1989). Training teachers to supervise their peers. *Teacher Education and Special Education, 12,* 27–32.

McClellan, M. (Ed.). (1987). *Child abuse.* Bloomington, IN: Phi Delta Kappa Hot Topics Series.

McDaniel, E., & DiBella-McCarthy, H. (1989). Enhancing teacher efficacy in special education. *Teaching Exceptional Children, 21*(4), 34–39.

Miller, J. (1993, March 24). Administration readies reform, assessment bill. *Education Week, 12*(26), 1, 44.

Miller, M. J., & Darling-Hammond, L. (1992). *Model standards for beginning teacher licensing and development: A resource for state dialogue.* Washington, DC: Council of Chief State School Officers.

Mirga, T. (1987, September 9). Textbooks do not imperil Christians' beliefs, 2 courts rule. *Education Week, 7*(1), 10, 23.

Mitchell, A. (1989). Old baggage, new visions: Shaping policy for early childhood programs. *Phi Delta Kappan, 70,* 664–672.

Naisbitt, J. (1982). *Megatrends.* New York: Warner Books.

National Commission on Excellence. (1983) *A nation at risk: The imperative for educational reform.* Washington, DC: United States Department of Education.

Nel, J. & Sherritt, C. (1992). Bridge building and student resistance: Increasing teacher commitment to multicultural education. In C. Grant (Ed.), *Multi-*

cultural Education for the Twenty-First Century.
Proceedings of the Second Annual Meeting of the
National Association for Multicultural Education.
New Jersey: Paramount Publications.

Newcomb, M., & Bentler, P. (1989). Substance use and
abuse among children and teenagers. *Children
and their development: Knowledge base, research
agenda, and social policy application* [Special
issue]. *American Psychologist, 44*(2), 242–248.

Oakes, J. (1986). Keeping track, part 1: The policy
and practice of curriculum inequality. *Phi Delta
Kappan, 68,* 12–17.

Olson, L. (1989, June 7). Dade County will solicit ideas
nationwide for design, structuring of 49 new
schools. *Education Week, 8*(37), 1, 21.

Olson, L., & Rodman, B. (1988, June 22). The
unfinished agenda, part II. *Education Week, 7,*
17–33.

Orlando, L. (1988, March). NSBA issues bold statement
to Washington about technology. *Electronic
Learning,* 8.

Patterson, G., DeBaryshe, B., & Ramsey, E. (1989). A
developmental perspective on antisocial behavior.
*Children and their development: Knowledge base,
research agenda, and social policy application*
[Special issue]. *American Psychologist, 44*(2),
329–335.

Peterson, K. (1993, April 7). Abuse of children is on the
rise. *USA Today,* p. D1.

Peterson, S., & Hudson, P. (1989). Coaching: A strategy
to enhance preservice teacher behaviors. *Teacher
Education and Special Education, 12,* 56–60.

Piechowski, P. (1987). *Project group work—An
innovative group counseling training program.*
Unpublished manuscript, Mississippi Bend Area
Education Agency, Bettendorf, IA.

Pugach, M., & Allen-Meares, P. (1985). Collaboration
at the preservice level: Instructional and evaluation
activities. *Teacher Education and Special Education, 8*(1), 3–11.

Raney, P., & Robbins, P. (1989). Professional growth and
support through peer coaching. *Educational Leadership, 46*(8), 35–37.

Raymond, G. (1986, April). *Teacher consultation skills.*
Paper presented at the conference of the American
Council on Rural Special Education, Tucson, AZ.

Reed, S. (1988). Children with AIDS: How schools
are handling the crisis [Special report]. *Phi Delta
Kappan, 69,* K1–K12.

Reeves, M. S., & McDonald, D. (1989, August 2). Stuck
in the horizon: A special report on the education
of Native Americans. *Education Week, 8,* 1–16.

Rothman, R. (1993, March 17). Taking account: From
risk to renewal. *Education Week, 12*(25), 9–13.

Safer, N., Burnette, J., & Hobbs, B. (1979). Exploration
1993: The effects of future trends on services to the
handicapped. *Focus on Exceptional Children,
11*(3), 1–24.

SCANS. (1991). Secretary's Commission on Achieving
Necessary Skills. *What work requires of schools:
A SCANS report for America 2000.* Washington, DC:
U.S. Department of Labor. (ERIC Document
Reproduction Service No. ED 332 054).

Schlecty, P., Ingwerson, D., & Brooks, T. (1988).
Inventing professional development schools.
Educational Leadership, 45(1), 28–31.

Schmoker, M., & Wilson, R. (1993). Transforming
schools through total quality education. *Phi Delta
Kappan, 74,* 389–395.

Schumaker, J., & Deshler, D. (1988). Implementing
the regular education initiative in secondary
schools: A different ball game. *Journal of Learning
Disabilities, 21,* 36–42.

Sickler, J. (1988). Teachers in charge: Empowering the
professionals. *Phi Delta Kappan, 69,* 354–356.

Sizer, T. (1992, November). School reform: What's
missing? *World Monitor, Social Issues Resources
Series, 4;* Article #79; p. 20.

Smith, G. (1992). Multicultural education: Implications
for the culturally responsive teaching of all our
children. In C. Grant (Ed.), *Multicultural Education for the Twenty-First Century.* Proceedings
of the Second Annual Meeting of the National Association for Multicultural Education. New Jersey:
Paramount Publications.

Snider, W. (1990, March 7). Children's Defense Fund
joins call to improve education of Hispanics.
Education Week, 9(24), 4.

Sommerfeld, M. (1993, March 3). Time and space:
From risk to renewal. *Education Week, 12*(23),
13–19.

Technology: Eyes on the Future. (1993, May 31).
Newsweek, pp. 38–50.

Tuma, J. (1989). Mental health services for children.
*Children and their development: Knowledge base,
research agenda, and social policy application*
[Special issue]. *American Psychologist, 44*(2),
188–199.

Viadero, D. (1989, May 3). 7 of 10 handicapped gradu-
ates found "productive." *Education Week, 8*(23), 6.

Viadero, D. (1993, March 10). The coherent curriculum. *Education Week, 7*(24), 10–15.

Villa, R., & Thousand, J. (1988). Enhancing success
in heterogeneous classrooms and schools: The
powers of partnership. *Teacher Education and
Special Education, 11,* 144–154.

Walberg, H., Bakalis, M., Bast, J., & Baer, S. (1989).
Reconstructing the nation's worst schools. *Phi
Delta Kappan, 70,* 802–805.

Walker, R. (1989, May 17). Welfare "sleeper": Schools
face brunt of law's training burden. *Education
Week, 8*(34), 1, 26.

Walsh, M. (1993, April 7). Signing up the public.
Education Week 12(28), 9–14.

West, F., & Idol, L. (1987). School consultation: Part 1.
An interdisciplinary perspective on theory, models,
and research. *Journal of Learning Disabilities, 20,*
388–408.

West, P. (1990, February 21). Interior Department sets
4 objectives for Indian education. *Education Week,
9*(22), 1, 24.

Wise, A. (1988). The two conflicting trends in school
reform: Legislated learning revisited. *Phi Delta
Kappan, 69,* 328–332.

Name Index

Subject Index